THE TROUBLE WITH TWIN STUDIES

The Trouble with Twin Studies questions popular genetic explanations of human behavioral differences based upon the existing body of twin research. Psychologist Jay Joseph outlines the fallacies of twin studies in the context of the ongoing decades-long failure to discover genes for human behavioral differences, including IQ, personality, and the major psychiatric disorders. This volume critically examines twin research, with a special emphasis on reared-apart twin studies, and incorporates new and updated perspectives, analyses, arguments, and evidence.

Jay Joseph, PsyD., is a licensed psychologist practicing in the San Francisco Bay Area. Since 1998 he has published two books, several book chapters, and many articles in peer-reviewed journals, where he has presented a critical appraisal of genetic theories and research in psychiatry and psychology.

THE TROUBLE WITH TWIN STUDIES

A Reassessment of Twin Research in the Social and Behavioral Sciences

Jay Joseph

NEW YORK AND LONDON

First published 2015
by Routledge
711 Third Avenue, New York, NY 10017

and by Routledge
27 Church Road, Hove, East Sussex BN3 2FA

Routledge is an imprint of the Taylor & Francis Group, an informa business

© 2015 Jay Joseph

The right of Jay Joseph to be identified as author of this work has been asserted by him in accordance with sections 77 and 78 of the Copyright, Designs and Patents Act 1988.

All rights reserved. No part of this book may be reprinted or reproduced or utilized in any form or by any electronic, mechanical, or other means, now known or hereafter invented, including photocopying and recording, or in any information storage or retrieval system, without permission in writing from the publishers.

Trademark notice: Product or corporate names may be trademarks or registered trademarks, and are used only for identification and explanation without intent to infringe.

Library of Congress Cataloging-in-Publication Data
Joseph, Jay.
 The trouble with twin studies : a reassessment of the research/ Jay Joseph.
  pages cm
 Includes bibliographical references and index.
 1. Twins. 2. Twins—Psychology. I. Title.
 HQ777.35.J67 2015
 306.875—dc23
 2014024510

ISBN: 978-1-138-81306-9 (hbk)
ISBN: 978-1-315-74838-2 (ebk)

Typeset in Sabon
by Swales & Willis Ltd, Exeter, Devon, UK

IN MEMORY OF MY PARENTS,
MARJORIE H. JOSEPH AND JAMES H. JOSEPH

CONTENTS

List of Illustrations   ix
Preface   x
Acknowledgments   xii
List of Abbreviations   xiii

PART I
Studies of Reared-Apart Twins: Scientific Proof or Scientific Illusion?   1

1 Introduction   3

2 Studies of Reared-Apart Twins: Origins, Publications, and Scandal   17

3 Studies of Reared-Apart Twins: The Critics Respond   61

4 Studies of Reared-Apart Twins: Basic Assumptions and Potential Fallacies   75

5 The Minnesota Study of Twins Reared Apart I: Biases, Assumptions, and Other Problem Areas   102

6 The Minnesota Study of Twins Reared Apart II: IQ and Personality Studies   128

PART II
Studies of Reared-Together Twins   151

7 The MZT–DZT Equal Environment Assumption: The Achilles Heel of the Classical Twin Method   153

CONTENTS

8 Twin Research in Psychiatry ... 179

PART III
Approaching a Post-Behavioral-Genetics Era? ... 205

9 Molecular Genetic Research: The Ultimate Test of Genetic Interpretations of Twin Studies ... 207

10 The Crumbling Pillars of Behavioral Genetics ... 222

11 A Human Genetics Parable ... 236

12 Summary and Conclusions ... 247

Appendix A: The Funding of MISTRA ... 253

Appendix B: A Little-Known Behavioral Genetic Adoption Study Whose Results Contrast with the MISTRA Personality Findings ... 259

Appendix C: List of Quotations from Twin Researchers and Others Invoking the "Twins Create Their Own Environment" *Argument A* in Defense of the MZT–DZT Equal Environment Assumption of the Twin Method: 1954–2014 ... 267

Glossary ... 273
References ... 279
Index ... 308

ILLUSTRATIONS

Figures

7.1	Circular Reasoning Used Since the 1950s in Support of the Twin Method: Twin Researchers' *Argument A*	159

Tables

1.1	Four Types of Pairs Studied in Twin Research	16
2.1	Environmental Similarities, Contact, and Relationship of "Reared-Apart" MZA Twin Pairs: Information on All 19 Pairs Reported in the 1937 Newman, Freeman, and Holzinger Study	25
2.2	Environmental Similarities, Contact, and Relationship of "Reared-Apart" MZA Twin Pairs: Information on All 44 Pairs Reported in the 1962 Shields Study	31
2.3	Environmental Similarities, Contact, and Relationship of "Reared-Apart" MZA Twin Pairs: Information on All 12 Pairs Reported in the 1965/1980 Juel-Nielsen Study	45
3.1	Summary of Problem Areas in TRA Studies as Identified by the Critics	73
4.1	Environmental Influences Shared by Reared-Apart Monozygotic Twin Pairs (MZAs)	96
4.2	Correlated Environments: Ascending Potential Shared Environmental Influences Experienced by Reared-Apart Monozygotic Twin Pairs (MZAs)	98
5.1	MISTRA Sample Sizes: 1981–2000	105
5.2	Some Implicit and Explicit MISTRA Assumptions	108
7.1	Environmental Dissimilarity among MZT and DZT Twin Pairs: Levels of Identity Confusion and Attachment	166
7.2	Behavioral Genetic and Psychiatric Genetic Interpretations of Research Findings: Family Studies versus the Twin Method	170

PREFACE

Many people have read that twin studies provide conclusive evidence that hereditary factors strongly influence IQ, personality, socially disapproved behavior, depression, schizophrenia, and most other types of behavior. Some people are undoubtedly skeptical of such claims, yet lack the arguments to be able to counter them. Based on my extensive knowledge of the twin studies of behavior literature, I decided to write this book to help supply such arguments in the context of the failure to discover genes for behavior at the molecular level.

While working on my dissertation on the genetics of schizophrenia in the late 1990s, I noticed that there weren't many critical writings on twin research. This was surprising, since it seemed obvious to me that genetic interpretations of twin studies were based on theoretical assumptions that were not true, even as most textbooks reported that they provided solid evidence in favor of genetics. I also became aware that twin research had been used in the past in support of harmful and unjust social and political policies. This provided additional motivation to examine twin research and other types of genetic studies very closely, which has resulted in two books and various other publications since 1998. In this book I bring the total twin research critical analysis together in one place and in much greater detail, with a special emphasis on reared-apart twin studies, and I incorporate new and updated perspectives, analyses, arguments, and evidence.

I am a clinical psychologist examining the methods and publications of academic research from the outside looking in. Although many psychotherapists are influenced by behavioral genetic research, most lean towards "environmentalism" because they witness the harmful effects of having experienced adverse environmental experiences every day in their clinical work. Although I am not a twin researcher by trade, the twin research critique is based largely on logic and statistics, on an understanding of human psychology and human societies, and on the lives and psychological makeup of twins growing up and living in these societies. Like most readers, I have encountered twins in daily life and have observed how they interact with each other, and how they are treated. The key assumptions of twin research run counter to what most people intuitively understand about twins, their relationship with each other, and their social environments.

My original intention had been to write a book that could be understood by a larger audience, but as the work progressed I realized that this would be a more difficult task than I first imagined. At the same time, I have tried to cover the main topics and controversies as simply as possible. I have done my best to review and analyze the twin research literature and the molecular genetic literature in a manner that can be followed and understood by people unfamiliar with these fields. This is a book about the fallacies of twin studies and the failure to discover genes for human behavioral differences, and the relationship between the two.

Jay Joseph

ACKNOWLEDGMENTS

Many people provided important assistance while I was writing this book. I have especially benefitted from the knowledge, wisdom, advice, and updates from the members of a critical genetics e-mail group, unofficially known as "The Forum." In addition, I want to thank Ken Richardson and M. C. Jones for reading and commenting on several key chapters. I would also like to thank Claudia Chaufan, David Cohen, Galina Gerasimova, David Jacobs, Andrew Kimbrell, Richard M. Lerner, *Journal of Mind and Behavior* Editor Raymond C. Russ, William H. Tucker, the Editors of *GeneWatch* magazine, and Stephanie Welch for their help and support. I also thank Routledge and the Taylor & Francis Group for their willingness to publish a controversial book such as this one, and I thank George Zimmar and Elizabeth Lotto of Routledge for their support and assistance.

All conclusions reached and opinions expressed in this book are entirely my own, and do not necessarily reflect the views of people who helped along the way. In addition, any errors in the book are entirely my responsibility.

ABBREVIATIONS

16PF	Sixteen Personality Factor Questionnaire
ADHD	attention-deficit/hyperactivity disorder
APA	American Psychiatric Association
BGA	Behavior Genetics Association
CAB	Comprehensive Ability Battery
CAP	Colorado Adoption Project
CCTI	Colorado Childhood Temperament Inventory
CNV	copy-number variant
CPI	California Personality Inventory
CTD	classic twin design
CU	callous-unemotional behavior
DNA	deoxyribonucleic acid
DSM	*Diagnostic and Statistical Manual* of the American Psychiatric Association
DZ	dizygotic (fraternal) twins
DZA	dizygotic twins reared apart
DZT	dizygotic twins reared together
EASI	self-report personality questionnaire purporting to measure "emotionality," "activity," "sociability," and "impulsivity"
EEA	equal environment assumption
GCA	general cognitive ability
GCTA	genomewide complex trait analysis
GWA	genomewide association
GWAS	genomewide association study
H-B	Hawaii Battery
HGP	Human Genome Project
IAAEE	International Association of for the Advancement of Ethnology and Eugenics
MD	major depression
MICTAR	Minnesota Center for Twin and Adoption Research
MISTRA	Minnesota Study of Twins Reared Apart
MMPI	Minnesota Multiphasic Personality Inventory

ABBREVIATIONS

MPQ	Multidimensional Personality Questionnaire
MZ	monozygotic (identical) twins
MZA	monozygotic twins reared apart
MZT	monozygotic twins reared together
ND	nicotine dependence
PKU	phenylketonuria
PTSD	post-traumatic stress disorder
QTL	quantitative trait loci
SATSA	Swedish Adoption/Twin Study on Aging
SE	shared environment
SEM	structural equation modeling
SES	socioeconomic status
SNP	single-nucleotide polymorphism
SRQ	Self-Rating Questionnaire
TEDS	Twins' Early Development Study
TRA	twins reared-apart (study)
WAIS	Wechsler Adult Intelligence Scale
WMH	World Mental Health

Part I

STUDIES OF REARED-APART TWINS
Scientific Proof or Scientific Illusion?

1

INTRODUCTION

> Because of their utility as a tool or method, twins are often referred to informally as the "Rosetta Stone" of behavior genetics.
> — Twin researcher Thomas Bouchard, 1999 (Bouchard, 1999, p. ix)

> Twin studies . . . provide the bulk of the evidence for the widespread influence of genetics on behavioral traits.
> — Behavioral genetic researchers Robert Plomin, John DeFries, Valerie Knopik, & Jenae Neiderhiser, 2013 (Plomin, DeFries, Knopik, & Neiderhiser, 2013, p. 82)

Decades of attempts to find genes for the normal range of IQ, personality, socially disapproved behavior, and psychiatric disorders have been tried, and they apparently have failed.[1] The search for genes that researchers believe underlie IQ and personality goes back to the early 1990s, while the search for the genes presumed to underlie psychiatric disorders goes back to the 1960s and earlier. Psychiatric genetic researchers of the 1980s were preparing for the discovery of genes in that decade, but the discoveries never came (American Psychiatric Association, 2013a; Faraone, 2013; see Chapters 8–10). Although researchers argue that they need better methods and larger samples to uncover these long-lost genes, an alternative explanation holds that the methods that led them to believe that genes exist are faulty. First among these methods is the study of twins.

Despite the stunning failures of molecular genetic research, many observers have concluded that the "nature–nurture" debate is now over because "everyone knows" that human behavior is the result of both genetic (nature) and environmental (nurture) influences. The nature–nurture (heredity–environment) issue refers to the question of whether genes or environments are the most important factors influencing differences in human behavior and ability, even when it is assumed that both play a role. Human intelligence (cognitive ability), which IQ tests are purported to measure, has been a major area of focus in the debate. Although claims of the obsolescence of the nature–nurture debate are sometimes made by people suggesting or implying that "nature" has won, the debate continues in full force and has major implications for social policy decisions. It also shapes how we view our fellow human beings and the human condition in general.

While it is obvious that all organisms are the product of both their genes and their environments, the controversy has centered on whether genetic or environmental factors have a predominant influence on human behavior, or more properly, on human behavioral *differences*. "The nature–nurture debate," as one author put it, "is essentially a question of the determinants of individual differences in the expression of specific traits among members of the same species" (Meaney, 2010, p. 41). When a behavior is called "genetic" it is often seen by the general public as unchangeable, or as largely resistant to change. When it is called "environmental" (non-genetic), attention may be drawn to the necessity of making changes in the environment. In both cases, the position that society takes on the issue often provides an impetus to take action of some kind. The developmental psychologist Richard Lerner pointed to words that are associated with the nature and nurture conceptions of development. Nature (genetic) terms include "genetic," "heredity," "inborn," "innate," "instinct," "intrinsic," "maturation," "nativism," and "preformed." Nurture (environmental) terms include "acquired," "education," "environment," "learning," and "socialization" (Lerner, 2002, p. 19). Another nurture term is "malleability," which refers to the ability to shape or change behavior.

Criminal behavior provides an example of the differing approaches society can take on the basis of whether a behavior is seen mainly as the result of heredity, or mainly as the result of the environment. For people taking an "environmentalist" position, strategies to reduce crime rates might include greatly increasing the funding of public education, paid maternity leave, increasing the minimum wage, passing laws and adjusting tax rates to greatly increase income equality, promoting full employment and job creation programs, fighting racism and other forms of oppression, restoring the "rehabilitation" aspect of incarceration, and so on. For people taking the "hereditarian" position that criminal behavior is largely the result of an individual's genetic predisposition to commit crimes or other "antisocial" acts, possible strategies include early intervention programs for people seen as being predisposed to criminal behavior, increasing the size and funding of the police force, lengthening jail terms, building new prisons, instituting (or increasing) capital punishment, increasing the availability of contraception and abortion in the inner cities, promoting genetic counseling programs, and even the promotion of "parental licensure" laws (Lykken, 1995, 2000). A more extreme strategy, based on eugenics, is captured in the words of the German author of the first twin study of criminal behavior, who concluded in 1931, "We must try to make it impossible for human beings with positive criminal tendencies to be born" (Lange, 1931, p. 198).

Even if differences in human behavior are accepted as having an important genetic component, society might still choose to focus on improving the environment. Responding to a 1977 comment by hereditarian psychologist Hans Eysenck (1916–1997) that genetic interpretations of a twin study on "earning capacity" suggested that the British Royal Commission on the Distribution of Income and Wealth should "pack up," the American economist Arthur Goldberger (1930–2009) wittily responded,

> If it were shown that a large proportion of the variance in eyesight were due to genetic causes, then the Royal Commission on the Distribution of Eyeglasses might as well pack up. And if it were shown that most of the variation in rainfall is due to natural causes, then the Royal Commission on the Distribution of Umbrellas could pack up too.
> (Goldberger, 1979, p. 337)

Research funding is also impacted by the approach society takes in dealing with the heredity–environment question. If it is directed in the genetic direction, other approaches suffer. As the historian of science Robert Proctor observed, "Scientific attention always comes at a certain cost: the decision to investigate one area is simultaneously a decision to ignore another" (Proctor, 1995, p. 243).

Since the late 1920s, the main technique used by supporters of genetic theories of human development and human behavioral differences has been twin research, which has been put forward as a scientifically validated research method that provides an ideal "natural experiment" for assessing the relative importance of heredity and environment. According to one estimate, by 2009 about 800,000 twin pairs had been studied (Johnson, Turkheimer, Gottesman, & Bouchard, 2009). Twin research has grown considerably over the past few decades, with studies now being conducted in 28 countries based on over 70 twin registries, and involving roughly 1.5 million participants (Hur & Craig, 2013). In almost all cases these studies are based on twin pairs reared together in the same family, while in an extremely small yet influential handful of studies, twin pairs were said to have been reared apart in different families.

Some critics, on the other hand, view most twin research as *pseudoscience* that is based on clearly unsupported theoretical assumptions and other biases, and is used to promote false hereditarian or "genetic determinist" ideas. A central aspect of this book, then, is an attempt to answer the crucial question of whether twin research is good science, uncertain science, or pseudoscience.

In this book I examine the use of twin research in the social and behavioral sciences. Behavioral science fields include psychology, psychiatry, and cognitive science. Social science fields include political science, economics, sociology, and anthropology. Although twin studies have been carried out by researchers in many fields, in the past few decades they have been promoted and defended by the (overlapping) fields of behavioral genetics and psychiatric genetics. The latter is a subfield of psychiatry, and will be examined more closely in Chapter 8. Twin research is also widely used in the study of non-psychiatric medical conditions.

Social and behavioral science research using human participants (subjects) is often referred to as "soft science," as opposed to "hard" sciences such as physics, biology, and chemistry. In the hard sciences researchers are often able to rigorously control and identify the environments and variables used in their experiments, whereas social and behavioral science researchers often must gather correlational data based on people growing up in environments that the researchers did not design, control, or observe. Twin studies are an example of "non-experimental" research of this type.

Researchers using such correlational data based on uncontrolled and unobserved environments are forced to make *assumptions* about these environments, and the conclusions they reach usually depend on the validity (truth) of these assumptions. An assumption is something taken for granted or accepted as true without proof. The project or investigation then treats it, and researchers arrive at conclusions, as if it were true. Whether an assumption is true or false can completely change the findings of a study—for example, a finding that the behavior is caused or influenced by genetic factors, or a finding that it is caused by non-genetic factors.

The sociologist Howard Taylor once asked, "What assumptions does the researcher make? Are the assumptions explicit or implicit? Would changing an assumption alter the researcher's conclusion a great deal or only slightly?" (Taylor, 1980, p. 9). These are very important questions, yet they are often overlooked. A major theme of this book relates to the question of whether the underlying assumptions of twin research, both stated and unstated, are true. If they are not true, a massive reevaluation of both twin studies and the theories based on them becomes the order of the day.

This book is divided into three parts. Part I focuses on investigations claiming to have studied "separated" twins reared apart in different family environments. The Minnesota Study of Twins Reared Apart is the most well-known and highly publicized study of this type, and is examined in detail. Leading up to that discussion, I will examine the three earlier "classical" reared-apart twin studies. I also look at some basic yet controversial concepts used in twin research and behavioral genetics in general, which include IQ testing, personality, and heritability. Part II looks at problem areas in the much more common studies of reared-together twins in the social and behavioral sciences. Here, I assess the validity of the most important theoretical assumptions underlying studies of reared-together twins, using the fields of political science and psychiatry as examples. I also examine other basic assumptions in psychiatry that have been the subject of criticism for many years, such as the reliability and validity of its diagnoses. In Part III, I examine the ongoing failure to uncover genes for behavioral characteristics and psychiatric disorders in the context of leading genetic researchers' unfulfilled gene discovery claims and predictions. Part III includes a story that shows the potentially harmful consequences of emphasizing genetic explanations of human behavior and many common medical conditions, with the final chapter devoted to an evaluation of twin research, and the conclusions that follow.

I focus on twin research used to assess the role of genetic influences on behavioral differences. I will not cover other areas of research where twins or twin data are used, including the much less frequent use of twins to investigate the role of environmental influences. An example is the "co-twin control method," where researchers assess the impact of environmental interventions or factors on monozygotic (MZ) twins, compared with their MZ co-twins who did not experience the interventions or factors. Another type of study using twins to assess environmental factors is the study of discordant MZ pairs, where researchers attempt to identify environmental differences between the twins that may have led to their differing psychiatric or medical diagnoses (see Mosher, Pollin, & Stabenau, 1971; the term discordant refers to one twin being diagnosed with a disorder, while the other is not).

The Historical Background

Chapter 2 of my 2004 book *The Gene Illusion* contained a detailed critical history of twin research, which should be consulted by those interested in this history (Joseph, 2004). Here I provide a brief summary. Twin research was initiated in the nineteenth century by the British statistician and founder of the eugenics movement, Francis Galton. The eugenics movement held that the human race can be improved by policies that promote selective breeding for "desirable" hereditary traits, and that prevent the reproduction of people and groups seen as harboring "undesirable" hereditary traits. Galton proposed the study of twins in an attempt to assess the relative roles of hereditary and environmental influences on intelligence and other psychological characteristics. In his article on twin research, he "was seeking some new method by which it would be possible to weigh in just scales the respective effects of nature and nurture" on the "intellectual ability of men." Galton concluded, "The life history of twins supplies what I wanted" (Galton, 1876, p. 391).

Galton believed that heredity maps out a behavioral life plan for each person, and that psychological characteristics are under as much hereditary control as are physical characteristics. Based on reports he received about the lives of twins, and on his preexisting beliefs, Galton concluded, "There is no escape from the conclusion that nature prevails enormously over nurture when the differences of nurture do not exceed what is commonly to be found among persons of the same rank of society and in the same country" (Galton, 1876, p. 404).

Twin research was developed more fully in the 1920s and 1930s by Galton's followers in Germany, the United States, the United Kingdom, and elsewhere. Many German eugenicists of the first half of the twentieth century preferred the term *racial hygiene* to eugenics (Joseph, 2004; Joseph & Wetzel, 2013; Proctor, 1988). Early twin studies based on reared-together pairs focused on IQ, criminality, schizophrenia, and several medical conditions.

Germany became the world center of twin research in the 1930s, but twin research fell into relative disrepute after World War II due to methodological issues and the questioning of its assumptions, and due to its association with Nazi-era German eugenic theories and practices, which helped provide a "scientific" justification for the killing of mental patients, and later the Holocaust (see Joseph & Wetzel, 2013; Müller-Hill, 1998; Proctor, 1988). As the Italian twin researcher Paolo Parisi recalled in 2004, in the post World War II era, "prompted by ill designed studies and somewhat simplistic conclusions, as well as by the previous political distortions of twin studies to serve racial discrimination policies, doubts were cast on the basic assumptions of the method." In the face of this criticism, "the study of twins was to appear obsolete by the late 1950s, when the emerging cytogenetic and molecular approaches allowed direct genetic analyses in man, overcoming, in the eyes of some, the need for the indirect approaches provided by twins." Although Parisi recognized that by the late 1950s twin research had almost been "sentenced to death," he triumphantly observed that "twin research did not die" (Parisi, 2004, p. 310).[2]

Three reasons why twin research survived this period, despite the shaky theoretical assumptions upon which it rested (and continues to rest) include: (a) that "molecular approaches" failed to uncover genes that underlie behavioral differences and psychiatric disorders; (b) that genetic theories supported by twin studies continued to be needed by powerful economic and political interests; and (c) that between 1961 and the early 1970s few major works critical of twin research were published.

After reaching its low point in the late 1950s and early 1960s, twin research began a comeback that has continued to this day, as twin studies are widely cited in support of important genetic influences on a great variety of behavioral characteristics, psychiatric disorders, and common medical conditions. At the same time, critics have pointed to many methodological issues and questionable assumptions, which they have argued call into question genetic interpretations of twin research data. The arguments put forward by these critics, however, have been largely ignored or dismissed.

A major reason why I decided to write this book is to encourage a healthy skepticism towards claims in textbooks, popular works, academic journals, magazines, newspapers, and online posts that twin studies provide solid evidence in favor of genetics. Many people intuitively doubt such claims, yet are unable to articulate effective counterarguments. In this book, I attempt to provide such counterarguments.

Human Behavioral Genetics

The field of behavioral genetics, or more specifically, human behavioral genetics, is a discipline rooted in the field of psychology that uses family, twin, adoption, and molecular genetic studies to assess the role of genetic influences on characteristics such as IQ, personality, psychiatric disorders, and other aspects of behavior. I use the term "behavioral characteristics" or simply "behavior" throughout this book to capture, in one concept, intelligence (cognitive ability), personality, abnormal or socially disapproved behavior, psychiatric disorders, and behavior in general.

The main research methods used by human behavioral genetics, briefly described below, are family, twin, and adoption studies, with twin studies playing a predominant role. As the genetically oriented child psychiatrist Michael Rutter and his colleagues put it, "For a variety of historical, as well as practical, reasons, behavioral genetics has tended to place most emphasis on the twin research strategy" (Rutter, Silberg, & Simonoff, 1993, p. 439). Based on the results of this body of research, the leaders of the field argue that genetic factors play an important role in causing human behavioral differences.

Behavioral genetic influence has grown steadily since the 1970s, as has its alliance with the psychology subfield of psychometrics. The online *Free Dictionary* defines psychometrics (also known as psychometry) as "the branch of psychology that deals with the design, administration, and interpretation of quantitative tests for the measurement of psychological variables such as intelligence, aptitude, and personality traits." The field focuses on individual differences in abilities and behavior. I will discuss several important issues related to psychometrics in Chapter 4. By the beginning of the twenty-first century, behavioral genetic methods, theories, and purported findings were integrated into the body of the mainstream psychological literature.

Although behavioral geneticists usually date the founding of their field to the publication of John Fuller and William Thompson's 1960 *Behavior Genetics* (Fuller & Thompson, 1960), most also recognize Galton as the "Father of behavioral genetics" (Plomin, DeFries, et al., 2013, p. 191).

According to behavioral geneticists Rowe and Jacobson, their field "was founded by Francis Galton in the second half of the nineteenth century" (Rowe & Jacobson, 1999, p. 13).

The first academic center for research in behavioral genetics, the Institute for Behavioral Genetics at the University of Colorado at Boulder, was founded in 1967. The Behavior Genetics Association (BGA) was established in the United States in 1972, and 1970 saw the first publication of what in 1974 became the BGA's official journal, *Behavior Genetics*. The founding editors were John DeFries and Steven Vandenberg. The BGA had 69 paid members at the time of its first conference in 1971, growing worldwide to 502 members by 2013 (Agrawal, 2013).

Having weathered the "racial differences in intelligence" storm reignited by Arthur Jensen and others in the late 1960s and early 1970s (see Chapter 2), the behavioral genetics field increased its influence into the 1980s. Towards the end of that decade psychologist Sandra Scarr, then the newly elected head of the BGA, proclaimed that "we have largely won the war" and worried that her discipline was "losing its identity" as its ideas continued to be integrated into mainstream psychology (Scarr, 1987, p. 228). Scarr concluded that, although the evidence did not support the position that racial differences in IQ were caused by genetic factors, IQ differences between social classes were rooted in hereditary factors.

In the early 1990s, Robert Plomin and other leading behavioral genetic researchers attempted to shift the field's focus in the direction of gene-finding efforts, believing that "quantitative genetic" studies of families, twins, and adoptees had definitively established that variation in "normally distributed" psychological characteristics such as personality and IQ had an important genetic component. They believed that the sequencing of the human genome would lead to the rapid discovery of the genes that they believed underlie behavior and psychiatric disorders (Plomin, 2003a; Turkheimer, 2000; see also Chapters 9 and 10).

Things didn't turn out that way, however, as the search for the genes believed to underlie IQ, personality, and the major psychiatric disorders has failed to bear fruit. The unexpected failure to identify genes has greatly increased the need to examine twin research much more closely, since gene-finding efforts are based largely on accepting the conclusion that twin research has established the genetic basis of human behavioral differences beyond any doubt.

Ironically, if molecular genetic research had delivered the genes for behavior promised by behavioral geneticists and other twin researchers, twin research today would be largely obsolete because the focus would have shifted to molecular genetic research, and a person's genotype would be determined directly from his or her DNA. Thus, twin research retains its current level of importance only because the genes believed to exist, on the basis of genetic interpretations of twin studies, have not been found.

At the approach of the twenty-first century, the field continued to consolidate its position "in the mainstream" (Rowe & Jacobson, 1999), and in 2000 behavioral geneticist Eric Turkheimer described what he called the "Three laws of behavior genetics." The first "law" held that "All human behavioral traits are heritable" (Turkheimer, 2000, p. 160). Behavioral genetic methods such as twin and adoption studies continued to be widely accepted, in addition to the omnipresent heritability statistics found in countless textbooks and academic journal articles (see Chapter 4).

Other theories the field has put forward include: (a) that most environmental influences on behavioral characteristics, rather than making children in the same family more similar, are "non-shared" influences and events that make members of the same family different (see Plomin & Daniels, 1987; Plomin, DeFries, et al., 2013); and (b) that many measures of the environment show genetic influence (the "nature of nurture"; see Plomin & Bergeman, 1991b). These theories will not be evaluated in this book, in part because they are based largely on the validity of twin research and its underlying assumptions. As some critics have argued, most behavioral genetic assumptions, models, "laws," and "discoveries" do not hold up under critical examination.

Primary Methods of Behavioral Genetics and Psychiatric Genetics

Family Studies

Family studies assess the behavioral resemblance or diagnostic status of biological relatives who share a common environment as well as common genes, and may include other biological relatives in different branches of the family. In the past, family behavioral resemblance was compared to the expected rate in the general population. In recent decades, the results often have been compared to a control group. A family study can establish that a behavior or disorder runs in families—and most behaviors and behavioral disorders do run in families—but cannot disentangle the potential roles of genetic and environmental influences in causing familial transmission or clustering. As Plomin and colleagues put it, "Many behaviors 'run in families,' but family resemblance can be due either to nature or nurture" (Plomin, DeFries et al., 2013, p. 74). Therefore, most behavioral geneticists and their critics are in agreement that the results of family studies can be completely explained on environmental (non-genetic) grounds.

Psychiatric genetic family studies were developed in Germany and were used extensively in the first half of the twentieth century. Ernst Rüdin and his "Munich School" psychiatric genetic colleagues developed the "empirical genetic prognosis" (*empirische Erbprognose*), which involved calculating the probability that (presumably hereditary) psychiatric disorders would eventually appear in the biological relatives and descendants of people diagnosed with these disorders. These calculations, which were based mainly on family studies, produced age-corrected "morbidity risk" percentage figures for various groups of relatives genetically related to the diagnosed "proband." For example, Rüdin and his colleagues found that the age-corrected schizophrenia risks among the parents and offspring of schizophrenia patients were higher than the rate expected in the general population, and concluded that these elevated rates were caused by genetic factors. In these studies the researchers did not diagnose relatives blindly, did not use control groups, and used vague and differing definitions of schizophrenia and other disorders. Rüdin and his Munich colleagues also performed these studies in support of eugenic (racial hygiene) legislation and policies both before and during the Third Reich (Joseph & Wetzel, 2013; Weber, 1996; Weiss, 2010).

However, like their fellow eugenicists in the United States, who based many of their theories and policy recommendations on widely reported yet subsequently discredited studies of allegedly "degenerate family lines" such as the "Jukes" and the "Kallikaks," on a purely scientific level Rüdin and his Munich colleagues committed the crucial error of assuming that hereditary factors explain the finding that psychiatric disorders and socially disapproved behavior (such as criminality) tend to "run in the family." As most contemporary psychiatric genetic researchers now understand, behavioral characteristics and disorders can aggregate in families for environmental (non-genetic) reasons, because family members share a common environment as well as common genes. A leading group of psychiatric genetic researchers recognized,

> It is critical to understand (and convey to clients) that familiality does not establish heritability. For example, religion and language are familial traits, as often all members of the same family practice the same religion and speak the same language. These facts are due ... to the common environment and upbringing that those family members share.
> (Glatt, Faraone, & Tsuang, 2008, pp. 6–7)

The Twin Method (Twins Reared Together)

Although family studies are widely recognized as being unable to disentangle genetic and environmental influences, most genetic researchers believe that twin studies *are* able to disentangle these potential influences. Apart from the small group of reared-apart twin studies that are the focus of Part I of this book, all twin studies in the social and behavioral sciences (and in medicine) have been based on twin pairs reared together in the same family home. Most of these studies are based on the "classical twin method" or simply the "twin method," which was developed in the 1920s and compares the resemblance of reared-together MZ (identical; believed to share 100 percent of their segregating genes) versus reared-together same-sex dizygotic twin pairs (DZ or fraternal; believed to share on average 50 percent of their segregating genes). If MZ pairs resemble each other more than DZ pairs for the characteristic or condition in question (on the basis of correlations or concordance rates), twin researchers conclude that it has a genetic component and then calculate heritability estimates based on the magnitude of the difference, or on more complex statistical methods (see Chapter 4).

Twin researchers and others arrive at this conclusion on the basis of several theoretical assumptions about twins, the most critical and controversial of which is the assumption that MZ and same-sex DZ twin pairs grow up experiencing roughly equal environments. This is known as the "equal environment assumption" or "EEA." The validity of this assumption has been challenged for decades, and many critics have been skeptical about claims that reared-together MZ–DZ comparisons prove anything about genetics, since researchers may be recording nothing more than MZ pairs' greater behavioral resemblance caused by their more similar environments, more similar treatment, and greater levels of emotional closeness and attachment. The validity of the twin method's MZ–DZ EEA is examined in Chapters 7 and 8.

Adoption Studies

An adoption study is another method researchers use in an attempt to separate out (disentangle) genetic from environmental influences. In an adoption study children carry the genes of their biological parents, but are reared in families with whom they share no genetic relationship. Although at first glance these studies would appear to be an ideal way to assess the influences of heredity and environment, they are subject to their own set of potentially invalidating problems, which include the restricted socioeconomic range of adoptive families, selective placement, late separation, parent–child attachment disturbance, problems with the tests, the non-representativeness of adoptees in relation to the population of non-adoptees (generalizability), and the reliability and validity of the characteristic under study (Bouchard & McGue, 2003; Faraone, Tsuang, & Tsuang, 1999; Horn & Loehlin, 2010; Joseph, 2004, 2006, 2010a; Kamin, 1974; Richardson & Norgate, 2006; Rutter, 2006; Stoolmiller, 1999).

Selective placement in adoption research refers to adoption agencies' practice of intentionally placing children into homes correlated with the socioeconomic and perceived genetic status of the birth (biological) parents. According to a leading group of behavioral genetic adoption researchers, "Selective placement seems to be an integral part of every adoption agency's operating procedures. Most agencies try to find the right 'match' between adoptive child and adopting parents" (Horn, Loehlin, & Willerman, 1979, p. 178).

Selective placement is a potentially confounding factor in IQ adoption studies, since adoption agencies often attempt to place children they perceive as "bright" (an assessment they make on the basis of socioeconomic status and the perceived intelligence of a child's biological parents) into better adoptive homes. (A "confound" is an unforeseen or uncontrolled-for factor that threatens the validity of conclusions researchers draw from their studies; an association between two factors could be caused by a third factor that influences both.) According to IQ adoption researcher Harry Munsinger, a "possible source of bias in adoption studies is the selective placement of adopted children in adopting homes that are similar to their biological parents' social and educational backgrounds." He recognized that "'fitting the home to the child' has been the standard practice in most adoption agencies, and this selective placement can confound genetic endowment with environmental influence to invalidate the basic logic of an adoptive study" (Munsinger, 1975, p. 627). Clearly, agency policies of "fitting the home to the child" are a far cry from the random placement of adoptees into a wide range of adoptive homes.

In psychiatry, adoption studies are sometimes seen as being less vulnerable to the effects of environmental confounds than are twin studies. Indeed, that was the stated rationale for the famous schizophrenia adoption studies performed by psychiatric researchers Seymour Kety, David Rosenthal, and their colleagues in Denmark (Kety, Rosenthal, Wender, & Schulsinger, 1968; Kety et al., 1994; Rosenthal, Wender, Kety, Welner, & Schulsinger, 1971). These studies are widely cited as having definitively established schizophrenia as a genetic disorder. However, in addition to the general adoption study problems mentioned above, psychiatric adoption studies contain a set of problem areas which include non-blinded diagnoses in some studies, inadequate and inconsistent definitions of the disorder in question, the questionable use of broader "spectrum disorder" diagnoses, inconsistencies in the way adoptee and relative group diagnoses were counted and assessed, the failure to find statistically significant results in some cases, investigator bias in favor of genetic interpretations, the failure to study adoptees' rearing environments, and other problems (critical analyses of psychiatric adoption research can be found in Boyle, 2002b; Cassou, Schiff, & Stewart, 1980; Jackson, 2003; Joseph, 2004, 2006, 2010a, 2013b; Lewontin, Rose, & Kamin, 1984; Lidz, 1976; Lidz & Blatt, 1983; Lidz, Blatt, & Cook, 1981; McMahon, 1980; Pam, 1995).

Based on a number of methodological issues and biases, therefore, adoption studies' presumed ability to make a clean separation between genetic and environmental influences on behavioral characteristics and psychiatric disorders is questionable in most cases.

INTRODUCTION

Reared-Apart Twin Studies

Due to the twin method's apparent environmental confounds, some have reasoned that studies of *reared-apart* MZ twin pairs (also known as "separated" pairs) are an ideal method of disentangling the potential influences of heredity and environment. Reared-apart twin pairs, while continuing to share a presumed 100 percent genetic resemblance, are raised in different family environments for much of their lives. A few researchers over the past 80 years have been able to pull together a sample of twins of this type, and have performed and published twins reared-apart (or "TRA") studies. Such studies are rare for the simple reason that twin pairs of this type are rare. Because these studies have been very influential, they will be examined in detail in the following chapters.

Researchers use several methods to accurately determine the zygosity of twins in all types of twin studies. Zygosity determination refers to whether twin pairs are MZ or DZ. The ability to accurately determine zygosity is not always straightforward, but is an important aspect of the work that twin researchers pay quite a bit of attention to. Throughout this book the original researchers' determination of the zygosity status of the twin pairs in question (MZ or DZ) is assumed to be accurate. This does not mean that the accuracy of zygosity is not an issue, and it likely was in the older studies, but there are other key aspects and assumptions of twin research that demand much greater attention and analysis. I focus mainly on postnatal environmental influences on twins' behavior, and largely avoid discussions of twins' prenatal environments even though the intrauterine environment experienced by MZ pairs is more similar than that experienced by DZs (Bulmer, 1970; Charney, 2012; Davis, Phelps, & Bracha, 1995).

Throughout this book I will use the researchers' term "MZA" for MZ twins reared apart, and "DZA" for DZ twins reared apart. As distinguished from these pairs, MZ pairs reared together are designated "MZT," and DZ pairs reared together are "DZT." Outside of the TRA context, these reared-together pairs are simply known as MZ and DZ. To avoid confusion, apart from instances where the terms MZ and DZ refer to the biological aspects of twinship, or are contained in a quotation, from this point forward I will refer to twin pairs as MZA, DZA, MZT, or DZT. These pairs are seen in Table 1.1.

Molecular Genetic Research

The final and most recent major method is molecular genetic research, where researchers search for causative genetic variants which they believe must exist on the basis of the results from previous twin and adoption studies. This area of research will be examined in Chapters 8–10.

Table 1.1 Four Types of Pairs Studied in Twin Research

	Reared Together	Reared Apart
Monozygotic (MZ, identical)	MZT	MZA
Dizygotic (DZ, fraternal)	DZT	DZA

MZT = Monozygotic twin pairs reared together; MZA = monozygotic twin pairs reared apart; DZT = dizygotic twin pairs reared together; DZA = dizygotic twin pairs reared apart.

In the following chapter I will review the paradigm-altering reared-apart twin study literature, focusing on studies that were able to obtain a sample of twins. According to one of the researchers, these studies "forever changed the way people think about the roots of human behavior" (Segal, 2012, p. 400). The goal of Part I is to determine whether TRA studies have provided evidence that supports this conclusion.

Although several single-case studies have been reported over the last 90 years, because anecdotal evidence of this type is rarely seen as supplying important evidence in favor of genetics, the only such twin pair I will describe is the first one, originally reported in 1922.

Notes

1 Readers may recognize this sentence as being based on reversing the implication of the opening sentence of Arthur Jensen's controversial 1969 article "How Much Can We Boost IQ and Scholastic Achievement?" Jensen opened his article by writing, "Compensatory education has been tried and it apparently has failed" (Jensen, 1969, p. 2; see Chapter 2).
2 By writing that twin studies were used in support of racial discrimination, and were subject to "previous political distortions," Parisi implied only that twin studies were misused by politicians, and he failed to mention the complicity of many twin researchers in the eugenic and racial hygienic policies in the United States, Germany, and elsewhere (Joseph, 2004; Joseph & Wetzel, 2013; Lifton, 1986; Weiss, 2010).

2

STUDIES OF REARED-APART TWINS

Origins, Publications, and Scandal

> When we come to the separated [twin] cases, a somewhat different situation exists. It seems possible that our group is more heavily weighted with extremely similar pairs than with identical twins of less striking similarity.
> — TRA researchers Horatio Newman, Frank Freeman, & Karl Holzinger, 1937
> (Newman, Freeman, & Holzinger, 1937, p. 31)

> In all 12 pairs there were marked intra-pair *differences* in that part of the personality governing immediate psychological interaction and ordinary human intercourse. . . . The twins behaved, on the whole, very differently, especially in their cooperation, and in their form of and need for contact. Corresponding with these observations, the twins gave, as a rule, expression to very different attitudes to life, and very divergent views on general culture, religion and social problems. Their fields of interest, too, were very different. . . . Those twins who had children treated, on the whole, their children differently, and their ideas on upbringing were, as often as not, diametrically opposed. Characterologically, the twins presented differences in their ambitions and in their employment of an aggressive behavior . . . . Various traits of personality found their expression in differences in taste, mode of dress, hair style, use of cosmetics, [and] the wearing of beard or of glasses.
> — TRA researcher Niels Juel-Nielsen, 1980
> (Juel-Nielsen, 1965/1980, Part I, p. 75, italics in original)

> Without exception [MZAs] were brought up in different homes for at least five years during childhood.
> — TRA researcher James Shields, 1962
> (Shields, 1962, p. 27)

> The most accurate description of this sample is "MZ twins partially reared apart."
> — Susan Farber, author of *Identical Twins Reared Apart: A Reanalysis*, 1981, writing of all pairs studied through 1980
> (Farber, 1981, p. 273)

The First Studied Reared-Apart Monozygotic Twin Pair

The first single-case MZA study published in the context of the nature–nurture question has gone down in history as the "Popenoe–Muller pair," based on the original 1922 report by Paul Popenoe, followed by a subsequent 1925 analysis of the same pair by future Noble Laureate H. J. Muller. Popenoe and Muller were prominent members of the American eugenics movement, and both were supporters of compulsory eugenic sterilization (e.g., Muller, 1933; Popenoe & Johnson, 1933), although Muller represented the left wing of the American eugenics movement, whereas Popenoe was a champion of the hardline eugenics positions put forward by Charles Davenport and others (Davenport, 1911).

In his original report, Popenoe discussed "Jessie and Bess," two American girls in their late 20s separated at 8 months and raised "by two families who lived on ranches" (Popenoe, 1922, p. 142). The twins had been reunited at age 18. Popenoe did not meet or study the twins personally, and relied on correspondence from Jesse. In her letters, Jesse wrote about herself and her twin sister, and their subsequent close relationship. For example, she wrote, "It is almost uncanny, the way we are always doing identical things at the same time," "We are both high strung," "An intelligence test would find our capacities very similar," and "We have never had a disagreement between ourselves, and while I am fond of my older sister and two brothers, yet [*sic*] they have never seemed as close to me as Bess" (p. 144). In the last passage Jessie spoke of her *close relationship* with Bess, a critical factor contributing to the similarity of supposedly "separated" MZ twin pairs. Thus, from the very first pair studied we see that, far from being "separated" with no subsequent contact, these twins had a close emotional bond with each other for nearly a decade.

On the basis of some differences in their upbringing, Popenoe concluded that, due to their "mental similarities, it is impossible to resist the conclusion that the psychical make-up of the individual is very largely settled by the time he is born" (1922, p. 144). It is indeed "impossible" to resist this conclusion when one already believes strongly that people are born largely with fixed mental properties and tendencies (see Popenoe & Johnson, 1918), and Popenoe is one of the first of a long line of twin researchers (reared together or reared apart) who interpreted twin data in ways that fit their strong preexisting beliefs in the importance of heredity.

Three years later, Muller reported on an examination and testing of Jessie and Bess. Muller (correctly) noted that pedigree charts showing that traits run in families could be explained by the common environments experienced by family members, leading to a "false appearance of inheritance" (Muller, 1925, p. 433). In the case of twins, however, he believed that "we are presented with material of the type sought for, namely, genetically identical individuals, in the cases of identical twins" (p. 433). He believed that the environments MZT pairs experience when growing up were not very different, and that instances in which twins are reared apart could supply important information about hereditary influences on psychological characteristics. Jessie and Bess were given psychological tests in the summer of 1923 while they were living in different states. They registered very similar IQ scores. On personality tests, however, they scored very differently, about as differently as two randomly selected unrelated persons would score.

Muller concluded,

> The responses of the twins to all these tests—except the intelligence tests—are so decisively different almost throughout, that this one case is enough to show that the scores obtained in such tests indicate little or nothing of the genetic basis of the psychic make-up. And yet the results of such tests have, it is claimed, been shown to be correlated distinctly with characteristics of importance.
>
> (p. 442)

Muller believed that, in the future, additional MZA pairs should be identified and tested in order to assess the relative importance of heredity and environment, although like most subsequent TRA investigators he already believed that "genetic differences ... undoubtedly do underlie much human psychological variation" (p. 444). Soon after, University of Chicago biologist Horatio Newman and his colleagues accepted this challenge.

The Classical Reared-Apart Twin Studies

By the early 1970s there were four recognized "classical" TRA studies, which included an IQ study by the British psychologist Cyril Burt that was subsequently discredited by the late 1970s (see below). The three remaining classical TRA studies were published by Horatio Newman (1875–1957) and colleagues in 1937, James Shields in 1962, and Niels Juel-Nielsen in 1965 (republished with an update in 1980). Each of the three studies was described in a carefully detailed book, which included case histories and test scores for most pairs.

TRA studies are sometimes referred to as "adopted twin studies," which reminds us that many of these twins/adoptees were abandoned children (Cassou et al., 1980), or "throwaway kids" (Pam, 1995), and most grew up in working-class, rural, or impoverished families. Their adopted family lives were often chaotic and nurtureless, and many twins undoubtedly suffered deeply by being kept apart from their co-twin. As Juel-Nielsen described his Danish sample, "If using a concept of 'broken homes' . . . the homes of every twin pair in the present investigation must be said to belong to this category" (Juel-Nielsen, 1965/1980, Part I, p. 126).[1]

Newman, Freeman, and Holzinger, 1937

The first TRA study was performed by Newman, Freeman, and Holzinger in the United States, and was published in 1937 as *Twins: A Study of Heredity and Environment*. The researchers studied 19 MZA pairs, and used MZTs and DZTs as controls (Newman et al., 1937). The study was divided into two parts. The first was a twin method comparison of 50 MZT pairs and 50 DZT pairs. The second part consisted of a study of 19 MZA pairs, whose results were compared mainly with the MZTs. The main areas of focus were IQ as measured by the Stanford-Binet test, and personality as assessed by the Woodworth-Mathews questionnaire.

In addition to assessing MZA correlations and behavioral similarities, a major goal of the study was to compare MZA correlations or mean difference scores to the same measures among MZTs:

> One obvious way to treat the data is to compare the average differences for the [MZA] group as a whole with the average differences in the case of the identical twins reared together [MZTs].
> (Newman et al., 1937, p. 356)

Newman and colleagues reported Stanford-Binet IQ correlations of 0.91 MZT, and 0.67 MZA. For the Woodworth-Mathews personality test, they reported an MZT correlation of 0.56, and an MZA correlation of 0.58. They also reported correlations for their DZT group.

According to Eysenck, writing 30 years later about the personality tests used by Newman and colleagues, "It is doubtful whether any psychologist would nowadays wish to make very strong claims for these measures. . . . the measures used would not now be regarded as either reliable or valid" (Eysenck, 1967, p. 192). Furthermore, according to Eysenck, these "were essentially tests for adults," and "it is quite inadmissible to use tests of this kind on children" (Eysenck, 1967, p. 193). Five of the 19 Newman and colleagues MZA pairs were under the age of 18

(Table 2.1). Newman and colleagues themselves recognized, in relation to the Woodworth-Mathews test, the "unreliability of the measure," casting further doubt on the validity of the reported correlations (Newman et al., 1937, p. 348).

The researchers came from different fields: Newman was a biologist, Freeman a psychologist, and Holzinger was a statistician. In their final section they recognized the differing viewpoints and interpretations each brought to the study, and, while concluding that hereditary factors play a role, they concluded that environmental factors also play a major role. Indeed, three years later Newman would write, "A fairly common criticism of our book on twins is that it plays up the environmental factors and tends to minimize the hereditary factors" (Gardner & Newman, 1940, p. 126). For example, they wrote:

> Differences in the environment which actually sometimes occur, as exemplified in our separated pairs, are sufficient to produce differences in weight, ability, and behavior large enough to overshadow the genetic differences which occur between siblings.
> (Newman et al., 1937, p. 359)

> There are a number of instances in which a rather large difference exists between the personalities of twins as shown by the tests or by observation, or by both, in which a large difference also exists between their environments, and in which it seems plausible to infer a relation between the two sets of differences.
> (p. 360)

They also found "consistent and significant positive correlations" between "educational ratings" and IQ scores (p. 341), and found that "the advantages of several years of schooling of one twin over the other produce marked differences in the broad educational test" (p. 341). Overall, their "correlations indicate that differences in education and social environment produce undeniable differences in intelligence and scholastic achievement as measured by our tests" (p. 341).

Newman and colleagues concluded that, if at the beginning of their project they had hopes of "reaching a definitive solution of the general nature–nurture problem . . . they were destined to be rather disillusioned" (p. 362). They believed that they had not "provided a comprehensive or final solution of the problem within our field of study," and invited others to evaluate their data and to arrive at their own interpretations (p. 363).

Sampling bias

In TRA studies it must be assumed that the MZA sample is representative of the total population of MZAs (which of course is not large), and is not systematically biased in favor of MZAs who are more similar to each other than are MZAs in general. Newman and colleagues, who recruited their MZA pairs through newspaper and radio appeals, were well aware of the likelihood that their MZA group was not representative of the population of MZAs, and therefore was biased in favor of more similar pairs:

> When we come to the separated [MZA] cases, a somewhat different situation exists. It seems possible that our group is more heavily weighted with extremely similar pairs than with identical twins of less striking similarity.
>
> (p. 31)

And later they wrote that "the separated group may very likely be a somewhat biased sampling" (p. 356). As most critics (and some twin researchers) have pointed out, MZA samples recruited through media appeals are biased because the twins had to have known of each other's existence to be able to respond to these appeals, and may have come forward because they believed themselves to be similar. MZA pairs who did not know of each other's existence and had no contact, and who therefore may have differed behaviorally and intellectually to a far greater degree, are missed in TRA studies based on media appeals.

Some examples of bias in the methods used to recruit twins are taken from pages 132–136 of Newman and colleagues' book. The investigators were describing the responses they received to their newspaper and radio appeals for twins to come forward in the interests of science. Following each passage, I will comment on the potential for bias, as well as the motivation for twins to exaggerate or even lie about themselves and their degree of separation. It is even possible that some pairs were not reared apart at all, but simply invented their separation for monetary gain or for publicity, especially under the severe hardship conditions of the Great Depression. I want to emphasize that I am speaking of the possible exaggeration and deception of the twins themselves as one of many potential pitfalls of TRA studies, not of Newman, Freeman, and Holzinger, who undoubtedly were honest and thorough investigators. Nevertheless, the financial limitations of this Depression-era study led to a biased sample in part because the investigators decided not to study dizygotic twins reared apart (DZAs), and therefore intentionally sought more similar MZA pairs in order to decrease the likelihood that they would incur the expense of bringing pairs to Chicago who would turn out to be DZAs.

- "The first case studied by us of identical twins reared apart gained considerable publicity through no fault of ours, for the twins themselves gave their photograph and their life-stories to an enterprising local reporter, who sent his news story to an American newspaper, from

which it was copied far and wide." **Comment:** These twins appeared to be seeking publicity and notoriety. They may have exaggerated their similarities and degree of separation for this reason.
- "The second pair of separated twins studied by us desired publicity in the hope that it might be the means of bringing them information about their unknown parents." **Comment:** This pair might have exaggerated their similarities and degree of separation for the purpose of locating their parents.
- "In one of the cases a man wrote that his twin brother, from whom he had been separated at four years, was now in Denmark and does not speak English. Apart from the prohibitive expense of bringing this man from Denmark, it would have been impossible to give him any of the mental tests we have been using." **Comment:** Twins who lived far apart and grew up in different cultures—and who may have greater IQ and personality differences because of these differing environments—were excluded from the study for financial and language reasons.
- "In another case one twin lived in Alaska and the sister in California. This case might have been managed by a Californian, but the distances were too great for us." **Comment:** The researchers were unable to study this pair because of their geographical distance both from each other and from the researchers' home base of Chicago. It is likely that this and other excluded pairs living far apart from each other were culturally and environmentally separated as well (Taylor, 1980).
- "In still another case the twins were separated by the whole width of the American continent, and, moreover, neither twin could leave her job long enough to come to Chicago unless we would pay their salaries during their absence." **Comment:** See the above comment.
- "Pair after pair, who had previously been unmoved by appeals to the effect that they owed it to science and to society to permit us to study them, could not resist the offer of a free, all-expense-paid trip to the Chicago Fair." **Comment:** This offer of an all-expense-paid trip to Chicago in the midst of the Great Depression may have induced twins to exaggerate their similarities and degree of separation (Kamin, 1974).
- "Because of the great expense involved in bringing these separated twins to Chicago, no chances were taken that any of them might prove to be fraternal twins. In every case an affirmative answer to the following questions was required before twins were asked to come to us for study:

1 Are you or have you been at some time so strikingly similar that even your friends or relatives have confused you?
2 Do you yourselves believe that you are far more alike than any pair of brothers or sisters you know of?

3   Can you send us a good photograph of yourselves, taken together in about the same positions?"
Comment: This meant that twins reporting dissimilarity, who nevertheless may have been dissimilar MZAs, were excluded on the grounds that they might be DZAs. The behavioral "alikeness" and "striking similarity" of twin pairs were *requirements* for participation in the study.

- "One case was excluded because the twins wrote: 'A good many people think we are identical twins, but we ourselves do not think we are so very much alike.' Another case failed to meet our requirements because one of the twins wrote that, while they look very much alike so that they were sometimes mistaken for each other, they were 'as different as can be in disposition, and I am almost as much like my older sister as I am like my twin.' These two cases may have been monozygotic, but the uncertainty was too great for us to advance the rather large sum of money required for their transportation."
Comment: Once again, the researchers described how they excluded dissimilar twins and recruited only twins reporting that they were similar. The study was therefore heavily biased by this fact alone, in that the researchers recruited only pairs who reported that they shared many similarities.

As Newman and colleagues recognized, their MZA sample was biased by more similar pairs. We will see in Chapter 3 that subsequent critics elaborated further on this point, and questioned the twins' accounts of their similarities and degree of separation.

Were these really "reared-apart" MZ twins?

A major issue in TRA studies is the question of whether the pairs under study were truly "reared-apart twins." Table 2.1 contains information provided by Newman and colleagues for all 19 MZA pairs they studied, including twins' degree of contact and association. The names, ages, and placements of each pair are listed, along with some passages from the case descriptions.

As seen in Table 2.1, the MZA age of separation ranged from 3 weeks to 6 years, and pairs often grew up in the same town or region. Rather than being "separated," many pairs had regular and prolonged contact and, more importantly, *had a relationship with each other*. For example, Pair I corresponded with each other and had been living together for 1 year when studied; Pair II had lived and worked together for 5 years; Pair IV had visited each other all their lives; Pair V lived together for 1 year and had visits and were regularly in correspondence; Pair VI was in regular contact their entire adult life and were living together at age 58 when studied; Pair VII had annual visits; Pair IX lived 3 miles apart and

Table 2.1 Environmental Similarities, Contact, and Relationship of "Reared-Apart" MZA Twin Pairs: Information on All 19 Pairs Reported in the 1937 Newman, Freeman, and Holzinger Study

Pair (Age)	Age at Separation	Placement	From the Case Descriptions
I. Alice & Olive (19)	18 months	Adopted Adopted	At age 18 "They met for a short time and have been apart again for 14 years but have corresponded more or less" (p. 144). "They had been living together in Olive's home for one year when they were examined" (p. 155)
II. Eleanore & Georgiana (27)	18 months	Adopted Adopted	"They had lived and worked together for over five years when we examined them" (p. 167)
III. Paul C. & Paul O. (23)	2 months	Adopted Adopted	"Separation complete. Had seen each other only once prior to taking of tests" (p. 144)
IV. Mabel & Mary (29)	5 months	"Adopted in families of close relatives"	"They have always lived rather near together in the same part of Ohio and have visited back and forth all their lives" (p. 187)
V. Edith & Fay (38)	14 months	Adopted Adopted	"Separation complete until 16 years old. Spent a year together when they were 20, but have lived apart except for occasional visits for the 18 years since then" (p. 144). "Since their marriage . . . . they have corresponded rather regularly" (p. 195)
VI. Ada & Ida (59)	3 years	Relative Relative	"Since [age 16] they have seen a good deal of each other, sometimes living together for months at a time" (p. 203). "Were living together when examined at the age of 58 years" (p. 144)

(continued)

Table 2.1 Continued

Pair (Age)	Age at Separation	Placement	From the Case Descriptions
VII. Raymond & Richard (13 ½)	1 month	Adopted Adopted	"The boys have had almost annual visits, chiefly in Raymond's home" (p. 211)
VIII. Mildred & Ruth (15)	3 months	"Two different families of relatives"	"They have always been acquainted but have spent very little time together" (p. 219)
IX. Harold & Holden (19)	6 months	"Two different families of relatives living in the same neighborhood"	"Their homes have been only three miles apart, and they have seen a good deal of each other" (p. 228)
X. Betty & Ruth (12½)	"Less than a year old"	Adopted Adopted	"Met first at 5 years and have had only a few short visits together. Both lived in Chicago until 7 years old, but R[uth] moved away some distance at that time. Visits have been infrequent since then" (p. 144)
XI. Gladys & Helen (35)	18 months	Adopted Adopted	"They were separated at about eighteen months of age, and did not meet again until they were twenty-eight years old" (p. 245)
XII. Thelma & Zelma (29)	18 months	Adopted Adopted	"Separation complete until nearly 30 years of age, when they met for the first time. Since then they have seen each other often during the last 5 years" (p. 144)
XIII. Kenneth & Jerry (19)	3 weeks	Adopted Adopted	"Kenneth first met his twin brother when three years old, but they have not visited back and forth to any great extent except during the last few years. Their homes are now not over one hundred miles apart" (p. 266)

XIV. Esther & Ethel (39)	6 months	Adopted Adopted	Separation "Complete until their first meeting at 24 years. Since then they have tried to spend a few weeks together each year and have corresponded" (p. 144)
XV. Edwin & Fred (26)	6 months	Adopted Adopted	"Both living in the same New England town. The two families were of essentially the same social and economic status" (p. 281). "Had attended school together for a short time" (p. 148). Separation "complete until their first meeting at 24 years. Only short visits together since then" (p. 144)
XVI. Maxine & Virginia (11½)	2½ years	Adopted Adopted	Separation "complete, except for visits of an hour or so two or three times a year, during recent years" (p. 145)
XVII. Gene & James (14)	2 years, 1 month	Orphanage/adoption Orphanage/adoption	Separation "complete except for occasional short visits one of the longest being when they were examined" (p. 145)
XVIII. James & Reece (27)	"Less than 12 months"	Mat. Grandparents Pat. Grandparents	Separation "complete except for rare short visits. Had never spent a night together before they came to Chicago for examination" (p. 145)
XIX. Augusta & Helen (41)	6 years	Orphanage/adoption Orphanage/adoption	"They spent 6 months studying nursing together when they were 17 years old, 11 years after their separation" (p. 145)

All information and case descriptions from Newman, Freeman, and Holzinger (1937).

saw each other regularly; Pair XII had seen each other often for 5 years leading up to the study; Pair XIII visited each other regularly in the years leading up to the study; Pair XIV corresponded and tried to spend a few weeks per year with each other for the 15 years leading up to the study; and Pair XIX was reared together for the first 6 years of life and studied nursing together at age 17.

Conclusion

Newman and colleagues performed the first systematic TRA study, but the claim that the study produced valid evidence in favor of genetics is highly questionable, and will be discussed later in this chapter. In the spirit of Newman and colleagues' decision to present the data and invite others to arrive at their own conclusions, I ask readers to consult Table 2.1 and to determine how many of these pairs deserve the status of having been "reared apart" or "separated."

Shields, 1962

Sample, goals, and biases

In 1962 British twin researcher James Shields (1918–1978) published the second TRA study, which as we saw in Chapter 1 was an era that marked the low point and near rejection of twin research for several reasons. Shields published his TRA study in the context of the struggle to validate twin research as a legitimate science, and twin researchers in that era wrote much more cautiously and defensively about their work than they do today.

Shields obtained a sample of 44 MZA pairs (his "Separated" or "S" group), which he compared with a group of 44 MZTs (his "Control" or "C" group). He also obtained a sample of 32 DZ pairs (the "DZ" group, consisting of 21 DZTs and 11 DZAs), but the main comparisons he made were between MZAs and MZTs. His goal was to determine whether early family influences play an important role in personality and IQ differences:

> The primary object of this research is, by means of a comparison of monozygotic twins brought up apart and monozygotic twins brought up together, to test the hypothesis that early environmental factors of the kinds that commonly differ from one family to another in Great Britain today are an important cause of variation in personality and intelligence.
>
> (Shields, 1962, p. 8)

Another goal was to assess the role of genetic influences on these characteristics. Shields had been mentored by psychiatric genetic twin researcher Eliot Slater, who had been trained at Rüdin's Munich school in the mid-1930s. Shields is also known for his collaboration with Irving Gottesman in the 1960s and 1970s. Together, he and Gottesman performed a schizophrenia twin study of MZTs and DZTs based on a British sample (Gottesman & Shields, 1966b, 1972).

Shields obtained his 1962 MZA group by arranging for a special appeal to be made on the 1953 British television program *Twin Sister, Twin Brother* for twins to come forward in the interests of scientific research. In the majority of cases one twin stayed with the mother or another family member, while the other twin was raised by someone in another branch of the family.

Like most TRA studies, Shields' sample was biased because twins had to have known of each other's existence to be able to respond to researchers' appeals. They also potentially shared psychological characteristics on the basis of being volunteers (Rosenthal & Rosnow, 1975). Shields was aware of this potential bias, recognizing that using volunteer participants is a "risky procedure in most types of research, but inevitable in this case" (p. 6).

Intelligence was assessed by using the Dominoes Intelligence Test, and the Synonyms section of the Mill Hill Vocabulary Scale, Form B. Shields and his colleagues administered and scored the tests. Personality was assessed by the Self-Rating Questionnaire (SRQ) developed by Eysenck, and by Shields' own personality ratings based on his non-blinded assessment of the twins. The SRQ personality tests were included in the booklet Shields mailed out to twins before they were interviewed, and therefore were completed by the twins at home, outside of the control of the researchers. Shields recognized that "the possibility of the twins comparing notes could not always be excluded" (p. 66). Clearly, we cannot even be sure that the twins were the ones who completed the tests.

Results and Shields' interpretations

Shields reported combined IQ correlations of 0.77 for MZAs, and 0.76 for MZTs. For personality, he found MZA and MZT "Neuroticism" correlations of 0.53 and 0.38 respectively, and 0.61 and 0.42 for "Extraversion" (p. 139). These latter personality scores were based on the SRQ. On the basis of comparing the MZA and MZT IQ correlations, Shields concluded that "the importance of heredity for intelligence is confirmed" (p. 61). For the SRQ personality tests, he concluded that the results "support the view that heredity is an important determinant not only of body build and intelligence, but also of personality as measured by tests" (p. 70). Based on Shields' additional method of assessing personality resemblance by interviews and booklets, he concluded that the "evidence for the importance of genetical factors in personality is very strong, while the differential effect of early environment is more difficult to demonstrate in the setting of the present investigation" (p. 76). Summing up in his concluding chapter, Shields wrote, "There is only a very slight support in the present material for the early environmental hypothesis" that family influences play an important role in shaping behavior and intelligence, and there is "much stronger support for the relative importance, for intelligence and personality as well as for physical traits such as height, of other factors, particularly genetical ones" (p. 141).

Degree of separation

Calling this a study of "reared-apart twins" or "separated twins," as twin researchers and their supporters have for decades with little qualification, depends on what counts as being "reared apart." For Shields, twins separated as late as age 9, or for only 5 years during childhood, counted as MZAs: "Without exception [MZAs] were brought up in different homes for at least five years during childhood" (p. 27). And pairs "living next door to each other, brought up by different aunts" were also counted as "separated" pairs (p. 48).

Table 2.2 lists all 44 MZA pairs studied by Shields, accompanied by excerpts from Shields' case history material for each pair. The information in Table 2.2 makes it abundantly clear that many pairs had a great deal of contact with each other, grew up together for prolonged periods, and sometimes had a close emotional relationship with each other. In a subsequent publication Shields wrote, "On average, the [MZA] environments were less alike than those of identical twins reared in the same home" (Shields, 1978, p. 85). This is undoubtedly true, but a study of "separated" twins should find that MZAs grew up in environments that were not at all alike, and were no more similar than a group consisting of (genetically unrelated) pairs of randomly selected members of the entire British population.

Examples from Shields' case descriptions of the 44 MZA pairs seen in Table 2.2 include, "have always been closely attached to each other," "have been in business together for the past 8 years," "were in cottages next door to one another and attended the same school," "went to school together," "came home to mother at 14," " were dressed alike . . . . They attended the same school," "met about once a fortnight during adolescence," "brought up within a few hundred yards from one another," "met about twice a week and sometimes spent holidays together," "met regularly," "now correspond frequently and meet at holidays," "until [separation at age 8] the twins had done everything together," "formed an extremely close association," "brought up together till the age of 7," "were reunited most of the

Table 2.2 Environmental Similarities, Contact, and Relationship of "Reared-Apart" MZA Twin Pairs: Information on All 44 Pairs Reported in the 1962 Shields Study

Pair (Age)	Age at Separation	Placement	From the Case Descriptions
Richard & Kenneth (14)	3 months	Mother / Maternal aunt	"From the age of 9 they met once a week when Kenneth's family came to live in the town" (p. 163)
Bertram & Christopher (17)	Birth	Paternal aunt / Paternal aunt	"The paternal aunts decided to take one twin each and they have brought them up amicably, living next-door to one another.... They are constantly in and out of each other's houses .... They have always been closely attached to each other.... When they were younger, Christopher used to follow Bertram around 'as if he were a younger brother'" (pp. 164–165)
Russell & Tristram (18)	20 months	Adopted / Mother	"They first met at 7 ... they met again at 10 and at 12 during holidays and still see each other only about once every one or two years" (p. 166)
Herbert & Nicholas (22)	Birth, reunited at 5 for less than a year (Both twins diagnosed with schizophrenia at age 22)	Maternal grandmother / Adopted	"It was at the beginning of the war that the twins first met .... The twins have had only occasional meetings of short duration .... Nicholas was taken to see [Herbert after his hospitalization for psychosis] on 22 December [1956] .... That evening he was found to be crying .... [Two weeks later] on returning home from work one evening, he amazed his father with strange, unintelligible talk .... He was admitted to [a] mental hospital" (pp. 170–171)
Frederick & Peter (30)	6 months	Paternal aunt / Friend of family	"Frederick was taken by a paternal aunt .... Peter was brought up at the other end of the same Kent town .... They have been in business together for the past 8 years" (pp. 172–173)

(continued)

Table 2.2 (Continued)

Pair (Age)	Age at Separation	Placement	From the Case Descriptions
Foster & Francis (32)	6 months	Paternal aunt Mother	"The twins have continued to live in the semi-industrialized villages on the outskirts of a large northern town where they were brought up about 5 miles apart, but meet only occasionally now" (p. 173). "The twins developed a close feeling for one another" (p. 121)
Rodney & Barry (34)	"Separated from birth to 9 years"	Paternal aunt Mother	"Rodney was taken straight away by the paternal aunt with whom he remained until the age of 9 when . . . he was returned to mother against his will . . . . Until then they were brought up about 3 miles apart" (p. 175)
Edward & Keith (38)	2 years	Orphanage Orphanage (different cottage homes)	At age 11 "they were in cottages next door to one another and attended the same school, but they continued to fight and were soon moved farther apart again" (p. 176)
Alfred & Harry (39)	Soon after birth	Father and stepmother Maternal aunt	"The twins went to school together." Both lived "in the same mining village" (p. 178)
William & Stanley (39)	4 years	Foster home Foster home	Separated at 4 years. "The twins then came home to mother at 14 . . . . Both twins say they thought a lot about one another as children. They went to different schools in the same north of England town" (p. 180)
Timothy & Kevin (45)	Birth	Mother Paternal aunt	"The twins lived a few roads away from each other in the same northern industrial town. They were dressed alike . . . They attended the same school . . . Until 36 they worked in . . . different departments of a glass factory" (p. 182)
James & Robert (49)	Birth	Mother Paternal uncle and aunt	"The twins met about once a fortnight during adolescence" (p. 183)

Patrick & Victor (51)	12 months	Paternal aunt Mother	"A paternal aunt took Patrick ... Victor [remained] with his parents in the same small town .... The twins went to the same school but did not get on well together" (p. 185)
Hubert & Brian (51)	12 months	Mother Maternal grandmother	"Met for their summer holidays, knowing they were twins" (p. 187). "The twins developed a close feeling for one another" (p. 121)
Benjamin & Ronald (52)	9 months	Mother Maternal grandmother	"Both brought up in the same fruit growing village, Ben by the parents, Ron by the grandmother .... They were at school together .... They have continued to live in the same village" (p. 188)
Jessie & Winifred (8)	3 months	Adopted Adopted	"Brought up within a few hundred yards of one another .... Attracted to each other at the age of 2, but meetings not encouraged." At age 5 "continued to meet in the park .... In their relationship to each other they are perfectly normal and friendly .... They play together quite a lot at school and during the evenings" (pp. 189–191). They "formed an extremely close association which was resented by one set of parents but not by the other" (p. 50)
Twins A & B Case 2 (23)	6 months	Mother Maternal aunt	"They were reunited from 5 to 7 years, then parted again. They meet every weekend now .... Though attending different schools, the twins met about twice a week and sometimes spent holidays together" (p. 192)
Valerie & Joyce (30)	13 months	Adopted Mother	An "acquaintance took Valerie ... temporarily, but he became so attached to her that he kept her permanently with mother's full agreement .... Joyce remained with the parents. Valerie was in a nearby small town .... Though attending different schools, the twins met about twice a week and sometimes spent holidays together" (p. 192)
Twins A & B Case 4 (32)	5 years	Aunt Mother	"Brought up in the same town, not always same school; met regularly" (p. 194)

(continued)

Table 2.2 (Continued)

Pair (Age)	Age at Separation	Placement	From the Case Descriptions
Megan & Polly (32)	Birth	Father and stepmother / Adopted	"They met a good deal aged 20–22 when Megan . . . was stationed near Polly. Since Polly's marriage at 22 they have met less often . . . but they correspond weekly" (p. 194). "Formed a close tie" (p. 51)
Twins A & B Case 6 (33)	Birth	Paternal aunt / Maternal aunt	[Limited information. Shields was not able to interview these twins.] "The mother died when the twins were born. A was with grandparents at first, later with paternal aunt (very strict). B was with maternal aunt" (p. 196)
Jenny & Kathleen (33)	Birth	Paternal aunt / Paternal aunt	"They were looked after by different paternal aunts, Jenny in a London suburb, Kathleen in a small seaside resort, where she was visited regularly by Jenny during the summer holidays for as long as they can remember" (p. 196)
Olive & Madge (35)	Birth (not met since 3)	Mother / Paternal aunt	"Until the age of 3 Madge was taken every week to visit her twin, but at that age the aunt suddenly refused to bring her any more" (p. 198)
Madeline & Lilian (36)	16 months	Adopted / Adopted	After meeting at age 36, "they spent the night together at Lilian's home and now correspond frequently and meet at holidays. . . . On the occasion of their first meeting they had a good deal of press publicity, probably through Lilian telling so many people the news" (pp. 200–202)
Marjorie & Norah (36)	22 months	Adopted / Adopted	"They first heard of their twinship when they were 19 and at this age they met for the first time . . . . They have met on only three subsequent short occasions, the last time 3 years ago" (p. 203)
Molly & Dorothy (38)	8 years	Maternal grandmother / Mother	"Until [separation at age 8] the twins had done everything together; thereafter they continued to attend the same school in the village where both families lived" (p. 206)

Pauline & Sally (38)	7 years	Mother Maternal aunt	"They were brought up together till the age of 7 . . . . The twins meet about once a fortnight when they visit their brother in [the] hospital" (pp. 208–209). "The twins developed a close feeling for one another" (p. 121)
Viola & Olga (39)	Birth to 11, then again at 16	Maternal grandmother Mother	"Viola was . . . taken by the by the grandparents, while Olga remained with the parents, living nearby in the same industrial area . . . At [11 Viola] went to live with the parents and was forbidden to see her grandmother . . . . For a short while after leaving school the twins worked together in a laundry" (p. 210)
Millicent & Edith (40)	3 months	Paternal grandmother Mother	"Edith was brought up in the home of her parents . . . . Millicent . . . was brought up nearby as an only child by her grandparents . . . and aunts" (p. 111). "The twins went to the same school . . . . They did not feel at home in each other's houses . . . . The twins have little in common" (p. 212)
Joan & Dinah (40)	Birth, reunited at 5	Mother Maternal aunt	"The twins . . . . were reunited most of the time from 5 to 15 . . . . Except for a year or two during the war they have not since lived near one another, apart from visiting each other one or two times a year" (p. 214)
June & Clara (41)	Birth	Adopted Adopted	After meeting at age 8 the twins "met for 2 or 3 weeks a year . . . but did not get on very well. Both went to elementary school till 14 . . . . After school they continued to meet at weekends three or four times a year at first and now rather less often" (p. 216)
Jacqueline & Beryl (41)	Birth	Paternal uncle Distant cousin of mother	The twins "did not meet until 16 . . . and they did not get to know one another well till 18 . . . . The twins are too busy to meet frequently, but they have a long telephone conversation weekly, both still living on the outskirts of London" (p. 218). After meeting, the twins "later kept house together for a while and remained closely attached to each other" (p. 51). "The twins developed a close feeling for one another" (p. 121)

(continued)

Table 2.2 (Continued)

Pair (Age)	Age at Separation	Placement	From the Case Descriptions
Christine & Nina (42)	Soon after birth	Father Paternal aunt	Growing up, "The twins generally spent summer holidays together in each other's homes. They knew all along they were twins.... They still live in the localities where they were brought up and now meet once every 2 or 3 months.... When they were children the twins fought when they met.... They get on quite well now" (pp. 219–220)
Herta & Berta (43)	4 years	Mother Adopted	"Though they have never met [since age 4] they have developed an intense affection for one another and derive great emotional satisfaction from their correspondence.... 'Your letters make me feel warm inside,' writes Berta.... Herta replies in similar terms. When Berta sends a letter with a lipstick kiss she presses it warmly against her lips. She longs for her twin so much that it hurts. They send one another generous presents" (p. 223)
Charlotte & Laura (45)	Birth	Maternal grandmother Mother	"From just before their ninth birthday they lived as close neighbors in a coastal town, attending the same school until they were 15. They were closely attached and went about a lot together" (p. 225)
Mary & Nancy (47)	Birth to 12 years	Maternal grandmother Mother	After separation, "First met again, aged about 8.... From then on they met in the coastal town for 1 week each August.... At age 12... Mary joined Nancy in the town where they attended the same school.... 9 months later the maternal grandparents decided that mother should bring both children home and they have lived in the same country village ever since.... The twins became very close.... They are mutually dependent.... Prefer to talk about 'we' rather than 'I'" (pp. 227–228)

Olwen & Gwladys (48)	2½ years	Adopted Adopted	"They were adopted by unrelated quarrymen.... Within 6 months of meeting [at age 24] they were living together in the small village where Olwen lived.... [later] They meet regularly, often spending weekends together" (pp. 228–229). After meeting, the twins "later kept house together for a while and remained closely attached to each other" (p. 51)
Annie & Trixie (48)	6 weeks	Paternal grandmother Mother	"The twins were brought up a mile apart in a north-country village.... They went to the same school.... On leaving school at 14, Annie worked in the village, Trixie in the nearby town; they might not meet for weeks" (p. 231)
Joanna & Isobel (50)	Birth to 5 years	Paternal grandmother Mother	"After reunion [at age 5] in the parental home the twins went to private schools together until ... 17 [twins reared together between ages 5 and 17]" (p. 233)
Odette & Fanny (51)	Birth to 12 years	Maternal grandmother Mother	Beginning at age 3 the twins "spent summer holidays together in the country, until they were 8 .... At 12 the father decided the twins should now be together and that Odette would be able to help her mother at home. They remained in the same home until after they left school.... [now] correspond four or five times a year and meet once or twice a year" (pp. 235–236). "The twins developed a close feeling for one another" (p. 121)
Amy & Teresa (55)	6 months	Maternal uncle Mother	Twins grew up "some 16 miles apart ... Since about 24 they have lived in different districts of the same town and get on fairly well when they meet, which is not often" (pp. 237–238)

(continued)

Table 2.2 (Continued)

Pair (Age)	Age at Separation	Placement	From the Case Descriptions
Dora & Brenda (56)	9 months to 12 years	Maternal grandmother Mother	Twins "were reunited at age 12 in the interests of Dora's schooling. Special point was made of seeing that the twins had the same clothes, the same presents and the same pocket-money. They met twice a year.... The twins meet twice a year still" (p. 240)
Maisie & Vera (59)	A few months to 12 years, and again at 17	Father Paternal uncle	"Both lived in the same town in northern England. The twins met for tea most Sundays.... When they were 12 the uncle and aunt emigrated to Canada and Vera at father's request came to live in his home" with Maisie, until age 17. "This pair has been less thoroughly investigated than the others" (pp. 242–243)
Adeline & Gwendolen (59)	9 years	Father Maternal aunt	"They were brought up together in a country village until their mother's death, when they were 9½" (p. 244)

All information and case descriptions from Shields, 1962. Twin pairs listed in the same order as described by Shields in his "Case Histories" section, pp. 163–246.

time from 5 to 15," "were closely attached and went about a lot together," "became very close . . . . they are mutually dependent," "After reunion [at age 5] in the parental home the twins went to private schools together until [age 17]," and "lived a few roads away from each other in the same northern industrial town. They were dressed alike."

In addition to these obvious examples of *non*-separation, the following passages from Shields' book illustrate many other ways that the sample was biased in favor of producing more behaviorally similar MZA pairs:

- "Based primarily on volunteers, our group of twins is self-selected and for this reason probably not a representative sample" (Shields, 1962, p. 29).
- "It can be argued that twins who are alike stand a greater chance of being investigated than those who differ" (p. 19).
- "Admittedly, [MZA] environments have not as a rule been extremely different" (p. 20).
- "One pair was separated at each of the following ages—5, 7, 8, and 9 years" (p. 46).
- "We did not reject eight pairs that were reunited at some time during childhood" (p. 46).
- 30 pairs were "brought up in different branches of the same family" (p. 47).
- "The twins with the greatest opportunity for contact in childhood were fourteen pairs who most of the time attended the same school" (p. 48).
- "Large differences in social class do not occur often, however, in the present material" (p. 48).
- "A distinct difference between the homes in religious persuasion (Roman Catholic–Church of England) occurred in only two pairs" (p. 49).
- "Some of the twins brought up apart had close contact as adults" (p. 50).
- "There are five pairs where contact as adults has been very close for some considerable period" (p. 51).
- "Thirty-three S [MZA] and twenty-nine C [MZT] pairs were thought to differ in this respect [socioeconomic status] if only to a modest extent" (p. 116).
- "The degrees of social and cultural differences between the families in the S [MZA] pairs were as a rule not remarkable" (p. 148).
- "Would similarity have been less if the homes had not been so alike, particularly if so many of the separated twins had not been brought up in different branches of the same family with, presumably, a good deal of resemblance culturally? To this objection one must answer 'quite possibly'" (p. 151).

An additional bias was introduced by the fact that, like Newman and colleagues, Shields' original intention had been to exclude DZA pairs from the study (p. 32). For this reason, during the correspondence stage he rejected several dissimilar MZA pairs because he did not want to take the risk that they were DZAs (p. 22; despite his original intention, Shields eventually included 11 DZA pairs in his study).

Conclusion

Based on the evidence presented here, the claim that Shields' study was based on "separated" or "reared-apart" twins can only be made by people: (a) who have not read the book describing the study; (b) who have a radically different definition of what constitutes "reared-apart" or "separated" twins than is commonly understood; (c) who rely on secondary sources that fail to discuss the nature of the sample or Shields' many cautions; (d) who accept Shields' definitions at face value; or (e) who consciously omit facts in the service of promoting a genetic agenda. As a critic observed, "the majority of Shields' separated pairs were never in any real sense separated at all" (Taylor, 1980, p. 79). Very true, yet it is rare to read such statements in mainstream or behavioral genetic accounts. And Shields himself must shoulder responsibility for presenting this work as a study of twins "brought up apart," and for reaching firm conclusions about genetic influences on personality and IQ on the basis of this sample of *partially* reared-apart twins. Simply put, due to its massive biases and the invalid transformation of partially reared-apart twin pairs into "separated" twin pairs, this was *not* a study of reared-apart twins.

Juel-Nielsen, 1965

Overview

The third classical TRA study was published by Niels Juel-Nielsen in Denmark in 1965. The original publication was accompanied by a follow-up study and was published in the 1980 book *Individual and Environment: Monozygotic Twins Reared Apart* (Juel-Nielsen, 1965/1980). Juel-Nielsen studied only 12 MZA pairs, and did not use a control group. Unlike the previous studies that relied on volunteer participants responding to media appeals, 8 of the 12 pairs were identified through the less biased method of population registers. The remaining four pairs were obtained "by chance." To be included in the study, the twins were required to be (1) "alive," (2) "reared apart from early life," and (3) "monozygotic" (Juel-Nielsen, 1965/1980, Part I, p. 38). Four pairs were separated during the first 6 weeks of life, five additional pairs were separated between 6 weeks and 12 months, with the remaining three pairs separated at 3½ years, 3½ years, and 5¾ years.

Most grew up in economically deprived (poor) working-class or rural Danish families.

Even though two-thirds of the pairs were identified by population registers, Juel-Nielsen still had to convince identified twins to participate in the study, and only twins willing to participate were included. Juel-Nielsen personally conducted all of the interviews. The MZA pairs were administered two intelligence tests (Wechsler-Bellevue Intelligence Scale, Form I, and Raven's Progressive Matrices), and two personality tests (Rorschach's Test, Rapaport's Word Association Test).[2] For reasons that included the small sample and the lack of Danish standardizations of the tests, he wrote, "The test results must be evaluated with caution, particularly with regard to the general conclusions" (Juel-Nielsen, 1965/1980, Part I, p. 58). Juel-Nielsen reported an MZA Wechsler-Bellevue IQ test correlation of 0.62, but did not calculate total sample personality test correlations. He concluded that, although intelligence is "to a certain extent, conditioned by environment and education," it "is quite predominantly determined by genetic factors" (Juel-Nielsen, 1965/1980, Part I, p. 132). He also concluded that, while "environmental factors play a decisive role in the development of personality," his results also indicated "that genetic factors play an important part in the development of the normal personality" (Juel-Nielsen, 1965/1980, Part I, p. 135).

Assumptions

Juel-Nielsen interpreted his findings of the basis of the assumption that "similarities in the twins' personality appearance and development have been shown," and that "these similarities must be related to the genotypical identity of the twins, and must be taken as an expression of the importance of genetic factors for the normal development of personality" (Juel-Nielsen, 1965/1980, Part I, p. 77). He restated this position in the context of describing the two main assumptions comprising the "theoretical framework" of his study:

> The theoretical framework of my investigation has been based on the assumption that differences between monozygotic twin partners reared apart from early life are conditioned by differences in their surroundings, and that similarities between them must be taken as expressions of their common genotype.
> (Juel-Nielsen, 1965/1980, Part III, p. 12)[3]

Juel-Nielsen, therefore, based his study and conclusions on a circular argument, since he assumed that MZA behavioral similarities "must be taken as expressions of their common genotype," and then concluded that above-zero behavioral correlations show that a characteristic such as intelligence "is quite predominantly determined by genetic factors." But that is the only logical conclusion he could have arrived at, since he already assumed that environmental factors do not contribute to MZA behavioral similarity. In other words, Juel-Nielsen both *assumed and concluded* that MZA behavioral similarity is caused by twins' identical genotypes—a circular argument that we will see in later chapters was repeated by the Minnesota TRA researchers.

Clearly, it is illogical to reach a conclusion that something is true based on the prior assumption that it is true, with the conclusion and the assumption serving to circularly cross-validate each other. A circular argument takes the form of "X is true because Y is true; Y is true because X is true." As an author writing about circular reasoning concluded, "A convincing argument for conclusion c can't rest on the prior assumption that c [is correct], so something has gone seriously wrong with such an argument" (Rips, 2002, p. 767).[4]

If all behavioral similarities among Juel-Nielsen's MZA pairs "must be taken as expressions of their common genotype," we must conclude that speaking the Danish language, practicing the Lutheran religion, and having *smørrebrød* and a cup of "boiled egg coffee" for lunch are genetically inherited traits. We would also have to conclude that being the same sex and being born at the same time, or being brought up in different social classes ranging from beggar to aristocrat, would have no behavior-influencing effects.

At the same time, Juel-Nielsen was well aware of the fact that, among MZAs, "a series of general cultural, social and psychological factors may well be common in their environments" (Juel-Nielsen, 1965/1980, Part I, p. 16). He also recognized that "all the twins were brought up in Denmark, the geographical distance between the childhood homes was on the whole small, and owing to the relatively uniform social, educational and cultural structure of the country, great diversities of environment are not to be expected" (Juel-Nielsen, 1965/1980, Part I, p. 97). However, he discounted the potential impact of these environmental similarities and instead focused on the "presumed . . . more relevant" role of "interpersonal relationships" and "attachments to objects" (Juel-Nielsen, 1965/1980, Part I, p. 16). These influences were emphasized by then-dominant psychoanalytic theories of development, and following Shields, Juel-Nielsen focused on examining the role of the early home environment on psychological development. Like Shields, Juel-Nielsen de-emphasized the role of common cultural influences on behavior, which will be examined in Chapter 4.

In contrast to Juel-Nielsen's "theoretical framework," Newman and colleagues recognized that even perfectly separated twins could experience similar behavior-shaping environments:

> Complete separation of a pair of twins guarantees that they shall have in common none of the random and casual experiences of childhood and shall have no friends and acquaintances in common, but it does not preclude the possibility that they may have been brought up in environments and lived through experiences which, if not specifically, at least generally, are the same.
>
> (Newman et al., 1937, p. 145)

This was a very astute observation in 1937! It is also one that has been largely ignored (or not properly controlled for) by TRA researchers ever since. Newman and colleagues not only implied that even perfectly separated MZA pairs might behave more similarly because they grow up in similar social environments, but also recognized the effect of having "lived through experiences" at the same time. In other words, two people born at the same time in the same region experience social and political environments at the same time during the same developmental periods of their lives (age, sex, and other "cohort" effects will be discussed in more detail in upcoming chapters).

Lack of a control group

Unlike all other TRA investigators, Juel-Nielsen decided against creating a control (comparison) group with which to compare his MZA results, believing that it was "doubtful" that a control group consisting of either MZTs or DZTs "was logically and theoretically ideal" (Juel-Nielsen, 1965/1980, Part I, pp. 35–36). In lieu of a control group, he decided to conduct a series of follow-up studies, which he felt would be easier to perform in a small country such as Denmark.

Interestingly, Juel-Nielsen considered, but then rejected, the formation of a control group far superior to MZTs or DZTs—a control group that has never been used in TRA research. As he described it, such a control group would consist of "unrelated persons matched for sex and age and brought up together, or perhaps, as is the case with separated twins and with other persons, brought up in different environments" (Juel-Nielsen, 1965/1980, Part I, p. 36). A control group consisting of genetically *un*related people, if matched properly on the basis of the environmental similarities shared by MZAs (appearance, age, sex, culture, religion, socioeconomic status and so on), would indeed constitute and interesting and much more appropriate group with which to compare the MZA sample. However, Juel-Nielsen decided that "such an investigation is hardly practicable" because "twins usually accept that a special interest is connected with them," whereas unrelated people presumably don't feel this way (Part I, p. 36).

Juel-Nielsen's decision to not use a control group obviously flowed from his "theoretical framework" assumption that MZA behavioral resemblance is the result of their common genotype. Once this is assumed, a control group does not seem necessary.

Degree of contact and environmental similarity

The 12 MZA pairs Juel-Nielsen studied clearly experienced less contact and emotional closeness when compared with the Newman and Shields pairs. Nevertheless, their degree of separation falls well short of what most people would consider to be truly reared-apart twins. Table 2.3 lists the 12 pairs, their ages at separation and at the time they were studied, along with excerpts from the detailed case histories provided by Juel-Nielsen.

As seen in Table 2.3, age at separation ranged from 1 day to almost 6 years, and 5 of the 12 pairs spent at least the first year of life together. In addition, Pair IV ("Ingegerd & Monika") was reared together with their mother between the ages of 7 and 14. Several pairs had a close relationship and years of mutual contact. Each of the 12 case histories Juel-Nielsen presented contained a section called "The Twin Relationship," which should not be found in a study of "reared-apart" twins where the common perception is that twins were separated at birth and had never met, and therefore had *no* relationship with each other. Most twins in this study grew up in impoverished rural or urban environments. This restricted range of rearing environments added an additional important similarity-producing bias to the study.[5]

Other sources of bias

Like Newman and Shields, Juel-Nielsen mentioned several potential biases in his study and raised several cautions:

- "The other four pairs ... were brought to our knowledge by chance .... these four pairs of twins may have either come forward voluntarily or been found by the very reason of a great resemblance, particularly in personality" (Juel-Nielsen, 1965/1980, Part I, p. 40).
- "To sum up, the methods of investigation employed, both by interview and by psychometrics, present from the start important limitations which must be taken into account in the evaluation of the final results of the investigation" (Juel-Nielsen, 1965/1980, Part I, p. 59).
- "The chief objection that may be made to this analysis of the differences and similarities between the early environments of the twins lies in the fact that the whole investigation was made by the same person" (Juel-Nielsen, 1965/1980, Part I, p. 103).
- "Where one is to put the limits for inclusion or exclusion [in the study] on account of the time of separation must be an arbitrary question" (Juel-Nielsen, 1965/1980, Part I, p. 125).

Table 2.3 Environmental Similarities, Contact, and Relationship of "Reared-Apart" MZA Twin Pairs: Information on All 12 Pairs Reported in the 1965/1980 Juel-Nielsen Study

Pair (Age)	Age at Separation	Placement	From the Case Descriptions
I. Palle & Peter (22)	10 months	Adopted Adopted	"The twins remained in close contact with each other ever since they were reunited. They met daily and acquired common friends, rowed in the same club, played chess together, and shared other interests" (p. 16). "Their homes do not seem to have differed particularly as regards social and economic status, housing conditions or general cultural influences" (p. 33)
II. Olga & Ingrid (35)	7 months	Foster child Foster child	"The twins were born out of wedlock. Shortly after birth they had been put into the care of foster-parents who lived in different parts of Jutland. The first saw each other again . . . at the age of 35" (p. 36)
III. Maren & Jensine (37)	6 weeks	Foster child Foster child	Grew up "in neighboring parishes" (p. 75). "After they had become adults . . . in spite of their differences they felt mutually bound to each other" (p. 76). "The childhood environments of the twins were very similar in their outer structure . . . . Both were brought up in stable, religious homes" (p. 84)
IV. Inggerd & Monika (42)	12 months	"Complicated foster childhood/ complicated foster childhood"	"The last part of their childhood, from their 7th to their 14th year, was spent together with their mother" (p. 113). "The twins always kept together when children, they played only with each other and were treated as a unit by their environment . . . . When Inggegerd was punished, it was Monika who cried" (p. 104). "It was a close relationship . . . during the last part of their childhood" (Part I, p. 97)

(continued)

Table 2.3 (Continued)

Pair (Age)	Age at Separation	Placement	From the Case Descriptions
V. Kaj & Robert (45)	9 months	Adopted / Adopted	"Nothing in common and did not like each other" (p. 115). "Robert was revolted by the glimpses he got of Kaj's way of living . . . . Kaj described his twin brother as 'the most unpleasant person I have ever come across'" (p. 132). "Proclivity of both twins to misrepresentation" (p. 135)
VI. Martha & Marie (49)	3½ years	Foster child / Foster child	At age 3½, "their mother placed her children in foster-homes in the neighborhood and the twins were sent to different families" (p. 148). Went "to the same school" (p. 148). "During the almost four years they were together in their home they resembled each other closely and were easily misidentified by strangers" (p. 151)
VII. Kamma & Ella (50)	1 day	Foster child / Natural father	"Kamma was taken care of by friends of the family. . . . Ella remained home with the parents" (p. 165). "Both had a feeling of strong solidarity since they met at the age of 12" (p. 176). As adults "they were always happy together but had little chance of seeing each other" (p. 176)
VIII. Signe & Hanna (54)	3 weeks	Foster child / Foster child	"The twins had known about each other's existence from about the age of 14 years. They corresponded with each other during the next few years, but did not meet until they were 20" (p. 201). Afterward, "they met each other at intervals of some years" (p. 201)
IX. Karin & Kristine (64)	3 weeks	Foster child / Foster child	After separation at three weeks, "they saw each other again at the age of six. During later childhood they attended different schools and only saw each other once a year" (p. 217). "The socio-economic circumstances of their foster-homes can hardly have differed very much" (p. 229)

X. Petrine & Dorthe (70)	12 months	Adopted Biological mother	"When 18 they lived together with their mother for six months but separated again, although they still keep in touch with each other" (p. 232). "They had always felt very much attached to each other.... Photographs [were] taken when they were 24 years old; they are fashionably dressed in high-necked lace frocks with exactly the same hair-style .... they were rather like good friends" (p. 246)
XI. Astrid & Edith (72)	3½ years	Biological mother Adopted	"They were separated when about three years and six months old" (p. 261). "The twins remained separated and were brought up in different quarters of Copenhagen" (p. 256). "When children the twins only saw each other at important family parties.... they were regarded as 'cousins'" (p. 267). "They did not think that there had been important differences in schooling" (p. 267)
XII. Vigo & Oluf (77)	5¾ years	Foster child Foster child	After separation when "nearly six years old," they "were brought up in neighboring villages, a few miles apart in North Zealand" (p. 276). Until separation at age six they "had been very closely attached to each other" (p. 283). "They had little schooling" (p. 291). "Since they had become adults, they had often not seen each other for several years. They still felt attached to each other, were happy to meet, and never disparaged each other" (p. 283)

From Juel-Nielsen (1965/1980). In this book, Part I (the main study), Part II (case material), and Part III (follow-up) each begin with page 1. All page numbers in Table 2.3 are taken from the Part II "Case Material" section unless cited otherwise.

- "An investigation of twins who have been exposed to unusually different environments in childhood was not the aim of this investigation" (Juel-Nielsen, 1965/1980, Part I, p. 126).

Conclusion

Like the previous investigations, Juel-Nielsen conducted a worthwhile and interesting study that was accentuated by the superbly detailed case histories he provided for each pair. Although his sample was very small, his MZA pairs clearly were more "separated" than the Newman and Shields MZAs.

Regardless of the great efforts and pioneering work of Juel-Nielsen and his predecessors, however, the fact remains that all three classical studies were subject to numerous biases and questionable assumptions. This will become even more apparent in the next two chapters, when I examine the writings of the critics as well as problems with claims that "intelligence" and "personality" can be measured and partitioned into genetic and environmental components. Therefore, while these studies help generate interesting ideas about the nature–nurture question, they have provided no scientifically acceptable evidence in support of genetic influences on human behavioral differences on the basis of having studied "reared-apart" twin pairs.

The Cyril Burt Scandal

In a widely reported example of probable fraud in science, noted British psychologist Cyril Burt (1883–1971) claimed to have given IQ tests to 53 MZA pairs. In the 1966 final report of the study, Burt reported an MZA IQ correlation 0.771 for his "group test" IQ (Burt, 1966, p. 146). Burt also reported that the twins had been placed into a wide range of families in different socioeconomic categories, yet he produced little case history information. However, irregularities and unchanging (invariant) correlations were reported by Leon Kamin in 1973, and were published in his 1974 book, *The Science and Politics of I.Q.* Kamin was the first to point out that the 0.771 MZA IQ correlation reported in 1966 was identical to Burt's 1955 correlation based on only 21 pairs, and to his 1958 correlation based on "over 30" pairs (Kamin, 1974, p. 38). The chances of obtaining identical correlations down to the third decimal place on the basis of such differing sample sizes were miniscule. Two years later, London *Sunday Times* reporter Oliver Gillie raised doubts that Burt's research assistants had ever existed (Gillie, 1976). British psychologist Leslie Hearnshaw, until then a supporter of Burt, published a biography of Burt in 1979 in which he convincingly argued that Burt had invented much of his twin data (Hearnshaw, 1979). Hearnshaw's conclusions were widely accepted by the early 1980s. Although subsequent investigations have led many genetic researchers and commentators to argue that the fraud charges leveled at Burt are unsubstantiated (see Fletcher, 1991; Joynson, 1989), all sides of the issue agree that Burt's data cannot be used.

While scientific fraud or misconduct is a serious charge, it is more widespread than commonly believed. According to the author of a 2009 study, roughly 2 percent of scientists admit to fabricating or falsifying research data, and about one-third admit to other questionable research practices. The investigator added further, "It is likely that this is a conservative estimate of the true prevalence of scientific misconduct" (Fanelli, 2009, p. 1). It is of course theoretically possible for a researcher to change data and results, or even to write up an entire study that was never performed. But more often, as the epidemiologist John Ioannidis pointed out, "False extravagant results are probably far more likely to arise from selective analysis and outcome reporting and data dredging of the analytical space rather than by fraud, but fraud does occur" (Ioannidis, 2014, p. 100).

In 2011 it came to light that the Dutch psychologist Diederik Stapel had fabricated data (unrelated to twin research), and even entire studies (Levelt Committee, Noort Committee, Drenth Committee, 2012). One of these "studies" was published in *Science*, one of the world's leading scientific journals. In November, 2011 the *New York Times* published an article about this case, whose author Benedict Carey mentioned that fraud is a particular problem area in the field of psychology. According to Carey, referring to a committee report on Stapel's activities:

> Experts say the case exposes deep flaws in the way science is done in a field, psychology, that has only recently earned a fragile respectability. The psychologist, Diederik Stapel, of Tilburg University, committed academic fraud in "several dozen" published papers, many accepted in respected journals and reported in the ... media.

Carey noted that the scandal is

> the latest in a string of embarrassments in a field that critics and statisticians say badly needs to overhaul how it treats research results. In recent years, psychologists have reported a raft of findings on race biases, brain imaging and even extrasensory perception that have not stood up to scrutiny.

Although "outright fraud may be rare, these experts ... contend that Dr. Stapel took advantage of a system that allows researchers to operate in near secrecy and massage data to find what they want to find, without much fear of being challenged." According to the committee, in Carey's words,

> Dr. Stapel was able to operate for so long ... in large measure because he was "lord of the data," the only person who saw the experimental evidence that had been gathered (or fabricated). This is a widespread problem in psychology, said Jelte M. Wicherts, a psychologist at the University of Amsterdam.

Carey also noted that in "a recent survey, two-thirds of Dutch research psychologists said they did not make their raw data available for other researchers to see. 'This is in violation of ethical rules established in the field,' Dr. Wicherts said" (Carey, 2011).

Although Burt is the only TRA researcher alleged to have fabricated data, the *Times* author noted that the field of psychology in particular has created conditions that allow unethical researchers to collect and selectively report data that support their theories, beliefs, and vested interests, with little fear that such data manipulation will be discovered or challenged. The temptation to manipulate and selectively report data is greater in fields where researchers are allowed to become "lords of the data."

Many years before he was unmasked as a fraud, Stapel wrote in 2000,

> The freedom we have in the design of our experiments is so enormous that when an experiment does not give us what we are looking for, we blame the experiment, not our theory. (At least, that is the way I work.) Is this problematic? No.
> (Stapel, 2000, quoted in Levelt Committee, Noort Committee, Drenth Committee, 2012, p. 40)

Here, Stapel candidly stated that when the results of an experiment do not produce the desired results, "we blame the experiment, not our theory." Instead of arguing for the need to reduce bias in the interpretation of research results, Stapel believed that blaming the experiment in the interest of keeping a theory intact is not "problematic."

In a related story, Leslie John and her colleagues surveyed over 2,000 psychologists about their involvement in "questionable research practices" such as failing to report data, or manipulating data and statistics in various ways. They found a "surprisingly high" percentage of anonymous respondents admitting to having engaged in such practices. The researchers went as far as concluding, "Some questionable practices may constitute the prevailing research norm" in the field of psychology (John, Loewenstein, & Prelec, 2012, p. 524).[6]

ORIGINS, PUBLICATIONS, AND SCANDAL

The Controversy Surrounding Arthur Jensen

Although by the end of the 1960s the four classical TRA studies (then including Burt) had an impact, they were not widely viewed as having provided evidence that called on social and behavioral scientists to radically reevaluate the role of genetic influences on psychological and behavioral characteristics, and these studies were not yet the subject of in-depth critical analyses.

All that changed in 1969, when University of California at Berkeley psychologist Arthur Jensen (1923–2012) published an analysis in the *Harvard Educational Review*, where he argued that IQ scores were roughly 80 percent heritable, and that some portion of the 15 point mean IQ score difference between American white and black people could be explained by genetic factors (Jensen, 1969). This was a modern reaffirmation of the mainstream psychology/psychometrics/eugenic position of the first four decades of the twentieth century (see Kamin, 1974). Jensen's publication touched off a storm of controversy on IQ, genetics, and racial differences in IQ that continued throughout the 1970s and afterwards (for arguments against Jensen's claims and theories, see Block & Dworkin, 1976, Gould, 1981; Hirsch, 1975, 1981; Lewontin, Rose, & Kamin, 1984; Mensh & Mensh, 1991; Montagu, 1999; Schiff & Lewontin, 1986; Taylor, 1980). The controversy was rekindled by Herrnstein and Murray's 1994 book *The Bell Curve*, whose authors cautiously endorsed Jensen's position that black people are genetically inferior in measured intelligence, and that social classes differ in intelligence as well (Herrnstein & Murray, 1994). More recently, science writer Nicholas Wade argued in *A Troublesome Inheritance* that there is an evolutionary basis for behavioral differences among various racial and ethnic groups (Wade, 2014; for a statement in opposition to Wade's arguments that was endorsed by over 100 population geneticists and evolutionary biologists, see Coop, Eisen, Nielsen, Przeworski, & Rosenberg, 2014).

Much of Jensen's 1969 argument was based on IQ correlations reported in the four TRA studies, with an emphasis on the Burt study whose "most important" characteristic was its wide range of MZA rearing environments. In Jensen's words,

> The separated [Burt] twins were spread over the entire range of socioeconomic levels (based on classification in terms of the six socioeconomic categories of the English census), and there was a slight, though nonsignificant, negative correlation between the environmental ratings of the separated twin pairs.
>
> (Jensen, 1969, p. 52)

Jensen speculated about the eugenic implications of his analysis, asking if there was

> a danger that current welfare policies, unaided by eugenic foresight, could lead to the genetic enslavement of a substantial segment of our population? The possible consequences of our failure seriously to study these questions may well be viewed by future generations as our society's greatest injustice to Negro Americans.
>
> (p. 95)

In other words, Jensen believed that eugenic measures were needed to reduce black people's rate of reproduction, which would reduce their numbers in the U.S. population and therefore raise the national intelligence level.

The following year Jensen published an article elaborating on his interpretation of the (then) four TRA studies, entitled "IQs of Identical Twins Reared Apart" (Jensen, 1970). Here, Jensen presented a "new analysis" based on pooling 122 MZA pairs across the four studies that had been tested for IQ, of which 53 pairs (43 percent) were derived from the subsequently discredited Burt data. Jensen calculated a pooled intraclass MZA IQ correlation of 0.824, which he believed "may be interpreted as an upper-bound estimate of the heritability (h^2) of IQ in the English, Danish, and North American Caucasian populations sampled in these studies" (Jensen, 1970, p. 133). He argued that data based on MZA pairs "is conceptually the simplest method of estimating the broad heritability of a characteristic" (p. 133). While allowing that some aspects of the twins' separation were not ideal (lack of random assignment, placement in different branches of the same family, shared intrauterine environment), Jensen portrayed the sample of 122 MZA pairs as largely uncontaminated by common environmental influences. He concluded that the pooled MZA data confirmed the high heritability of IQ, and that the roughly six-point average IQ difference he calculated between MZA pairs "may be attributable to prenatal intrauterine factors rather than to later effects of the individual's social-psychological environment" (Jensen, 1970, p. 146). For Jensen, then, a person's IQ score is largely determined at birth.

Jensen spent the rest of his long career defending the validity of IQ tests and the concept of "general intelligence" or g, the high heritability of IQ scores, and the position that IQ score differences between classes, and between races, are mainly the result of genetic factors (for example, see Jensen, 1980, 1998; Rushton & Jensen, 2010). Thirty years after his 1969 *Harvard Educational Review* article, Jensen and psychologist co-author J. Philippe Rushton discussed the need for "race realism," and continued the theme that "racial group differences, and the associated gaps in living standards, education levels etc., are rooted in factors that are largely heritable, not cultural" (Rushton & Jensen, 2008, p. 638). Jensen played a major role in strengthening hereditarian theories of IQ in the United States and elsewhere, even though many of his followers were not willing to publically support his views on IQ racial differences.

In 1994, however, 52 of the world's leading IQ genetic researchers (at least ten of whom had publically supported the position that genetic factors influence IQ racial differences) endorsed a carefully worded "Mainstream Science on Intelligence" statement published in the *Wall Street Journal* in support of many positions put forward in *The Bell Curve* (Arvey et al., 1994). While not explicitly endorsing genetic causes of IQ racial differences, according to the statement, "There is no definitive answer to why IQ bell curves differ across racial-ethnic groups." The statement held that "most experts" believe that environmental influences are involved in racial differences in IQ, and that these experts also believe that "genetics could be involved too." Among the 52 signatories of this statement were Jensen and Robert Plomin, as well as Minnesota TRA researchers Richard Arvey, Thomas Bouchard, and David Lykken.

The Minnesota Study of Twins Reared Apart

By far the most well-known and influential TRA study is the Minnesota Study of Twins Reared Apart (MISTRA), which was carried out by Thomas Bouchard, Jr. and colleagues between 1979 and 2000, with many additional publications based on the MISTRA data appearing since 2000. Bouchard was awarded the American Psychological Foundation's 2014 Gold Medal Award for Life Achievement in the Science of Psychology, which cited the MISTRA as "groundbreaking and inventive, exciting and controversial," and a "stunning achievement, a body of work in which all psychologists can take pride" (Anonymous, 2014, p. 477). Here I will briefly introduce and describe this study and the media attention given to individual pairs, and then return in Chapters 5 and 6 for a detailed analysis of the results reported by the researchers, the conclusions they drew from their results, and the various claims made about the study in the context of a comprehensive book published by MISTRA researcher Nancy Segal (Segal, 2012).

In 1990, Bouchard and his MISTRA colleagues David Lykken, Matt McGue, Nancy Segal, and Auke Tellegen published their results in *Science* (Bouchard, Lykken, McGue, Segal, & Tellegen, 1990), reporting MZA and MZT correlations for physical variables, IQ, and personality test scores. The reported full-scale Wechsler IQ intraclass MZA correlation was 0.69 (48 pairs), while the MZT correlation was 0.88 (40 pairs). For personality measures, MZA and MZT correlations were each about 0.50. Based on the size of the MZA correlations, the investigators concluded that IQ, personality, and other psychological characteristics are strongly influenced by genetic factors. Because MZA and MZT correlations were similar, they concluded that "shared family environments" have little influence, and framed their results in the context of evolutionary psychology and sociobiology. The MISTRA researchers subsequently published results for various other behavioral characteristics. In most cases they reached similar conclusions about the influences of genes and environment.

Bouchard and colleagues began this famous 1990 *Science* publication by stating,

> Monozygotic and dizygotic twins who were separated early in life and reared apart (MZA and DZA twin pairs) are a fascinating experiment of nature. They also provide the simplest and most powerful method for disentangling the influence of environmental and genetic factors on human characteristics.
> (Bouchard, Lykken, et al., 1990, p. 223)

However, as I will discuss in more detail in Chapter 6, they decided not to report the correlations for their 30 DZA pairs "due to space limitations and the smaller size of the DZA sample (30 sets)" (p. 223).

The MISTRA has had a major impact on the nature–nurture debate in the social and behavioral sciences, and its authors' conclusions in support of a major role for genetic influences on IQ and various dimensions of personality have been celebrated and popularized in countless textbooks and articles, and in many popular books that could be characterized as "Mistraphile" (for examples of the latter, see Cassill, 1982; Harris, 1998; Pinker, 2002; Ridley, 2003; Watson, 1981; L. Wright, 1997; W. Wright, 1998). As one author wrote, "The science of behavioral genetics, largely through twin studies, has made a persuasive case that much of our identity is stamped on us from conception" (L. Wright, 1997, p. 143).

A theme of many of these popular works has been that unbiased and apolitical TRA researcher-scientists of high integrity discovered, often to their own astonishment, that genetic factors play a major role in most aspects of human behavior and abilities. For example, barely one year into the investigation with no more than 15 MZA pairs and no published data, Bouchard was quoted in a 1980 magazine article as saying, "The genetic effect pervades the entire structure of personality. If someone had come to me with results like this I wouldn't have believed him. I was aghast" (Jackson, 1980, p. 53). In another 1980 article, *Science* writer Constance Holden quoted Bouchard as saying, "I frankly expected far more differences [between twins] than we have found so far. I'm a psychologist, not a geneticist" (Holden, 1980, p. 1323). Another journalist wrote that Bouchard was "boggled by the unexpected discoveries" (W. Wright, 1998, p. 41).

At times, the authors of these popular accounts can't get the story straight. For example, in his 2003 book *The Agile Gene*, popular genetics writer Matt Ridley quoted Bouchard as saying in an interview, "Look, when I started I did not believe these kinds of things [personality traits] could be influenced by genes. I was persuaded by the evidence." Yet in the very next paragraph Ridley wrote, "When Bouchard began, he expected to find that some measures of personality were more heritable than others" (Ridley, 2003, p. 82). From a scientific perspective it really doesn't matter what Bouchard thought or expected to find, or whether he was "aghast" or "boggled," and these authors' accounts of Bouchard's reactions to what he believed he had found, in contrast to what he supposedly expected to find, seem much more like disingenuous marketing strategies than they do science.

At the same time, critics are often portrayed in the Mistraphile literature as politically motivated outsiders who employ faulty arguments against real scientists in the service of their (political) "ideologies," and/ or their naïve sentimental attachment to outmoded ideas about human equality that "science" has shown to be false. The supposedly objective and non-ideological TRA researcher "scientists" and "scholars" are portrayed as having being hounded, ridiculed, persecuted, and even physically attacked for simply telling the unpleasant truth, with the critics and their supporters often being portrayed as the persecutors. In a glowing tribute to Jensen and his work, Sandra Scarr wrote about the "mobs" that disrupted and threatened Jensen in the 1970s. Even worse, in her view, were the intellectual "thugs with pens," who are "politically driven liars, who distort scientific facts." Scarr saw these critics, some of whom she named, as "despicable" because they "deliberately corrupt science" (Scarr, 1998, p. 231).

Selectively Reported MZA Pairs

From 1979 until the first major publication of the MISTRA data in 1988, there were many reports in the press and in popular works describing the lives and supposed similarities of selectively reported pairs. The most celebrated pair was Jim Lewis and Jim Springer, commonly referred to as the "Jim Twins." The "Jims" of Ohio were separated at birth and were reunited at age 39. They were said to share a "spooky" set of similarities, such as the names of their wives and children, career choices, preferences for particular brands of beer and cigarettes, and favorite holiday vacation spots as teenagers. Newspaper accounts of the Jim Twins inspired Bouchard to study reared-apart twin pairs, and Bouchard invited them to the University of Minnesota and they became the first studied MISTRA MZA pair.

A typical account of the Jim Twins, seen below, is taken from journalist Peter Watson's 1981 book *Twins: An Investigation into the Strange Coincidences in the Lives of Separated Twins.*

> Both had married a girl named Linda, divorced her, *then* married a second time, to a woman called Betty. Lewis had named his first son James Alan, Springer had called his son James Allan. Both had owned a dog as a boy, and named it Toy.... Both spent their holidays at the same beach near St. Petersburg in Florida.... Both drove there and back in the same kind of car, a Chevrolet. Both bit their fingernails—right down until there is nothing left.... Both have basement workshops and work in wood, building frames and furniture. Both chain-smoke Salems.... Both enjoy stock car racing and dislike baseball.... Both scatter love notes around the house.
> (Watson, 1981, pp. 10–11, italics in original)

Similar accounts of the Jim Twins were widely disseminated in the decades that followed (for some examples, see Begley, 1987; Cassill, 1982; Harris, 1998; Lykken, 1999; Miller, 2012; Ridley, 2003; L. Wright, 1997; W. Wright, 1998).

Although stories about the Jim Twins and other pairs, which include the "Fireman Twins," the "Giggle Twins," the "Talking Twins," the "Nazi and the Jew Twins," the "Seven Rings on Seven Fingers Twins," the "Necklace Twins," and so on, have been told and retold by both researchers and journalists *ad nauseam* since 1979, there is an important and simple point to be made about such stories: *They prove absolutely nothing about the importance of genetic influences on human behavior.*[7] Yet in most cases, both journalists and scientists suggest that the supposed behavioral similarities of these pairs are caused by their genetic identity.

The Jim Twins came to the attention of journalists and researchers *because of* their reported similarities. Most pairs of this type had incentives to invent similarities, and there is little doubt that some who had previously led uneventful lives enjoyed their celebrity status which in some cases included television talk show appearances and having book chapters written about them. In some cases reunited twins hired talent agents and sought book and movie deals (Jackson, 1980).[8]

Moreover, it is likely that any two randomly selected people of the same age and sex will discover many common interests, attitudes, memories, preferences, and so on. As Minnesota twin researchers David Lykken, Bouchard and their colleagues conceded, "When any two biographies are avidly compared, at least some overlap is likely to be found" (Lykken, McGue, Tellegen, & Bouchard, 1992, p. 1556). Bouchard also recognized, "some of those similarities are surely coincidental—complete strangers at cocktail parties routinely discover 'astonishing' occurrences in their lives; imagine what they might find after fifty hours of filling out questionnaires" (Bouchard, 1997c, p. 53).

Researchers and journalists claiming that MZA pairs have many similarities usually highlight the reported similarities, and downplay or ignore the differences. As Juel-Nielsen pointed out, twin researchers are "consciously or unconsciously, in a position to choose to emphasize similarities between the twins, and at the same to omit to register, or be inclined to belittle, the differences" (Juel-Nielsen, 1965/1980, Part I, p. 57). And Shields recognized that twin researchers risk being "taken in" not only by twins, but by their own preexisting biases: "It could be objected that almost any pair of individuals will be alike in some odd way and that it is all too easy to pick on such coincidences and to exaggerate others so that the twin investigator is easily taken in" (Shields, 1962, p. 98).

Philosophy professor Val Dusek published a 1987 essay describing the selective and misleading reporting of reared-apart pairs (Dusek, 1987). For Dusek, a striking aspect of the anecdotal reunited twin material "is its similarity to the sort of evidence often offered as proof for astrology or parapsychology" (p. 21). In the astrology and extrasensory perception literature, he wrote, cases where forecasts came true are presented as evidence, whereas cases where forecasts did not come true are not mentioned. Dusek also commented that twins "may wish to exaggerate similarities of behavior or wear identical dress to receive publicity and scientific approval for themselves" (p. 21).

Other TRA Studies

Two additional TRA studies have been performed since 1980. These studies, which are much less well known and cited than the MISTRA, are a study from Finland, and the Swedish Adoption/Twin Study on Aging (SATSA). In the Swedish study the investigators considered pairs to be "reared apart" if they had been separated before age 11: "By definition, the twins reared apart were separated by the age of 11" (Pedersen, Plomin, Nesselroade, & McClearn, 1992, p. 347). About 75 percent had some degree of contact after separation. According to the researchers, the SATSA twins (average age 65.6 years) were "separated" for an average of only 10.9 years at the time of testing (Pedersen et al., 1992, p. 347). Twins supplied information by mail, and many were not investigated personally (for other major problem areas of the SATSA, see Kamin & Goldberger, 2002). Bouchard saw his study as superior to the SATSA in several respects: "Their instruments are very inferior to ours . . . . Their zygosity diagnosis is entirely by questionnaire and their data collected by mail" (Bouchard, 1993b, p. 26).

In the Finnish study (Langinvainio, Koskenvuo, Kaprio, & Sistonen, 1984), 12 of the 30 MZA pairs were separated after the age of 5, and the degree of post-separation contact is unclear. The Finnish TRA researchers were unsure about the generalizability of their findings to the rest of the population. In a statement that could be applied to all TRA studies published to date, they believed that because their study did not present an "ideal experimental situation," the "generalization of results may meet with some problems" (Langinvainio, Koskenvuo, Kaprio, Lönnqvist, & Tarkkonen, 1981, p. 198).

For reasons such as late separation and the fact that much of the SATSA and Finnish data were based on mailed questionnaires, the MISTRA publications have been the main focus of scientific and journalistic attention. Therefore, they are the main focus of TRA attention in this book.

Conclusions

There have been six systematic studies of pairs designated by the original researchers as "reared-apart" twins. These include the three classical studies by Newman and colleagues in 1937, Shields in 1962, and Juel-Nielsen in 1965/1980, the Swedish SATSA, a study from Finland, and the MISTRA. The IQ correlations produced by Cyril Burt have been discredited and are no longer counted.

The evidence I have presented in this chapter challenges the claim that the three classical studies were truly studies of reared-apart twins. As seen in Tables 2.1–2.3, in addition to other evidence I have presented, these were studies of monozygotic twin pairs only *partially* reared apart, which invalidates any claim that they provide data on pairs of reared-apart twins. This means that, as of 1979, there existed no valid study of reared-apart twins in the scientific literature. The same observation holds for the more recent Swedish and Finnish studies. Writing in 1980 about the three classical TRA studies, Howard Taylor concluded: "About two-thirds of the . . . identical twin pairs originally studied by Shields, Newman et al., and Juel-Nielsen do not fit any reasonable definition of being raised separately in uncorrelated environments" (Taylor, 1980, p. 110).

As we will see in the following chapters, TRA study results are open to various interpretations even if all pairs were separated at birth and randomly placed into the full range of available adoptive families (which we have seen was not the case). This position receives further support from the works of several critically minded authors who analyzed these studies, and whose work is the subject of the following chapter. The all-important question of whether the MISTRA qualifies as a valid TRA study that has supplied important information about genetics—indeed potentially the *only* valid TRA study supplying this information—is the subject of subsequent chapters.

Notes

1 In the 1980 revised edition of the book reporting the study (Juel-Nielsen, 1965/1980), Part I (the main study), Part II (case material), and Part III (follow-up) each begin with page 1. All citations from this book will list the page number and the corresponding Part I, II, or III assembled by Juel-Nielsen.
2 Twin pairs were administered other tests, but Juel-Nielsen did not include the results in his book (see Juel-Nielsen, 1965/1980, Part I, p. 53).
3 Juel-Nielsen also wrote, "Intra-pair similarities, to the extent that they are not attributable to similarities, or 'insufficient' dissimilarities of the environment, must, presumably, be attributed to the twins' genotypical identity" (Juel-Nielsen, 1965/1980, Part I, p. 64).
4 Another faulty aspect of Juel-Nielsen's basic assumption was that, while allowing that environmental factors can contribute to MZA differences, he assumed that environmental factors cannot contribute to MZAs' similarities. Logically speaking, if environmental factors are capable of making MZAs (and people in general) differ behaviorally, environmental influences must also be capable of making them behave more similarly. It is almost as if he assumed that MZAs are programmed at birth with very similar potentials for personality and intelligence, and that dissimilarities subsequently found between them are caused by environmental differences or events. Yet he discounted the possibility that MZA resemblance could be increased, if not be totally attributable to, environmental similarity.
5 Half of the pairs were born out of wedlock. The professions of three of the 12 biological fathers were listed as "laborer," with the remaining nine listed as "brushmaker," "farmer," "herdsman," "wholesale merchant," "carpenter," "baker," "decorator," "butcher," and "staff sergeant." Of the 12 biological mothers, five were unmarried "domestic servants," and the remaining seven were listed as "housewife" (Juel-Nielsen, 1965/1980, Part I, p. 46). The adoptive families in which some twins were placed were of similar low socioeconomic status. As Juel-Nielsen recognized, this group of biological parents "cannot, with regard to the distribution of their occupations, be said to be representative of the Danish nation as a whole" (Juel-Nielsen, 1965/1980, Part I, p. 46).
6 Another study published in 2005 in the prestigious journal *Nature*, which surveyed U.S.-based early- and mid-career scientists, found that 33% of the respondents had engaged in one of the top ten unethical behaviors during the past 3 years. These behaviors included "falsifying or 'cooking' research data," failing to disclose the involvement of firms whose products are the subject of study, "failing to present data that contradict one's own previous research," and "changing the design, methodology or results of a study in response to pressure from a funding source" (Martinson, Anderson, & de Vries, 2005, p. 737).
7 As one commentator noted, "Anecdotal examples of [MZA] behavioral convergence tell us nothing about the biological bases of behavior" (Prinz, 2012, p. 34).
8 Stories about reunited pairs have even led to calculations of the mathematical probability that pairs would have so many things in common. Watson devoted an entire chapter to such calculations in his 1981 book, implying that the twins' common genes play a role in these similarities (Watson, 1981). The Minnesota researchers supplied Watson with information at a very early stage of their investigation. In perhaps the most ridiculous chapter or article in the history of journalistic accounts of twin research, Watson calculated the chances that the Jim

twins would both drive Chevrolets, would both bite their fingernails, and would both be heavy smokers and drinkers. By Watson's calculations, the chances were 1 in 15,152. For Barbara Herbert and Daphne Goodship, another selectively reported MISTRA pair, Watson calculated that the odds that they would share five other characteristics in common were 1 in 333,000,000 (Watson, 1981, p. 130). These calculations are ridiculous because, among other reasons, similar odds could be calculated between most pairs of randomly selected biologically unrelated people comparing common behavioral characteristics.

3
STUDIES OF REARED-APART TWINS
The Critics Respond

> On the one hand, the investigator is, consciously or unconsciously, in a position to choose and emphasize similarities between the twins, and at the same to omit to register, or be inclined to belittle, the differences.
> — TRA Researcher Niels Juel-Nielsen, 1980 (Juel-Nielsen, 1965/1980, Part I, p. 57)

> We have never had and presumably never will have available a large sample of human monozygotic twins who have been reared from conception on in environments differing to the same degree as do those of members of the population at large. Any inferences from the existing studies of identical twins reared apart must be tempered by this fact.
> — Behavioral genetic researcher John Loehlin, 1978 (Loehlin, 1978b, pp. 71–72)

The claims of the original TRA researchers and subsequent commentators in favor of genetics have not gone unchallenged. This chapter will examine the arguments of several critics of TRA studies. The groundwork for much of the analyses of the Newman, Shields, and Juel-Nielsen studies in Chapter 2 was laid by earlier authors such as Leon Kamin, Susan Farber, Howard Taylor, Arthur Goldberger, Richard Lewontin, Ken Richardson, Richard Rose, Steven Rose, and others. Let us now review the works of these authors.

Leon Kamin, 1974

Princeton psychologist Leon Kamin published a groundbreaking critical analysis of the four TRA studies published up to the early 1970s in his widely discussed 1974 book, *The Science and Politics of I.Q.* (Kamin, 1974). As seen in Chapter 2, Kamin played a major role in showing that Burt's TRA IQ data could not be trusted.

In 1974 Jensen published an article (Jensen, 1974) where he recognized several problems in the figures left behind by Burt (who died in 1971). This article appeared to be a preemptive attempt to limit the damage while Kamin's book was still in press (Hirsch, 1981). In a footnote Jensen did recognize that Kamin was "the first person" to point out that Burt's MZA IQ correlations did not change even though sample sizes did (Jensen cited an unpublished 1972 speech by Kamin; Jensen, 1974, p. 12). Jensen belatedly recognized that Burt's publications lacked information and detail, and that there were errors and "inconsistencies" in his data. He also recognized Kamin's documentation of Burt's unchanging 0.771 MZA IQ correlations even though the (alleged) MZA sample had increased from 21 pairs to 53 pairs (p. 13). Jensen ended by noting "the often unknown, ambiguous, or inconsistent sample sizes and invariant correlations" found in Burt's data, and concluded that Burt's "correlations are useless for hypothesis testing" (p. 24). That is, Burt's MZA data cannot be used.

Moving on to the Newman, Shields, and Juel-Nielsen studies, Kamin highlighted many problem areas, which included:

- the late or incomplete separation of pairs;
- the fact that pairs had to have known of each other's existence to be able to participate in the Newman and Shields studies;
- the researchers' assessment of the degree of twins' separation frequently depended on the (potentially unreliable) verbal accounts of the twins themselves;
- the samples were biased in favor of the recruitment of more similar MZA pairs;
- many MZA pairs experienced similar or "correlated" environments (see Tables 2.1–2.3);
- the existence of confounding influences such as age and sex effects, which increase twin IQ correlations for non-genetic reasons;
- the existence of "unconscious experimenter bias," which may have led researchers who tested both members of an MZA pair to score them more similarly;
- problems with the tests, including a lack of test standardization in some cases;
- that subsequent reviewers performed questionable statistical practices, which included deriving standard scores from raw data, and the upward adjustments of some correlations;
- that secondary sources, including textbooks, usually fail to mention twins' correlated environments and other biases.

Kamin concluded, "To the degree that the case for a genetic influence on I.Q. scores rests on the celebrated studies of separated twins, we can justifiably conclude that there is no reason to reject the hypothesis that I.Q. is simply not heritable" (p. 67).

To a certain extent Kamin accepted the validity of heritability estimates and IQ tests, despite considering the latter to be an "instrument of oppression against the poor" (p. 2). This is seen in a frequently cited passage, where Kamin wrote, "There exist no data which should lead a prudent man to accept the hypothesis that I.Q. test scores are in any way heritable" (p. 1). He also believed that, as long as a TRA study's assumptions were met, "The intraclass I.Q. correlation of separated MZ twin pairs would in fact be an estimate of the heritability of I.Q." (p. 34). Kamin argued, however, that these assumptions were not met. I discuss the controversial topics of IQ and heritability in Chapter 4.

The Science and Politics of I.Q. was a work of major importance and scholarship, and paved the way for others to perform similar critical analyses of genetic claims, research, and theories. Along with Don Jackson's never-refuted 1960 critique of schizophrenia twin research (Jackson, 1960; Joseph, 2004), it serves as a model of how to perform a critical analysis of genetic research in the social and behavioral sciences. It is also a model of IQ historical research. In his first two chapters, Kamin documented how early twentieth-century psychologists, eugenicists, and politicians united to condemn entire groups of people, including immigrants from southern and eastern Europe, to the status of genetic inferiority on the basis of the alleged science of IQ testing.

Howard Taylor, 1980

Sociologist Howard Taylor published a major critical analysis of TRA studies in his 1980 book, *The IQ Game* (Taylor, 1980). In a statement that applies to personality research as well, Taylor argued that "the literature on IQ heritability" relies heavily on "assumptions that are arbitrary, implausible, or both" (p. 7). In greater detail than Kamin, Taylor showed that many MZA pairs in the classical studies grew up in similar environments, experienced late separation, had frequent reunions after separation, were brought up in different branches of the same family, and experienced similar educational and socioeconomic environments. He also discussed how methods of twin recruitment influenced twin similarity, and that researchers had to rely on the twins' accounts of their degree of separation. Taylor wrote that roughly two-thirds of the pairs studied in the three classical TRA studies (excluding Burt) "do not fit any reasonable definition of being raised separately in uncorrelated environments" (p. 110). He concluded that it is a "myth" that these were truly "separated identical twins" (p. 75), even as "countless articles and textbooks in behavioral genetics, psychology, education, and even sociology, have sustained the myth that these twins were separated virtually at birth and raised apart in ignorance of each other" (p. 76).

Taylor performed a statistical analysis of the Newman, Shields, and Juel-Nielsen MZA data categorized in terms of whether twins were late or early separated, whether they had been reunited prior to testing, the degree of relatedness of the adoptive families, and the similarity of their social environments. He found that, in general, IQ correlations were higher among MZA pairs that had experienced more similar environments, and lower for pairs that had experienced less similar environments. Taylor concluded that MZA correlations among pairs experiencing "absolutely uncorrelated environments would be extremely low" (p. 101).

An important aspect of Taylor's work was his detailed documentation of the numerous questionable statistical and social assumptions genetic researchers must accept in order to arrive at the conclusion that important genetic factors underlie IQ differences, and by implication other behavioral areas as well. Quite often, genetic researchers fail to list the explicit and implicit assumptions underlying their conclusions, while secondary sources such as textbooks discuss them even less frequently. Taylor saw IQ genetic research and accompanying heritability estimates as being based on a "string of flimsy and implausible assumptions" (p. 7).

Taylor concluded that genetic theories of IQ derived from TRA data published to that point were based on "a mass of faulty methods and data, which do not permit one to conclude in favor of a significant genetic effect on IQ score[s]" (p. 216). The MISTRA was in its beginning phases in 1980, and (based on personal communication he had received from Bouchard) Taylor believed that the Minnesota study "showed some promise" in being able to meet the requirements of a study in which MZAs are "separated at birth and randomly allocated over a wide range of environments" (p. 216).

Taylor accepted the validity of the heritability concept, but argued that problems in various types of kinship studies (including TRA studies) rendered them unable to produce accurate IQ heritability estimates.

Although others had praised Taylor's book in their reviews (e.g., Hirsch, 1983), Bouchard called Taylor's study a "pseudoanalysis" (Bouchard, 1983, p. 182), a dismissing term that Bouchard applied to the works of other critics of TRA studies (see Bouchard, 1982a, 1982b, 1993a, 1993b). Bouchard subsequently treated critics even more harshly, referring to "an entire industry [that] has evolved up around the reanalysis of kinship data, particularly the large body of published data on identical twins reared apart" (Bouchard, 1993a, p. 43). Given the claims and social policy decisions based on TRA studies, however, it is not surprising that many people would want to take a close look at them.[1]

Susan Farber, 1981

Psychologist Susan Farber jumped into the TRA study debate with her amazingly detailed 1981 book *Identical Twins Reared Apart: A Reanalysis*. This book remains the most in-depth work ever published on the subject, and contained a wealth of thoughtful discussion and detailed statistical analysis. Although her work has been interpreted in various ways, Farber presented a devastating indictment of the logic and methods of the existing TRA studies.

Like Kamin and Taylor, Farber observed that both the Newman and Shields samples were biased in favor of similarity because they were based on twins recruited through media appeals. "The most blatant bias," wrote Farber, "results from the way the data were collected in the first place" (p. 15). Looking at all 121 pairs reported in the literature up to 1980 (including single-case studies, and excluding the Burt data), Farber showed that, due to ascertainment bias, "approximately 90 percent of the known cases of separated MZ twins have been studied precisely because they were so alike," and that conclusions about their similarity were therefore based on "circular reasoning" (p. 36). She pointed to "quite stunning omissions in elementary design requirements such as random sampling or assignment," which are "rarely, if ever, mentioned in reports." She believed that because "the material is so rich and intriguing," researchers "become blinded to the biased nature of their samples" (p. 15).

Farber argued that the twins recruited to these studies, whose similarities were so eagerly generalized to the non-twin population, were not even representative of the population of reared-apart twins, and she questioned the twins' degree of separation. She found that only three of the 121 pairs were separated during the first year of life, were reared with no knowledge that they had a twin, and were studied at the time of their first meeting. "Of the 121 cases reported in the last fifty years," wrote Farber, "only three are 'twins reared apart' in the classical sense" (p. 60). The "most accurate description of this sample," she concluded, is "MZ twins partially reared apart" (p. 273).

Turning to the twins' socioeconomic environments, Farber showed that about 90 percent of MZAs were born into poor families, and that "anywhere from 50 to 75 percent of the twins were reared in clearly deprived homes.... Only two or three individuals were adopted into professional families" (p. 62). She argued that the pooled data were "not good and do not meet even elementary design requirements" (p. 22). In her view a well-designed study would use randomly selected and assigned MZAs, who were "reared as single individuals with no contamination from twinning" (p. 30).

Farber believed that Juel-Nielsen's study was less affected by similarity bias, because he "discovered his subjects by tracing them through twin registries and other official listings, thus ensuring that their knowledge of each other was not the prerequisite for selection" (p. 17). Although ascertainment through population registers is indeed a less biased method of obtaining a twin sample (Kendler & Prescott, 2006), we saw in Chapter 2 that only eight of Juel-Nielsen's 12 pairs (67 percent) were discovered through a register (Juel-Nielsen, 1965/1980, Part I, p. 40). One of the four non-register pairs was Palle and Peter, who were identified after the latter "approached us in 1956 at the Institute of Human Genetics in Copenhagen," with the twins stating that "due to the possible scientific interest of their case they were prepared to submit to detailed examination" (Juel-Nielsen, 1965/1980, Part II, p. 1). We have also seen that even when twin pairs are identified through a register, both must still be willing to participate in the study, which might reflect similarities in personality.

Farber also addressed the issue of cohort effects, which refer to similarities in people's behavior, preferences, physical condition, and other attributes that arise from the characteristics of the historical periods and cultural milieu in which they experience stages of life at the same time. In reference to dental records, Farber wrote that MZAs are "not so much similar to each other as they are similar to people of their eras and SES [socioeconomic status]" (p. 77). This is a very important point, and has major implications for the interpretation of all MZA data, including IQ and behavioral correlations. What researchers believe are genetic effects may actually be cohort effects based on same-sex pairs growing up in similar (non-familial) environments in the same era (see Chapter 4).

Importantly, Farber called for the creation of a central registry for TRA data to enable others to have access to the data. She believed that "biographical outlines, raw test profiles, and case summaries are the best safeguards against the disreputable claims and use of data that have occurred in the past and undoubtedly will occur in the future" (pp. 273–274):

> Probably the most fruitful avenue would be to have a central registry for all such [MZA] cases . . . . This registry need not infringe in any way on an investigator's ability to publish part or all of his data under his own name in any way he sees fit or to continue to use the information from his study in whatever way he wishes. However, access to a core of explicit, detailed, and reputable data might contribute greatly to unraveling issues touching on many aspects of human development and functioning. A central library also could help with the issues of privacy and disguise that, by right, we owe our subjects.
>
> (p. 274)

Earlier, in the wake of Kamin's exposure of the Burt study, Jensen wrote that "especially rare data, such as those of monozygotic twins reared apart . . . should be published in full." He continued, "Perhaps this should be a general requirement for the publication of studies based on such valuable data, so that quantitative analytical techniques other than those used by the original author can be applied to the data by anyone who wishes" (Jensen, 1974, pp. 26–27).

Jensen therefore welcomed others to apply "quantitative analytical techniques" to MZA data, and to analyze them in ways that differed from the original investigators—a process that Bouchard would later denounce as "pseudoanalysis."

Farber (1981, p. 30) listed five required features of a future TRA study (paraphrased below):

1. Pairs should consist of genetically identical individuals (MZ twins).
2. Pairs should be selected randomly.
3. Pairs should be randomly assigned to various rearing conditions.
4. Pairs should be reared as single individuals with no contamination from twinning.
5. Pairs should not have experienced non-genetic features, such as prenatal or perinatal traumas, that would affect heritability estimates.

She concluded,

> To the question of how close the actual data are to the ideal (or even minimal) requirements, the answer is that they approach them hardly at all. The only requirement that seems fulfilled is the assumption [#1] that MZ twins are genetically identical
>
> (p. 30).

She believed that "no conclusion from twin-reared-apart data as they now exist is generalizable" to the non-twin population, and that the analysis of TRA data up to 1981 "should be construed only as speculation" until "a reputable and rigorous study is done" (p. 31). Interestingly, we will see in Chapter 4 that subsequent scientific findings suggest that even Farber's intuitively correct yet crucial TRA study requirement #1— that both members of an MZA pair are genetically identical—may not hold (Charney, 2012).

We therefore can conclude that, through 1981, TRA studies met, at best, only one of the five minimum requirements outlined by Farber, and even that requirement is questionable. The central question then becomes: was the subsequently performed MISTRA able to overcome these problems?

Leon Kamin, in Eysenck vs. Kamin, 1981

In the 1981 book *The Intelligence Controversy*, Kamin squared off with the hereditarian psychologist Hans Eysenck in a debate on the "genetics of IQ" question (Kamin, in Eysenck vs. Kamin, 1981). In his sections,

Kamin reviewed for a wider audience the case against the TRA studies of Newman and colleagues, Shields, and Juel-Nielsen. He took this opportunity to review the evidence that Burt's data were not reliable, and updated the account to include Gillie's article and Hearnshaw's biography of Burt.

Kamin again reviewed the early history of IQ testing in the context of racism, the eugenics movement, and psychologists' and eugenicists' use of IQ testing to label entire groups of people as inferior (see also Chase, 1980; Tucker, 1994, 2009). Moving on to the three remaining classical TRA studies, he reviewed the evidence that these studies were subject to biases such as incomplete separation, correlated environments, age and sex effects, poor test standardization, that the same researchers administered tests to both twins, and that the methods of recruiting twins biased the samples in favor of MZA similarity.

Kamin was more critical of heritability estimates than he had been in 1974, pointing out that genetically determined human traits such as the number of eyes ("two-eyedness") have a heritability of zero, because all eyedness *variation* is caused by environmental factors (such as accidents). At the same time, he wrote, "The heritability of a trait in a human is, to say the least, very difficult to estimate, some would say impossible" (p. 96).

Kamin concluded,

> Taken as a whole, the studies of separated identical twins provide no unambiguous evidence for the heritability of IQ. The apparently most impressive study has been unmasked as a fraud. The most obvious defect of the remaining three studies is the glaring tendency for the environments of so-called separated twins to be highly correlated. This tendency, no less than identical genes, might easily be responsible for the observed resemblance in IQs. We cannot guess what the IQ correlation would be if, in a science fiction experiment, we separated pairs of identical twins at birth and scattered them *at random* across the full range of available environments. It could conceivably be zero—which would force us to conclude that the heritability of IQ is zero.
>
> (Kamin, in Eysenck vs. Kamin, 1981, p. 113, italics in original)

Richard Rose, 1982

Behavioral genetic twin researcher Richard Rose published a 1982 review of Farber's *Identical Twins Reared Apart: A Reanalysis* in *Science*. Although an advocate of twin research and aspects of TRA research, in this review he raised some important cautions in relation to TRA research (Rose, 1982). "In principle," he wrote, "separated twins permit a direct estimate of heritability; in practice, MZA data are so limited that, as

Farber documents, any generalization is suspect." He believed that MZA data "generate many hypotheses but rarely if ever confirm them" (p. 960). Addressing the selected pairs that had been reported in the media and by researchers, Rose saw such "drama" as "good show biz but uncertain science" (p. 960).

Rose believed that cohort effects were an important confounding factor in the interpretation of TRA data, arguing that we cannot know the importance of MZA correlations "without necessary control data on similarities found in pairs of age-matched strangers." As we saw in Chapter 2, Juel-Nielsen considered, but then rejected, the idea of forming a control group of this type. Continuing on this theme, Rose argued, "Were one to capitalize on cohort effects by sampling unrelated but age-matched pairs, born, say, over a half-century period, the observed similarities in interests, habits, and attitudes might, indeed, be 'astonishing'" (p. 960).

Rose mentioned Farber's observation that cohort effects had an impact on twins' dental records, and wrote that her argument that twins are not so much similar to each other as they are to people growing up in the same era "is by no means limited to dental health. Cohort effects will be operative in interest, attitudes, and education, and Farber's box-score analysis of twin pairs born from the 1890's to the 1950's [sic] may be severely confounded by cohort effects" (p. 960).

It "is not necessary to rely on the MZA data" to make the argument in support of genetics, Rose concluded, and such data "by all accounts including Farber's, may not warrant generalization" to the non-twin population (p. 960).

Richard Lewontin, Steven Rose, and Leon Kamin, 1984

Kamin teamed up with American evolutionary geneticist Richard Lewontin and British neurobiologist Steven Rose in their 1984 classic anti-hereditarian work *Not in Our Genes* (Lewontin, Rose, & Kamin, 1984). This book remains one the most important statements against biological determinist ideology and the political implications that flow from it. Their discussion of TRA studies was based largely on Kamin's previous work. The authors provided an updated account of the Burt scandal, adding that "the implausibility of Burt's claims should have been noted at once by any reasonably alert and conscientious scientific reader" (p. 102).

Turning to the classical TRA studies, Lewontin and colleagues outlined many biases discussed by Kamin in *The Science and Politics of I.Q.*, and pointed to the questionable "separation" of the twin pairs in these studies:

> The reader whose knowledge of separated twin studies comes only from the secondary accounts provided by textbooks can

have little idea of what, in the eyes of the original investigators, constitutes a pair of "separated" twins.

(Lewontin et al., 1984, p. 107)

In this passage the authors not only criticized the original researchers for passing off only partially separated twins as "separated" twins, but in addition took the authors of some secondary sources to task for failing to inform their readers of the "massively correlated" environments experienced by the twins under study (p. 108). "The technical use of the word 'separated' by the scientists of IQ," wrote Lewontin and colleagues, "obviously differs from the usage of the same word by ordinary people" (p. 108).

The authors questioned many aspects of IQ testing itself, seeing it as a flawed attempt to "rank order the world." While also criticizing aspects of heritability estimates, they did not call for discarding the concept entirely and were closer to the position of Kamin in 1974 and Taylor in 1980 that such estimates for IQ were difficult, if not impossible, to calculate, and may well turn out to be zero. They concluded that when the major biases of the TRA studies published up to that time "are added to the overwhelming flaw of highly correlated environments, and when it is recalled that the apparently most impressive study has been unmasked as a fraud, it seems clear that the study of separated identical twins has failed to demonstrate a heritable basis for IQ test scores" (pp. 109–110).

Ken Richardson, 1998

In his 1998 book *The Origins of Human Potential*, British psychologist Ken Richardson questioned the degree of twin separation in TRA studies, and pointed to the fact that many MZAs were reared in different branches of the same family. Turning to the SATSA and the MISTRA, he pointed out that some SATSA pairs were reared together until age 11, and that the MISTRA "is far from a meticulously controlled investigation" (Richardson, 1998, p. 142).

Richardson questioned the MISTRA pairs' degree of separation, and noted that the recruitment procedures tended "to favour those who live in close proximity to one another" (p. 142). He criticized the researchers' failure to provide case history information and the "irritating insufficiencies in basic information" (p. 144), with an accompanying failure to provide information on separation and reunion. He wrote that "a blanket correlation simply conceals a host of imponderables about this question" (p. 143). Also, the MISTRA "contact time" formula used to assess the amount of contact the twins experienced "tells us nothing about the *quality* of such contact" (p. 143, italics in original).

Other important issues Richardson covered included the influence of cohort effects (including age and sex effects), the lack of randomization, the MISTRA reliance on questionable assumptions, problems with "model-fitting" techniques, and doubts that the researchers were able to control for environmental influences on IQ. He concluded, "There seems little doubt... that studies of 'separated' twins are universally – and probably intrinsically – flawed" (p. 144).

Leon Kamin and Arthur Goldberger, 2002

Kamin and Arthur Goldberger published a 2002 analysis of more recent TRA research, focusing on problem areas in both the MISTRA and the SATSA (Kamin & Goldberger, 2002). Here I will highlight their critique of the MISTRA. Goldberger had written several papers in the 1970s challenging Jensen's calculations, the usefulness of heritability estimates in general, and the questionable assumptions underlying behavioral genetic models (for example, see Goldberger, 1978, 1979).

Kamin and Goldberger noted that "apart from producing a copious technical literature," the MISTRA "has had popular impact via worldwide newspaper, magazine, and television accounts" (p. 84). Although MZAs are assumed to grow up in uncorrelated environments, like the previous studies the MISTRA "initially attracted disproportionate numbers of highly similar pairs" (p. 85). They questioned the MISTRA "contact time" formula (see Chapter 5), which attempts to quantify the amount of time pairs spent together, asking how "so crude a measure can capture the extent of a pair's influence on each other, or validly index the effects of contact on similarity of experience?" (p. 86). In direct contrast to how the MISTRA researchers reported their personality correlations, Kamin and Goldberger showed that the researchers failed to publish their full-sample DZA IQ correlations. This question will be examined more closely in Chapter 6.

They also pointed to the researchers' dependence on twins' own accounts of their similar behavior and degree of separation, suggesting the "unreliability of such accounts" (p. 86). They documented instances where the twins lied about their behavioral similarity, and another case where a MISTRA researcher explained unexpected MZT findings on the grounds that twins "compare notes when asked about developmental milestones" (Eckert, Bouchard, Bohlen, & Heston, 1986, p. 424). Kamin and Goldberger wondered whether "twins reared apart, who come to Minneapolis for a week-long assessment, also compare notes?" (p. 86). Because MZA pairs recruited to TRA studies on the basis of media appeals already know of each other's existence, and in many cases had frequent contact and a close relationship, they often do have many opportunities to "compare notes."

The authors concluded, "We have described what seem to us to be a number of serious problems in the design, reporting, and analyses by the psychologists engaged in the MISTRA and SATSA projects under the rubric of behavior genetics." They also questioned the continuing use of heritability estimates in behavioral genetics, seeing "no indication of the usefulness" of such estimates (p. 93).

My Previous Analyses

My own first critical analysis of TRA research is found in a 2001 article (Joseph, 2001), which appeared in an expanded and revised form in a chapter of *The Gene Illusion* (Joseph, 2004[2]). This was followed by a summary of the main points in a 2010 chapter in the *Handbook of Developmental Science, Behavior, and Genetics* (Joseph, 2010a). In Part I of the present book I greatly expand on these points, and investigate several other potential problem areas. I now list the main arguments that I made in the above publications, many of which followed the lead of previous critics:

- Individual cases of reunited twins reported by researchers and journalists, though at times entertaining and interesting, fail to provide scientifically acceptable evidence in favor of genetic influences on human behavior.
- Previous critics were correct in observing that MZA samples were biased in favor of more similar pairs, that most MZA pairs did not meet the requirements necessary to attain the status of being "reared-apart" twins, and that most pairs grew up in similar environments.
- The status of IQ and personality as valid and quantifiable concepts is questionable.
- Heritability estimates are misleading, and should not be used in the study of human behavior.
- The behavioral resemblance of MZAs can be explained by cohort effects which (as we have seen) refer to similarities in people's behaviors and preferences that arise from the characteristics of the historical periods and cultural milieu in which they experience stages of life at the same time. In most cases, MZAs share at least seven different cultural influences with MZTs: national, regional, ethnic, religious, economic class, birth cohort, and gender cohort.
- Important problem areas with the MISTRA include the researchers' failure to publish full case histories and/or to make their data available to others for inspection, the questionable degree of "separation" of the pairs, the failure to account for cohort effects (other than their attempt to control for age and sex effects), inconsistent and incomplete reporting of their DZA IQ correlations, and the impact that the investigators' genetic biases may have had on their methods and conclusions.
- A valid TRA study would compare the behavioral resemblance of a group consisting of MZAs unknown to each other and reared apart from birth, versus the resemblance of a control group consisting

not of MZTs or DZAs, but rather of biologically unrelated pairs of strangers sharing the non-genetic characteristics and influences also shared by MZAs. Therefore, in all TRA studies utilizing a control group, the wrong control group was used.

Table 3.1 Summary of Problem Areas in TRA Studies as Identified by the Critics

- Many twin pairs experienced late separation, and many pairs were reared together in the same home for several years
- Most twin pairs were placed in, and grew up in, similar socioeconomic and cultural environments
- MZA correlations were impacted by non-genetic cohort effects, based on age, sex, and other factors
- Twins share a common prenatal (intrauterine) environment
- TRA study findings might not be (or are not) generalizable to the non-twin population
- In studies based on volunteer twins, a bias was introduced because pairs had to have known of each other's existence to be able to participate in the study
- Many pairs had a relationship with each other, and the relationship was often emotionally close
- TRA studies and their authors' conclusions are based on a circular argument
- MZA samples, in general, were biased in favor of more similar pairs
- The more similar physical appearance and level of attractiveness of MZAs will elicit more similar behavior-influencing treatment by people in their environments
- There was a reliance on potentially unreliable accounts by twins of their degree of separation and behavioral similarity
- There are many questionable or false assumptions underlying the statistical procedures used in several studies
- MZA pairs were not selected randomly, and are not representative of MZAs as a population
- MZA pairs were not assigned to random environments
- There was researcher bias in favor of genetic interpretations of the data
- There were problems with the IQ and personality tests used
- The validity of concepts such as IQ, personality, and heritability are questionable (see Chapter 4)
- Due to differences in epigenetic gene expression, many previously accepted biological and genetic assumptions about MZA (and MZT) twin pairs may not be true, meaning that such pairs might not be genetically identical, as previously assumed (see Chapter 4)
- The researchers conducting the classical studies used the wrong control group (Juel-Nielsen did not use a control group)
- There was a potential for experimenter bias in cases where evaluations and testing were performed by the same person
- The authors of textbooks and other secondary sources often fail to mention the lack of MZA separation, and many other problem areas of TRA research
- A registry should be established to house raw TRA study data, which should be made available for independent inspection

Calling for the creation of a control group of biologically unrelated pairs, however, implies that if such a group were formed, a valid comparison could then be made between this group and the MZA group. But even in this case, the question would remain as to how "intelligence," "personality," and other behavioral characteristics would be assessed. In the following chapter we will see that these concepts, and the tests based on them, are controversial in and of themselves.

Conclusions

Several critically minded authors have pointed to many areas of TRA research that potentially invalidate the original researchers' conclusions in favor of genetics. Major problem areas in TRA research, as outlined by these authors, are summarized in Table 3.1.

In Chapters 5 and 6 we will see how these and other problem areas played out in the MISTRA. But first, some of the issues listed above, as well as additional flaws, pitfalls, and questionable assumptions in behavioral genetic and TRA research, must be examined in greater detail.

Notes

1 Bouchard and other genetic researchers failed to criticize the original TRA researchers when they performed after-the-fact analyses of trends within their own data. Such analyses were performed by Newman and colleagues in their Chapter 12, by Shields in his Chapters 11 and 13, and by Juel-Nielsen when he compared the IQ variance between his "completely separated" and "incompletely separated" MZA groups, finding little difference between these two categories that he created (Juel-Nielsen, 1965/1980, Part I, p. 109).
2 This 2004 Algora edition was a revised version of the original U.K. edition of the book, published by PCCS Books in 2003.

Chapter 4

STUDIES OF REARED-APART TWINS

Basic Assumptions and Potential Fallacies

> The method of separated identical twins [has] limitations, such as the confounding variable that identical twins tend to be placed in similar, and hence correlated, environments, so that effects that may appear to be a result of genetic factors may, in fact, not be a result of such factors.
> — Psychologist Robert Sternberg, 2007
> (Sternberg, 2007, p. 273)

> There is a danger of concealing assumptions which have no factual basis behind an impressive façade of flawless algebra.
> — Eugenics critic Lancelot Hogben, 1933
> (Hogben, 1933, p. 121)

Howard Taylor described many IQ genetic researchers' "use of assumptions that are implausible as well as arbitrary to arrive at some numerical value for the genetic heritability of human IQ scores on the grounds that no heritability calculations could be made without benefit of such assumptions" (Taylor, 1980, p. 7). Taylor called this "the IQ game." As I attempted to show in two previous books and in other publications, there are similar grounds for characterizing genetic research in other areas as "the schizophrenia game," "the personality game," "the autism game," "the attention-deficit hyperactivity disorder (ADHD) game," "the bipolar disorder game," "the genetics of criminal and antisocial behavior game," "the genetics of political attitudes and behavior game," and so on. Decades of failures to identify genes at the molecular level for these behaviors and conditions provide additional support to this view (see Chapters 8–10).

In this chapter I discuss some major issues and concepts that relate to behavioral genetic and psychiatric genetic research, which of course include TRA studies and studies of twins reared together.

Psychometrics

We saw in Chapter 1 that psychometrics has been defined as "the branch of psychology that deals with the design, administration, and interpretation of quantitative tests for the measurement of psychological variables such as intelligence, aptitude, and personality traits." The psychometric approach to intelligence is based on three main assumptions (based on Ceci, Rosenblum, de Bruyn, & Yee, 1997, p. 306): (a) there exists a singular pervasive mental ability called *general intelligence*, or *g*; (b) general intelligence is biologically and genetically based; and (c) IQ tests are a good measure of general intelligence, and general intelligence permeates most aspects of intellectual functioning. Behavioral genetics has adopted the psychometric approach to human intelligence. The two disciplines have a long-running historical association with each other (Rose, 1997), and both trace their origins back to Galton (for example, see Cohen, Swerdlik, & Smith, 1992; Plomin, DeFries, Knopik, & Neiderhiser, 2013). Both fields are concerned with the study of individual differences in the population.

The psychometric approach to understanding human intelligence and other types of behavior is only one of many approaches, however, even as behavioral geneticists tend to present it as the only valid approach. Sociologist Claude Fischer and his colleagues contrasted the psychometric view with other approaches in their 1996 book *Inequality by Design* (Fischer et al., 1996). They noted that many psychologists question the psychometric position, and that psychometrics is concerned with individual differences in the population, as opposed to studying how people think, learn, and solve problems. Psychometrists also claim that intelligence and other behavioral characteristics are normally distributed in a "bell-shaped curve," when in reality psychometrists create bell-shaped distributions by methods of test construction to match their assumptions about people and society (Simon, 1997).[1]

Some commentators have pointed out that the concepts of "intelligence" and "IQ" are different, and should not be used interchangeably. As Taylor put it in *The IQ Game*, "IQ and intelligence are by no means one and the same: IQ is an observed empirical score; intelligence is an abstract concept" (Taylor, 1980, p. 12). Nevertheless, at times these terms are used interchangeably, and readers should keep in mind the important "IQ" versus "intelligence" distinction in upcoming chapters if the distinction is not made clear enough.

According to Plomin and his behavioral genetic colleagues, "despite the massive amount of data pointing to the reality of *g*, considerable controversy continues to surround *g*, especially in the media. There is a wide gap between what laypeople . . . believe and what experts believe" (Plomin, DeFries, et al., 2013, p. 187). Critics such as Lewontin, Rose, and Kamin, on the other hand, questioned the views of these experts and described what they called "the grand illusion of psychometry," which they argued is based on numerous questionable assumptions and concepts (Lewontin, Rose, & Kamin, 1984, p. 92).

It is therefore important to recognize that the psychometric/behavioral genetic approach to human behavioral differences, including the magnification of these differences and their distribution in a bell-shaped curve, is only one of many approaches. Many have argued that it is the wrong approach, and that there are many different conceptions of human intelligence.

Heritability

A key behavioral genetic concept is *heritability*, which was developed in agriculture to predict the results of selective breeding programs. As Bouchard recognized, "The term 'heritability' comes to us from the agricultural geneticists [sic] J. L. Lush. Its initial use was to allow estimation of 'breeding values' in order to predict 'response to selection'" (Bouchard, 2009, p. 527). There are two types: "broad" heritability, and "narrow" heritability. The latter refers to additive genetic variance and is symbolized h^2. Behavioral geneticists currently define heritability as "the proportion of phenotypic differences among individuals that can be attributed to genetic differences in a particular population" (Plomin, DeFries, et al., 2013, p. 419). Heritability estimates, which range from 0.0 to 1.0 (0 to 100 percent), are usually calculated from twin data by doubling MZT–DZT correlation differences, or by claiming that the MZA correlation "directly estimates" heritability, or are derived from more complex "biometrical model fitting" analyses, discussed below. Using basic twin method data, if a sample of MZT pairs correlates at 0.8 on an IQ test, and a DZT sample correlates at 0.5, behavioral geneticists would double the difference and estimate the heritability of IQ as 0.6 (60 percent).

Although heritability estimates are widely used in behavioral genetic and psychiatric genetic research, their usefulness and validity have, in the words of psychologist David Moore, "been the subject of unrelenting criticism from philosophers, biologists, and psychologists for nearly four decades" (Moore, 2013, p. 636). Some objections to the practice of producing heritability estimates, and to the heritability concept itself, include the following points:

- Heritability estimates *do not* estimate the relative weight of genetic and environmental influences in a population, and are misleading and potentially harmful when presented this way.
- Although heritability estimates are based on the assumption that genetic and environmental factors do not interact, they clearly do (see the model-fitting section below).

- Heritability is the property of a population, not of the characteristic or disorder itself.
- Heritability refers to the genetic contribution to behavioral variation in a particular population; it does not describe the importance of genetic factors as they relate to an individual.
- Heritability estimates apply only to a specific population, at a specific time, and in a specific environment.
- Heritability estimates are based on research methods that are unable to disentangle the potential influences of genes and environment on behavior, such as family and twin studies.
- The finding of high heritability *within* populations says nothing about whether genetic differences exist *between* different populations.
- High heritability, or even 100 percent heritability, does not mean that even simple environmental changes or interventions cannot have an important impact.

Heritability ≠ Inherited

Some writers have noted the common confusion between two different uses of the word heritability. The technical meaning of "heritability" refers to the proportion of individual differences in a population that can be attributed to genetic factors. In contrast, people commonly yet mistakenly use the word "heritable" to mean "inherited," or "hereditary" (Hirsch, 1997; Keller, 2010; Stoltenberg, 1997). According to the critical behavioral genetic researcher Jerry Hirsch (1922–2008), "heritability" and "heredity" are "two entirely different concepts that have been hopelessly conflated" in several texts. "Because of their assonance," he wrote, "when we hear one of the two words, automatically we think the other" (Hirsch, 1997, p. 220). As Hirsch repeatedly pointed out, a heritability estimate *is not* a "nature–nurture ratio" of the relative contributions of genes and environment (e.g., Hirsch, 1997). The author of *The Mirage of a Space Between Nature and Nurture*, Evelyn Fox Keller, found it unfortunate that "authors and readers alike routinely slide from one meaning [of heritability] to the other, wreaking havoc on the ways in which legitimate scientific measurements are interpreted" (Keller, 2010, p. 59). According to behavioral geneticist Douglas Wahlsten, a critic of heritability estimates, "the only practical application of a heritability coefficient" is its original purpose of "predict[ing] the results of a program of selective breeding" (Wahlsten, 1990, p. 119).

Variation ≠ Cause

Lewontin has shown that a "trait can have a heritability of 1.0 in a population at some time, yet could be completely altered in the future by a simple environmental change" (Lewontin, 1974, p. 400). An example is phenylketonuria (PKU), a genetic disorder of metabolism that causes intellectual disability (mental retardation). Although PKU is a "highly heritable" single-gene disorder, the administration of a low-phenylalanine diet to the at-risk infant during a critical developmental period prevents PKU from causing intellectual disability.

As an example of how heritability estimates do not measure the "strength" or "magnitude" of genetic influences, imagine a country in which all citizens (100 percent) carry the gene predisposing them to favism, a disease marked by the development of hemolytic anemia. Favism is caused by an inherited deficiency of glucose-6-phosphate located on the X chromosome, combined with the consumption of fava (broad) beans or the inhalation of fava bean pollen. In other words, both "beans and genes" are necessary for favism to appear. Let us then imagine that 3 percent of the citizens, all of whom are of course genetically predisposed to develop favism, consume fava beans and are subsequently diagnosed with favism. In this case, because all citizens carried the gene but only some ate fava beans, all favism *variation* in the population would be caused by environmental factors (fava bean exposure), and the heritability of favism therefore would be *zero* (0.0). Even though favism heritability would be 0 percent in this example, it obviously would be mistaken to conclude that genes play no role in developing the disorder, or that the genetic influence was weak or irrelevant. A genetic predisposition is, in fact, a prerequisite for developing favism.

On the other extreme, if all citizens ate a diet that included fava beans but only some carried the gene, all favism *variation* would now be caused by genetic factors (carrying or not carrying the gene), and the heritability of favism would be 100 percent (1.0). As we see, heritability estimates assess variation as opposed to cause, and do not indicate the "strength" of the genetic influence (Moore, 2013).[2]

As another example, imagine a society where everyone (like MZ twin pairs) is born with identical genotypes. In such a society, all variation in intelligence and behavior would be caused by environmental factors, meaning that the heritability of all behavioral characteristics, psychiatric disorders, medical conditions—basically everything—would be zero. Once again, population variation and cause are different concepts.

Several critics of behavioral genetics have argued that focus should be placed on causal mechanisms relating to how individuals develop characteristics, and not on the causes of variation in the population (Gottlieb, 2003; Tabery & Griffiths, 2010). As the developmental psychologist Gilbert Gottlieb (1929–2006) put it, behavioral genetic practice

> is mainly a purely statistical enterprise derived from population genetics. The population view of behavioral genetics is not

developmental. It is based on the erroneous assumption that a quantitative analysis of the genetic and environmental contributions to individual differences sheds light on developmental process of individuals.

(Gottlieb, 2003, p. 338)

According to the biologist Steven Rose, the "heritability measure . . . except in the very specific context for which it was originally devised (agricultural breeding experiments) [is] rarely applicable, widely misunderstood and in most cases meaningless" (Rose, 1997, p. 293).

Heritability and Psychiatric Disorders

While the authors of mainstream psychiatric and psychiatric genetic publications claim that conditions such as schizophrenia, bipolar disorder, major depression, and ADHD are "moderately to highly heritable," the irrelevance of heritability in psychiatry is seen in the example of autism. For many years, based mainly on the results of three or four small twin studies, leading researchers variously described autism as showing "strong genetic determination" (Folstein & Rutter, 1977, p. 728), as being "under a high degree of genetic control" (Bailey et al., 1995, p. 63), as having "very high heritability" (Rutter, 2006, p. 52), and as being "one of the most heritable mental disorders" (Plomin, DeFries, et al., 2013, p. 259). Reviewers commonly estimate autism heritability at roughly 0.9 (90 percent), based on a 1995 twin study and review by Bailey and colleagues (Bailey et al., 1995; for a critical review of autism genetic research, see Joseph, 2006).

Suppose a team of epidemiological researchers conclusively proves that all children who eventually develop autism had eaten "Baby Delight Apricot Baby Food" between the ages of 6 and 8 months, and that further investigation had shown that the ingestion by genetically predisposed children of a rare chemical found only in this brand of apricot baby food, during this sensitive developmental period, caused autism. The government immediately removes Baby Delight Apricot Baby Food from the market, confiscates existing inventories of the product, and issues warnings to parents. What would happen to the rate of new autism diagnoses a few years later? The answer is that it would be reduced to virtually zero. Thus, like PKU, presumed genetic factors appear to be "under a high degree of genetic control" (and difficult to change) only in the absence of (or denial of) identified environmental triggers.

An example in the twin research literature illustrating this important point is found in Segal's description of a British MISTRA MZA pair who suffered from headaches and irritability, due to their shared allergy to foods containing gluten. Although medical researchers believe that gluten sensitivity is "strongly heritable" (Hadjivassiliou et al., 2010, p. 320), and that "genetic predisposition plays a key role" (Sapone et al., 2012, p. 4), according to Segal, one twin's "health and spirit improved dramatically" upon "eliminating wheat from his diet," and his twin brother "agreed to make the same dietary changes when he returned home" (Segal, 2012, p. 227). As this example shows, an environmental intervention cured a "strongly heritable" condition in the same way as it would have cured a "weakly heritable" condition. This pair's story again shows that a heritability estimate does not indicate the strength of the genetic component, or the potential effectiveness or non-effectiveness of an environmental intervention.

Some Leading Behavioral Geneticists Now Recognize that Heritability Estimates "Are Not Very Important"

Some contemporary behavioral genetic researchers, while continuing to support twin research and other basic positions of their field, now recognize that heritability estimates have little meaning. According to Eric Turkheimer, "the relative magnitudes of the various components were supposed to tell us something about the importance of genetic and environmental causes underlying a trait, but they do not" (Turkheimer, 2011a, p. 598). He continued,

> In the real world of humans, in a given context everything is heritable to some extent and environmental to some other extent, but the magnitudes of the proportions are variable from situation to situation, and have nothing whatsoever to do with the causal properties of genes and environment for the trait in question.
> (p. 598)

Elsewhere, Turkheimer wrote that "heritability is a distraction" (Turkheimer, 2011b, p. 239).

Behavioral genetic twin researchers Wendy Johnson, Turkheimer, Bouchard, and Gottesman wrote in 2009 that "little can be gleaned from any particular heritability estimate and there is little need for further twin studies investigating the presence and magnitude of genetic influences on behavior" (Johnson, Turkheimer, Bouchard, & Gottesman, 2009, p. 218). In their view, "Once we accept that basically everything—not only schizophrenia and intelligence, but also marital status and television watching—is heritable, it becomes clear that specific estimates of heritability are not very important" (p. 220). They saw heritability estimates as having "some importance" only "in areas of the social sciences in which genetic influences have not been acknowledged" (p. 218).

In a 2011 article, Johnson, Penke, and Spinath wrote that a heritability estimate may be useful in showing that genes are involved, but "beyond that" it

> provides little information about the trait's evolutionary importance, the kinds of genetic and environmental transactions involved in its development, the degree to which we can expect the heritability to be stable across different populations and environmental circumstances, or the degree to which the trait may be responsive to environmental manipulation.
> (Johnson, Penke, & Spinath, 2011, p. 260)

The obvious conclusion is that the use of heritability estimates as a measure of the relative importance of genes and environment should be abandoned (for an opposing view, see Sesardic, 2005).

The words "heritability" and "inherited" have different meanings, and heritability estimates do not indicate the relative magnitude of genetic and environmental influences. Although researchers will continue to use twin studies to claim that various behavioral characteristics are influenced by genetic factors, assigning a heritability estimate to this finding is meaningless and misleading. Therefore, the use of heritability estimates in the social and behavioral sciences should be discontinued.

In the chapters that follow I will continue to assess the common claim that twin studies have provided indisputable evidence in favor of genetics. For the reasons mentioned above, however, I will not engage in an analysis of what proper heritability estimates should be, or whether heritability is too high or too low.

Model Fitting

In the past few decades behavioral genetics has moved away from comparing simple correlations and has embraced "biometrical model fitting" statistical procedures (also known as "structural equation modeling," or SEM). Model fitting, according to leading behavioral geneticists, is a "technique for testing the fit between a model of genetic and environmental relatedness against the observed data. Different models can be compared, and the best-fitting model is used to estimate genetic and environmental parameters" (Plomin, DeFries, et al., 2013, p. 412). Model-fitting analyses attempt to partition (A) genetic, (C) "shared environment," and (E) "non-shared environment" contributions to behavioral variation in a population, and are often accompanied by path diagrams providing "a visual and intuitive way to describe and explore any kind of model that describes some observed data" (Purcell, 2013, p. 392). This "ACE Model" is widely used in behavioral genetic research in the social and behavioral sciences. Behavioral genetic researchers prefer model-fitting techniques for the additional reason that they are able to factor data from different types of family relationships into the same analysis. Both the SATSA and the MISTRA researchers based many of their conclusions on the results of model-fitting procedures.

An "Important First Step"

A preliminary first step prior to performing a model-fitting analysis is the requirement that the observed familial correlations are consistent with genetic influences. In TRA studies, it must be determined that the MZA intraclass correlation is significantly higher than the DZA intraclass correlation. In a description of model fitting in his appendix to Plomin and colleagues' 2013 edition of *Behavioral Genetics*, Sean Purcell wrote, "Simple comparisons between twin correlations can indicate whether genetic influences are important for a trait. This is the important first question that any quantitative genetic analysis must ask" (Purcell, 2013, p. 383). According to Segal, the "simple comparison of the MZ (or MZA) and DZ (or DZA) intraclass correlations is an important first step in behavioral–genetic analysis because this demonstrates whether or not there is genetic influence on the trait" (Segal, 2012, p. 62).

In a SATSA IQ publication, Pedersen, Plomin and their behavioral genetic colleagues wrote, in reference to their MZA and DZA results, "When MZ correlations are not greater than DZ correlations, twin similarity may reflect correlated environments rather than genetic similarity. This appears to be the case for the Figure Logic, Digit Span Forward, and Names and Faces-Immediate tests" (Pedersen, Plomin, Nesselroade, & McClearn, 1992, p. 350).

Plomin also made this point in several other publications. For example, Plomin, Chipuer, and Loehlin cautioned in 1990 that model fitting "has the disadvantage of being complex and sometimes seems to be a black box from which parameter estimates magically appear." Furthermore, they wrote,

> We should not stand too much in awe of model fitting or allow it to obfuscate the basic simplicity of most behavioral genetic designs. For example, the twin design estimates genetic influence on the basis of the difference between MZ and DZ correlations. If the MZ correlation does not exceed the DZ correlation for a particular trait, there is no genetic influence (unless assortative mating approaches unity), and model-fitting analyses must come to that conclusion or there is something wrong with the model.
> (Plomin, Chipuer, et al., 1990, p. 235)

As Plomin stressed here and in the Second and Third Editions of his textbook *Behavioral Genetics*, a twin study model-fitting analysis finding genetic influence would be wrong if the MZT correlation does not (significantly) exceed the DZT correlation, a conclusion that applies to MZA–DZA comparisons as well.[3] While correlations often occur in patterns predicted by genetic theories (although many critics argue that these patterns are also predicted by environmental theories and are therefore confounded), we will see in Chapter 6 that there are important exceptions in the MISTRA results.

It is important to emphasize that when researchers write that the MZT (or MZA) correlation must be "higher than" or "exceed" the DZT (or DZA) correlation, the difference must be statistically significant at the conventional 0.05 level of probability (if not lower). If it is not, from the basic statistical perspective of comparing sample populations, these sample correlations do not differ. In TRA studies, which are necessarily based on relatively small sample sizes, it is not enough for researchers to show that the MZA correlation is higher than the DZA correlation. If the MZA correlation is not higher at a statistically significant level, the researchers must conclude that the MZA and DZA correlations do not differ, and that the study failed to detect genetic influences on the behavior or condition in question. As Plomin and others have stressed, model-fitting techniques cannot find genetic influences if the preliminary twin comparison fails to provide evidence that there is a genetic influence.

Questionable Assumptions

Critics have charged that model-fitting techniques are based on numerous questionable theoretical assumptions. In *The IQ Game*, Taylor discussed and listed many such assumptions (Taylor, 1980). In models based on twin method data, for example, researchers assume that the implausible MZT–DZT equal environment assumption (see Chapter 7) is valid: "We make the assumption that components of variance are identical for all individuals.... This assumption implies that the effects of genes and environments on an individual are not altered by that individual being a member of an MZ or DZ twin pair" (Purcell, 2013, p. 385). Model-fitting procedures and path models have also been used extensively in twin research in psychiatry since the 1980s (see Kendler & Prescott, 2006).

In addition to incorporating previous questionable assumptions found in twin and adoption studies, model-fitting analyses assume that genetic and environmental influences are additive, and that behavioral characteristics are the result of the independent influence of both factors. Behavioral geneticists represent this as $P = G + E$, where P represents the measured phenotypic value (for example, an IQ score), G represents genetic influences (estimated from the variation among relatives), and E represents environmental influences (Purcell, 2013). Model fitting was introduced to the study of human behavioral differences by John Jinks and David Fulker in their frequently cited 1970 "Birmingham School" publication (Jinks & Fulker, 1970). Among the model-fitting assumptions listed by these authors are "no genotype–environment interaction," and "no correlated environments" (p. 317).

Many critics have argued, however, that genetic and environmental factors *are* correlated, and that gene–environment interaction reduces or even invalidates heritability estimates produced by model-fitting procedures (for example, see Goldberger, 1979; Layzer, 1974; Lewontin, 1974; McGuire & Hirsch, 1977; Taylor, 1980; Wahlsten, 1990, 1994; Zuk, Hechter, Sunyaev, & Lander, 2012). As Lewontin wrote, "If these causes 'interact' in any generally accepted meaning of the word, it becomes conceptually impossible to assign quantitative values to the causes of that individual event. Only if the causes are utterly independent could we do so" (Lewontin, 1974, p. 402). According to developmental researcher Michael Meany, "research in biology reveals that the genome cannot possibly operate independent of its environmental context" (Meaney, 2010, p. 42).

Even Shields believed that attempts to calculate a "numerical value for the extent of heredity or environmental determination of the traits measured . . . have little meaning," in part because such calculations do "not take into account any interaction between heredity and environment" (Shields, 1962, pp. 53–54). Examples of potential gene–environment interactions include physically attractive people who experience much different responses from the social environment than do physically unattractive people, and children with great musical talent who are sent to an expensive music academy to maximize their talent.

Behavioral geneticist Lindon Eaves helped pioneer model fitting along with his Birmingham School colleagues. In a 1989 book describing model fitting and personality research, Eaves and his colleagues Hans Eysenck and Nicholas Martin recognized that the "elementary model . . . makes a number of very strong assumptions which may not be generally true" (Eaves, Eysenck, & Martin, 1989, p. 48). Thus, a pioneer of model fitting in the behavioral sciences and his colleagues admitted that their method is based on assumptions that may not be true. Eleven years earlier, behavioral geneticist John Loehlin called the Birmingham model-fitting assumptions "inconsistent" (Loehlin, 1978a, p. 427), and held that "its assumption of a zero genotype–environment correlation in the children's generation cannot be strictly correct . . . . and it cannot be correct for the parent generation either" (p. 428). Loehlin concluded that the model is based on "somewhat arbitrary assumptions" (p. 430).

The genetically oriented (yet critical where appropriate) researcher Michael Rutter noted in his 2006 book *Genes and Behavior* that "statistical modeling is . . . often based on quite implausible assumptions," which while they "may be justified for some characteristics, they quite definitely are not so for others" (Rutter, 2006, p. 50). For Rutter, the most "seriously misleading" (p. 51) error in model-fitting techniques is the practice of counting gene–environment correlations and gene–environment interactions as genetic effects, using the example of cigarette smoking to show the "falsity of this argument" (p. 50). Even though, in Rutter's view, genetic and environmental factors lead people to smoke cigarettes, none of these factors account for the diseases caused by the tars of cigarette smoke. In other words, model-fitting techniques incorrectly count environmental effects as genetic effects.

We will also see in Chapter 5 that Bouchard and his MISTRA colleagues concluded that several assumptions of their model "are likely not to hold for cognitive abilities" (McGue & Bouchard, 1989, p. 23), and in Chapter 6 that the assumptions "are generally oversimplifications of the actual situation, and their violation can introduce systematic distortions in the estimates" (Johnson et al., 2007, p. 548). Subsequently, Johnson questioned the assumption that genetic and environmental influences are independent: "All estimates of heritability rely on the assumption that genetic and environmental influences are independent, yet the more we learn about genetics, the clearer it is that this assumption does not hold." She believed that this assumption does not hold for general cognitive ability, and concluded that "genetic and environmental influences tend to be correlated," and that "environmental influences tend to interact: Genes will influence individual differences in the effects environments have on people" (Johnson, 2010, p. 178).

Purcell wrote that the assumption of no gene–environment correlation is "not necessarily true." As he put it, "Another assumption that we may wish to make (but one that is not necessarily true) is that genetic and environmental influences are uncorrelated" (Purcell, 2013, p. 377). As Ken Richardson observed, "never before in any field of science have so many arbitrary assumptions been gathered together, *in full knowledge of their invalidity*, as the basis of substantive claims about the nature of people, with so many potentially dire consequences for them" (Richardson, 1998, p. 135, italics in original). Richardson was criticized for this statement, yet we have just seen several leading researchers admit that model-fitting assumptions are arbitrary and may not be true—while at the same time making strong claims about the relative influences of genes and environments based on model-fitting analysis.

Circular Reasoning

According to Segal, model-fitting analyses "assume that shared genes underlie similarity between relatives" (Segal, 2012, p. 63). It is illogical, however, for researchers to both assume and conclude that "shared genes underlie similarity between relatives," which we saw Juel-Nielsen do in his 1965/1980 TRA study (see Chapter 2). As Taylor wrote in reference to the original Jinks and Fulker model-fitting paper, "The technique assumes a priori the very conclusion it is attempting to demonstrate.... This means that high heritability (and zero measurement error) must be presumed beforehand. But heritability is the very thing being estimated" (Taylor, 1980, pp. 160–161). In upcoming chapters we will see that TRA study model-fitting analyses, as well as MZT–DZT twin method comparisons, are based on the acceptance of assumptions built on circular arguments.

The *Penguin Dictionary of Psychology* provides an example of the "futility" of circular reasoning. An instinct theorist was asked why all the sheep in an open field clustered together, and he answered, "Because all sheep have a gregarious instinct." When he was asked how he knew that sheep had such an instinct, he replied, "It's obvious, just look at them all clustered together in that open field" (Reber, 1985, p. 123). In a similar fashion, when we ask TRA researchers why we should accept their claim that MZA correlations are caused by genetic factors they reply, in effect, "It's obvious, just look at our assumption that MZA correlations are completely explained by genetic factors."

Goldberger observed that "the models involve as much social science theorizing as genetic theorizing," and noted that social and family "processes are reflected in the biometrical-genetic models." He concluded, "Implausible assumptions are needed to identify the parameters and produce the estimates, and thus keep the model-fitters happy. But estimates produced in that manner do not merit the attention of the rest of us" (Goldberger, 1979, p. 336).

Although model-fitting analysis is a mainstay of TRA and behavioral genetic research, including the MISTRA and SATSA studies, like most behavioral genetic methods and concepts it is based on a very questionable set of assumptions about genes, people, and the world in which they develop—assumptions that even several behavioral genetic researchers recognize may not be true. Moreover, the model assumes the very thing it is attempting to assess.

Random Assignment

In a controlled social or behavioral science experiment, participants are assigned randomly to experimental and control groups, and researchers attempt to control for all variables other than those being tested. As we have seen, Farber argued that a valid TRA study would require twin pairs to be selected randomly, and to be randomly assigned to a wide range of rearing conditions.

In TRA studies, the environments in which twins grow up are far from random, and many pairs are reared nearby to each other in different branches of the same family. As Bouchard once recognized, although clearly "unethical," a "real experiment" would consist of twin pairs "literally separated at birth, randomly assigned to homes, and evaluated as adults prior to any social contact" (Bouchard, 1993a, p. 56). For this reason, behavioral geneticists Scarr and Carter-Saltzman wrote that, although many people find TRA studies to be "compelling, reasons of nonrandom selection and nonrandom assignment to environments render the study of MZs apart less useful than research on adopted children" (Scarr & Carter-Saltzman, 1982, p. 832).

Although prior to conceiving the MISTRA Bouchard held that random assignment was a "methodological necessity" in behavioral research among relatives (Bouchard, 1976, p. 173), he and his colleagues later recognized, in an understatement, that "reared-apart twin studies are not truly randomized experiments" (Bouchard, McGue, Hur, & Horn, 1998, p. 310).

IQ Tests

Since the time of Galton, "the nature–nurture controversy has been virtually synonymous with debate on whether genetic factors influence IQ" (McGue, Bouchard, Iacono, & Lykken, 1993, p. 59). We have seen that some of the implied assumptions of the MISTRA, and indeed all behavioral genetic research, include the psychometric positions that general intelligence exists and can be measured and quantified, that IQ scores fall into a bell-shaped curve, and that general intelligence exists as a biological substrate in the brain.

The two main IQ tests used in the MISTRA were the Wechsler Adult Intelligence Scale (WAIS; currently in its fourth edition), and the Raven Progressive Matrices. The WAIS is the most widely used IQ test, and consists of six Verbal and five Performance subtests. The Verbal subtests ask questions assessing knowledge, reasoning, arithmetic, vocabulary, and other skills that psychometrists believe are components of intelligence. The Performance subtest assesses skills related to solving puzzles, completing pictures, arranging blocks, and so forth. Three scores are calculated: Verbal IQ, Performance IQ, and the combined Full Scale IQ. The tests are designed to have a mean score of 100, with a 15-point standard deviation. The Raven test is a non-verbal measure of problem-solving ability, where test takers are asked to identify the missing element that completes a pattern. From the psychometric/behavioral genetic standpoint, both the WAIS and the Raven tests are excellent measures of general intelligence, or g. Other types of cognitive ability tests assess "special mental abilities," which include verbal, perceptual, spatial, and memory tasks.

Criticism of IQ Testing

Genetic studies of IQ are based on the assumption that standardized IQ tests accurately measure "general intelligence." This claim, however, has been the subject of intense debate for many decades. Over the years, critics have highlighted many problems in IQ testing, which include: (a) that general intelligence is merely a statistical artifact, and therefore has no physical reality; (b) that there is no consensus definition of "intelligence"; (c) that IQ tests measure school-related learning more than general cognitive ability; (d) that there are different types of intelligence, as opposed to a single general factor; (e) that IQ tests measure only narrow abilities and ignore "real-world" intelligence; (f) that IQ tests serve the interests of the upper classes to "scientifically" legitimatize their position in society based on the alleged biological reality of human inequality; and (g) that IQ tests are biased on the basis of race, culture, and economic class (examples of the works of critics can be found in Block & Dworkin, 1976; Gould, 1981; Jacoby & Glauberman, 1995; Lewontin et al., 1984; Mensh & Mensh, 1991; Montagu, 1999).

Some critics have designated IQ testing as a form of pseudoscience, exemplified by IQ critic Stephen J. Gould (1941–2002). In response to Jensen and his supporters, Gould wrote, "The racist arguments of the nineteenth century were primarily based on craniometry, the measurement of human skulls. Today, these contentions stand totally discredited. What craniometry was to the nineteenth century, intelligence testing has been to the twentieth" (Gould, 1974/1999, p. 185; see also Gould, 1981).[4]

An important criticism of IQ testing has been that the test creators' beliefs about the lower intelligence of the working class and different racial and ethnic groups are built into IQ tests. Psychologist Ken Richardson captured this position in the following quotation:

> In effect, then, Galton's aim, and that of his followers, became simply an attempt to reproduce an existing set of ranks (social class) in another, the test scores, and pretend that the latter is a measure of something else. This is, and remains, the fundamental strategy of the intelligence-testing movement.
> (Richardson, 2000, p, 27)

Richardson pointed out that test developers "decide in advance . . . who is or is not intelligent, and then the superior scoring of such individuals becomes guaranteed by a long, drawn-out process known as 'item selection'" (Richardson, 1998, p. 113). In direct contrast to how they approach racial and ethnic group IQ score differences, test creators assume that men and women are equally intelligent, and then create tests whose scores reflect this assumption.

In reality, then, IQ tests are designed to match their creators' assumptions about which members of society are and are not intelligent, as opposed to their claim that they are merely recording the distribution of intelligence "in nature." As Jensen acknowledged, "It is claimed that the psychometrist can make up a test that will yield any kind of score distribution he pleases. This is roughly true, but some types of distributions are much easier to obtain than others" (Jensen, 1980, p. 71). This statement speaks to the arbitrary nature of IQ testing and test creation.

The widely discussed work of James Flynn (the "Flynn Effect") has shown that IQ scores have been making "massive gains" worldwide since the 1930s, and that tests are periodically renormed and made more difficult in order to maintain a mean score of 100 (Flynn, 1984, 1999). The obvious implication is not that people have increasing levels of "g," but rather that rising IQ test scores are the result of improved education, nutrition, and other environmental factors.

IQ Score Differences Based on Accepted and Rejected Assumptions

Taylor documented the "string of flimsy and implausible assumptions . . . made merely for the sake of cranking out numerical values for the quantitative 'heritability' of IQ" (Taylor, 1980, p. 7). Behavioral geneticists and psychometrists accept the validity of the implausible MZT–DZT "equal environment assumption" of the twin method (see Chapter 7), while at the same time most reject the assumption that blacks and whites, or professionals and the working class, should score equally on IQ tests.[5] These rejected assumptions could be called the black–white, or working class–professional class "equal IQ score assumptions."

Thus, the entire enterprise of claiming that intelligence and other behavioral characteristics are strongly influenced by genetics is based on an elaborate set of accepted *and rejected* assumptions about genetics and human beings. Behavioral geneticists and others accept many implausible theoretical assumptions—or recognize that they do not hold, but then go on to calculate heritability estimates anyway—while rejecting many plausible assumptions, which include the assumption that races and classes should score equally on IQ tests.

It is not the task of critics to establish the "true heritability" of IQ, or to demonstrate that it is zero, but rather to show that the "heritability of IQ" does not qualify as a valid concept.[6] This does not necessarily mean that "intelligence," however one understands it, has no genetic component at all. But it does mean that people cannot be scored and ranked according to how much "general intelligence" they have, nor can people and groups be assessed on the basis of heritability estimates of how much IQ variation in the population is caused by genetic factors.

"Personality" and Personality Tests

Personality testing in behavioral genetic research is based on the assumption that "personality traits are relatively enduring individual differences in behavior that are stable across time and across situations" (Plomin, DeFries, et al., 2013, p. 273), and can be measured and quantified with psychometric tests. These are controversial positions, however, and represent an additional set of questionable assumptions and positions underlying behavioral genetic research and twin studies. An opposing view within psychology, put forward by Walter Mischel in 1968, argues that "global traits and states are excessively crude, gross units to encompass adequately the extraordinary complexity and subtlety of the discriminations people make," and that trait theory "misses both the richness and the uniqueness of individual lives" (Mischel, 1968, p. 301).

Moreover, the psychometric/behavioral genetic emphasis on "individual differences" magnifies and emphasizes human behavioral differences, and tends to de-emphasize the common behaviors, abilities, longings and many other qualities that most human beings share (Fischer et al., 1996; Rose, 1997). Personality testing, as a pair of critics put it, "has never been uncontroversial in psychology" (Blinkhorn & Johnson, 1990, p. 671).

There are several differences between ability tests (IQ, for example) and personality tests (Willerman, 1979, p. 222). In ability tests, participants try to do their best, the questions are usually clear, there are right and wrong answers, participants are motivated and know what is expected of them, and the examiner's goal is to maximize performance. In self-report personality tests, participants are told to be honest, questions are less clear, there is no correct answer, participants are sometimes unaware of the examiner's expectations, motivation may vary considerably, and the examiner is usually interested in typical performance.

Personality Tests Rejected by Leading Personnel Psychologists

Psychologists such as Frederick Morgeson and five former personnel psychology journal editors rejected self-report personality tests as a predictor of personnel selection and job performance (Morgeson et al., 2007b). Although it is not possible to "fake smart" on an IQ test, it is quite possible to "fake good" on a personality test, even though test developers usually create validity scales in an attempt to catch such faking. There are also many situations in which personality test takers attempt to "fake bad" on a personality test (a plaintiff in a lawsuit alleging psychological damage by her employer, for example). Although personnel selection and twin research are different domains, twins might also be expected to answer personality test questions less than honestly in order to deny their own deficiencies, or to impress the researchers and possibly even their co-twins. Morgeson and colleagues reached a consensus on the following points (Morgeson et al., 2007b, pp. 720–721):

- "Faking on self-report personality tests should be expected, and it probably cannot be avoided."
- "Corrections for faking do not appear to improve validity."
- "Personality tests have very low validity for predicting overall job performance."
- "Due to the low validity and content of some items, many published self-report personality tests should probably not be used for personnel selection."
- "Personality constructs certainly have value in understanding work behavior, but future research should focus on finding alternatives to self-report personality measures."

Organizational psychologists working for companies seek methods to help these companies perform better, hire better people, and increase profits. They are not in the business of continuing to promote the use of low-validity tests that do not help their employers achieve these goals. If self-report personality tests are unable to satisfactorily predict performance based on what are supposed to be stable personality traits, in part because people can and do "fake" responses, organizational psychologists are compelled to "provide a sobering reminder about the low validities and other problems in using self-report personality tests for personnel selection" (Morgeson et al., 2007a, p. 1046).

On the other hand, as psychometrists going all the way back to Galton have understood, supporters of genetic theories and approaches are unable to provide scientific evidence in support of the "heritability of personality" position without first claiming (a) that personality traits exist and are stable and enduring across varying situations, and (b) that personality tests or assessments accurately measure and quantify these traits. Corporations will continue to operate, probably more efficiently as we have seen, by eliminating the use of personality tests in personnel selection. Behavioral geneticists studying personality, on the other hand, would be out of business if they decided to eliminate personality tests, and their claims in support of an important genetic basis for personality would disappear.

Cultural Influences

Behavioral genetic accounts of the underlying causes of personality differences often overlook other major factors shaping behavior and development, such as schools and neighborhoods, social class, religion, the effects of oppression, and culture (Winter, 1996). As the pioneering personality psychologist Gordon Allport wrote, "Everyone admits that culture is vastly important in shaping personality.... The impact of culture is so indisputable that some writers regard it as the *all*-important factor." (Allport, 1961, p. 165, italics in original). Narrowly focusing on correlations between family members fails to capture the "indisputable" larger role of cultural, religious, social class and other non-genetic influences on personality and behavioral development. Amazingly, the concept of social and political oppression and its negative psychological impact on people hardly exists in the behavioral genetic literature.

Twins' Answers on Personality Test Questions

Another issue in TRA and other twin studies based on self-report personality tests is that researchers compare each twin's score with a standardization (norm) group established by the test developers, after which twins' scores versus this standardization group are compared to each other. Researchers do not assess how many questions twins answer the same way. Theoretically, members of a twin pair could answer very differently on individual questions, yet their scale or total scores could be "highly correlated" based on similar raw or standardized scores.

Critical psychometrist Paul Kline noted in relation to "empirically keyed" self-report personality tests such as the Minnesota Multiphasic Psychological Inventory (MMPI) and the California Psychological Inventory (CPI), both of which were used in the MISTRA, that "if two subjects have the same score on the scale, the scores are not necessarily psychologically equivalent" (Kline, 1993, p. 129). Empirically keyed tests ask hundreds of true–false questions that are claimed to differentiate people on various characteristics, and each scale is based on a set of individual test questions.

The MMPI was designed to assess psychopathology, whereas the CPI was designed to assess "folk concepts" that predict people's normal behavior across various settings. MMPI clinical scales include "Depression, "Hysteria," "Schizophrenia, and "Hypomania," while CPI scales attempt to assess concepts such as "Sociability," "Responsibility," "Empathy," "Flexibility," and "Self-acceptance." According to its creator, the CPI attempts to "assess individuals by means of variables and concepts that ordinary people use in their daily lives to understand, classify, and predict their own behavior and that of others" (Gough & Bradley, 1996, p. 1). Test takers are instructed to answer the questions, and each question is keyed and scored on the basis of its placement in the test's various validity and clinical scales. In the CPI, for example, the "Responsibility" (Re) scale is based on 36 out of a total of 434 questions. These questions are dispersed widely throughout the test. Empirically keyed self-report personality tests ask test takers to answer yes or no (or uncertain) to items such as "I enjoy socializing," "At times I do not feel useful," "I sometimes feel as if I am being watched," "One should read the newspaper every day," and so on.[7]

In a TRA study of personality based on tests of this type, imagine a "Happiness" scale based on 20 questions. Twin A might answer only the even-number questions in the keyed direction, while Twin B might answer only the odd-number questions in the keyed direction, yet the pair would have correlated raw scores of ten despite having answered each question differently. As one of the developers of the revised MMPI recognized, "The same total raw score on a clinical scale can be achieved by individuals endorsing combinations of quite different kinds of items" (Graham, 1987, p. 116).

Although he recommended the use of other types of personality tests, in Kline's view the MMPI "is not a reliable or valid test," and "the validity of the CPI is dubious" (Kline, 1995, p. 514). Aside from these questions, it would be interesting to see how similarly MZAs and DZAs answer individual personality test items, but this is not assessed in TRA studies.

Do MZA Pairs Grow Up in Different (Uncorrelated) Environments?

In the public imagination, MZA pairs are separated at or near birth and are placed into a wide variety of available adoptive homes headed by a married couple unknown to the twins or to their biological parents, and the twins would meet for the first time when studied. In most cases, however, it doesn't happen this way. We saw in Chapter 2 that most MZA pairs were only partially reared apart, and in many cases the twins grew up together for extended periods and had a close emotional bond with each other (see Tables 2.1–2.3). We saw in Chapter 3 that Farber found that only three of the 121 reported MZA pairs were separated during the first year of life, were reared with no knowledge that they had a twin, and were studied at the time of their first meeting.

Similar Appearance

A common criticism of TRA studies has been that because MZAs are very similar in physical appearance, they will elicit more similar behavior-influencing treatment from their social environments. As Cropanzano and James observed, in their critical review of a MISTRA "work attitudes" TRA study, "MZ twins are very similar in appearance, and appearance has been demonstrated to have important effects on how individuals are perceived and treated, including, as we have noted, how they are treated on the job." They concluded that "the great similarity in appearance that generally holds for MZ twins may lead them to be treated similarly even if they are reared apart, which may predispose them to similar job satisfaction" (Cropanzano & James, 1990, p. 435). They cited several studies in support of the position that appearance has an important effect on how people are perceived and treated, and I will refrain from listing such studies here simply because it is good common sense that factors such as facial features, weight, height, overall attractiveness, acne in adolescence, and so on lead to different types of treatment by the social environment, which have an obvious effect on behavior and "personality" (for an opposing view, see Segal, 2013). Psychologist B. Douglas Ford argued that TRA studies "are inherently confounded" by MZAs' similar appearance (Ford, 1993, p. 1294).

It is also true that MZAs are more similar in appearance than are DZAs due to their more similar genetic makeup. Behavioral geneticists sometimes defend twin studies by claiming that the effects of similar appearance on behavior count as a genetic effect, but this is a mistaken position (see Chapter 7).

Other Cohort Effects

Even in the extremely rare cases of twins separated near birth who are studied at the time of their first reunion, MZAs share many behavior-influencing environmental factors. A central aspect is the question of what is meant by "uncorrelated" environments. TRA researchers, while recognizing that some studied pairs grew up experiencing some environmental similarities, define "correlated environments" mainly as they relate to correlated *family* environments. However, even in cases where twins grew up in completely different family environments with no contact, most studied MZA pairs grew up in correlated *social* environments—a point that TRA researchers Newman and colleagues were well aware of:

> It is obvious that the environmental differences of pairs of children picked from the same family are small as compared with those pairs picked at random from the community. Again, the amount of such differences depends on the size and diversity of the community from which the pairs are chosen. A small, homogeneous New England town would yield relatively small differences, a large metropolitan city much greater differences, a whole nation still greater, and the whole world still greater.
> (Newman, Freeman, & Holzinger, 1937, p. 358)

Newman and colleagues recognized the behavior-shaping influence of pairs being reared in the same small community (albeit in different family homes), as opposed to being randomly selected from "the whole world." This relates to the influences of cohort effects.

Environmental influences shared by even perfectly separated MZA pairs are reviewed in Table 4.1. Based on these influences, we should expect any two newborns of the same sex (whether 100 percent genetically MZA pairs, or genetically unrelated pairs), who are placed into different families around the same time, to later share many adult characteristics and behaviors simply because they are the same sex and grow up in the same era (Joseph, 2004; McGue & Bouchard, 1984; Rose, 1982). As seen in Table 4.1, pairs of this type usually also share cohort effects related to national, regional, ethnic, religious, and economic class influences. Together with age, sex, and appearance-related effects, these numerous common environmental influences plausibly explain any additional reported MZA behavioral resemblance.

The following example illustrates the potential impact of behavior-shaping cohort effects. Imagine that male MZAs are separated at birth and are raised in different Pennsylvania Amish families. The Amish (population approximately 280,000) are traditionalist Christians known for simple living, plain dress, and a reluctance to adopt many conveniences of modern technology. The largest population of Amish live in Lancaster County, Pennsylvania, United States. If these twins met each other for the first time at age 35, they would likely display many similarities in personality, IQ, behavior, religious beliefs, clothing, facial hair, and so on because, although they were reared in completely different families and homes, they were raised in the same behavior-molding *culture* at the same time. In a similar way, it is likely that a pair of age-matched yet *genetically unrelated* male infants placed into different Pennsylvania Amish families around the same time would also display many similarities for the same reasons.

Table 4.1 Environmental Influences Shared by Reared-Apart Monozygotic Twin Pairs (MZAs)

- They shared the same prenatal (intrauterine) environment
- They are exactly the same age (birth cohort)
- They are the same sex
- They are almost always the same ethnicity
- Their appearance is strikingly similar (which will elicit more similar treatment)
- They usually are raised in the same socioeconomic class
- They usually are raised in the same culture
- They usually are raised in the same country
- They usually are taught similar religious beliefs and religious behaviors
- They volunteered to be studied. Volunteers share several common psychological characteristics (Lykken, 1978; Rosenthal & Rosnow, 1975)
- Most studied pairs spent a certain amount of time together in the same family environment, were aware of each other's existence when studied, and often had regular contact over long periods of time

Source: Adapted from Joseph, 2004, p. 126.

Taking the opposite approach with a pair sharing only common age, common sex, prenatal environment, and similar appearance, we could imagine a pair of separated-at-birth Arab-American female MZAs born in Berkeley, California (Joseph & Ratner, 2013). One twin is raised in a liberal non-religious Berkeley family, while the other is sent to Saudi Arabia and is raised there in a conservative Islamic Saudi Arabian family, and they have no contact with each other and do not know of each other's existence. In Saudi Arabia, women experience "gender apartheid" in a strict Islamic society, are not allowed to interact with men much of the time, and are required to be covered in black from head to toe when in public (Ratner & El-Badwi, 2011). If these twins are reunited for the first time at age 40, how much would we expect them to have in common? As even Lykken recognized, "If twins were separated as infants and placed, one with a middle-class Minnesota family and the other with an 18-year-old unmarried mother living on AFDC [welfare program] in the South Bronx, the twins will surely differ 30 years later" (Lykken, 1995, p. 87).

Table 4.2 provides a rough outline of the ascending levels of environmental similarity experienced by MZA pairs. The "Genetically unrelated pairs" category in Table 4.2 is used as a baseline to indicate the most randomly selected non-twin pairs that can be found in the population. Even though people unfamiliar with TRA research might expect MZA pairs to fall into Category 1 or 2, even these pairs are subject to common age, sex, prenatal, appearance, and ethnic group influences. And in fact, most studied pairs fall into Categories 5–10.[8] Thus, although genetic factors are one possible (partial or complete) explanation for MZA's behavioral resemblance, the resemblance is plausibly explained by cohort effects and other *non*-genetic factors.

Range Restriction

The restricted socioeconomic range of MZA family environments is another non-genetic factor biasing MZA correlations upwards. Since MZAs are usually placed in similar (poor or working-class) environments, on the basis of this restricted socioeconomic range alone we would expect them to correlate to a certain extent on IQ tests. This is an empirical argument, for the moment unrelated to why social classes differ in measured IQ. Psychometrist Mike Stoolmiller showed in a 1999 publication that the restricted range of adoptive families inflates adoption study correlations that behavioral geneticists usually attribute to genetic influences. TRA studies are a type of adoption study, and Stoolmiller showed that these studies also "do not escape biases due to range restriction." He argued that "heritability estimates for related siblings adopted apart will also be seriously inflated by range restriction of SE [shared environment]" (Stoolmiller, 1999, p. 404).

Table 4.2 Correlated Environments: Ascending Potential Shared Environmental Influences Experienced by Reared-Apart Monozygotic Twin Pairs (MZAs)

Genetically unrelated pairs	Genetically unrelated pairs of strangers, different sex, randomly selected from the entire range of ages, randomly selected from the entire national or world population
Category 1	Common prenatal, separated at birth, same sex, same age, similar appearance
Category 2	Common prenatal, separated at birth, same sex, same age, similar appearance, same ethnicity
Category 3	Common prenatal, separated at birth, same sex, same age, similar appearance, same ethnicity, similar socioeconomic status
Category 4	Common prenatal, separated at birth, same sex, same age, similar appearance, same ethnicity, similar socioeconomic status, common culture
Category 5	Common prenatal, separated at birth, same sex, same age, similar appearance, same ethnicity, similar socioeconomic status, common culture, common religion
Category 6	Common prenatal, late separation, same sex, same age, similar appearance, same ethnicity, similar socioeconomic status, common culture, common religion, partially reared together
Category 7	Common prenatal, late separation, same sex, same age, similar appearance, same ethnicity, similar socioeconomic status, common culture, common religion, partially reared together, contact as adults
Category 8	Common prenatal, late separation (after several years) same sex, same age, similar appearance, same ethnicity, similar socioeconomic status, common culture, common religion, partially reared together, contact as adults, close emotional twin relationship
Category 9	Common prenatal, late separation (after several years), same sex, same age, similar appearance, same ethnicity, similar socioeconomic status, common culture, common religion, partially reared together, contact as adults, close emotional twin relationship, raised by different members of the same family
Category 10	Common prenatal, late separation (after several years), same sex, same age, similar appearance, same ethnicity, similar socioeconomic status, common culture, common religion, partially reared together, contact as adults, close emotional twin relationship, raised by different members of the same family, lived together as adults

A study performed in France found that the adopted-away children of unskilled workers, who were reared in the homes of adoptive families in the upper 13 percent of the socioprofessional scale, scored 14 points higher on IQ tests when compared with children who were reared in the homes of their unskilled worker biological parents (Schiff, Duyme, Dumaret, & Tomkiewicz, 1982; see also Schiff & Lewontin, 1986). This finding suggests that socioeconomic environments are an important factor in determining IQ scores, which has important implications for TRA studies because MZA pairs are usually reared in similar socioeconomic environments.

Epigenetics

In recent years much attention has focused on epigenetics, which refers to genes switching expression on and off in response to environmental events and challenges, without alteration in the DNA sequence. Furthermore, these epigenetic changes can be passed down to the next generation independently of DNA inheritance. As the psychologist John Read and his colleagues Richard Bentall and Roar Fosse put it, "epigenetic processes turn gene transcription on and off through mechanisms that are highly influenced by the individual's socio-environmental experiences." They believed that "the implications, for research, mental health services and primary prevention, are profound" (Read, Bentall, & Fosse, 2009, p. 299).

In an extensive review of the scientific literature, Evan Charney, a political scientist writing critically about behavioral genetic research and affiliated with the Duke Institute for Brain Science, showed that recent findings call into question several assumptions by twin researchers and others relating to the biology and genetics of twinning. These assumptions include: (a) that 100 percent of the genes of MZ twin pairs are genetically identical; (b) that the percentages of the genetic identity of MZ twin pairs never change; and (c) that "all causes of phenotypic variation that impact human behavior can be attributed to a latent genetic (G) or environmental (E) parameter, or the interaction of the two (G × E)" (Charney, 2012, p. 333). As Charney showed, "recent developments in molecular genetics call into question every one of these assumptions" (p. 334).[9]

If so, behavioral genetic assumptions about inheritance face additional challenges, and call into question the basic assumption in twin research that MZT or MZA pairs share 100 percent genetic similarity, while DZT or DZA pairs share an average 50 percent genetic similarity. Because genes are expressed throughout one's lifetime on the basis of differing environmental influences, both types of twin pairs may differ genetically more than previously believed. Epigenetic discoveries also challenge traditional behavior genetic arguments that DNA is the all-important form of inheritance (see Plomin & Crabbe, 2000), because some of what is inherited is the result of gene expression based on environmental experiences independent of DNA inheritance.

Although some genetically oriented researchers have attempted to integrate epigenetics into their existing arguments and theories (e.g., Plomin, DeFries, et al., 2013, pp. 146–149), recent findings in epigenetics and other areas provide additional support to environmental theories of behavioral differences. This is because it is now known that the environment, and especially the perinatal environment, can influence gene expression. This is, according to Charney, "particularly prevalent in the human brain and probably [is] involved in much human behavior" (Charney, 2012, p. 331; see also Meaney, 2010).

Conclusions

All topics I have discussed in this chapter relate directly to the interpretation of twin studies, and most are key concepts and positions of the field of behavioral genetics. The psychometric/behavioral genetic perspective accepts the validly of concepts such as IQ (and IQ tests), stable personality traits, personality tests, heritability, model fitting, the biological reality of bell-shaped distributions (curves), and the ranking of people on the basis of numerical test scores with an assumed genetic basis to such ranking.

Although we will see in upcoming chapters that twin studies contain an additional set of assumptions that must be true in order to interpret their results in favor of genetics, the psychometric/behavioral genetic positions on most of the topics covered in this chapter must be true in order to uphold the claim that important genetic influences underlie behavioral characteristics and psychiatric disorders. However, there is good reason to believe that the critics have correctly identified the major invalidating flaws of these concepts and assumptions.

In the following two chapters I will further assess the assumptions, methods, results, and conclusions of the MISTRA. Continuing the themes of the earlier chapters, I will arrive at some conclusions about what, if anything, TRA studies prove about genetic influences on human behavioral differences. In Chapter 7, I will examine the critical assumptions underlying studies of reared-together twin pairs.

Notes

1 In this context, a psychometrist is defined as a psychologist who devises, constructs, and standardizes psychological tests.
2 Paradoxically, in this example if fewer citizens were genetically predisposed (say 60 percent), some favism variation in the population would be attributable to genetics, and heritability would be well above zero.
3 The Second and Third Editions of Plomin and colleagues' *Behavioral Genetics* contained similar "black box/something wrong with the model" cautions about

BASIC ASSUMPTIONS AND POTENTIAL FALLACIES

model fitting (see Plomin, DeFries, & McClearn, 1990, p. 246; Plomin, DeFries, McClearn, & Rutter, 1997, p. 310).

4 As IQ critics Elaine and Harry Mensh (1991) pointed out in *The IQ Mythology*, by the time he published *The Mismeasure of Man* in 1981, Gould qualified this statement to read, "What craniometry was for the nineteenth century, intelligence testing has become for the twentieth, when it assumes that intelligence (or at least a dominant part of it) is a single, innate, heritable, and measureable thing" (Gould, 1981, p. 25).

5 Psychometrists' failure to assume that racial and class IQ scores should be equal does not imply that they assume that genetic factors explain group differences, since environmental factors could still completely explain IQ score differences.

6 As Wahlsten put it, instead of focusing on the "heritability of intelligence," we should instead assess the "intelligence of heritability" question (Wahlsten, 1994).

7 These questions were not taken from the tests, but are similar to real test questions.

8 Even in a perfectly randomized study, some pairs are likely to share several factors due to chance.

9 Charney discussed three additional assumptions underlying molecular genetic studies, which are not listed here.

5

THE MINNESOTA STUDY OF TWINS REARED APART I

Biases, Assumptions, and Other Problem Areas

> If one thing is clear in our results it is that fairly large environmental differences do modify physical, mental and temperamental traits and produce proportionately large differences even between hereditarily identical individuals.
> — TRA researchers Iva Gardner and Horatio Newman, 1940 (Gardner & Newman, 1940, p. 126)

> The MZA intraclass correlation of 0.50 for a personality trait directly estimates the heritability of the trait because MZA twins share only their genes.
> — Nancy Segal, 2012 (Segal, 2012, p. 334)

> It must always remain possible for the conclusions to be traced back to the original data. Journals should only accept articles if the data concerned has been made accessible in this way.
> — Committee report on the activities of Dutch psychologist Diederik Stapel, 2012 (Levelt Committee, Noort Committee, Drenth Committee, 2012, p. 58)

In 2012, former MISTRA researcher Nancy Segal published a book summarizing the findings of the study, entitled *Born Together—Reared Apart: The Landmark Minnesota Twin Study* (Segal, 2012). This book provides an excellent opportunity to review the major problem areas associated with TRA studies in general, and the MISTRA in particular. Considering the claims that have been made about this study, and the impact it has had, the MISTRA researchers' methods, assumptions, and conclusions must be examined in detail, which is the task of this chapter and the next. In Appendix A, I discuss Segal's defense of her colleagues' decision to accept major funding from the controversial Pioneer Fund.

One might have expected a purely "scientific" work detailing the MISTRA research findings, yet Segal's book, like the numerous popular works and textbooks that preceded it, is filled with stories of the supposed similarities of selected MISTRA pairs that have been reported for decades. She even made several references to journalistic accounts of the Jim Twins' similarly named wives and sons, their tendency to smoke Salem cigarettes, their vacations at the same Florida beach, and so on (Segal, 2012, pp. 10, 19, 27, 111, 226, 326, 342; see Chapter 2).

The book's title is itself problematic, since there is every reason to believe that the MISTRA, like the previous studies, consisted mainly of MZA pairs only *partially* reared apart, most of whom grew up reared *together*—at the same time—in similar social, political, and cultural environments. We saw in previous chapters that TRA researchers' use of the word "apart" refers mainly to family environments, and that twins' behavioral similarity is influenced by cohort effects related to experiencing similar national, cultural, age and sex-related, religious, and appearance-related environments during the same stages of life. Travelers to several Middle Eastern countries, for example, will encounter the remarkable (non-genetic) behavioral similarity that most women wear head covering, even though almost all were "reared apart" from each other in different family environments.

After reviewing the assembled research and the investigators' conclusions in favor of important genetic influences, Segal wrote, "Science rests on data, not dialogue" (p. 305). It is wrong, however, to counterpose the concepts of data and dialogue, since a major aspect of science is the *interpretation* of data, which involves dialogue among scientists and others. In response to Segal's position on data versus dialogue, *Born Together—Reared Apart* reviewer Michael Rossi wrote that Segal "gets it exactly wrong," because the "building blocks of science are data of one form or another, but dialogue is the basis on which science rests; discussion is what gives meaning to the numbers; the tales that we tell about data are what give it substance." Rossi concluded,

> Whatever Bouchard and Segal's protestations, it's stories about data—interpretations of observation, assumptions underlying test design, explanations of statistical correlation—on which the Mistra scientists based their findings of "genetic" behaviours given that not a single gene was actually examined in the study.
> (Rossi, 2013)

Rossi's comments apply especially to "soft science" social and behavioral science fields, where in some instances non-scientific opinion can make more sense than the conclusions of researchers based on their closely held theories and beliefs. As an obvious example, the opinions of leading American political scientists about the best political direction for the country are no more valid than anyone else's opinion. This is not an "antiscience" position, but merely the recognition that social and behavioral scientists' strongly held opinions and affiliations can sometimes lead them to confuse their own worldviews with scientific facts. As psychologists Brent Slife and Richard Williams put it, "The facts of science are themselves theory laden. A prominent misconception of scientists is that they are objective observers of the world." They continued that "data have little or no meaning without the researchers' interpretation of them," and that "scientists may be so accustomed to seeing the world through their particular theoretical 'glasses' that they forget they are wearing them" (Slife & Williams, 1995, pp. 5–6).

The MISTRA Twin Sample

The MISTRA researchers did attempt to reduce the potential bias described by Kamin and others. Twins were tested separately, and different people administered the tests. This reduced the possibility of unconscious experimenter bias. They also attempted to minimize ascertainment bias by recruiting all pairs they became aware of regardless of whether they were MZA or DZA, and were the first TRA researchers to attempt to correct for age and sex environmental confounds inflating twin correlations (see below). At the same time, the sample was not random and consisted of self-referred pairs.

The following description of the sample as it stood in 1990 is taken from the MISTRA *Science* publication (Bouchard, Lykken, McGue, Segal, & Tellegen, 1990, p. 223). According to Bouchard and colleagues, "the sample consists of adult twins, separated very early in life, reared apart during their formative years, and reunited as adults." The sample included

> more than 100 sets of reared-apart twins or triplets from across the United States and the United Kingdom [who] have participated in the Minnesota Study of Twins Reared Apart since it began in 1979. Participants have also come from Australia, Canada, China, New Zealand, Sweden, and West Germany.... participants complete approximately 50 hours of medical and psychological assessment. Two or more test instruments are used in each major domain of psychological assessment to ensure adequate coverage (for example, four personality trait inventories, three occupational interest inventories, and two mental ability batteries).

The researchers used "separate examiners [to] administer the IQ test, life history interview, psychiatric interview, and sexual life history interview. A comprehensive mental ability battery is administered as a group test. The twins also complete questionnaires independently, under the constant supervision of a staff member." MZA and DZA pairs "have been ascertained in several ways . . . friends, relatives, or the reunited twins, themselves, having learned of the project, contact the Minnesota Center for Twin and Adoption Research (MICTAR)." They wrote that "selection on the basis of similarity is minimized by vigorously recruiting all reared-apart twins, regardless of known or presumed zygosity and similarity" (Bouchard, Lykken et al., 1990, p. 223).

At the time of the 1990 *Science* article, the MISTRA MZA sample consisted of 56 MZA pairs and 30 DZA pairs. More pairs were added between 1990 and the close of the study in 2000, with the final total consisting of 81 MZA pairs, and 56 DZA pairs (38 same-sex and 18 opposite-sex DZA pairs; Segal, 2012, p. 42). Table 5.1 shows the MISTRA sample sizes as reported in various publications appearing between 1980 and 2000.

The investigators assessed pre-study contact through their development of a "contact time" formula, which assessed the time twins spent before and after separation. According to the investigators, "Twins who met for a week at Christmas and for a week in the summer each year over a 10-year period are credited with 20 weeks of contact" (Bouchard & McGue, 1990, pp. 266–267). The total reflects the amount of time (measured in months) that twins spent together before being studied. Bouchard stated that MZAs had "minimal contact" before entering the study (Bouchard & McGue, 1990, pp. 266–267), thereby assuming that twins are only able to influence each other's behavior when they are physically together, a questionable assumption for which the investigators provided no evidence

Table 5.1 MISTRA Sample Sizes: 1981–2000

Year	TWIN PAIRS	
	MZA	DZA
1981[1]	15	(NR)
1982[2]	30	9
1984[3]	28	12
1988[4]	44	27
1990[5]	56	30
1996[6]	65	54
1998[7]	71	53
2000[8]	81	56

[1]Eckert, Heston, & Bouchard (1981); [2]Lykken (1982); [3]Bouchard (1984); [4]Tellegen et al. (1988); [5]Bouchard, Lykken, McGue, Segal, & Tellegren (1990); [6]DiLalla, Gottesman, Carey, & Bouchard (1996); [7]Bouchard, McGue, Hur, & Horn (1998); [8]Segal (2012); final total. NR = not reported. Opposite-sex pairs were generally about one-third of the DZA total. The study was closed to new twin pairs in 2000.

in support. In addition, "contact time" makes no distinction between time spent together as infants versus time spent together as children or adults, and does not assess the quality of the contact (Richardson, 1998). The 1990 MZA sample had a mean age of 41.0 years, with a range of 19–68 years, and a "Total contact time" mean of 112.5 weeks, with a range of 1–1,233 weeks (Bouchard, Lykken et al., 1990, p. 24). This meant that the average MZA pair had over 2 years of contact with each other, and that one pair had over 23 years of contact (Richardson, 1998).

Attempting to assess similarities in twins' rearing environments, in their 1990 *Science* article Bouchard and colleagues described their use of a "checklist of available household facilities (for example, power tools, sailboat, telescope, unabridged dictionary, and original artwork)," which they believed "provides an index of the cultural and intellectual resources in the adoptive home." Each twin completed an environmental similarity questionnaire "describing the individual's retrospective impression of treatment and rearing provided by the adoptive parents during childhood and adolescence." The investigators concluded that the "measured similarity of the adoptive rearing environments" had a minimal effect on MZA behavioral similarity (Bouchard, Lykken et al., 1990, p. 225). They also believed that the effects of selective placement on their twin sample "appear to be modest" (Bouchard & McGue, 1990, p. 278).

We recall from Chapter 2 that Shields saw the use of volunteers as a "risky procedure in most types of research, but inevitable in this case." And Lykken recognized, "It is well established that volunteers tend to be more intelligent than nonvolunteers" (Lykken, 1978, p. 6). Lykken also recognized that volunteer subjects are better educated and frequently hold middle-class values, which will further increase twin behavioral resemblance. Volunteer twin samples tend to be overrepresented by female pairs, reflected in the fact that the final MISTRA MZA sample was 60 percent female, while the same-sex DZA sample was 68 percent female (Segal, 2012, p. 42; see also Lykken, 1978).

In this chapter I will examine major problems and biases in the MISTRA, many of which were also in evidence in the classical studies examined in previous chapters. As I showed in Chapter 4, the validity and usefulness of concepts such as heritability, IQ testing, general intelligence (g), stable personality traits, personality tests, and model fitting have been debated for many years. Moreover, we saw that the many common cultural influences experienced by MZAs plausibly explain above-zero behavioral and cognitive ability correlations. I will attempt to show that the MISTRA was subject to most of the errors and biases of the classical studies, and in some respects it was subject to more errors and biases. In Chapter 6 I focus on how these problem areas came into play in specific MISTRA IQ and personality studies, and in Chapters 9 and 10 we will see that molecular genetic researchers have failed to uncover genes for the behavioral characteristics studied in the MISTRA, a study in which, as Rossi reminded us, "not a single gene was actually examined."

The main explicit and implicit assumptions underlying the study are seen in Table 5.2. Assumptions 1 through 7 must be true in order to validate the researchers' conclusions in favor of genetics, while genetic findings probably could withstand violations of Assumptions 8 through 18 to a certain degree. A major aspect of Part I of this book is to show that these assumptions range from probably true, to questionable, to doubtful, to outright false.

DZA Pairs: The MISTRA Designated Control Group

In an introductory chapter of *Born Together—Reared Apart*, Segal wrote that intraclass correlations "are calculated separately for MZA and DZA twin pairs and compared," and that "genetic effects on a trait are demonstrated when MZ (or MZA) intraclass correlations exceed DZ (or DZA) intraclass correlations" (Segal, 2012, p. 59). In most MISTRA publications reported by Segal, the researchers concluded in favor of genetics on the basis of twin data used in their model-fitting procedures, which we have seen were based on the assumption that all behavioral resemblance is caused by genes. This was true for MISTRA studies of personality (Segal, 2012, pp. 97–104), cardiac characteristics (pp. 123–125), religiosity (pp. 141–147), dental parameters (pp. 151–162), vocational interests (pp. 165–170), workplace values (pp. 179–181), reproductive outcome (pp. 184–186), sensation seeking and control (pp. 207–208), "morningness–eveningness" (pp. 221–222), headaches (pp. 225–227), dietary preferences (pp. 227–230), authoritarianism (pp. 230–233), social attitudes (pp. 253–256), and reading comprehension (pp. 257–261).

Segal wrote that "Bouchard's decision to use DZA twins as controls was made in a very early memo to the 'Twin Research Team'" (Segal, 2012, p. 12, see also Footnote 69 on Segal's p. 343). This memo was dated March 5th, 1979, and indicates that from the very beginning Bouchard decided to use DZAs as the control group. Segal regarded this decision as "an important methodological improvement over past projects" (p. 12). In Chapter 6 we will see how the researchers discussed DZA pairs and their correlations in the various publications, but for now the main point is to establish that, according to Segal's account, from the beginning of the study in 1979, Bouchard had designated DZA pairs as the MISTRA control group.

According to the MISTRA genetic "general model," the DZA correlation should be one-half of the MZA correlation (McGue & Bouchard, 1989, p. 24). This is seen in a frequently reproduced MISTRA diagram, where the DZA correlation is said to represent one-half of the heritability estimate

Table 5.2 Some Implicit and Explicit MISTRA Assumptions

1. There are only two types of twin pairs, monozygotic and dizygotic
2. MZAs are genetically identical throughout their life
3. MISTRA MZA pairs qualify as "reared-apart twin pairs"
4. The MISTRA results are generalizable to the non-twin population
5. Human intelligence is accurately measured by IQ tests, which measure general intelligence, or g
6. Personality can be measured and quantified with personality tests
7. Apart from age and sex effects, MZA and DZA behavioral correlations are not influenced by cohort effects related to common socioeconomic status, culture, religion, and other social influences
8. MZAs create more similar environments for themselves than DZAs because they are more similar genetically, which counts as a genetic effect
9. Heritability estimates provide a valid indicator of the magnitude of genetic influences on human behavioral characteristics
10. Personality traits exist as stable and enduring descriptions of how people behave in varying situations
11. Biometrical model fitting is a valid method for the partitioning of genetic and environmental influences
12. Biometrical model-fitting assumptions, including those relating to genetics and human relationships, are valid
13. Genetic and environmental influences are additive
14. Behavioral characteristics in a population are distributed in a bell-shaped curve
15. The more similar prenatal environments of MZA versus DZA pairs did not contribute to the greater behavioral resemblance of the former
16. The great physical and appearance similarity of MZA pairs does not influence their greater behavioral similarity versus DZA pairs. If it does, it is counted as a genetic effect
17. "Substantial" age and sex effects on twin correlations were eliminated through the use of MISTRA-developed statistical corrections
18. The MZA correlation for IQ, personality, and other behavioral characteristics directly estimates heritability (sometimes qualified by requiring a lack of selective placement)

($^r dza = 0.5h^2$), and the MZA correlation is the same as the heritability estimate ($^r mza = h^2$; for example, see Bouchard & McGue, 2003, p. 8).

MZA versus DZA Correlations

We saw in the previous chapter that if the MZA correlation is comparable in magnitude to the DZA correlation, or if the MZA correlation is not higher than the DZA correlation at a statistically significant level, according to basic statistical principles relating to the comparison of sample populations, the MZA and DZA correlations are the same (do not differ) because the difference may have occurred by chance. A finding that MZA and DZA sample correlations do not differ argues against the genetic position because MZA pairs' more similar genetic relationship versus DZA pairs (presumed to be 100 percent versus an average 50 percent) did not lead to their greater behavioral resemblance, as predicted by genetic theories. This finding would suggest that non-genetic factors alone are responsible for raising both the MZA and the DZA correlations above zero. As seen in Chapter 4, the SATSA researchers recognized, "When MZ[A] correlations are not greater than DZ[A] correlations, twin similarity may reflect correlated environments rather than genetic similarity" (Pedersen, Plomin, Nesselroade, & McClearn, 1992, p. 350).

In cases where the MZA correlation is significantly higher than the DZA correlation, the difference could be accounted for by environmental influences because DZA pairs clearly experience less similar environments than MZA pairs due to their less similar physical appearance, placement decisions, and their less frequent pre-study contact. For example, the MISTRA MZA–DZA sample ratio included far more MZAs than would be expected by chance, and the MISTRA MZAs experienced twice as much pre-study contact time than experienced by the DZAs (Bouchard & McGue, 1990, p. 267). As the researchers acknowledged, "In the MISTRA pool, on average, MZA co-twins have had more contact and have spent a smaller percentage of their lifetimes apart than DZA co-twins" (McCourt, Bouchard, Lykken, Tellegen, & Keyes, 1999, p. 1007).

According to Segal, who chose to emphasize the point, "Bouchard agreed with our critics that MZA twins probably do have more similar environments than DZA twins, *but they are environments of the twins' making*" (Segal, 2012, p. 104, italics in original). In other words, Segal argued that MZAs create more similar environments for themselves because they are more similar genetically, which in her view counts as a genetic effect (see Chapter 7 for an analysis of this argument).

Therefore, because the MISTRA genetic model implies that the MZA correlation should be significantly higher than the DZA correlation, in cases where this occurs a major aspect of the MISTRA argument in favor of genetics comes down to whether the behavior-shaping influences of MZA pairs' more similar environments count as a genetic effect, as Segal and other MISTRA investigators contend, or count as an environmental effect, as most critics contend.

How the Researchers Arrived at Conclusions in Favor of Genetics

In their 1990 MISTRA personality publication, Bouchard and McGue wrote, "A major assumption underlying the present analysis is that twins were separated early in life and placed in rearing environments that are uncorrelated with respect to factors influencing the development of personality" (Bouchard & McGue, 1990, p. 276). We saw in Chapters 3 and 4 that this assumption is false, regardless of whether adoption agencies (when used) did or did not selectively place MZA pairs. In fact, taking Shields' British study as a prime example, many pairs were raised nearby to each other in different branches of the same family and had ongoing relationships with each other, and fully one-third of the MISTRA MZA pairs also grew up in the culture of Great Britain (Segal, 2012, p. 45). We also saw that cohort effects and many types of cultural influences, shared by even perfectly separated MZA pairs, exert important influences on behavior.

As will be explored in more detail below and in Chapter 6, the MISTRA researchers' conclusions in favor of important genetic influences on human behavioral differences (including IQ and personality) were based on three findings.[1] I will list these findings, and provide some comments on each:

Finding # 1: The MZA correlation is significantly higher than the DZA correlation (a preliminary "first step").

Finding # 2: The MZA correlation is well above zero. The MZA correlation is assumed to directly estimate heritability, and the environments experienced by MZAs (other than age and sex effects) are assumed to play little, if any, role in explaining these MZA correlations.

Finding # 3: Model-fitting procedures produce substantial heritability estimates. These estimates are assumed to be roughly accurate, and are assumed to indicate the degree (strength) of the genetic influence on the behavioral characteristic in question.

Finding # 1: The MZA Correlation is Significantly Higher than the DZA Correlation

We have seen that the preliminary "first step" of a valid TRA study using MZAs and DZAs is a determination that the MZA correlation is significantly higher than the DZA correlation. However, despite designating DZAs as the MISTRA control group, in their publications the researchers bypassed this crucial preliminary determination, and based their conclusions on Findings # 2 and # 3. When encountering and commenting on DZA correlations that did not fit their genetic models, they developed various explanations that were consistent with these models (see Chapter 6).

The decision to skip the preliminary step of directly comparing MZA and DZA correlations is seen in the first major MISTRA peer-reviewed publication, the 1988 personality study by Tellegen, Bouchard, Segal, and colleagues. Here they wrote, "Although intraclass correlations are often informative . . . for analytic purposes they can be misleading if MZ and DZ variances differ. Biometric geneticists . . . therefore, prefer analyzing variances over correlations. We also take this approach in this article" (Tellegen et al., 1988, p. 1034). Their decision to bypass or skip the necessary first step of determining that the MZA correlation is significantly higher than the DZA correlation was then repeated in all subsequent major MISTRA publications.

As we have seen, Plomin and colleagues wrote that

> the twin design estimates genetic influence on the basis of the difference between MZ and DZ correlations. If the MZ correlation does not exceed the DZ correlation for a particular trait, there is no genetic influence . . . and model-fitting analyses must come to that conclusion or there is something wrong with the model.
> (Plomin, Chipuer, & Loehlin, 1990, p. 235)

Leaving aside model-fitting problem areas seen in Chapter 4, the models used in TRA studies cannot find genetic influences on a behavioral characteristic unless the MZA correlation is significantly higher than the DZA correlation. Segal also endorsed this "important first step" position, yet in practice she and her colleagues skipped over it and based their conclusions on Findings # 2 and # 3 (Segal, 2012, p. 62; Segal did not state the need to show a statistically significant difference between MZA and DZA pairs).

Bouchard and colleagues seemed to place more emphasis on the importance of their DZA correlations at an earlier stage of the study in 1986, writing, "DZA twins allow us to test the two most common competing hypotheses proposed as alternatives to the genetic hypothesis as an explanation of the similarity between MZA twins" (Bouchard, Lykken, Segal, & Wilcox, 1986, p. 300). Yet by 1988, with the data at hand, they decided against making a preliminary Finding # 1 "test" of these "competing hypotheses."

Finding # 2: The MZA Correlation is Assumed to Directly Estimate Heritability

The researchers based many of their conclusions on the Finding # 2 "MZA correlation directly estimates heritability" assumption, which would seem to override any contradictory results based on Findings # 1 and # 3, and even though it is interrelated with Finding # 3 because model-fitting calculations assume that all twin behavioral resemblance is due to genetics.

This "MZA correlation directly estimates heritability" position assumes that MZAs do not share any environmental similarities that cause their similar behavior. For example, if the MZA IQ correlation is 0.70, the heritability of IQ is estimated to be 0.7 (70 percent). We have seen, however, that there are three major problems with this position:

1. Most pairs were only partially reared apart.
2. Even perfectly separated MZA pairs share many environmental similarities.
3. There are major problems with the heritability concept itself.

Some examples from the MISTRA literature of this "directly estimates heritability" assumption are seen below. At times this assumption was qualified by the requirement that it applies only if there was no placement bias, but it was usually put forward without qualification:

- **Bouchard, 1984**: "If there is no placement bias . . . then the intraclass correlation between [reared-apart] MZ twins is a direct estimate of heritability" (Bouchard, 1984, p. 150).
- **Bouchard, Lykken et al., 1990**: "The power of the MZA design is that for twins reared apart from early infancy and randomly placed for adoption [the genetic variance, or heritability] can be directly estimated from the MZA correlation" (Bouchard, Lykken et al., 1990, p. 224).
- **McGue, Bouchard, Iacono, and Lykken, 1993**: "The MZA correlation provides a direct estimate of heritability" (McGue et al., 1993, p. 65).
- **Segal, 1999**: "If identical twins are separated in early infancy, and raised in contrasting environments, they provide a direct estimate of genetic influence on behavior. This is because the only factor they share is their genes" (Segal, 1999, p. 19).
- **Lykken, 2006**: "The intraclass correlations of monozygotic twins who were separated in infancy and reared apart (MZA twins) provide estimates of trait heritability" (Lykken, 2006, p. 306).
- **Bouchard, 2008**: "The correlations for monozygotic twins reared apart directly estimate the heritability of the trait" (Bouchard, 2008, p. 12).
- **Segal, 2013**: "The MZA intraclass correlation directly estimates heritability" (Segal, 2013, p. 23).

In addition to the controversial concept of heritability itself (see Chapter 4), the MISTRA (and behavioral genetic) position that the MZA correlation directly estimates heritability because "the only factor they share is their genes" (Segal, 1999, p. 19) is contradicted not only by the influence of cohort effects, but even by the recognition by Bouchard, McGue, Segal, and others that age and sex effects alone can "substantially" influence MZA behavioral correlations (see below).

Finding # 3: Model-Fitting Procedures Produce Substantial Heritability Estimates

In Chapter 4 we saw that model-fitting techniques assume "that shared genes underlie similarity between relatives" (Segal, 2012, p. 63). This means that the model assumes the very thing it is attempting to determine, and is therefore based on a circular argument. It also means that Findings # 2 and # 3 are not independent, because both are based on the assumption that the MZA intraclass correlation is caused only by genetic influences. Moreover, simply because data "fit" a model does not mean that the model is correct, and other means are necessary to validate this finding.

Because the MISTRA researchers decided to skip Finding # 1 (and because it was potentially superseded by Finding # 2), direct MZA–DZA comparisons did not play a role in determining the researchers' conclusions. And because Finding # 3 is based on assuming Finding # 2, the MISTRA researchers' entire argument in favor of genetics rested on the Finding # 2 position/assumption that MZA correlations are caused only by genetic factors, and on the accompanying assumption that the MZA correlation directly estimates heritability. As I argue throughout Part I of this book, the numerous environmental influences shared by MZA pairs indicate that this assumption has little, if any, support.

Assumptions That Are "Likely Not to Hold"

The standard set of biometric model-fitting assumptions used in most MISTRA publications is found in a 1989 publication by McGue and Bouchard on information processing and special mental abilities, where a stated assumption was that the "phenotype (i.e., character of interest)" is expressed as the additive effect of genetic and environmental effects. "Additional assumptions" included

> (a) All resemblance between reared apart relatives is because of genetic factors, (b) there is no assortative mating, (c) all genetic effects are additive (i.e., there is no dominance or epistasis), and (d) genetic and environmental effects are independent (i.e., there no genotype–environment co-variance) and combine additively in the determination of the phenotype (i.e., there is no genotype by environment interaction).
>
> (McGue & Bouchard, 1989, pp. 22–23)

All of these assumptions are questionable, and McGue and Bouchard admitted that "several of these assumptions are likely not to hold for cognitive abilities" (p. 23). In other words, they recognized that the assumptions underlying their attempts to "resolve the magnitude of the genetic and environmental sources of phenotypic variability" (p. 22) are "likely not to hold" for cognitive abilities, by far the most important area of behavioral genetic investigation.

These assumptions also apply to personality and other behavioral areas, and the assumption that genetic and environmental effects are independent and do not interact (MISTRA assumption "d" above) is clearly false, as we saw in Chapter 4. In addition, the MISTRA "assumption c" that there is no dominance or epistasis may also be false. Epistasis occurs when the effect of one gene depends on the presence of one or more "modifier genes." Some research suggests that epistasis is "strong" and "pervasive" in mice and rats (Shao et al., 2008, p. 19910), and is reported to influence human characteristics as well (Hemani et al., 2014; Zuk, Hechter, Sunyaev, & Lander, 2012). At the same time, the MISTRA genetic "findings" continue to be reported in textbooks and in the media, and its lead investigator is awarded a Gold Medal by the American Psychological Foundation (Anonymous, 2014), with no mention of the assumptions the study was based upon, some of which the researchers themselves recognized are "likely not to hold," that is, are likely to be false.

Moreover, we have seen that the MISTRA assumption that all MZA IQ and behavioral resemblance "is because of genetic factors" (MISTRA assumption "a" above) uses the same circular reasoning employed by Juel-Nielsen in his TRA study, as well as by researchers using subsequently developed model-fitting techniques. Segal wrote that the MISTRA personality studies showed "that personality similarity between relatives seems to come mostly from their shared genes" (Segal, 2012, p. 102), a conclusion based on the MISTRA *assumption* that, as Segal wrote elsewhere, "shared genes underlie similarity between relatives" (p. 63).

Taylor recognized the "important flaw" of circular reasoning underlying the Jinks and Fulker model, which formed the basis of the MISTRA models (for example, see Tellegen et al., 1988, p. 1034). We saw earlier that, according to Taylor, "The technique makes sense only if one presumes, as do Jensen, Jinks, and Fulker, that the mean IQ score of a twin pair 'reflects the genotypic value.' This means that high heritability (and zero measurement error) must be presumed beforehand" (Taylor, 1980, pp. 160–161). Indeed, the MISTRA researchers' models "presume beforehand" their subsequent finding that most behavioral characteristics are "substantially heritable."

Ironically, Bouchard was critical of circular arguments when he believed he spotted them in studies by researchers emphasizing the importance of the family environment. He wrote on several occasions that developmental psychologists' interpretations of parent–child correlations in support of important environmental factors "are completely confounded by genetic factors. Interpretation of such correlations in terms of environmental causation presumes the theory they are purporting to test" (Bouchard, 1993b, p. 30). Yet Bouchard and colleagues themselves "presume the theory they are purporting to test" when they assumed (and concluded) that "all resemblance between reared apart relatives is because of genetic factors."

In *Born Together—Reared Apart,* Segal wrote that the MISTRA was "unique" in several respects, including its use of "sophisticated biometrical modeling techniques that partition genetic and environmental effects on behavior that have been developed since the 1970s" (Segal, 2012, p. 99). Regardless of how "sophisticated" model-fitting techniques may be, if they are based on false assumptions and circular reasoning they will produce false and misleading results, and we have seen that the MISTRA researchers admitted that the assumptions their cognitive ability model-fitting procedures are based upon do not hold. The computer science saying "garbage in, garbage out" applies as well to behavioral genetic model-fitting results based on false assumptions about genes, people, and society. As we have seen, over 80 years ago Hogben warned of the "danger of concealing assumptions which have no factual basis behind an impressive façade of flawless algebra" (Hogben, 1933, p. 121).

Did the MISTRA MZA Pairs Experience Less Similar Environments than Pairs in the Previous Studies?

The answer to the question posed in this section is simple: Only the researchers know for sure, since they have chosen to become the MISTRA "lords of the data" (see Chapter 2, and below). We saw in Chapter 4 that even perfectly separated MZA pairs share many environmental similarities that were not controlled for, or even thought of, by TRA researchers prior to 1979. And, as seen in Tables 2.1–2.3, most classical study pairs had much contact over many years and had ongoing relationships with each other. In other words, despite countless characterizations of these investigations as "reared-apart twin studies," most of the twin pairs in these studies were only partially reared apart.[2]

Recruitment Bias

Segal wrote that "the methods by which MISTRA participants (and reared-apart twins in other studies) were identified have been criticized for attracting or favoring assessment of the relatively more similar MZA pairs" (Segal, 2012, p. 304; she cited my 2001 and 2004 publications, and Lewontin, Rose, & Kamin, 1984 as examples of such critics). We saw in previous chapters that several critics have indeed argued that TRA recruitment methods led to samples biased in favor of similarity. The key word here is "methods," which does not imply that the researchers intentionally sought biased samples for the purpose of artificially inflating IQ and personality correlations. Nevertheless, there is little doubt that the MISTRA MZA sample was biased in favor of more similar pairs for many of the same reasons that the classical TRA studies were so biased.

Bouchard recognized in 1984 that "twins who are willing to participate in [a TRA] study are to a large extent, a self-selected population and this further exacerbates the sampling problem. Placement of these children in adoptive homes is also unlikely to be random" (Bouchard, 1984, p. 151). Two years later, Bouchard, Segal, and colleagues recognized, "We cannot claim that our sample of MZA twins is a random sample of the population of twins" (Bouchard et al., 1986, p. 301). We saw in Chapters 2 and 3 that MZA samples recruited through media appeals are biased because twins had to have known of each other's existence in order to respond to such appeals, and they may have discovered each other because of their similarities. In the words of SATSA researchers Nancy Pederson, Robert Plomin and colleagues, studies such as the MISTRA "typically relied on identification by third parties or response to media appeals. Pairs may have come to the investigator's (and to each other's) attention because of their remarkable similarity" (Pedersen, Plomin, McClearn, & Friberg, 1988, p. 955).

Shields recognized that the degree of social and cultural differences among his MZA pairs' families "were as a rule not remarkable," and speculated that "had the material consisted mostly of pairs where one twin was brought up in the criminal underworld, the other in a 'respectable' upper-middle-class home, no doubt many interesting differences would have emerged" (Shields, 1962, p. 148). Indeed they would have, yet TRA studies based on media appeals are unavoidably biased by the fact that pairs of this type are rarely examined, due to the unlikelihood that both would agree to participate in the study. Shields wrote of his inability to study "fourteen probably MZ[A] pairs where co-operation was blocked by one of the twins" (p. 27). Clearly, when one twin "blocks" cooperation in a TRA study, this unstudied (and untested) pair is much more likely to be behaviorally dissimilar compared with pairs who are both eager to cooperate.

In *The Gene Illusion* (Joseph, 2004) I discussed a 1940 account by Iva Gardner and Horatio Newman, who wrote about an MZA pair they had identified after the publication of Newman and colleagues' 1937 study (of which Newman was the lead researcher). Gardner and Newman corresponded with a pair of separated male twins in Pennsylvania. Although one of the twins was "anxious to have their case studied," his brother "is, we fear, somewhat of a hoodlum and refuses to submit to examination." The researchers commented, "This is unfortunate in view of the fact that the two brothers now seem to be so different in their personality traits" (Gardner & Newman, 1940, p. 119). I pointed out that such pairs are less likely to participate in a TRA study *because of* their differing personalities. This introduces unintended bias in favor of the recruitment of more behaviorally similar pairs.

Segal wrote of Newman and colleagues "possibly excluding dissimilar MZA sets" (p. 304). This was not just a possibility, as Newman and colleagues clearly stated that they attempted to exclude dissimilar MZA sets due to the possibility that they might be DZA sets. As they acknowledged, "It seems possible that our [MZA] group is more heavily weighted with extremely similar pairs than with identical twins of less striking similarity," which they viewed as an unintended bias resulting from their recruitment methods (Newman, Freeman, & Holzinger, 1937, p. 31). This is an inevitable aspect of TRA studies that recruit volunteer twins on the basis of media appeals. Although the MISTRA reduced bias by recruiting all pairs regardless of their zygosity, its twin sample remained subject to the biases introduced by a reliance on volunteer twin pairs recruited through media appeals.

Age and Sex Confounds

Kamin argued in *The Science and Politics of I.Q.* that TRA IQ correlations are influenced by cohort effects such as common age and common sex (gender), which constituted major environmental confounds that the earlier researchers did not control for, or even notice. The Minnesota researchers attempted to adjust their data to eliminate age and sex effects. According to Bouchard, "Simply because twins are matched in age, they are going to be similar in ability. So you have to control for age" (Bouchard, 1984, p. 183). In a 1984 publication, McGue and Bouchard described their statistical strategy to remove age and sex confounds, recognizing, "For most psychological, physiological, and medical variables there are substantial age and sex effects" (McGue & Bouchard, 1984, p. 325). We saw in Chapter 4 (Table 4.1), however, that the common age and sex of MZA pairs are only two of many non-genetic social and cultural factors contributing to their behavioral similarity. Imagine the folly of attempting to control only for age and sex confounds in a TRA study carried out among the Pennsylvania Amish (see Chapter 4), where age and sex effects, though important, would be only two of many non-genetic factors contributing to MZA behavioral similarity.

McGue and Bouchard concluded that the best method to adjust correlations to account for age and sex effects is a "twin-based" approach using information from the twin data itself. Their formula, as described in a 1984 publication, is extremely complicated and indecipherable to almost anyone not holding the unofficial title of "statistical guru," and there is no reason to accept that age and sex effects were eliminated through the use of this formula (McGue & Bouchard, 1984). Nevertheless, it was used to adjust all subsequent MISTRA MZA and DZA correlations.[3]

Reliance on Twins' Accounts of Separation and Behavioral Similarity

As Kamin noted in the 1970s, another key, yet usually overlooked, aspect of TRA studies is that the degree of MZA separation is based mainly on the acceptance of the twins' verbal accounts. Segal mentioned that "all travel and hotel expenses were covered by the project" (plus an honorarium) for twins and their spouses to come to Minneapolis for the week (Segal, 2012, p. 54), and "it became clear that having spouses, children, or friends travel with the twins provided an added incentive for the twins to participate" (p. 25). It may have also provided an added incentive for twins to exaggerate, or even lie about, their degree of contact and behavioral similarity. Almost 50 percent of the MISTRA pairs came from overseas (p. 45), adding the additional incentive of an all-expense-paid international vacation for some who could not have afforded one otherwise.

Perhaps many MZA pairs were truthful, but there were incentives for them to exaggerate their degree of separation (or even to invent their separation), or to concoct "eerie" similarities between themselves. Some motivations for MZAs to present themselves as more separated and more similar than they actually were include:

- financial, since they could potentially sell their stories to the media or to movie studios. Some MISTRA pairs hired agents and appeared on television programs (Jackson, 1980)
- the desire to impress the researchers
- the desire to be the center of scientific attention and to feel important
- the opportunity to enjoy a fully paid vacation in Minneapolis for themselves and their spouses. Almost 50 percent of the MISTRA pairs came from overseas
- to feel that they have more of a bond with their co-twin.

Even Shields questioned the credibility and memories of the twins he studied. In a largely unknown passage from *Monozygotic Twins Brought up Apart and Brought up Together*, he wrote,

> Twins themselves will take delight in relating stories of their buying identical presents and perhaps asking an aunt to hide them in the same place. Or they claim, perhaps, to have changed their

hair styles at the same time and to have decided independently to have their watches repaired before coming to London. They are said in many instances to come out with nearly the same remarks at the same time or to know what the other twin is thinking. Nearly all such stories have in common that they cannot be independently confirmed, and one sometimes suspects retrospective falsification of memory. Stories of twins falling ill at exactly the same time are not usually borne out by medical histories.

(Shields, 1962, p. 94)

In this passage the author of one of the three classical TRA studies, indeed the classical study with by far the largest MZA sample, recounted with apparent amusement that reunited twins told him many lies, or at least embellished stories that "cannot be independently confirmed." As Shields put it, many pairs suffered from "retrospective falsification of memory." When twins told similar stories to the MISTRA team, they were (and continue to be) put forward by journalists, textbook authors, and the researchers themselves as "eerie" examples of the powerful influence of genetics. Shields attempted to verify many of the stories his twins told him. Did the MISTRA researchers attempt to verify their twins' stories as well?

In his case history of MZAs Kaj and Robert (Case V), Juel-Nielsen noted the "proclivity of both twins to misrepresentation"—in other words, to lie about themselves (Juel-Nielsen, 1965/1980, Part II, p. 135). Peter Watson's account of the early MISTRA years found that British MZAs Daphne and Barbara (the "Giggle Twins") "had told Bouchard the same lie," and then broke into laughter about it. "We both said we wanted to be opera singers and neither of us can sing a note," one of the twins confessed (Watson, 1981, p. 43). Kamin and Goldberger pointed out that this story "makes it clear that twins could and did lie about themselves to the investigators" (Kamin & Goldberger, 2002, p. 86).

The psychologist Donald Dorfman noted in 1995 that "the detailed case-study records of the Minnesota MZAs have never been released and have therefore not been subjected to public scrutiny to determine the degree to which assumptions have been met and the degree to which the MZAs told the truth to the Minnesota group" (Dorfman, 1995, p. 420). We know that Daphne and Barbara lied about wanting to become opera singers only because they decided to come clean about it. The number of other lies invented by various pairs that were not uncovered by the researchers, and were therefore passed off as truth, remains unknown. The credibility of reunited (partially) reared-apart pairs is therefore open to serious doubt, which by itself calls into question both the "statistical" and "anecdotal" evidence presented by the MISTRA researchers and others (Bouchard himself made this distinction, see Segal, 2012, p. 27).

Sample Size

The question of whether a particular study's sample is large or small, or modest or sufficient, is often a subjective one. Bouchard and colleagues defended the adequacy of their 1990 *Science* study sample size against criticism, stating that this question "is answered by our statistical analyses, which take sample size into account" (Bouchard, Lykken, McGue, Segal, & Tellegen, 1991, p. 192). They did not, however, explain how a statistical procedure can compensate for an inadequate sample size. In their famous *Science* article, the researchers viewed their MZA sample of 48 pairs as large enough to be able to conclude:

> For almost every behavioral trait so far investigated, from reaction time to religiosity, an important fraction of the variation among people turns out to be associated with genetic variation. This fact need no longer be subject to debate; rather, it is time instead to consider its implications.
> (Bouchard, Lykken et al., 1990, p. 227)

Segal recognized that "many critics claimed that the reared-apart twin sample was too small to generate valid findings," but defended the study's validity by claiming that "the quality of twin pairs that were studied was excellent" (Segal, 2012, p. 302). Continuing a theme that will be explored in more detail in the following chapter, the MISTRA researchers usually mentioned problems with sample sizes only when the results based on the sample were not consistent with genetic explanations of the data.

Confirmation Bias

In contrast to the authors of the classical studies, the MISTRA researchers recognized no conclusions or interpretations other than their own, and usually criticized (or ignored) those attempting to challenge their conclusions. Rossi noted Newman and colleagues' reluctance to reach definitive conclusions, and contrasted this with the Minnesota researchers: "Didn't the Mistra scientists ever experience divergent interpretations of their own data? Didn't they ever argue among themselves over what their data meant? If not, on what basis did they conclude that their results made sense?" (Rossi, 2013). There is no indication that leading MISTRA researchers, who were psychometrically oriented psychologists, had any major disagreements or greatly differing perspectives, and in a 2004 interview Bouchard recalled that he had co-authored many papers with MISTRA colleagues David Lykken and Auke Tellegen, "and we never had a disagreement in 20 years" (Bouchard, 2004). Segal also mentioned in a positive tone that Bouchard had said, in relation to his colleague David Lykken, "We never really disagreed" (Segal, 2012, p. 22).

Three years prior to initiating the MISTRA in 1979, Bouchard held tightly to the psychometric position on IQ and heredity: "Human intelligence can be usefully construed as a single relatively coherent trait whose phenotype variance is largely under genetic control" (Bouchard, 1976, p. 193). He also believed that "class differences in intelligence have an appreciable genetic component," and that some evidence suggests a "decline in the intelligence of the population," a topic that "should be subject to continual scrutiny" (p. 193). Thus, well before he conceived the MISTRA, Bouchard believed that human intelligence is a single entity measurable through IQ testing, is "largely under genetic control" and shows social "class differences," and may be declining in the population.

A Gene for Pinkie Finger Curling?

In *The Gene Illusion* I argued that the Minnesota researchers' genetic biases influenced the way they interpreted MZA data, and pointed to their tendency to highlight behavioral similarities and downplay differences. As one example, I took Segal to task for her description of "Fireman Twins" Jerry Levey and Mark Newman, a pair of well-publicized reunited MZA New Jersey firefighters. There is a photo of Jerry and Mark together holding up a can of beer while posing for the photo, with each twin holding the can with his pinkie (little) finger curled under the can. Segal wrote in her 1999 book *Entwined Lives* that "distinctive physical expressions co-occurring in identical twins reared apart suggest that genetic factors are involved." As evidence, she captioned this photo by pointing out that "the twins' little fingers support their cans of beer," and wrote that Jerry and Mark "held pinky fingers under cans of Budweiser long before they met" (Segal, 1999, p. 144).

I listed seven very plausible non-genetic explanations in *The Gene Illusion* for why the twins held beer cans this way, and referred to another photograph of Jerry and Mark where they *did not* curl their pinkies under the can. I concluded that, although it was perhaps understandable that journalists would want to write about this photograph in terms of genetics, it was improper for Segal to provide a scientific seal of approval to such rampant (unscientific) speculation. The photo showing Jerry and Mark holding beer cans differently appeared in a 1987 article in the magazine *U.S. News and World Report* (Lang, 1987, p. 63), and has been reproduced elsewhere (for example, in the psychology textbook by Wade & Tavris, 2006, p. 469).

Nevertheless, in *Born Together—Reared Apart* Segal continued to imply that Jerry and Mark's pinkie-curling styles were caused by their common genes no fewer than three times (pp. 28, 64, 178). Segal was familiar with the *U.S. News and World Report* article, having referred to it in another context in *Born Together—Reared Apart* (Segal, 2012, p. 354, footnote 4). She also claimed that a photograph of five other MZA pairs posing for photographers with television host Lesley Stahl provided additional evidence in support of genetic influences on "hand and leg positions," without mentioning that these pairs were dressed alike as well (pp. 263–264). Returning to Mark and Jerry, there are only three possible places one can position one's pinkie finger while holding a can of beer: pointing away from the can (an extremely unlikely pinkie position for male New Jersey firefighters in the 1970s and 1980s), on the side of the can, or under the can. (I ask readers to take a quick break and test this for themselves with a nearby canned beverage, if one is available.)

Failure to Make the Data Available for Inspection and Analysis

In *The Gene Illusion* I argued that, given the MISTRA researchers' refusal to make their raw data available for inspection, on this basis alone we must reject any interpretation of their results in favor of genetics. Today, I reaffirm this position with even more emphasis. Because it is extremely difficult for independent researchers to replicate the study due to the increasing rarity of separated twin pairs, it is critically important—actually mandatory—that independent analysts and researchers have access to all of the raw data. For this reason we have seen that reviewers from differing perspectives have called for making TRA data available to "anyone who wishes" (Jensen, 1974, p. 27), or for the creation of "a central registry for all such cases" (Farber, 1981, p. 274).

In addition to the lack of published case history material, the MISTRA researchers failed to produce a table with basic demographic, degree of separation, and test score information for each studied pair, even though *Born Together—Reared Apart* provided an excellent opportunity to provide this information. In an early 1981 report, Bouchard and colleagues provided a table containing some information for each of the 15 MZA pairs they had studied up to that point, but no subsequent table of this type appeared after that (Eckert, Heston, & Bouchard, 1981, pp. 182–184).

In contrast, in her 1981 *Identical Twins Reared Apart: A Reanalysis*, Susan Farber compiled numerous tables containing a wealth of previously published TRA data and test scores (including IQ scores) as reported by the original researchers, much of it appearing in painstaking detail in her 44-page Appendix E (Farber, 1981, pp. 319–362). In an earlier table spanning six full pages, Farber listed all studied pairs from the combined sample, providing information such as sex, handedness, birth order, age at separation, whether twins knew they had a twin prior to reunion, age met, age studied, degree of contact over the lifespan, years apart, and who they were reared by (Farber, 1981, pp. 54–59).

In his 1974 article about Burt's IQ correlations, Jensen described his attempts to obtain Burt's raw data after his death. After corresponding with Burt's secretary, he traveled to London and was told that "many boxes of old data, which Burt had kept for many years, were disposed of in the course of vacating his flat in Hampstead." Jensen was told that these boxes "were either poorly labeled or not labeled at all, so that their exact contents were not apparent to casual inspection. And so, unfortunately, the original data are lost" (Jensen, 1974, pp. 24–25).

Even though Jensen apparently felt that he had a right to inspect Burt's purported data on the grounds of scientific principles and inquiry, the MISTRA raw data, although they exist, are just as "lost" to the world as are Burt's data.

The committee established to investigate the fraudulent activities of Dutch psychologist Diederik Stapel (see Chapter 2) made the following recommendations:

> Research data that underlie psychology publications must remain archived and be made available on request to other scientific practitioners. This not only applies to the dataset ultimately used for the analysis, but also the raw laboratory data and all the relevant research material, including completed questionnaires, audio and video recordings, etc. It is recommended that a system be applied whereby on completion of the experiment, the protocols and data used are stored in such a way that they can no longer be modified. It must be clear who is responsible for the storage of and access to the data. The publications must indicate where the raw data is located and how it has been made permanently accessible. It must always remain possible for the conclusions to be traced back to the original data. Journals should only accept articles if the data concerned has been made accessible in this way.
>
> (Levelt Committee, Noort Committee, Drenth Committee, 2012, p. 58)

According to the committee, "it must always remain possible for the conclusions to be traced back to the original data." To reduce the possibility of misconduct in future research: (a) data must be made available to other scientists; (b) data should be stored in a way that ensures that they cannot be modified; and (c) someone should be designated as being responsible for safeguarding the data, and publications should be required to state where the data are located and how they can be accessed. The committee recommended that "journals should only accept articles if the data concerned has been made accessible in this way."

If TRA studies could be replicated in the same way as normal scientific experiments are replicated, other groups could try to obtain similar results using comparable samples. Of course, even if these groups obtain similar results, various and vastly different interpretations of the results could still be offered.

A 1991 Exchange in Science

Following the MISTRA 1990 *Science* publication, Harvard geneticist Jonathan Beckwith and his colleagues wrote a letter to *Science* criticizing the MISTRA team for "not publishing in a format that permits independent scrutiny. Investigators in this field should indicate the precise nature of being 'reared apart,' including, for example, whether it involved only being raised in separate households within the same community" (Beckwith, Geller, & Sarkar, 1991, p. 191). Beckwith and colleagues concluded that "it is imperative that case studies be fully published." In another letter, mathematician Richard Dudley questioned the researchers' assumption of "no environmental similarity" (Dudley, 1991, p. 191).

In response, Bouchard and colleagues argued that it is "highly unlikely" that MZAs experienced environmental similarities (Bouchard et al., 1991, p. 192). As evidence, they cited studies that found no IQ correlations between biologically unrelated individuals reared together, implying that common environment does not lead to IQ resemblance.

From the psychometric/behavioral genetic perspective, most aspects of the human condition can be explained and understood not by studying and understanding the larger picture of human beings in their social contexts, but by calculating correlation coefficients and fitting data to models. Beckwith and colleagues requested much more information about the twins' life circumstances and degree of separation—Bouchard and colleagues answered this request with a (non-twin) correlation coefficient.

The MISTRA Researchers and Leon Kamin

According to Segal, Leon Kamin "was a severe critic of the MISTRA, continually demanding the original data to conduct the analyses himself" (Segal, 2012, p. 101). Note Segal's wording here; Kamin's initial requests only became "demands" after Segal and others denied him access to the data.[4] Kamin's analysis was not expected to support the researchers' positions, so he was not granted access to the raw data. As I reported in *The Gene Illusion*, Bouchard refused to make MZA data available to Kamin even under conditions where pairs are identified only by code numbers, and where information about age is omitted to guarantee non-identification (Leon Kamin, personal communication of 4/8/2001). Bouchard told journalist Lawrence Wright that he "wouldn't let Leon Kamin anywhere near" the MISTRA raw data, although he was available to answer a "legitimate question" (Wright, 1997, p. 69). Segal reported that "Bouchard shared his data (albeit carefully) with interested colleagues" (p. 242), but Kamin apparently was not a qualified "interested colleague" in Bouchard's eyes. Therefore, the result of this well-known credentialed Princeton psychologist's attempts to gain access to the raw data: *Access denied.*

In contrast, Segal told a different story about a friendly researcher seeking access to the MISTRA raw data. In this account, she described the attempt of evolutionary psychologist Linda Mealey, who later became a "close friend" of Segal's, to gain access to the data (Segal, 2012, p. 184; Segal is an evolutionary psychologist as well). As Segal described it,

> Linda was interested in how genetic and environmental variables affected reproduction-related variables, such as age at marriage and number of children. She asked Bouchard for access to the reared-apart twin data, and he agreed—Bouchard was careful about releasing his files outside the department, but he was generous and encouraging when he trusted colleagues and believed they were serious about their work.
>
> (p. 184)

In this case Bouchard and Segal provided access to a supportive colleague, and Mealey did not have to "demand" anything. Therefore, the result of "trusted" and "serious" MISTRA supporter Linda Mealey's attempt to gain access to the raw data: *Access granted.*

Use of the MISTRA Findings by Disreputable Groups

The MISTRA results are frequently cited by white supremacist and Nazi groups in support of their theories of the importance of genetics and race, and in support of their claims that racial differences in intelligence and behavior have a genetic basis. For example, Segal spoke of "our findings being misused," such as the posting of their 1990 *Science* article "on the Web site of former Louisiana Republican State Representative and Ku Klux Klan member David Duke under the tags 'Intelligence: Heredity Vs. Environment' and 'Racial Differences.' Race differences were never discussed in our article" (Segal, 2012, p. 114).

It is true that race differences were not discussed in this 1990 article or any other MISTRA study publication (although elsewhere, Bouchard wrote in favor of the position that genetic factors influence racial differences in IQ scores; see Bouchard, 1995). It is also true that Segal and her colleagues are not responsible for the way others may want to interpret or promote their research (although strong public disclaimers are often made in such cases). However, given that the MISTRA results and conclusions continue to be cited worldwide by racists and Nazis in support of their agendas, Bouchard and colleagues, instead of portraying their critics as the purveyors of "pseudoanalysis," could at least display a degree of sympathy for people who—if for no other reason than the fact that these studies are used to promote the views of these groups—are motivated to take a very close look at their findings. Yet, as Rossi noted, "Segal and her colleagues appear baffled and exasperated that Mistra's findings have met with resistance" (Rossi, 2013).

Access to the Data Must Become a Requirement

In summary, providing qualified reviewers of all opinions and perspectives access to the raw data must become a requirement for accepting the results of any TRA study, including the MISTRA. Therefore, *in TRA studies that cannot be replicated (or are extremely difficult to replicate), the researchers' conclusions must be automatically rejected until qualified independent analysts are allowed to inspect, and publish findings from, the raw data.*

Conclusion: The MISTRA was Based on a Large Number of Questionable Assumptions and Concepts

In this chapter we have seen that major problem areas of the MISTRA studies include the failure to recognize or adequately control for obvious environmental confounds, the failure to determine whether the MZA correlation significantly exceeds the DZA correlation for the behavioral characteristic in question, faulty logic and a reliance on false or unsupported theoretical assumptions, the doubtful status of many of the pairs as "reared-apart twins," recruitment bias in favor of more similar pairs, confirmation bias, issues related to the control group and sample sizes, the questionable credibility of twins' accounts of their degrees of separation, contact, and behavioral similarity, a lack of published information on twins, and the failure to provide access to the raw data. In addition, like most behavioral genetic studies, the MISTRA was based on a number of concepts that we saw in Chapter 4 have been challenged for decades.

After stripping away the study's complex statistical analyses and concepts, we saw that the researchers' conclusion that genetic factors play a major role in causing human behavioral variation was based almost entirely on the assumption that the MZA correlation "directly estimates heritability," and the assumption that MZA correlations are caused only by genetic factors. In addition to the fact that many non-genetic factors influence MZA behavioral similarity, the study was based on a circular argument because it assumed the very thing it was attempting to determine.

By default, all MISTRA MZA pairs should be classified as "partially reared-apart monozygotic twin pairs" until proven otherwise. Segal believed that the "burden of proof lies with the critics" to show that the study contained important biases. "Bias must be demonstrated, not assumed," she wrote (Segal, 2012, p. 299). This places critics in a classic "Catch-22" position because if they are known to be inclined to look for bias, Bouchard, Segal and colleagues deny them access to the raw data.

Given the lack of information provided, and the similar biases affecting all TRA studies, there is no reason to believe that the MISTRA pairs were any more "separated" than the Newman, Shields, or Juel-Nielsen pairs. Until proven otherwise through examination of the raw data by independent analysis, we must assume that the reared-apart status of the MISTRA MZAs was similar to the 44 partially separated Shields MZA pairs, seen in Table 2.2.

In the following chapter, I will examine the MISTRA IQ and personality studies more closely in the context of the major problem areas discussed in this chapter and previous chapters, at which point I will arrive at some final conclusions about how these studies should be evaluated.

Notes

1 In previous publications I mistakenly wrote that the MISTRA researchers' conclusions in favor of genetics were sometimes based on comparing MZA versus MZT correlations, and I failed to emphasize the key role that model-fitting analysis and the "MZA correlation directly estimates heritability" assumption played in these studies (for example, Joseph, 2001, 2004, 2010a). At the same time, the main conclusions I reached about TRA research in these publications continue to hold.
2 Although Bouchard, Segal, Lykken and their colleagues usually failed to acknowledge the massive problems in the classical studies, on at least one occasion Bouchard discussed the "common illusion, fostered by secondary reports that the [classical] MZA twins were separated at birth and not reunited until they were studied by the authors of the research reports," adding that "the authors of the original reports maintained no illusions about the quality of their cases" (Bouchard, 1987, p. 59). In fact, these authors maintained enough illusions to enable them to reach conclusions in favor of genetics on the basis of twin pairs they chose to designate as "reared apart."
3 On many occasions the researchers highlighted the three classical study MZA IQ correlations as being consistent with their own findings, without mentioning the need to adjust *these* correlations for "substantial" age and sex confounds (for example, see Bouchard, Lykken, McGue, Segal, & Tellegen, 1990; Segal, 2012, p. 107).
4 Segal herself was granted "access to all files and documents associated with the MISTRA" (Segal, 2012, p. 15).

6

THE MINNESOTA STUDY OF TWINS REARED APART II

IQ and Personality Studies

> Human behavioral genetics has been an insufficiently self-critical discipline. It adopted the quantitative models of experimental plant and animal genetics without sufficient regard for the many problems involved in justifying the application of those models in human research.
> — Thomas Bouchard, 1987
> (Bouchard, 1987, p. 68)

> The simple comparison of the MZ (or MZA) and DZ (or DZA) intraclass correlations is an important first step in behavioral-genetic analysis because this demonstrates whether or not there is genetic influence on the trait.
> — Nancy Segal, 2012
> (Segal, 2012, p. 62)

> Clearly, MZA [pairs] provide one of the tools in the kits of behavioral and medical geneticists, but you could no more build an adequate structure for these domains with one tool than you could build an entire house with only a pair of pliers.
> — Twin researcher Irving Gottesman, 1982
> (Gottesman, 1982, p. 351)

In previous chapters I argued that studies of reared-apart twins suffer from a number of methodological problems, logical fallacies, reliance on false or questionable assumptions, failing to place the word "partially" in front of the term "reared-apart twins," and researcher bias in favor of genetic explanations and theories. Having surveyed the classical studies and the MISTRA, and highlighting these studies' major problem areas, this chapter examines the publications reporting MISTRA data in the two main areas of TRA study investigation: IQ and personality.

Cognitive ability (including IQ and special mental abilities) is the most important area of psychometric and behavioral genetic focus, with the IQ results being the most frequently cited area of the MISTRA work as well. As Segal put it, "Studies of general intelligence were a mainstay of the MISTRA's research program" (Segal, 2012, p. 284). I will first examine these IQ studies, followed by a briefer assessment of the personality studies. We saw that various other MISTRA investigations examined areas such as cardiac characteristics, religiosity, dental parameters, vocational interests, ego development, workplace values, reproductive outcome, sensation seeking and control, "morningness–eveningness," headaches, dietary preferences, authoritarianism, social attitudes, and reading comprehension. Clearly, many problems with the MISTRA IQ and personality studies apply to these areas as well. In *Born Together—Reared Apart* Segal reviewed the reported data and findings from various MISTRA studies, but provided little previously unpublished information or data on individual twin pairs and their test scores.

MISTRA IQ Studies

Behavioral geneticists and psychometrists view IQ tests as a measure of general intelligence, or *g* (see Chapter 4). According to Bouchard and colleagues, "The study of IQ is paradigmatic of human behavior genetic research" (Bouchard, Lykken, McGue, Segal, & Tellegen, 1990, p. 224). By the mid-1990s, Bouchard would claim that hereditarian theories of human intelligence had made "the long journey from plausibility to proof" (Bouchard, 1996, p. 527).[1]

Like the earlier investigations, the MISTRA researchers based their conclusions on the implied assumption that if IQ score differences in the population were solely the result of environmental influences, the MZA IQ correlation would be 0.0. They assumed that "all resemblance between reared apart relatives owes to genetic factors" (Bouchard, Segal, & Lykken, 1990, p. 198). Thus, like Juel-Nielsen and others, the researchers based their conclusions on the assumption that MZA correlations are caused mainly by the common genes they share, although we saw in previous chapters that this is a false assumption due to the influence of cohort effects and other non-genetic factors.

The main MISTRA IQ tests were the WAIS, and the Raven test. The latter was usually combined with the Mill-Hill test of word knowledge, which produced MISTRA "Raven/Mill-Hill Composite" scores. We recall from Chapter 4 that the WAIS (in its various editions) has been the most widely used IQ test, and that the Raven test is claimed to be a "culture-free" test of cognitive ability (for a dissenting view on that claim, see Richardson, 1998, 2000). In addition, MISTRA twins performed test batteries assessing "special mental abilities," which we have seen include verbal, perceptual, spatial, and memory tasks. The two special mental abilities batteries used were an expanded version of the battery used in the Hawaii Family Study of Cognition (the Hawaii Battery, or H-B), and the Comprehensive Ability Battery (CAB). The Raven IQ test was a component of the H-B.

The researchers believed in the importance of using multiple tests, with Bouchard writing in 1984 that the MISTRA corrected the "dependence on a single instrument" flaw found in "previous MZA studies" (Bouchard, 1984, p. 174). According to Segal, this "multiple measure" approach "would allow assessment of the stability and consistency of participant behavior, thereby increasing confidence in the findings" (Segal, 2012, p. 68). At the outset of the study in 1981, Bouchard saw general intelligence as his main focus of investigation, placing secondary focus on special mental abilities (Bouchard, 1981).

We saw in Chapter 5 that the MISTRA researchers assessed the role of genetic influences on behavioral characteristics on the basis of three main findings: (a) by determining, as a first step, that the MZA correlation is significantly higher than the DZA (control group) correlation; (b) by assuming that the MZA correlation directly estimates heritability and is not influenced by environmental factors (other than age and sex effects); and (c) by accepting the assumptions and results of model-fitting analyses based on MZA, MZT, DZA, and other familial data. Although Segal and other leading behavioral genetic researchers recognized that determining that the MZA correlation is (significantly) higher than the DZA correlation is a necessary "first step" in the genetic analysis, in practice the MISTRA researchers bypassed this step and based their conclusions on the assumption that the "MZA correlation directly estimates heritability."

The following sections provide a brief outline of the most important MISTRA publications presenting IQ and special mental abilities data published through 1990. The results published after 1990 will be discussed in relation to the reporting, or the lack of reporting, of the DZA IQ correlations. Unless otherwise noted, the number of pairs (N) reported in each study reflects the cumulative number of pairs tested between 1979 and 2000.

In addition to the MISTRA researchers' failure to publish the full-sample WAIS IQ correlations of their DZA control group, they failed to publish the full-sample Raven MZA or DZA IQ correlations (with one possible exception, that will be examined below). This is puzzling, since many leading IQ researchers view the Raven test, which is non-verbal and involves problem-solving skills, as a highly "g-loaded" test that is not biased by the culturally loaded questions found in standard IQ tests such as the WAIS (Jensen, 1969, 1998). According to Bouchard and colleagues, "The Raven Progressive Matrices (Standard Set) is a widely used nonverbal measure of problem-solving ability" (Bouchard, Lykken, et al., 1990, p. 224).

Early Reports

Lykken published early MISTRA IQ correlations in 1982, reporting that, as of November, 1981, the researchers had brought 30 MZA and nine DZA pairs to Minneapolis to be studied and tested (Lykken, 1982). He reported MZA, MZT, and DZT correlations, with the MZA sample consisting of 29 pairs. The Raven/Mill-Hill composite MZA correlation was 0.71. The WAIS MZA correlation was 0.73. Lykken did not provide correlations for the DZA pairs. In 1984, the researchers published a paper reporting various correlations for information-processing tests, and included MZA and DZA correlations (McGue, Bouchard, Lykken, & Feuer, 1984).

McGue and Bouchard published a MISTRA study on special mental abilities and information processing in 1989. As seen in the previous chapter, in this publication the researchers admitted that several of their model-fitting assumptions "are likely not to hold for cognitive abilities" (McGue & Bouchard, 1989, p. 23). They concluded that, for most special mental abilities, "a genetic component was needed to statistically account for the twin data," although on several subtests the MZA correlations "were no more similar than the DZA twins." They accounted for "the relatively large DZA correlations" on the basis of "statistical variation" and the "relatively small size of the DZA sample" (pp. 31, 41).

Two 1990 Publications

The 1990 Science article

We saw in previous chapters that, as Segal put it, "the long awaited [MISTRA] IQ data" were published in the 1990 *Science* article. As Segal described it, "the *Science* IQ paper was a significant moment in the history of the study" (Segal, 2012, p. 104). The researchers reported MZA IQ correlations for several different tests of "general factor mental ability" in the 0.64–0.78 range (based on MZA samples ranging in size from 42 to 48 pairs), and MZT correlations ranging from 0.76 to 0.88 based on similar sample sizes. However, no DZA control group correlations were presented or discussed in the 1990 *Science* article.

On the basis of their assumption that the MZA correlation directly estimates heritability, in addition to model-fitting results based on this assumption, Bouchard and colleagues concluded, "General intelligence or IQ is strongly affected by genetic factors" (Bouchard, Lykken, et al., 1990, p. 227). Based on the similarity of the MZA and MZT correlations (in addition to other factors), they reached the additional conclusion "that common rearing enhances familial resemblance during adulthood only slightly and on relatively few behavioral dimensions" (Bouchard, Lykken, et al., 1990, p. 227).[2]

We have seen that Bouchard and colleagues began their 1990 *Science* publication by writing,

> Monozygotic and dizygotic twins who were separated early in life and reared apart (MZA and DZA twin pairs) are a fascinating experiment of nature. They also provide the simplest and most powerful method for disentangling the influence of environmental and genetic factors on human characteristics.
> (Bouchard, Lykken, et al., 1990, p. 223)

However, they *decided* not to publish their DZA correlations "due to space limitations and the smaller size of the DZA sample (30 sets)" (p. 223). I emphasize the word "decided" to make the general point that scientific researchers are presented with numerous decisions about what to study, how to define variables, whether to publish, where to publish, what comparisons to make, and so on. We only get to see what they decide to publish, and in this case Bouchard and colleagues had the DZA results at hand when they made this decision.

In her chapter on the MISTRA IQ and personality studies published in the period 1988–1990, Segal wrote that the *Science* paper "reported IQ analyses for forty-eight MZA twin pairs for whom we had processed data; the DZA twin sample was still modest (thirty pairs)" (Segal, 2012, p. 105). Although she believed that "DZ twins reared apart (DZA) constitute an important control group" (Segal & Johnson, 2009, p. 85), Segal provided no other explanation for the researchers' decision not to publish the DZA control group IQ correlations, and proceeded to discuss the study and its findings of major genetic influences on IQ. (Segal also missed an opportunity in *Born Together—Reared Apart* to finally reveal what the 1990 DZA WAIS IQ correlation actually was.) This indicates that the researchers decided that potentially paradigm-altering conclusions about the nature of human intelligence can be reached on the basis of 48 reared-apart MZA pairs, but that *30 DZA pairs* constitute a "modest sample" that can be arbitrarily omitted due to "space considerations." The researchers made a completely different decision about whether to include DZA correlations in a concurrently published 1990 MISTRA personality publication, where data for only *26 DZA pairs* were published in full and were included in the model-fitting analysis (Bouchard & McGue, 1990, p. 263).

Studies published in *Science* carry great prestige and are noticed by the scientific community as well as by the media. The "results from the *Science* paper," wrote Segal, "appeared in hundreds of newspapers, magazines, and broadcasts across the country and around the world" (p. 112). It is unlikely that any of these reports mentioned that the DZA control group correlations were missing, and that their inclusion might have led to a very different set of interpretations and conclusions.

The 1990 Acta Geneticae Medicae et Gemellologiae article

In the same year, Bouchard, Segal, and Lykken published the results of another MISTRA study of special mental abilities in the relatively obscure twin research journal *Acta Geneticae Medicae et Gemellologiae*, published in Rome (Bouchard, Segal, & Lykken, 1990; this study assessed different areas of special mental abilities than did the McGue & Bouchard 1989 study). The researchers assessed four domains of special mental abilities: verbal, spatial, perceptual speed, and accuracy and memory. Based on model-fitting procedures, they concluded that the heritability of special mental abilities is about 0.50. In this *Acta* study the researchers reported correlations for 49 MZA pairs, and, in direct contrast to the concurrently published *Science* article, they reported correlations for 25 DZA pairs. For the two special mental ability test batteries, the H-B and the CAB, MZA and DZA mean correlations were, respectively, 0.45 and 0.34 on the H-B, and 0.48 and 0.35 on the CAB. These differences are not large and do not appear to differ at a statistically significant level, and do not match the researchers' reasoning that, according to their genetic model, the DZA correlation should be one-half of the MZA correlation. Moreover, for the separate variables assessed in the batteries (such as "word beginnings and endings," "word fluency," "memory span," and "perceptual speed"), DZA correlations were higher on nine of the 28 variables, which runs counter to genetic predictions (Bouchard, Segal, et al., 1990, p. 199).

In this *Acta* paper's concluding section, Bouchard, Segal, and Lykken argued that "the relatively large DZA correlations have been accounted for by statistical variability." Although they were willing to "explore" non-genetic "alternative explanations," for the researchers "it would be difficult to account for the MZA correlations without reference to the genetic factors" (Bouchard, Segal, et al., 1990, p. 205). They concluded, "These data also show that only modest weight should be given to the results of any single study with modest sample sizes utilizing only one or a few brief subtests" (p. 205).

The 1990 *Science* WAIS IQ correlation was based on 48 MZA pairs, and the MISTRA researchers put forward no cautions about the modest size of this sample. In their *Acta* article, on the other hand, they wrote that "only modest weight" should be given to results from its MZA special mental abilities sample of 49 pairs.[3] Over seven billion people currently inhabit our planet, and psychological studies based on double-digit twin pair sample size data generalized to most of the human population are from this perspective all "modest."

Subsequent Reporting (and Non-Reporting) of the MISTRA DZA IQ correlations

In their 2002 critical review, Kamin and Goldberger documented the researchers' failure to publish their full-sample DZA WAIS IQ correlations: "For cognitive measures, MISTRA researchers have been slow to publish DZA *r*'s [correlations] despite their emphasis on the importance of DZAs as a control group" (Kamin & Goldberger, 2002, p. 87). The story has changed little since then, apart from Raven IQ correlations published in 2007, and unpublished WAIS correlations included in Segal's book that will be discussed shortly.

I will now review several MISTRA publications appearing after 1990 that discussed TRA study IQ findings. To the best of my knowledge, the MISTRA researchers—over 35 years after the study was launched—have failed to publish and discuss their full-sample DZA WAIS IQ correlations.

Bouchard, 1991

In this chapter in a book honoring University of Minnesota psychologist Paul Meehl, Bouchard reviewed the MISTRA findings. He reported MZA and DZA correlations for special mental abilities, information processing, personality, and other behaviors studied by the MISTRA. For IQ, however, Bouchard reported only MZA correlations (Bouchard, 1991).

Bouchard, 1993

In this major 1993 review of genetic research on human intelligence, Bouchard did not report any MISTRA DZA IQ correlations, but he did report a SATSA DZA IQ correlation of 0.52 based on 29 pairs, and included this finding in a graph (Bouchard, 1993b, p. 58). According to Bouchard, "At the time of the Bouchard and McGue (1981) review no studies of dizygotic twins reared apart had been reported. Since that time only one such study has appeared" (p. 57). Bouchard could make this statement only because the MISTRA team decided against publishing *their* DZA correlations, despite having a larger sample (reported as 30 DZA pairs in the 1990 *Science* article).

McGue, Bouchard, Iacono, and Lykken, 1993

The researchers contributed a 1993 chapter on behavioral genetic research from the "Life-span perspective" to the textbook *Nature, Nurture, and Psychology* (McGue, Bouchard, Iacono, & Lykken, 1993). They reported no DZA correlations, while reviewing the 1981 Bouchard and McGue

"Familial studies of intelligence: A review" article without updating it to include either their own or the SATSA DZA correlations.

Bouchard, 1994

This was Bouchard's "Twin Studies of Intelligence" contribution to Robert Sternberg's *Encyclopedia of Intelligence* (Bouchard, 1994b). Bouchard provided the MZA IQ correlations for the classical studies, the MISTRA, and the SATSA. He also reported the SATSA DZA IQ correlation, but did not report the MISTRA DZA IQ correlation.

Bouchard, Lykken, Tellegen, and McGue, 1996

In this publication Bouchard and colleagues presented a figure showing "correlations of IQ, for adults, for five critical kinship relationships under two conditions of rearing, together and apart," with DZA pairs constituting one of these "critical kinship relationships" (Bouchard, Lykken, Tellegen, & McGue, 1996, pp. 10–11). The figure showed a DZA IQ correlation of 0.35 based on 112 pairs. Bouchard and colleagues did not mention what tests these figures were based on, or which study samples the 112 DZA pairs were taken from.

Bouchard, 1996

This was Bouchard's "Galton Lecture." He listed the MZA IQ correlations from the various TRA studies (including his own), and listed the SATSA DZA IQ correlation, but not the MISTRA DZA IQ correlation (Bouchard, 1996, p. 539).

Bouchard, 1997

Bouchard published a chapter entitled "IQ Similarity in Twins Reared Apart: Findings and Responses to Critics" in *Intelligence, Heredity, and Environment*, edited by Robert Sternberg and Elena Grigorenko (Bouchard, 1997b). Here he reported MZA IQ correlations and discussed them in some detail, yet did not mention any DZA IQ correlations.

Bouchard, 1997

Bouchard wrote this article for a wider audience in the magazine *The Sciences*. He discussed the MISTRA personality findings by referring to its MZA and DZA correlations (50 percent and 25 percent respectively). Turning to IQ, "the single most heritable trait of all the traits studied by programs such as ours," he did not report any MZA or DZA IQ correlations (Bouchard, 1997c, p. 55).

McGue and Bouchard, 1998

In this article appearing in the *Annual Review of Neuroscience*, McGue and Bouchard (1998) reported MZA IQ correlations from the various TRA studies, but again failed to report the MISTRA DZA control group correlation. In contrast, they discussed their DZA personality correlations in the context of estimating the heritability of personality traits.

Newman, Tellegen, and Bouchard, 1998

This study of "ego development" contained the first-ever publication of the MISTRA DZA WAIS full-scale IQ intraclass correlations, yet only for a *subsample* of DZAs. The researchers reported full-scale WAIS IQ correlations derived from this subsample as MZA = 0.75, DZA = 0.47 (Newman, Tellegen, & Bouchard, 1998, p. 992). The DZA subsample was based on 28 pairs, even though about twice as many pairs had been assessed by the MISTRA team up to that point. The WAIS scores were discussed mainly in relation to the authors' theories of ego development.

Bouchard, 1998

In this solo-authored article published in the academic journal *Human Biology*, Bouchard discussed published MISTRA DZA IQ correlations for the first time in the context of IQ genetic research—that is, almost two decades after the study was initiated, and 8 years after the publication of the 1990 *Science* article. Still, he referred only to Newman and colleagues' 1998 0.47 DZA subsample correlation (Bouchard, 1998, p. 263). While Bouchard recognized that the DZA correlation "is reported as a control variable" in the MISTRA, he wrote that "the MISTRA [DZA] correlations have not yet been fully analyzed," and that he and his colleagues "are awaiting completion of the study before conducting a full analysis" (Bouchard, 1998, p. 262).

Are we to believe that the researchers had not yet conducted a "full analysis" of their DZA IQ results, almost 20 years into the study? This is consistent with Bouchard's October 29th, 1997 reply to a query from Kamin, where he wrote to Kamin, "I can't pass on the IQ results for our MZAs or DZAs because I have not published them yet. Indeed, I have not even calculated them" (quoted in Kamin & Goldberger, 2002, p. 87).

How is it possible that the DZA control group IQ correlations had "not yet been fully analyzed" or "calculated" 8 years after the publication of the 1990 *Science* article, with an entire team of researchers and graduate students presumably available to perform such analyses, while many other MISTRA correlations had been analyzed and published long before? And why did Bouchard decide to postpone the "full analysis" of the data until after the "completion of the study"—an analysis that remains unpublished to this day?

Segal, 1999

In her book *Entwined Lives*, Segal mentioned that DZA correlations had been reported in both the SATSA and the MISTRA, referring to the 0.47 subsample correlation reported by Newman and Bouchard a year earlier. Following Bouchard's 1998 *Human Biology* article, she wrote that Bouchard "cautioned that the Minnesota data are preliminary and require further analysis" (Segal, 1999, p. 136). She failed to explain, however, why only these data were "preliminary" and were in need of "further analysis."

Bouchard and Pedersen, 1999

In this 1999 book chapter, Bouchard and SATSA researcher Nancy Pedersen discussed MZA IQ correlations in the various studies, in addition to MZA and DZA personality correlations, but failed to report any DZA IQ correlations (Bouchard & Pedersen, 1999).

McCourt, Bouchard, Lykken, Tellegen, and Keyes, 1999

This was a MISTRA study of "right-wing authoritarianism." McCourt and colleagues published MZA and DZA "general cognitive ability" correlations from a subsample of 39 MZA and 38 DZA pairs in the context of assessing how cognitive ability might be related to authoritarian attitudes. Ten of the 38 DZA pairs were opposite-sex. The reported subsample correlations were MZA = 0.74, DZA = 0.53 (McCourt, Bouchard, Lykken, Tellegen, & Keyes, 1999, p. 1001).

Bouchard and McGue, 2003

In this review article Bouchard and McGue did not report any MISTRA DZA IQ correlations, whereas they reported several MISTRA DZA correlations in other areas of behavior (Bouchard & McGue, 2003).

Segal, 2003

In an article highlighting the pioneers of TRA research, Segal wrote in relation to a 1985 SATSA publication, "I will always recall SATSA as being the first study to publish IQ findings on DZ twins reared apart" (Segal, 2003, p. 76). At the same time, she failed to discuss the reasons behind her own study's failure to report its DZA IQ findings, even though the SATSA and MISTRA DZA sample sizes were comparable (MISTRA unpublished 1990 DZA IQ sample $n = 30$; SATSA published 1985 DZA sample $n = 29$; Pedersen, Plomin, McClearn, & Friberg, 1985).

Johnson, Bouchard, McGue, Segal, Tellegen, Keyes, and Gottesman, 2007

This publication contained what appears to be the first-ever MISTRA stand-alone Raven MZA and DZA IQ correlations not combined with other tests. Wendy Johnson, Bouchard, Segal and their colleagues were assessing the MISTRA data in the context of testing a particular model of mental abilities, and reported the Raven correlations in a table listing the individual components of the H-B. The sample consisted of 74 MZA and 52 DZA pairs (less than the final full MISTRA sample of 81 MZAs and 56 DZAs). The Raven IQ correlations were reported as MZA = 0.55, DZA = 0.42 (Johnson et al., 2007, p. 552). These sample correlations do not differ significantly at the 0.05 level, meaning that from the statistical perspective they are the same.[4] The researchers did not discuss or evaluate these Raven IQ correlations. The average WAIS correlations were listed as MZA = 0.51, DZA = 0.34.

Johnson and colleagues admitted that one of their model-fitting assumptions (no assortative mating) was "contrary to [the] evidence," and that other assumptions "are generally oversimplifications of the actual situation, and their violation can introduce systematic distortions in the estimates" (p. 548). Or, as critics sometimes argue, these false assumptions completely invalidate the researchers' conclusions in favor of genetics. The researchers, however, speculated that "several combinations of violations of assumptions can act to offset each other" (Johnson et al., 2007, pp. 548–549). Arriving at scientific conclusions on the basis of the hope that several questionable or false theoretical assumptions somehow cancel each other out in favor of genetic theories, however, is dubious.

Rather than conclude that high DZA correlations suggested a lack of genetic influence on intelligence, Johnson, Bouchard, Segal and colleagues chose to attribute this finding to "sampling variability." Clearly referring to their MZA and DZA pairs they wrote, in a footnote,

> For 4 tests, DZ correlations actually exceeded MZ correlations, a situation we attribute to sampling variability. In such situations, [the] Mx [software program] gives greater weight to the larger MZ than DZ sample, providing estimates of genetic influence based primarily on the MZ correlations.
>
> (Johnson et al., 2007, p. 551)

Note the decision to "attribute" high DZA correlations to "sampling variability," and not to attribute them to powerful environmental influences on IQ scores—*in essence ignoring the correlations of their designated control group*. The researchers simply assumed that higher DZA correlations, unexplainable by genetic theories, were the result of sampling variability, and then used their software to disregard the DZA correlations and base genetic estimates mainly on the MZA correlations, which they assumed directly estimate heritability. This can be seen in their table of MZA and DZA mental test correlations (p. 552), where, for example, WAIS Information subscale correlations of MZA = 0.57, DZA = 0.64 still produced an "estimated genetic influence" (heritability) figure of 0.65! In addition, the Coding subscale MZA and DZA correlations were both 0.38, which produced an estimated genetic influence of 0.64 (based on the "MZA correlation directly estimates heritability" assumption, it should have been 0.38). This appears to be little more than programming a computer to produce results that fit the researchers' assumptions about genetic influences on IQ. Or put another way, the researchers apparently used the software program to disregard the DZA control group correlations if they did not fall in line with genetic predictions. Once again, genetic theories are guaranteed to prevail using such maneuvers. As Richardson pointed out, behavioral genetic researchers make "certain assumptions about 'what to expect' in the patterns of scores, and adjusted their analytical equations accordingly: not surprisingly, that pattern emerges!" (Richardson, 1998, p. 121).

Segal and Johnson, 2009

In their chapter entitled "Twin Studies of General Mental Ability" appearing in the *Handbook of Behavior Genetics*, Segal and Johnson recognized that DZAs "constitute an important control group, providing opportunities to assess interactions between genotypes and behavior." They believed that it was "unfortunate" that "DZA pairs were not included in studies prior to the 1970s," yet discussed only MZA IQ correlations while providing no explanation for why they failed to publish the MISTRA full-sample DZA WAIS IQ correlations (Segal & Johnson, 2009, p. 85).

Segal, 2012

In *Born Together—Reared Apart*, Segal wrote that Bouchard believed that the 1990 *Science* article "legitimated the study" (p. 104). In her chapter covering this key article that she co-authored, we saw that Segal supported her colleagues' original position that the "DZA twin sample was still modest (thirty pairs)" (p. 105). She made no further attempt to explain why the DZA control group correlations were missing, or how a sample of 30 DZA pairs was too "modest" to report, whereas concurrently published MISTRA personality studies reported full-sample DZA correlations based on fewer than 30 pairs.

Segal also mentioned that, in the early 1980s, Bouchard had submitted a MISTRA IQ article to *Science* based on 29 MZA and 12 DZA pairs. The editors of *Science* rejected the article, according to Segal, "largely due to the small sample size," which led Bouchard to "delay publishing the IQ data until additional pairs were assessed" (Segal, 2012, p. 104). Segal did not explain how Bouchard believed that 12 DZA pairs constituted a large enough sample to submit to *Science* in the early 1980s, but that a larger sample of 30 DZA pairs was too "modest" to submit to *Science* several years later.

After discussing other MISTRA IQ studies published after 1990, almost as an afterthought Segal mentioned that she received unpublished Wechsler IQ (WAIS) correlations from Bouchard "when I visited Minnesota in October, 2009" (Segal, 2012, pp. 285–286). Segal reported these unpublished WAIS intraclass correlations as MZA = 0.62, DZA = 0.50 (p. 286).[5] Although Segal did not provide enough information about these unpublished MZA and DZA WAIS IQ correlations for others to make a precise assessment, these sample correlations do not appear to differ at a statistically significant level.[6] Segal wrote that Bouchard's WAIS correlations of MZA = 0.62, DZA = 0.50 showed that the MZA correlation was "larger" than the DZA correlation and therefore was "consistent with genetic influence on IQ" (Segal, 2012, p. 286). However, the lack of a statistically significant difference between these sample correlations does not allow for the conclusion that the MZA correlation is "larger," because from the standpoint of basic statistical principles these sample correlations are equal (the null hypothesis stating that the samples do not differ is not rejected). But even if we do view them as differing slightly, the difference can be explained on the grounds that, as Segal and Bouchard recognized, DZAs experience less similar environments than experienced by MZAs, and were separated at a later age than were the MZA pairs (Segal, 2012, p. 42; see also Chapter 5).

It therefore appears that there is no statistically significant difference between the MISTRA MZA and DZA pairs on either the WAIS or the Raven IQ tests. We saw previously that Segal recognized that the "simple comparison of the MZ (or MZA) and DZ (or DZA) intraclass correlations is an important first step in behavioral-genetic analysis because this demonstrates whether or not there is genetic influence on the trait" (Segal, 2012, p. 62). It appears that the results of this "important first step" in determining "whether or not there is genetic influence" show that, contrary to most of what has been written about this study by the researchers and countless others since 1979, the study found no genetic influence on IQ.

Bouchard, 2013

In this review article, Bouchard reported MZA IQ correlations for the MISTRA and previous TRA studies, but again failed to publish or mention MISTRA DZA IQ correlations. At the same time, he referred to the SATSA study's MZT, MZA, DZT, and DZA IQ results and included them in his Figure 2 on the "estimates of genetic and shared environmental influence on *g* by age" (Bouchard, 2013, p. 924).

Bouchard, 2014

In an article entitled "Genes, Evolution and Intelligence," published in *Behavior Genetics*, Bouchard reproduced his Figure 2 from his 2013 publication, which referred to the SATSA IQ results (Bouchard, 2014). Bouchard did not list any type of IQ correlations in this publication.

Evaluation of the MISTRA Cognitive Ability Studies

The researchers' failure to publish their full-sample DZA control group IQ correlations by itself calls into question the MISTRA IQ results and conclusions because the researchers have, for decades, withheld important data *produced by their own designated control group* that may have cast doubt upon their conclusions in favor of genetics.

Bouchard and McGue wrote that "behavior genetic methods are unbiased with regard to whether genetic or environmental sources of variance are more important," concluding, "if there is no genetic source of variance the methods will reveal this fact" (Bouchard & McGue, 2003, p. 5). And Segal wrote, "We were interested in results of any kind on any topic that was studied. We did not decide how the data turned out, *the twins did*" (Segal, 2012, p. 244, italics in original). However, the twins did not decide to base the study's findings on several questionable key assumptions, to not publish the MISTRA DZA IQ correlations, and to deny access to the raw data—the researchers did.

The failure to publish or calculate their DZA IQ correlations runs counter to the researchers' claims that they had no interest in what their study found, and that they were prepared to conclude that they found no evidence in favor of genetics if that is what the data showed. The findings "revealed" by behavioral genetic methods do not speak for themselves, and are clearly subject to the genetic biases of the researchers who report and interpret them.

Although the investigators decided not to publish and evaluate their full-sample WAIS or Raven IQ DZA correlations, they did decide to publish their DZA correlations for special mental abilities and most other MISTRA behavioral areas. We saw that the researchers explained these sometimes anomalous DZA correlations in ways that were consistent with genetic theories. If the DZA correlation was one-half of the MZA correlation, they of course concluded that genetic factors account for this finding. If the DZA correlation was low versus the MZA correlation, or even negative, they had "flagged a possibly emergenic trait," which provided a genetic explanation for a DZA correlation not significantly above zero (Segal, 2012, p. 172; see also Lykken, McGue, Tellegen, & Bouchard, 1992).[7] If the DZA correlation was close to or even higher than the MZA correlation, the researchers assumed that the culprit was "assortative mating," "statistical variation," or "sampling variability" (for example, see Hur, Bouchard, & Eckert, 1998, p. 636; Johnson et al., 2007, p. 551; McGue & Bouchard, 1989, pp. 23, 31; Segal, 2012, pp. 62, 222).[8]

Thus, when they chose to publish it, the researchers had a genetic explanation for their control group DZA correlation regardless of its value. This approach guarantees that genetic explanations will prevail. As Gould showed, there is a long history of human genetic researchers "shifting criteria to work through good data toward desired conclusions" (Gould, 1981, p. 102), and creating conditions in which "data" are not allowed to "overthrow . . . assumptions" (p. 89). At the same time, the researchers' interpretation of their DZA correlations in favor of genetics makes sense from the standpoint of their assumption that the MZA correlation is completely caused by genetic factors. This serves to underscore the point that, from the perspective of that assumption, the DZA correlations were not important, and that the study's conclusions were based mainly on calculating heritability estimates based on the assumption that the "MZA correlation directly estimates heritability."

In the TRA study context, we have seen Segal write that "genetic effects on a trait are demonstrated when" the MZA intraclass correlation exceeds the DZA intraclass correlation (Segal, 2012, p. 59), which is consistent with her previously stated behavioral genetic position that "quantitative genetic theory holds that the degree of resemblance between family members should vary as a function of their genetic relatedness" (Segal, 1993, p. 944). Although the information is incomplete, *there does not appear to be a statistically significant difference between the MISTRA near full-sample MZA and DZA correlations for either the WAIS IQ or Raven IQ scores, which runs counter to genetic theories which require the MZA correlation to be significantly higher than the DZA correlation.*

Adding TRA study problem areas discussed in previous chapters to the unique flaws and biases of the MISTRA leads to the general conclusion that genetic interpretations of the MISTRA IQ studies are invalid, and should be expunged from the scientific record at least until an independent analysis of the raw data is performed and published.

MISTRA Personality Studies

We have seen that the MISTRA team reported complete full-sample MZA and DZA correlations in publications investigating areas other than IQ. Regarding the personality data, although the investigators published their CPI data in full, they decided not to publish their 16 Personality Factors Questionnaire (16PF) results. The 16PF is a widely used personality test that was included in the MISTRA battery (Bouchard, 1984). The CPI is also a widely used psychological test, and is said to assess "folk concepts" and normal personality characteristics (see Chapter 4). According to Segal's description in *Born Together—Reared Apart*,

> The twins' four (later five) questionnaire booklets were presented in the order of their importance. The Multidimensional Personality Questionnaire [MPQ] was the first item in Booklet 1, closely followed by a second major personality questionnaire, the Minnesota Multiphasic Personality Inventory [MMPI].... The personality assessment forms, variously distributed across the questionnaire booklets, also included the 16 Personality Factor Questionnaire [16PF], and the California Psychological Inventory [CPI], among others.
>
> (Segal, 2012, p. 99)

Although the MISTRA MPQ and CPI data were reported in several publications and were reproduced in Segal's book, to the best of my knowledge the researchers have not published their 16PF results for any type of twin pair. Once again, with little explanation, they appear to have arbitrarily decided what data to publish, and what data not to publish.

Segal (2012) also failed to mention the results of a major 1998 longitudinal (non-twin) adoption study produced by behavioral geneticists Robert Plomin and colleagues of the Colorado Adoption Project (CAP). This study found an average personality test score correlation between the birthparents and their 240 adopted-away biological offspring, a resemblance that the researchers believed "directly indexes genetic influence," of 0.01 (Plomin, Corley, Caspi, Fulker, & DeFries, 1998, p. 211). In other words, there was no correlation or genetic effect. The results of this 1998 CAP adoption study, which was methodologically superior to the MISTRA in many respects (though flawed in other respects; see Richardson & Norgate, 2006), stand in striking contrast to, and were based on much larger samples than, the published MISTRA personality results (see Appendix B, and Joseph, 2013a for more on this "lost" behavioral genetic adoption study).[9]

Based on his MISTRA work and other behavioral genetic research, Bouchard wrote in a 1994 *Science* article that the "well-replicated finding in behavior genetics, and its implications are straightforward. The similarity we see in personality between biological relatives is almost entirely genetic in origin" (Bouchard, 1994a, p. 1701). This bold statement conveyed to the average reader that similarity in personality and human behavior are largely determined at conception. According to Segal, "our findings showed that personality similarity between relatives seems to come mostly from their shared genes" (Segal, 2012, p. 102).

Segal acknowledged the critics' argument that "personality inventories do not faithfully capture the behaviors that people express in real life," and responded that, while "inventories are imperfect, they are superior to observational data gathered on just a few unrepresentative occasions" (Segal, 2012, p. 301). It should be stressed, however, that "superior" does not equal "valid."

I will now survey the major MISTRA personality publications. I will be brief because the main issues are the potentially invalidating biases, questionable concepts, and false assumptions of TRA studies outlined in previous chapters.

Tellegen and Colleagues, 1988

The first MISTRA personality paper published in a peer-reviewed scientific journal appeared in 1988, with Bouchard and Segal among the co-authors (Tellegen et al., 1988).[10] We saw in the previous chapter that the investigators based their conclusions on model-fitting techniques, which assume that the MZA correlation is caused by genetic factors, choosing to bypass the question of whether the MZA correlation was significantly higher than the DZA correlation. The researchers reported correlations for 44 MZA pairs, 217 MZT pairs, 27 DZA pairs, and 114 DZT pairs. The twins had completed Tellegen's MPQ self-report personality test. The researchers found similar MZA and MZT correlations (MZA correlations ranged from 0.29 to 0.61 on the 14 scales; MZT correlations ranged from 0.41 to 0.65), and lower DZA correlations (ranging from –0.07 to 0.39). Based on their model-fitting procedure (and its accompanying assumptions), they concluded, "on average, about 50% of measured personality diversity can be attributed to genetic diversity" (p. 1035), and that personality differences are influenced more by genetic variation than by environmental variation (p. 1036). They also concluded, "The overall contribution of a common family–environment component was small and negligible" (p. 1031).

Two 1990 Publications

The 1990 MISTRA *Science* article contained personality as well as IQ data (Bouchard, Lykken, et al., 1990). We have seen that DZA correlations for all studied behavioral characteristics were completely missing from this article, and that the investigators reported only MZA and MZT correlations for personality, IQ, psychological interests, and social attitudes. MPQ and CPI data appeared in this article's master correlation table, but the 16PF correlations did not.

Also in 1990, Bouchard and McGue published a MISTRA study based on the CPI (Bouchard & McGue, 1990). This study reported a mean MZA correlation of 0.45 based on 45 pairs, and a mean DZA correlation of 0.18 based on 26 pairs. Bouchard and McGue concluded that personality heritabilities are in the 0.50 range, and that there is little evidence of shared family environment influences. In both the 1990 *Science* and CPI publications, the investigators reached their conclusions on the basis of the assumption that MZA personality correlations of roughly 0.50 directly estimated heritability, and on their model-fitting results.

Subsequent MISTRA Personality Studies

MISTRA personality studies published after 1990 included a study based on the MMPI (DiLalla, Gottesman, Carey, & Bouchard, 1996), another CPI study with a larger cumulative sample of 71 MZA and 53 DZA pairs (Bouchard, McGue, Hur, & Horn, 1998), and McCourt and colleagues' study of "right-wing authoritarianism" (McCourt et al., 1999). These studies again were based on MZA and DZA data used in model-fitting procedures, and the investigators reached their usual conclusions about the roles of genes and environment.

Reviewing the MISTRA and other behavioral genetic personality results in 2001, Bouchard and Loehlin wrote that "enough empirical evidence ... has now been gathered to convince anyone but the most extreme skeptic that virtually all human psychological traits are influenced by genetic factors to a significant degree" (Bouchard & Loehlin, 2001, p. 243). They went further and favorably cited a non-MISTRA study that assessed "personality factors" among non-human species such as pigs, donkeys, hyenas, guppies, and gorillas, implying that personality differences are inherited and manifested in varying degrees by most species, from guppies to humans (p. 245).[11] Subsequently, in 2008 Bouchard wrote that "the findings of moderate heritabilities reported from recent quantitative genetic studies of 'avian personalities' in wild birds are eerily similar to those found for 'human personalities'" (Bouchard, 2008, p. 5).

Evaluation of the MISTRA Personality Studies

I have attempted to show that there is little reason to accept the MISTRA researchers' claims that their studies prove something about genetic influences on personality, and the controversial position that stable personality traits exist and can be accurately measured by psychometric tests has been disputed for decades. We have seen that the MISTRA and other TRA studies are built on many layers of biases, circular reasoning, and a reliance on questionable or outright false assumptions, which render the original researchers' conclusions invalid.

Summing up the MISTRA as a whole, Segal concluded,

> The MISTRA's biggest contribution to psychology was showing that behaviors found to be familial, such as intelligence, personality, and religiosity, have substantial genetic components. The study also showed that shared environments have little effect on the behavioral resemblance of relatives living together.
> (Segal, 2012, p. 319)

I have attempted to show in this book that, in fact, the MISTRA has failed to produce acceptable evidence in support of these conclusions.

Conclusions

We have seen that the MISTRA was subject to most of the invalidating flaws and false assumptions found in the classical studies. The extent to which the MISTRA twins were truly reared apart in different non-familial homes with minimal contact is known only to the researchers, since they have kept their raw data secret since 1979 and have provided only minimal information. Social and behavioral science researchers, especially those conducting studies of great social importance that are not easily replicated, must not become "lords of the data," permitting others to see only selected data that they choose to release. *Born Together—Reared Apart* provided an excellent opportunity to publish all MISTRA test results in full, and to provide detailed information and test scores for each studied pair. Unfortunately, the opportunity was missed.

From the very beginning, Bouchard designated DZAs as the MISTRA control group he intended to use to assess the meaning of MZA correlations. Yet the researchers decided to follow two tracks in reporting their DZA control group correlations. For the personality studies, they reported the full-sample correlations consistently since 1988. For the IQ studies, on the other hand, the study was initiated in 1979 (Jimmy Carter was President of the United States), and the world continues to await the publication and evaluation of the full-sample DZA WAIS IQ correlations. In addition, the 16PF personality correlations, and the full-sample Raven IQ correlations, have never been published and evaluated. Although DZA correlations were reported for most non-IQ behavioral characteristics studied in the MISTRA, we saw that the investigators explained anomalous DZA correlations in ways that were consistent with genetic interpretations of the data.

The researchers arrived at their conclusions on the basis of their decision to accept several controversial concepts and theoretical assumptions, while at the same time recognizing that the main assumptions of their model-fitting procedures "are likely not to hold." We saw in Chapter 5 that their conclusion that important genetic influences underlie behavioral characteristics was based almost entirely on the clearly false assumption that all MZA behavioral resemblance is caused by genetics. The study was therefore based on assuming the very thing it was attempting to determine.

Segal quoted Bouchard as saying that the finding of an absence of shared environmental effects on personality was "counter-intuitive, but true," adding that this finding was "certainly one of the most provocative and controversial findings from our study" (Segal, 2012, p. 188). However, it is much more likely that the massive flaws and biases of the study led the researchers to arrive at a set of mistaken interpretations and conclusions relating to the role of genetics and shared environments.

Although his subsequent work with the MISTRA suggested a shift in his views, Irving Gottesman evaluated the twins reared-apart approach in 1982 as follows:

> After a quarter century of experience with twins reared together and twins reared apart, it is my conviction that twins reared apart are a wonderful source of hypothesis generation, but not a useful source for hypothesis testing.
>
> (Gottesman, 1982, p. 351)

TRA studies have certainly helped generate some interesting hypotheses, but they have completely failed to provide scientifically acceptable evidence in support of genetic influences on human behavioral differences, which include IQ and personality.

And yet there remain the bulk of twin studies, the "99 percent" as it were, which have capitalized on the far more plentiful occurrence of reared-together twins. In Part II, I will focus on the Achilles heel of the twin method, which is the assumption that MZTs and DZTs experience similar or equal childhood and adult environments.

Notes

1 Bouchard has referred positively to his work as "hereditarian" (Bouchard, 1987), and Segal referred to Bouchard as a "steadfast reductionist" (Segal, 2012, p. 400).
2 Given the researchers' selective and incomplete presentation of their data, it is interesting that the Editor of the journal *Intelligence* went out of his way to praise the MISTRA researchers' 2011 publication of a correlation matrix of some of their cognitive ability data. On the first page of this article, the "Editor's note" read, "I would like to thank Johnson and Bouchard for their generosity in making this data available to everyone. This gesture embodies

3 the highest scientific altruism of sharing data that have, for some, taken a lifetime to collect. I encourage others to follow their example" (Editor's note in Johnson & Bouchard, 2011, p. 82).
3 In 1985, Bouchard and Segal had "refrained from placing too much emphasis on" a French adoption study showing large IQ gains among 32 working-class adoptees who had been reared in professional families, due to what they saw as that study's "very small sample size" (Bouchard & Segal, 1985, p. 424).
4 The VassarStats website http://vassarstats.net/rdiff.html provides a test of the significance level between two correlation coefficients. Johnson et al. reported that the sample consisted of 74 MZA and 52 DZA pairs (148 individual MZA twins, 104 individual DZA twins), and reported the Raven IQ correlations as MZA = 0.55, DZA = 0.42. Significance tests run on the above-mentioned website produce the following results based on the correlations and samples sizes listed above. Basing the correlation N on the number of twin pairs, the difference between these Raven IQ correlations is not statistically significant at the conventional 0.05 level, one-tailed ($Z = 0.92$, probability = 0.18). Basing the N on the number of individual twins (which doubles the N), the comparison remains statistically non-significant ($Z = 1.32$, probability = 0.09). The same results were obtained from another website, http://www.quantpsy.org/corrtest/corrtest.htm (Preacher, 2002).
5 In a discussion of migraine headaches, Segal noted that a MISTRA study found an MZA correlation of 0.52, and a DZA correlation of 0.46. Although she wrote that "a genetic component to migraine headache was indicated," she believed that the "relatively high DZA correlation urges a cautious interpretation" (Segal, 2012, pp. 226–227). Perhaps the publication of the full-sample MZA and DZA IQ correlations might have urged a similarly "cautious interpretation."
6 The VassarStats website http://vassarstats.net/rdiff.html again provides a test of the significance level between two correlation coefficients. Segal did not state the number of twin pairs that the full-scale WAIS MZA 0.62 and DZA 0.50 correlations reported to her by Bouchard were based upon. The full MISTRA sample consisted of 81 MZA and 56 DZA pairs (162 individual MZA twins, 112 individual DZA twins). Significance tests run on the above-mentioned website produce the following results based on the reported correlations and the full MISTRA MZA and DZA sample. Basing the correlation N on the number of twin pairs, the difference between these WAIS IQ correlations is not statistically significant at the conventional 0.05 level, one-tailed ($Z = 0.99$, probability = 0.16). Basing the N on the number of individual twins (which doubles the N), the comparison remains statistically non-significant ($Z = 1.41$, probability = 0.08). The same results were obtained from another website, http://www.quantpsy.org/corrtest/corrtest.htm (Preacher, 2002).
7 The controversial concept of emergenesis and "emergenic traits" was put forward by Lykken in 1982 (Lykken, 1982). According to Segal, "Emergenesis refers to genetically influenced traits that do not run in families. Emergenic traits are thought to emerge out of complex configurations of polymorphic genes that come together by chance in an individual" (Segal, 2012, p. 171).
8 In a 1992 MISTRA study of "work values" by Keller, Bouchard, and colleagues, based on 23 MZA and 20 DZA pairs, the researchers found few statistically significant differences between these groups, and concluded that "small sample sizes severely restricted the power to detect differences" (Keller, Arvey, Bouchard, Segal, & Dawis,1992, p. 83).

9 Plomin believed so strongly in "the power of adoption studies" that in 1977 he and his colleagues argued that "the use of separated identical twins is by no means necessary," because "the use of any genetically related family members living in unrelated environments . . . is sufficient" (Plomin, DeFries, & Loehlin, 1977, p. 320).
10 Bouchard had published some preliminary MISTRA personality correlations in a 1984 book chapter (Bouchard, 1984).
11 In the same year, Plomin argued that g can be found in non-human primates, rodents, and even in marine mollusks (Plomin, 2001).

Part II

STUDIES OF REARED-TOGETHER TWINS

7

THE MZT–DZT EQUAL ENVIRONMENT ASSUMPTION

The Achilles Heel of the Classical Twin Method

> If monozygotic twins are significantly more alike in a trait than dizygotic twins, it follows that the characteristic has an inherited component.... If the two kinds of twins were treated differently, the results of a twin study would be questionable.
> — Behavioral genetic twin researchers Arnold Buss, Robert Plomin, & Lee Willerman, 1973 (Buss, Plomin, & Willerman, 1973, p. 515)

> In contrast with identical twins, fraternal twins are not as close, nor are their lives as intimately entwined.
> — Nancy Segal, 1999 (Segal, 1999, p. 101)

> MZ cotwins model their behavior upon each other to a greater extent than DZ cotwins.
> — *Behavior Genetics* authors John Fuller and William Thompson, 1960 (Fuller & Thompson, 1960, p. 110)

In Part II we leave the realm of TRA studies to examine by far the most common way that twins have been used to support genetic theories—the classical twin method comparison of *reared-together* MZ pairs (MZTs) and reared-together same-sex DZ pairs (DZTs).[1] If the estimate of about 800,000 total studied twin pairs reported in Chapter 1 is accurate, all but a few hundred of these pairs were reared together in the same family home, and many had strong bonds well into adulthood. As seen in Chapter 1, the twin method is based on a comparison of these two types of reared-together twin pairs. Because twin researchers believe that MZTs share 100 percent of their segregating genes, whereas DZTs share only 50 percent on average, they conclude that the greater behavioral resemblance of MZTs versus DZTs indicates that the behavior has an important genetic component.

From the very beginning in Hermann Siemens' 1924 study (Siemens, 1924), twin researchers have based this conclusion on the MZT–DZT "equal environment assumption" (EEA), which holds that the childhood and adult environments of both types of twin pairs are roughly equal. Therefore, they argue, the greater behavioral resemblance of MZT versus DZT pairs can only be caused by genetic factors. Other assumptions of the twin method include that there are only two types of twin pairs, that researchers are able to reliably distinguish between these two types of twin pairs, that twins do not differ from non-twins for the characteristic in question, and that twin method results are generalizable to the entire non-twin population (generalizability). The validity or non-validity of the EEA, however, has always been the central issue of contention.

The twin method has been the mainstay of behavioral genetics for decades, and we will see in Chapter 8 that it constitutes a major pillar of support for genetic theories in psychiatry and psychiatric genetics as well. Indeed, as Lindon Eaves and colleagues wrote in 2003, "For several decades, twin studies have provided a critical facet of psychiatric and behavior-genetic research" (Eaves, Foley, & Silberg, 2003, p. 486). According to Segal, MZT–DZT comparisons are "a powerful investigatory tool," and "a simple and elegant natural experiment for examining genetic and environmental influences on behavior" (Segal, 2012, pp. 1–2).

The perceived validity of TRA studies is frequently cited in support of the twin method and its underlying assumptions. As one of numerous examples, political science twin researcher John Alford and his colleagues, in their 2005 twin study of political attitudes, argued that "the most powerful refutation" of criticism of the twin method "comes in recent studies utilizing MZ and DZ twins raised apart. These studies uniformly validate MZ and DZ differences found in earlier studies of twins raised together" (Alford, Funk, & Hibbing, 2005, p. 155).

Researchers in psychology and psychiatry have used the twin method since the 1920s to assess whether genetic factors underlie psychological characteristics such as IQ and personality, major psychiatric disorders such as schizophrenia and bipolar disorder, criminality, and many other areas of human behavior. They usually find significantly higher MZT versus DZT resemblance for the behavior in question, and conclude that genetic factors play an important role in causing the behavior, and in explaining a significant portion of its variation in the population (heritability).

At the same time, most critics have argued that MZTs experience much more similar environments than DZTs, and that this greater environmental similarity confounds genetic interpretations of twin method data.[2] As it turned out, by the mid-1960s most critics and many twin researchers were in agreement that MZT pairs experience much more similar environments, are treated more alike, and are socialized to be more alike than DZT pairs. Indeed, as twin researchers Sandra Scarr and Louise Carter-Saltzman concluded in 1979, "the evidence of greater environmental similarity for MZ than DZ twins is overwhelming" (Scarr & Carter-Saltzman, 1979, p. 528). According to Loehlin, in his 1976 study (Loehlin & Nichols, 1976) he "found, as nearly everybody else has found who has investigated the point, that identical twins are indeed treated more alike—they are dressed alike more often, are more often together at school, play together more, and so forth" (Loehlin, 1978b, p. 72). Others have pointed to MZTs' greater psychological closeness, identity confusion, and "ego fusion" when compared with DZT pairs (Dalgard & Kringlen, 1976; Husén, 1959; Jackson, 1960; Joseph, 2004; Koch, 1966; Kringlen, 1967; Shields, 1954). In the words of twin researcher Ricardo Ainslie, "twins often encounter ambiguity and confusion with respect to their sense of identity" (Ainslie, 1997, p. 2).

The Traditional Definition of the EEA

During the first 40 years of the twin method (roughly 1924 to 1964), twin researchers in psychology and psychiatry defined the EEA—without qualification—as the assumption that MZT and DZT pairs grow up experiencing roughly equal environments. Some examples of twin researchers' "traditional" definition of the EEA are presented below:

> It has been assumed that the mean nurture difference . . . is the same for identical and fraternal twins.
> (Holzinger, 1929, p. 244)

> [The twin method] assum[es] that environmental differences are the same for both identical and fraternal twins.
> (Newman, Freeman, & Holzinger, 1937, p. 21)

> The [twin] formulas usually involve the assumption that the nurture influences are approximately equal for fraternal and identical twins.
> (Carter, 1940, p. 246)

> The "twin method" developed in Germany . . . and much used here in the last two decades for the study of heredity and environment . . . . [rests] on the assumption that the environment is as similar for a pair of fraternals as for a pair of identicals.
> (Woodworth, 1941, p. 9)

[One assumption of the twin method is] that nurture influences are the same for both types of twins.

(Eysenck & Prell, 1951, p. 461)

In the comparison of MZ with DZ twins the assumption is made that the individual members of a twin-pair enjoy comparable or equivalent environments.

(Neel & Schull, 1954, p. 280)

[The twin method assumes] that the "average nurture difference" is the same for the two types of twins.

(Jones, 1955, p. 102)

An underlying assumption [of the twin method] has been that the environments of the members of the identical pairs are not, on the average, more similar than those of the members of the fraternal pairs.

(Tienari, 1963, p. 10)

The traditional use of the twin method entails the assumption that the environmental factors are, on an average, just as alike, or just as unlike, for monozygotic as for dizygotic twins.

(Juel-Nielsen, 1965/1980, Part I, pp. 25–26)

The basic underlying assumption for the classical twin method is, of course, that environmental conditions of monozygotic twins do not differ from those of dizygotic twins.

(Kringlen, 1967, p. 20)

Upon discovering that MZT and DZT environments are very different, some commentators were prepared to reject the twin method on this basis alone. For example, the psychologist R. S. Woodworth concluded in his 1941 review, "Having convinced ourselves (in considering the 'twin method') that the environment differs more for fraternal than for identical twins, we cannot derive much information from a comparison of the results from the two classes of twins" (Woodworth, 1941, p. 21). And James Neel and William Schull, in their 1954 textbook *Human Heredity*, concluded that because it is "rarely ... the case" that MZT and DZT environments are comparable, "twins have contributed little which may be extrapolated to other genetic situations" (p. 280).

The "Fallacy" of the Twin Method

By the mid-1960s it was clear to most critics that the twin method was based on the "fallacy" that MZT and DZT environments were equal (Bleuler, 1978, p. 432; Penrose, 1973, p. 90; Stocks, 1930, p. 104). Several leading researchers and psychologists of the postwar era were themselves unsure of the validity of the EEA. For example, according to the Finnish schizophrenia twin researcher Pekka Tienari,

> It is doubtful... whether the difference in concordance rate between identical and fraternal groups of twins can, as such, be ascribed to hereditary factors. In all likelihood, the environment, too, is more similar in the case of identical than in the case of fraternal twins... Furthermore, it is obvious that the intensity of the mutual relationship of identical twins is considerably greater than that of siblings in general and, also, of fraternal twins.... It is apparent that differences in concordance rates between groups of identical and fraternal twins, as well as between female and male twin pairs, are partly attributable to environmental (psychological) factors.
>
> (Tienari, 1963, pp. 119–121)

Mid-1960s researchers in the fields of behavioral genetics, psychiatric genetics, and medical genetics were therefore presented with a major problem, since their theories and claims in favor of the importance of heredity, and at times advocacy of eugenic policies (Joseph, 2004), were based largely on twin method data. And yet, the evidence strongly suggested that the EEA—as it had been defined until then—was false. This indicated that conclusions in favor of genetics based on twin studies were confounded by environmental factors, and that the twin method should have been discarded.

We will see, however, that twin researchers were successful in preserving the twin method mainly on the basis of: (a) using circular arguments and committing other logical fallacies; (b) changing the definition of the EEA; or (c) denying, ignoring, or downplaying the evidence that MZT and DZT environments are different (Joseph, 2004, 2010a, 2012; Lewontin, Rose, & Kamin, 1984; Pam, Kemker, Ross, & Golden, 1996).

Thus, in the twenty-first century the twin method lives on as twin studies, and their authors' conclusions that they prove something about genetic influences on behavior, continue to be published and discussed in leading social and behavioral science journals and textbooks, with little critical analysis. More recently, researchers in social science fields such as political science and economics have used twin method data to argue in favor of an important role for genetic factors (e.g., Alford et al., 2005; Cesarini, Johannesson, Wallace, & Lichtenstein, 2009), and have created the subfields of "genopolitics" and "genoeconomics."

The analysis I present here, including an examination of the "EEA-test" study by Kevin Smith and his colleagues, applies broadly to the twin method's use in psychology (including IQ and personality), psychiatry, the social and behavioral sciences in general, and some areas of medicine. All assumptions, data, and studies I discuss and analyze in this chapter are based on samples of twin pairs reared together in the same family home (MZT versus DZT), which form the basis of twin method investigations.

The Two Main Arguments Put Forward in Defense of the Equal Environment Assumption

Argument A

Since the 1960s, most twin researchers have moved away from the traditional EEA definition and have defended the validity of the twin method on the basis of two main arguments, sometimes invoking both arguments at the same time. What I have called *Argument A* (Joseph, 2013c) states that, although MZT environments are more similar than DZT environments, the twin method retains its validity because MZT pairs "create" or "elicit" more similar environments for themselves because they are more similar genetically. Three examples of the *Argument A* defense of the EEA read as follows:

> A series of ingenious studies . . . have all pointed to the conclusion that, for the most part, the more similar treatment of MZs is not the cause of their greater phenotypic similarity but, rather, a consequence of their genetic identity and the more similar responses this elicits from the environment.
> (Martin, Boomsma, & Machin, 1997, p. 390)

> It is important to note that if MZ twins are treated more alike than DZ twins, it is most likely associated with their genetically based behavioral similarities.
> (Segal & Johnson, 2009, p. 82)

> A subtle, but important, issue is that identical twins might have more similar experiences than fraternal twins because identical twins are more similar genetically. That is, some experiences may be driven genetically. Such differences between identical and fraternal twins in experience are not a violation of the equal environments assumption because the differences are not caused environmentally.
> (Plomin, DeFries, Knopik, & Neiderhiser, 2013, p. 82)

In addition, the following passage appeared in a 2010 twin study published in a political science journal:

> If MZ twins are treated more similarly because they are biologically more alike, this can hardly be considered a violation of the

EEA. For the reason that MZ environments are more similar than DZ environments (if indeed they are) is *because of the initial difference in genetic predispositions.*

(Sturgis et al., 2010, p. 222, italics in original)

Many other leading behavioral genetic researchers have defended the validity of the twin method on the basis of *Argument A*, examples of which can be found in Appendix C.

Although twin researchers have used *Argument A* consistently since the 1950s, the argument is a circular one because twin researchers' conclusion that MZT–DZT differences are explained by genetics is based on assuming the very same thing. In other words, as seen in Figure 7.1, twin researchers using *Argument A* simultaneously and circularly assume and conclude that the greater behavioral resemblance of MZT versus DZT twin pairs is caused by the former's greater genetic similarity, and their position that genetic factors explain the greater behavioral resemblance of MZT twin pairs is both a *premise and a conclusion* of the twin method. They commit the logical fallacy of arguing, as we saw in Chapter 2, that "X is true because Y is true; Y is true because X is true."

We have seen that circular reasoning is "empty reasoning in which the conclusion rests on an assumption whose validity is dependent on the conclusion" (Reber, 1985, p. 123). A circular argument consists of "using as evidence a fact which is authenticated by the very conclusion it supports," which "gives us two unknowns so busy chasing each other's tails that neither has time to attach itself to reality" (Pirie, 2006, p. 27). As seen in Figure 7.1, the *Argument A* premise and conclusion are the same—that MZTs' greater genetic resemblance causes their greater behavioral resemblance—and they are too busy "chasing each other's tails" to provide any evidence in favor of genetics. We also saw in previous chapters that some

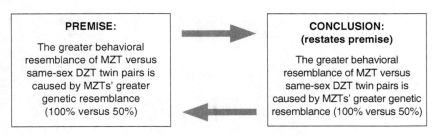

Figure 7.1 Circular Reasoning Used Since the 1950s in Support of the Twin Method: Twin Researchers' *Argument A*.

Modified from Jay Joseph (2012). "The 'Missing Heritability' of Psychiatric Disorders: Elusive Genes or Non-Existent Genes?" *Applied Developmental Science, 16* (2), p. 71. © Taylor & Francis Group, LLC, New York, New York.

of the conclusions reached by the MISTRA and other TRA researchers were based on circular arguments.

According to the psychologist Lance Rips, in circular arguments, "the arguer illicitly uses the conclusion itself . . . as a crucial piece of support, instead of justifying the conclusion on the basis of agreed-upon facts and reasonable inferences." We saw in Chapter 2 that he concluded, "A convincing argument for conclusion c can't rest on the prior assumption that c [is correct], so something has gone seriously wrong with such an argument" (Rips, 2002, p. 767). In their attempts to answer the critics' objections, in Figure 7.1 and Appendix C we see that twin researchers invoke *Argument A* as they refer to the premise in support of the conclusion, and then refer back to the conclusion in support of the premise, in a continuously circular loop of faulty reasoning.

An additional problem with *Argument A* is that, even if it is accepted, MZT pairs could still resemble each other more than DZT pairs for behavioral characteristics, psychiatric disorders, and medical conditions for purely environmental reasons. For example, MZT pairs with strong genetic predispositions for enjoying tennis would probably correlate higher than DZT pairs for tennis elbow, but this condition would not be caused by any genes for tennis elbow.

A final problem with *Argument A* is that it portrays twins as behaving according to an inherited environment-creating blueprint, but portrays *parents* and other adults as easily able to change their behavior and treatment in response to the twins' behavior—in effect being flexible enough to allow the twins to "create their own environments." However, according to the logic of *Argument A*, adults' "environment-creating" behavior and personalities should be far more unchangeable than twin children's because, in addition to their presumed genetic predispositions, adults have experienced decades of behavior-molding peer, family, religious, and other socialization influences (Joseph, 1998).

Summing up, the *Argument A* defense of the EEA is based on a "seriously wrong" error in reasoning, in addition to other problems, and we must therefore reject it as a valid argument in support of the twin method.

Argument B

Like supporters of *Argument A*, proponents of what I have called *Argument B* (Joseph, 2013c) recognize that MZTs experience more similar environments than DZTs, but argue that, in order to invalidate the twin method and the EEA, it must be shown that MZT and DZT environments differ in aspects that are relevant to the behavior in question. This is the "trait-relevant" definition of the EEA, and is seen in the following EEA definition by a group of leading psychiatric twin researchers:

> The traditional twin method, as well as more recent biometrical models for twin analysis, are predicated on the equal-environment assumption (EEA) — that monozygotic (MZ) and dizygotic (DZ) twins are equally correlated for their exposure to environmental influences *that are of etiologic relevance to the trait under study.*
>
> (Kendler, Neale, Kessler, Heath, & Eaves, 1993, p. 21, italics added)

Bouchard and McGue also endorsed the *Argument B* position:

> Behavioral geneticists call this assumption the "equal environmental similarity assumption," a term that is somewhat misleading in that the issue is not whether [reared together] MZ twins experience more environmental similarity than [reared together] DZ twins, but rather whether they are more likely to share trait-relevant features of their environments.
>
> (Bouchard & McGue, 2003, p. 9)

Bouchard has argued that the twin method is valid even if MZTs and DZTs "experience quite different environments" (Bouchard, 2009, p. 532).

An example of an *Argument B* environmental factor relevant to a characteristic or disorder is the relationship between exposure to trauma and post-traumatic stress disorder (PTSD). Because trauma exposure is (by definition) an environmental factor known to contribute to the development of PTSD, a finding that MZT pairs are more similarly exposed to trauma than DZT pairs means that MZTs experience more similar "trait-relevant" environments than DZTs. Many twin researchers using *Argument B* would conclude that the EEA is violated in this case.

It appears that *Argument B* was first put forward in 1966, without explanation or theoretical justification, by Irving Gottesman in a twin study of personality. Gottesman subtly redefined the traditional definition of the EEA by inserting one italicized qualifying term into it, writing that the twin method is based on the assumption "that the average intrapair differences in *trait-relevant* environmental factors are substantially the same for both MZ and DZ twins" (Gottesman, 1966, p. 200, italics in original). In the same year, Gottesman and James Shields (author of the 1962 TRA study) wrote that, in schizophrenia twin studies, the EEA would be wrong if "the environments of MZ twins are systematically more alike than those of DZ twins in features which can be *shown* to be of etiological relevance in schizophrenia" (Gottesman & Shields, 1966a, pp. 4–5, italics in original). In defining the assumption using this new "trait-relevant" formulation, Gottesman and Shields appeared to place the burden of proof on critics to "show" that MZT and DZT environments differ in trait-relevant aspects.

In an earlier 1963 twin study of personality, Gottesman had defined the EEA as the traditional unqualified assumption that "the within-pair environmental variance is the same for the two types of twins." He cautioned, however, that "this is not necessarily true for the personality traits as measured by the tests, but one can proceed only on the assumption that such variance is not too different for the two types of twins" (Gottesman, 1963, p. 8).

Three years later Gottesman attempted to solve the unequal environment problem for twin researchers, not by showing that MZT and DZT childhood and adult environments are in fact equal, but simply by inserting the qualifying term "trait-relevant" into the 40-year-old traditional definition of the EEA, and then charging critics with the responsibility of showing that MZT environments are more similarly "trait-relevant" than are DZT environments. We saw in Chapter 1 that the early 1960s were a difficult time for twin researchers, and Gottesman's modification of the traditional EEA played a role in keeping twin research alive.

Although other twin researchers explicitly place the burden of proof on critics for demonstrating that MZT pairs experience more similar trait-relevant environments than DZT pairs (e.g., Alford, Funk, & Hibbing, 2008; Bouchard, 1993b, 1997b; DeFries & Plomin, 1978; Faraone & Biederman, 2000; Lyons, Kendler, Provet, & Tsuang, 1991), at other times, such as the Smith and colleagues study I will review shortly, twin researchers perform "EEA-test" studies in an attempt to test the assumption for environmental biases. Nevertheless, most EEA-test researchers uphold the assumption on the basis of *Argument A*, *Argument B*, or both (for critical reviews of the EEA-test literature, see Felson, 2014; Joseph, 2004, 2006; Pam et al., 1996; Richardson & Norgate, 2005; see also Chapter 8).

As seen in Kendler and colleagues' *Argument B* definition above, the MZT–DZT EEA also underlies more complex biometrical model-fitting analyses based on twin data, which were discussed in previous chapters. We have seen that these analyses attempt to partition genetic, "shared environment," and "unshared environment" contributions to behavioral variation in a population (the "ACE Model"). A critical point, however, is that, regardless of the apparent complexity of twin method statistical formulations, path diagrams, model-fitting procedures, and so forth, all depend on the validity of the MZT–DZT EEA.

Although most proponents of *Argument B* implicitly or explicitly place the burden of proof on critics to show that MZT and DZT environments differ on "trait-relevant" dimensions for the behavior or behavioral disorder in question, the burden of proof rests with those who make a scientific claim, twin researchers in this case, and not on those who question it. For example, people claiming that Bigfoot exists bear the burden of proof for demonstrating this; skeptics are not charged with the responsibility of proving that Bigfoot does not exist. Supporters of *Argument B* appear to commit the *argumentum ad ignorantiam* logical fallacy (argument from ignorance), which is the fallacy of asserting that something is true simply because it has not been proved false, which usually involves shifting the burden of proof onto skeptics (Walton, 1999). Twin researchers invoking *Argument B* in defense of the validity of the EEA assert, despite recognizing that MZTs experience more similar environments, that critics have not disproved twin researchers' claim that MZTs and DZTs usually experience similar trait-relevant environments.

Most participants in the twin method debate recognize that MZTs experience much more similar environments than experienced by DZTs, and most also recognize that environmental factors play a role in explaining behavioral differences in the population. Unless twin researchers are able to identify and rule out specific and exclusive "trait-relevant" factors that contribute to the cause of the behavioral characteristic they are studying, these two widely recognized facts combine to invalidate genetic interpretations of MZT–DZT correlational differences based on *Argument B*.

Argument A Potentially Renders Argument B Irrelevant

Interestingly, the *Argument A* position that twins create their own environments because they are more similar genetically potentially renders *Argument B* irrelevant because, even if critics or researchers show that MZT pairs experience more similar "trait-relevant" environments than DZT pairs, twin researchers could still argue in favor of the validity of the twin method and the EEA on the basis of MZT pairs having "created" or "elicited" more similar "trait-relevant" environments for themselves (Joseph, 2006).

An example of researchers making this argument is seen in a 1993 twin study of PTSD among combat veterans. William True and his colleagues found that MZT pairs did indeed experience more similar PTSD trait-relevant combat experiences than did the DZT pairs. However, they concluded that "inheritance makes a substantial contribution to PTSD symptoms" based on their *Argument A* claim that "inherited factors . . . increase the likelihood of exposure to traumatic events and responding to exposure by developing PTSD" (True et al., 1993, p. 263). The researchers therefore chose to conclude that their results supported a genetic basis for PTSD, despite the finding that their MZT pairs experienced more similar trait-relevant combat experiences than experienced by the DZT pairs.

Another group of twin researchers led by Dutch genetic investigators Eske Derks and Dorret Boomsma explicitly stated that, even if trait-relevant environmental influences are found, the "twins create their own environment" argument would trump this finding and validate the twin method. "It has been shown," they wrote, "that MZ twins in childhood more often share playmates, share the same room, and dress more alike than same-sex DZ twins." However, they believed that "this does not necessarily imply that the EEA is violated," because

> the greater environmental similarity in MZ than DZ twins does not have to be related to a greater phenotypic similarity. Second, even if a greater environmental similarity *is* related to a greater phenotypic similarity, this association could be mediated by a greater genetic similarity in MZ than DZ twins.
> (Derks, Dolan, & Boomsma, 2006, p. 403, italics in original)

Like most twin researchers, Derks and colleagues recognized that MZT and DZT environments are different. In the language I use in this chapter, they then wrote that the EEA may be valid on the basis of *Argument B*, but even if *Argument B* does not hold, researchers could still fall back on *Argument A* and validate the twin method, because the trait-relevant environmental "association could be mediated by a greater genetic similarity in MZ than DZ twins." For this and other reasons, the validity of the EEA—and therefore of the twin method itself because it is based on the validity of this assumption—rests mainly on the acceptance or rejection of the "twins create their own environment" *Argument A*.

Identity Confusion and Attachment

Twin researchers typically assess environmental similarity by inquiring whether, as children, twins shared the same bedroom, attended school together, dressed alike, and played together. Some earlier critics of the twin method argued that environmental similarity measures used by most twin researchers are limited, and while they assess some aspects of this similarity, they fail to adequately assess the nature of the attachment, conscious attempts to be alike, identity confusion, and ego fusion experienced by MZT twin pairs to a far greater degree than DZT pairs.

Family therapy pioneer Don Jackson described "the intertwining of [MZT] twin identities, in the ego fusion that in one sense doubles the ego (because the other is felt as part of the self) and in another sense halves it (because the self is felt as part of the other)" (Jackson, 1960, p. 66). According to the psychoanalytically oriented twin researcher Dorothy Burlingham, "Identical twins when they grow up often fail to develop into separate human entities" (quoted in Jackson, 1960, p. 66). And in a little-quoted passage from their field-defining 1960 textbook *Behavior Genetics*, John Fuller and William Thompson recognized that "MZ cotwins model their behavior upon each other to a greater extent than DZ cotwins" (Fuller & Thompson, 1960, p. 110). The founders of the behavioral genetics field thus agreed with critics that MZTs model their behavior on each other to a greater degree than DZTs, viewing this as a "possible source of error" in the twin method without adding any *Argument A* or *Argument B* qualifications to this finding.

Looking at earlier twin studies whose authors attempted to assess twins' emotional closeness and attachment, James Shields (in a 1954 MZT–DZT study) found that 47 percent of his MZT pairs experienced a "degree of attachment" that was "very close," whereas only 15 percent of the DZTs experienced a very close degree of attachment (Shields, 1954, p. 234). Swedish researcher Torsten Husén calculated an "index of attachment" for twins, and found "a considerable mean difference" between MZT and DZT pairs (Husén, 1959, p. 143). Husén concluded that MZT pairs "are much more prone to emphasize the desire to be alike, to be together, to share the same interests, and to have a feeling of loyalty" (p. 142). The Norwegian twin researcher Einar Kringlen performed a "global evaluation of twin closeness" and found that 65 percent of MZT pairs had an "extremely strong level of closeness," which was true for only 17 percent of the DZT pairs (Kringlen, 1967, p. 115). And in a 1966 twin study, Helen Koch of the University of Texas found that "Identical [MZT] cotwins tended to be closer to each other than fraternals [DZTs]" (Koch, 1966, p. 132).

Some findings by twin researchers that relate to twins' emotional attachment and identity issues are seen in Table 7.1.[3] I have excluded questions such as whether twins shared the same bedroom, played together, and other questions of this type listed above. Some of the results in Table 7.1 were obtained by twin researchers using or developing zygosity determination questionnaires attempting to more easily and economically distinguish MZT from DZT pairs for future twin studies. Although there are various methodological issues in these studies, the trend is clear that MZT pairs experience much greater levels of identity confusion and attachment than experienced by DZT pairs, which we would expect to contribute significantly to their greater resemblance for the behaviors studied in the social and behavioral sciences.

The findings in Table 7.1, which plausibly explain at least a portion of MZT–DZT behavioral correlation differences, are rarely cited by contemporary twin researchers and their supporters. Of the Table 7.1 researchers using or developing zygosity determination questionnaires, only the Cohen group commented on the irony of needing to demonstrate the great dissimilarity of MZT and DZT childhood environments as a method to reliably distinguish between MZT and DZT twin pairs. As we have seen, the twin method assumes that these environments are *not* dissimilar. According to Cohen and colleagues, "The impact of such

Table 7.1 Environmental Dissimilarity among MZT and DZT Twin Pairs: Levels of Identity Confusion and Attachment

Study	Characteristic of Reared-Together Twin Relationship	MZT	DZT
von Bracken, 1934	"Closely attached"	87%	21%
Wilson, 1934	"Never separated from twin"	44%	27%
Mowrer, 1954	"Other twin as member of family that understands me best"	61%	24%
Mowrer, 1954	"Should be closer to my twin than other siblings"	70%	44%
Shields, 1954	"Very close degree of attachment"	47%	15%
Husén, 1959	"Very keen on always being together"	50%	25%
Cederlöf et al., 1961*	"As like as two peas"	54%	0%
Koch, 1966	"Sees likeness between himself and twin"	78%	54%
Nichols & Bilbro, 1966*	"Mistaken for each other by parents (as children)"	27%	0%
Kringlen, 1967	"Identity confusion in childhood"	90%	10%
Kringlen, 1967	"Mistaken for each other by parents and/or sibs"	21%	0%
Kringlen, 1967	"Considered alike as two drops of water"	76%	0%
Kringlen, 1967	"Inseparable as children to an extreme degree"	73%	19%
Kringlen, 1967	"Inseparable as adults to an extreme degree"	18%	0%
Kringlen, 1967	"Brought up 'as a unit'"	72%	19%
Kringlen, 1967	"Global evaluation of twin closeness"	65%	17%
Cohen et al., 1973*	"Confused for each other by mother or father"	78%	10%
Cohen et al., 1973*	"Sometimes confused by other people in family"	94%	15%
Cohen et al., 1973*	"Hard for strangers to tell them apart"	99%	16%
Cohen et al., 1975*	"Confused for each other by mother or father"	79%	1%
Cohen et al., 1975*	"Sometimes confused by other people in family"	93%	1%

Study	Question	%
Cohen et al., 1975*	"Hard for strangers to tell them apart"	99% 8%
Dalgard & Kringlen, 1976	"Extreme or strong interdependence in childhood"	86% 36%
Dalgard & Kringlen, 1976	"Brought up as a unit"	92% 75%
Dalgard & Kringlen, 1976	"Extreme or strong closeness in childhood"	86% 36%
Kasriel & Eaves, 1976*	"Confused for each other in childhood"	98% 6%
Torgersen, 1979*	"As alike as two peas in a pod"	83% 1%
Torgersen, 1979*	"Twins mixed for each other up as children"	71% 2%
Morris-Yates et al., 1990	"Parental treatment of twins as two individuals"	55% 83%

Adapted from Jay Joseph (2013c), "The Use of the Classical Twin Method in the Social and Behavioral Sciences: The Fallacy Continues." *Journal of Mind and Behavior, 34*, p. 22. © The Institute of Mind and Behavior, Inc., P.O. Box 522, Village Station, New York City, New York, 10014.

Sources (same-sex twin pair samples sizes; country): Cederlöf et al., 1961, p. 344 (MZT = 81, DZT = 100; Sweden); Cohen et al., 1973, p. 467 (MZT = 94, DZT = 61; U.S.); Cohen et al., 1975, p. 1374 (MZT = 181, DZT = 84; U.S.); Dalgard & Kringlen, 1976, p. 224 (MZT = 49, DZT = 89; Norway); Husén, 1959, p. 141 (MZT = 26, DZT = 24; Sweden); Kasriel & Eaves, 1976, p. 265 (MZT = 94, DZT = 84; U.K.); Koch, 1966, p. 233 (MZT = 70, DZT = 72; U.S.); Kringlen, 1967, p. 115 (MZT = 75, DZT = 42; Norway); Morris-Yates et al., 1990, p. 323 (MZT = 186, DZT = 157; Australia); Mowrer, 1954, pp. 469–470 (based on "612 twins," status not stated; U.S.); Nichols & Bilbro, 1966, p. 270 (MZT = 82, DZT = 41; U.S.); Shields, 1954, p. 234 (MZT = 36, DZT = 26; U.K.); Torgersen, 1979, p. 228 (MZT = 98, DZT = 117; Norway); von Bracken, 1934, p. 299 (MZT = 23, DZT = 19; Germany); Wilson, 1934, p. 334 (MZT = 70, DZT = 55; U.S.).

MZT - monozygotic twin pairs reared together; DZT- same-sex dizygotic twin pairs reared together. Includes studies whose authors provided percentage figures for environmental similarity, or enough information to calculate percentages. Excluded are studies whose authors provided only correlations or mean scores, or correlations between twins' environmental similarity and the characteristic under study. Excludes questions such as whether twins shared the same bedroom, attended school together, dressed alike, played together, etc. The Cohen et al. 1973 and 1975 studies were based on different twin samples

*Studies obtaining information in the context of using or developing questionnaires designed to distinguish between MZT and DZT pairs

repeated confusion on individual twinships, or the effect of these differences between MZT and DZT twins is not known with certainty. However, such information must cast doubt upon the assumption of environmental equivalence" (Dibble, Cohen, & Grawe, 1978, pp. 246–248). In other words, in the process of developing a questionnaire designed to help future twin researchers reliably distinguish between MZT and DZT pairs, the researchers noticed that their data, which showed greatly unequal MZT–DZT childhood environments, cast doubt on the validity of the twin method itself.

Segal also recognized that MZT pairs are emotionally closer to each other than are DZT pairs, devoting an entire chapter to this topic in her 1999 book *Entwined Lives: Twins and What They Tell Us about Human Behavior* (Segal's Chapter 6). Segal described "the bond between identical twins" as "a *friendship extraordinaire* . . . stronger than the bonds between other siblings" (Segal, 1999, p. 97, italics in original), and referred to "the special intimacy shared by many identical twins" (p. 100). While recognizing that "identical twins share closer social bonds than fraternal twins" (p. 97), she framed this discussion in terms of the "general principle" in the field of evolutionary psychology that people direct "increased altruism toward close relatives," which for her explained the emotional closeness of MZTs, and even reunited MZAs. However, she dismissed the idea that MZT pairs' strong emotional bond and "special intimacy" had negative implications for the twin method and the EEA on the basis of her *Argument A* position that "fraternal twins receive differential treatment from parents . . . because they are genetically different and, therefore, behaviorally different and their parents respond to their uniqueness" (p. 101).

Attempting to uphold the validity of twin research in political science, Sarah Medland and Peter Hatemi wrote in 2009, "it is difficult to conceive of a population where parents of MZ[T] twins would purposely or unconsciously socialize their children [more than DZT twins] to support the same political party" (Medland & Hatemi, 2009, p. 199). However, it is *not* difficult to conceive of a population in which MZTs' greater attempts to model their behavior on each other, in addition to their much greater levels of closeness, loyalty, attachment, and identity confusion (seen in Table 7.1), would cause them to hold similar political views, support the same candidates and parties, and behave more alike in general, much more often than DZT pairs.

Family Studies and the Twin Method

It is noteworthy that twin researchers and behavioral geneticists do not make the "trait-relevant" or "create their own environment" arguments when discussing potential environmental confounds in *family studies*, despite the fact both family studies and the twin method compare groups experiencing very different environments. That is, most behavioral genetic researchers recognize that family members share much more similar family and physical environments than shared by randomly selected members of the population, and recognize that MZT pairs share much more similar environments than shared by DZT pairs. However, they approach the unequal environments in each type of study very differently. Table 7.2 shows the differing ways that most leading behavioral geneticists approach and interpret family study data, versus the ways they approach and interpret data produced by twin method MZT–DZT comparisons.

In Table 7.2 we see that most behavioral genetic researchers recognize that the comparison groups in both family studies and twin studies experience different environments. In assessing the results of family studies, they make no "family members create their own environments" or "trait-relevant" qualifications about how they should interpret data derived from these differing environments. For most behavioral geneticists, the simple recognition that family members share common environments is enough to invalidate genetic interpretations of family studies. Leading behavioral genetic researchers such as Robert Plomin and colleagues then correctly conclude that "family studies by themselves cannot disentangle genetic and environmental influences" (Plomin, DeFries, et al., 2013, p. 191).

However, with the twin method and *its* differing environments, behavioral geneticists usually invoke *Argument A* and/or *Argument B* and conclude the opposite—that the twin method is, according to Plomin and colleagues, one of the "workhorses of human behavioral genetics that help to disentangle genetic and environmental sources of familial resemblance" (Plomin, DeFries, et al., 2013, p. 35). Whereas behavioral genetic researchers correctly see family studies as unable to disentangle potential genetic and environmental influences, they see the twin method as *able* to disentangle these influences. In doing so, however, they arbitrarily choose to apply a standard to family studies that they choose not to apply to the twin method, and then arrive at entirely different conclusions about each research method.

The error lies in the contrasting behavioral genetic and psychiatric genetic evaluations of family studies and the twin method. There should be no such contrast because these two research methods are equally either able, or unable, to disentangle the potential influences of genes and environment. Therefore, because the comparison groups in both types of studies experience very different environments, both must be assessed in the same way.

A 2012 Defense of the Equal Environment Assumption

Beginning with a twin study of political attitudes and ideology published in 2005 (Alford et al., 2005), the political science field has seen a major growth of genetic research.[4] At the same time, like other social

Table 7.2 Behavioral Genetic and Psychiatric Genetic Interpretations of Research Findings: Family Studies versus the Twin Method

Type of Study	Environments of Comparison Groups	Qualifications Invoked by Behavioral Geneticists and Psychiatric Geneticists	Conclusion Reached by Most Behavioral Geneticists and Psychiatric Geneticists
Family Studies	**Different:** Family members experience much more similar environments than those experienced by members of the general population	**None** (No claim that family members create or elicit more similar environments for themselves because they are more similar genetically; no requirement that family members must be shown to experience more similar *trait-relevant* environments than those experienced by members of the general population; no denial that families share a common environment as well as common genes)	*Unable* to disentangle potential environmental and genetic factors. Therefore, a family study by itself provides no conclusive evidence in support of genetics "Many behaviors 'run in families,' but family resemblance can be due either to nature or nurture." (Plomin, DeFries, Knopik, & Neiderhiser, 2013, p. 74)
The Twin Method	**Different:** Reared-together monozygotic twin pairs (MZTs) experience much more similar environments than those experienced by reared-together same-sex dizygotic pairs (DZTs)	1. *Argument A:* MZT pairs create or elicit more similar environments for themselves because they are more similar genetically, *and/or* 2. *Argument B:* It must be shown that MZT pairs experience more similar *trait-relevant* environments than those experienced by DZT pairs (they usually conclude that this has not been shown), *or* 3. *Ignoring or denying:* Failure to address the issue of MZT and DZT environments (thereby tacitly accepting twin method assumptions), or occasional claims that the environments are not different	*Able* to disentangle potential genetic and environmental factors. Therefore, the twin method by itself provides conclusive evidence in support of genetics *"The twin method is a valuable tool for screening behavioral dimensions and disorders for genetic influences."* (Plomin, DeFries, et al., 2013, p. 83)

Adapted from Jay Joseph (2013c), "The Use of the Classical Twin Method in the Social and Behavioral Sciences: The Fallacy Continues." *Journal of Mind and Behavior*, 34, p. 11. © The Institute of Mind and Behavior, Inc., P.O. Box 522, Village Station, New York City, New York, 10014.

and behavioral science areas, attempts to identify genes for political characteristics have been unsuccessful (Charney & English, 2012; Hatemi & McDermott, 2012; Hatemi et al., 2014).

Here I focus on an attempt by Kevin Smith and a group of leading genetic researchers in political science (Smith et al., 2012)[5] to test the validity of the EEA and the twin method in the face of challenges both from within their field (Charney, 2008a, 2008b; Suhay, Kalmoe, & McDermott, 2007) and outside of their field (Beckwith & Morris, 2008; Joseph, 2010b). Indeed, Alford, Funk, and Hibbing had previously written, correctly, that the EEA "is crucial to everything that follows from twin research" (Alford et al., 2005, p. 155).

Smith and colleagues believed that twin research has shown that "political attitudes are inherited" to some degree (p. 17), and seemed puzzled that despite the "consistency" of twin study results, "their validity has been consistently challenged on a number of key issues" (p. 18). What many critics have argued, however, is that twin researchers have *consistently misinterpreted* the results of twin studies in the social and behavioral sciences in favor of genetics. Smith and colleagues wrote that the critics' "central argument" is that studies using the twin method "inflate heritability estimates and do not accurately account for environmental-based sources of variance in political attitudes due to several specific shortcomings in the model" (p. 19). As we saw in Chapter 4, however, some critics have entirely rejected the validity of heritability estimates in the social and behavioral sciences and have also argued that, in most cases, MZT–DZT differences are caused entirely by non-genetic factors.

The investigators chose to emphasize the point that, according to their definition of the EEA, "the assumption is *not that MZs and DZs have equal environmental experiences*" (Smith et al., 2012, p. 19, italics in original). They recognized that it is "well known, for example, that MZs are more likely to be dressed alike, share the same bedroom, and have the same friends." However, "the EEA assumes that these more similar environmental experiences do not lead to a greater co-twin similarity on the specific trait being studied" (p. 19). Their defense of the EEA, therefore, initially was based on *Argument B*.

Smith and colleagues focused on a 2007 critique of twin research in political science by Elizabeth Suhay and colleagues, who summarized four common arguments that critics have put forward for decades (Suhay et al., 2007). *Point 1* states that MZT pairs have more similar experiences than DZT pairs; *Point 2* is that MZTs experience a greater mutual influence than DZTs; *Point 3* is that MZT pairs are treated more similarly than DZT pairs; *Point 4* is that MZT pairs share more similar prenatal (intrauterine) environments than DZT pairs. Let us now briefly examine how Smith and colleagues responded to these four major points.

Points # 1 and # 2: MZT Pairs Have More Similar Experiences, and Influence Each Other More, Than DZT Pairs

Smith and colleagues saw Points 1 and 2 (similar experiences and mutual influence) as being related to "similarities in the social environment and as such are consistent with traditional social science explanations for political attitudes and behaviors" (p. 29). In an attempt to test the potential impact of similar experiences and mutual influence on twin resemblance for political characteristics, they analyzed data they obtained from 596 reared-together adult twin pairs (356 MZT, 240 DZT) based on the University of Minnesota Twin Registry.[6]

The political characteristic they chose to test was "ideology," as assessed by the Wilson-Patterson Index. The Index is said to measure political conservatism, and consists simply of labels or catchphrases of supposedly controversial issues (e.g., "socialism," "mixed marriage," "bible truth," "pyjama parties," "jazz," "women drivers," "learning Latin," "chaperones," and "striptease shows"), to which respondents answer "yes," "no," or "?" (uncertain; Wilson & Patterson, 1968, p. 266). Smith and colleagues provided no evidence or citations in support of the validity of the Wilson-Patterson Index.[7]

The researchers produced a table of MZT and DZT Wilson-Patterson correlations as a product of varying levels of environmental similarity, assessed by twins' answers to questions such as how often you "See your twin," "Talk to your twin on the telephone," "Communicate with twin via text/email," "Attended same classes at school," "Dressed alike when growing up," "Shared the same bedroom at home," and "Had the same friends growing up" (Smith et al., 2012, p. 22). Instead of listing twin correlations for each response, the authors arbitrarily combined differing responses into one score. To the question of whether twins were dressed alike when growing up, the only correlations listed in the table were the combined response categories "always/usually" and "sometimes/rarely/never." For the "Shared the same bedroom at home?" question, the possible responses were "always," "usually," "sometimes," "rarely," and "never." However, the researchers decided to combine these five possible responses into only two categories: "always," and "usually/sometimes/rarely/never." Perhaps a much different picture of the relationship between twin environmental similarity and Wilson-Patterson correlations would have emerged had the researchers decided to show the correlations for each of the possible responses (for more details, see Joseph, 2013c).

Although Smith and colleagues noted "relatively stable MZ correlations" (p. 22), in part because of the restricted and combined environmental similarity categories they used, they found, "In contrast, DZ ideological similarities display extreme variation depending on levels of adult contact/similarity in childhood experiences" (p. 23). Nevertheless, they continued to weakly uphold the validity of the EEA because "overall, these results strongly suggest that MZ–DZ ideological similarities are not based solely in environmental similarities" (p. 23). Clearly, as the researchers recognized, environmental similarity *does* lead to greater co-twin similarity for political attitudes and behavior. They concluded that "patterns of ideological similarity between MZ and DZ twins do not seem to be fully explained by the mechanisms proposed by EEA critics" (Smith et al., 2012, p. 30). This is hardly a ringing endorsement of the twin method. In fact, it could serve as the epitaph of the twin method.

From Argument B . . . to Argument A

Although Smith and colleagues initially defined the EEA in its *Argument B* form, they worked *Argument A* into their analysis as well, writing that "it is . . . possible that ideological similarity leads to environmental similarity":

> If, *as twin studies suggest*, there is a genetic predisposition toward ideology, this in turn raises the possibility that there is a genetic component underlying the environmental variation reported by twins. This latter view already has considerable empirical support.
> (Smith et al., 2012, p. 28, italics added)

Here they argued that "there is a genetic component underlying the environmental variation reported by twins," which they supported with the claim that "twin studies suggest" that this is the case—thereby assuming the validity of previous twin studies in an attempt to validate current twin studies. They concluded, "Environmental similarities seem to influence similarities in political temperament, but this influence is mediated by genes" (Smith et al., 2012, p. 23). This means that they ultimately validated the EEA more on the basis of *Argument A* than on *Argument B*.

Point # 3: Is More Similar Treatment (Based on Similar Appearance) a Genetic Effect?

We have seen that most twin researchers have recognized for decades that MZT pairs are treated more alike by parents and others than are DZT pairs, and we saw in Table 7.1 that MZT pairs experience much greater levels of identity confusion and attachment than DZT pairs. Rather than focus on the role of treatment in general, Smith and colleagues chose to focus only on the more similar treatment elicited by MZTs' more similar *physical appearance*, conceding that "there is some basis for such an expectation" (p. 29). However, they mistakenly counted this as a genetic effect, arguing that "whatever variation in ideological similarity [that] can be attributed to physical appearance has an indisputably genetic basis. Even critics of twin studies concede that MZ twin pairs look more alike than DZ pairs because of their close genetic relationship" (p. 29). This position, in fact, is very disputable.

Charney has pointed to the "fallacious nature" of counting treatment effects based on appearance as genetic effects. As an example, people with the inherited trait of black skin color were forced into slavery, and he asked, "Are we to assume then, that the effects upon blacks of their enslavement by European whites were *genetic,* because slavery was 'caused' or 'elicited' or 'created' by the genetic trait of black skin color?" (Charney, 2008b, p. 337, italics in original). Based on the logic of Smith and colleagues' position, the status of being a slave should have been seen as an "indisputably" strongly genetic trait, because virtually all variation in the population of the Confederacy for the status of being a "slave" or a "non-slave" was attributed to the inherited trait of dark skin color.

Smith and colleagues wondered "whether physical appearance systematically creates an environment that socializes individuals into a particular set of political attitudes" (p. 29). To the extent that this might be occurring, however, it is clearly an environmental effect on twin behavioral resemblance.

Point # 4: Do Prenatal (Intrauterine) Environmental Differences Support Genetic Interpretations?

Continuing the theme of counting what are in fact environmental influences on twin pair resemblance as genetic influences, and of conflating potential biological and genetic influences on behavioral characteristics, Smith and colleagues addressed the argument that MZTs' more similar prenatal (intrauterine) environment might further confound MZT–DZT comparisons. They argued that this position "brings critics of twin studies into agreement with proponents on a key issue, namely the importance of biological precursors of adult ideology that are present at birth, and strengthens rather than weakens our call to reexamine the epistemological foundations of the discipline" (p. 30).

Biological and genetic influences are not, however, the same thing, and in many cases biological causes are *environmental* causes. Although it is true that every genetic influence must have a corresponding biological impact, the reverse is not true: many biological influences are not genetic or inherited. The measles virus is one of countless such examples. Death caused by rattlesnake venom is another. As Gottesman and Hanson pointed out, "Everything that is genetic is biological, but not all things biological are genetic" (Gottesman & Hanson, 2005, p. 265).

Another example would be a twin study of birth defects. In such a study, all twin pairs would be born to mothers who had been prescribed the drug thalidomide in the 1950s and 1960s, which was subsequently shown to cause birth defects in children born to these mothers. As Smith and colleagues recognized (p. 29), in the intrauterine setting, MZT pairs share a more similar placental and chorionic environment than experienced by DZTs (Bulmer, 1970). This means that MZT pairs would be more similarly exposed to thalidomide and other potential toxins prenatally than would DZT pairs.

Suppose a group of twin researchers finds that the MZT correlation for thalidomide-related birth defects is 60 percent, but only 15 percent for the DZT pairs. This finding would be the result of a biological agent (thalidomide) affecting MZTs more similarly than DZTs prenatally. The differing correlations would be explained by biological factors, but *not* by genetic factors, and any conclusion in favor of genetics and a 90 percent heritability estimate for birth defects would clearly be mistaken (though welcomed by the manufacturers of thalidomide). As Shields correctly pointed out in 1962, "Differences between monozygotic twins can still be regarded as environmentally determined even when due to factors whose onset is natal or prenatal" (Shields, 1962, p. 5).[8]

So even in the unlikely event that biological agents shared to a greater degree by MZT versus DZT pairs in the intrauterine environment contribute to the former's greater resemblance for political characteristics as adults, this would do nothing to support the theoretical basis of the twin method. On the contrary, this finding would constitute yet another environmental influence confounding genetic interpretations of twin method data.

Smith and colleagues concluded that even if the critics are "wholly correct" that the causes of MZT–DZT differences are "exclusively environmental," this finding would "provide reasons for political science to pay more rather than less attention to the biological basis of attitudes and behaviors" (p. 17). It is illogical, however, to state that political scientists should "pay more attention" to biological influences on political attitudes and behaviors if explanations for MZT–DZT differences are "exclusively environmental." This is similar to calling "heads" when flipping a coin with a "genetic/biological" heads stamped on both sides, and by no means were Smith and colleagues the first group of twin researchers to employ such faulty reasoning.

"An Obviously Confounded, Unreliable Methodology"

Smith and colleagues thus join a long list of twin researchers who, based on their acceptance of the MZT–DZT EEA fallacy, mistakenly concluded in favor of genetic influences on behaviors intuitively and traditionally understood as being caused by non-genetic factors. Twin studies of this type include those looking at characteristics such as breakfast eating patterns (Keski-Rahkonen, Viken, Kaprio, Rissanen & Rose, 2004), the status of being a "born again Christian" (Bradshaw & Ellison, 2008), cell phone use (Miller, Zhu, Wright, Hansell, & Martin, 2012), drunk driving convictions (Anum, Silberg, & Retchin, 2014), ethnocentrism (Orey & Park, 2012), finger-sucking and nail-biting in childhood (Ooki, 2005), frequency of orgasm in women (Dawood, Kirk, Bailey, Andrews, & Martin, 2005), happiness (Bartels & Boomsma, 2009), loneliness (Boomsma, Willemsen, Dolan, Hawkley, & Cacioppo, 2005), physical activity in young adults (Mustelin et al., 2012), problematic masturbatory behavior in children (Långström, Grann, & Lichtenstein, 2002), tea and coffee drinking preferences (Luciano, Kirk, Heath, & Martin, 2005), and voter turnout (Loewen & Dawes, 2012).

Perhaps the twin method has shown that all of these characteristics have an important genetic basis, but a much better interpretation of the results is that the twin method's EEA is false, and that genetic interpretations of MZT–DZT comparisons are mistaken. As Charney concluded, "That twin studies generate results that even partisans of the methodology acknowledge as absurd is further evidence that they are to many what they have always seemed to be: an obviously confounded, unreliable methodology" (Charney, 2013a, p. 560).

Conclusions

Although the twin method is based on the assumption that MZT and DZT pairs experience roughly equal childhood and adult environments, twin researchers have acknowledged for decades that these environments are in fact very different. In this chapter I have attempted to show that efforts by twin researchers to uphold the validity of the twin method and its all-important EEA, by using *Argument A* and/or *Argument B*, do not hold up to critical examination.

The two main competing explanations for the usual twin method finding that MZTs resemble each other more (correlate higher) than same-sex DZTs for IQ, personality, psychiatric disorders, criminality, and other behavioral characteristics are:

1. Based on *accepting* the EEA, the greater behavioral resemblance of MZT versus DZT pairs indicates that important genetic influences underlie most human behavioral differences and behavioral (psychiatric) disorders; or
2. Based on *rejecting* the EEA, the greater behavioral resemblance of MZT versus DZT pairs is caused entirely by non-genetic influences, and all interpretations of MZT–DZT comparisons in favor of genetics must be rejected.

Based on the much more plausible "Explanation #2" position, we can conclude that previously reported twin method MZT–DZT comparisons in the social and behavioral sciences have recorded nothing more than the role of *non*-genetic influences on human behavioral characteristics.

Critics have argued for decades that the twin method is unable to disentangle the potential roles of genetic and environmental influences, and genetic researchers in political science have been no more able than their predecessors in behavioral genetics, psychiatric genetics, and other areas of psychology and psychiatry to provide convincing arguments otherwise. Acceptance of the Explanation #2 position does not mean that twin studies "overestimate heritability," or that researchers should assess the EEA on a study-by-study basis, but instead indicates that the twin method is no more able than a family study to disentangle the potential influences of genes and environment. In other words, the twin method is clearly unable to disentangle these influences. This leads to the conclusion that *genetic interpretations of all past, present, and future MZT–DZT twin method comparisons in the social and behavioral sciences must be rejected outright.*

Notes

1 Chapter 7 is based on a condensed, updated, and revised version of an article appearing in *The Journal of Mind and Behavior* (Joseph, 2013c).
2 My own first attempt to articulate this position appeared in 1998 (Joseph, 1998).
3 The results in Table 7.1 are taken from all twin studies I am aware of that provided percentage figures (or enough information to calculate percentages) based on twins' responses to questions relating to attachment and identity issues.
4 In political science, the twin method is frequently called the "CTD," or "classic twin design."
5 Coauthor Lindon Eaves is not a political scientist, but has worked with others in the field.
6 Afterwards, they decided to replicate their analysis on the basis of additional data they obtained from a different twin sample.
7 According to Bouchard and colleagues, writing about the Wilson-Patterson Conservatism Scale, its "'catch phrase' format strikes many psychologists as inadequate and of doubtful validity. We concurred with this judgment, but because of the scale's brevity and the strong genetic influence on the Conservatism score derived from this instrument reported by Martin and colleagues (1986), we incorporated it into the MISTRA assessment" (Bouchard et al., 2004, p. 97). Thus, despite its "doubtful validity," Bouchard and colleagues decided to use the Index in their TRA study because of its "brevity," and because a previous group of twin researchers (Martin et al., 1986), based on their acceptance of the validity of both the Index and the MZT–DZT equal environment assumption, concluded in favor of strong genetic influences on conservatism.
8 Political scientist John Hibbing, one of the co-authors of Smith and colleagues' 2012 study, in an essay published the following year listed the idea that

"biology is genetics" as the "#1 misconception concerning neurobiology and politics" (Hibbing, 2013, p. 476). Hibbing listed three examples of the "misconception" that biology and genetics are the same, one of which was related to the intrauterine (prenatal) environment, and wrote, "Note that none of these examples has anything to do with genetics yet each is heavily biological" (Hibbing, 2013, p. 476). Hibbing was right, yet one year earlier he and his colleagues conflated potential biological and genetic influences in their defense of the EEA and the twin method.

8
TWIN RESEARCH IN PSYCHIATRY

> Twin studies are a more compelling form of genetic data [than family studies], but even twin studies depend on the assumption that the only thing that differentiates monozygotic from dizygotic twins is their genetic relatedness, and that environmental factors are somehow canceled out or randomized. But that is not the case. Monozygotic twins share much of their environment as well as their genetic endowment. They live together; they sleep together; they are dressed alike by parents; they are paraded in a double parambulator [sic] as infants; their friends cannot distinguish one from the other. In short, they develop a certain ego identification with each other that is very hard to dissociate from the purely genetic identity with which they were born.
> — Psychiatric Genetic Adoption Researcher Seymour Kety, 1978 (Kety, 1978, p. 48)
>
> In addition to the problems of diagnosis of zygosity, the validity of the [twin method] assumption of equal environmental variance within sets of fraternal and identical twins is questionable.
> — Pioneering Behavioral Geneticist John DeFries, 1967 (DeFries, 1967, p. 328)

Twin studies supply the main pillar of support for the position that genetic factors play an important role in causing psychiatric disorders. Adoption studies are much fewer in number and are subject to several potentially invalidating methodological problems and questionable assumptions (see Chapter 1).[1] The leaders of psychiatry, and its subfield of psychiatric genetics, have argued for decades that the evidence shows conclusively that conditions such as depression, schizophrenia, bipolar disorder (manic depression), autism, antisocial personality disorder, and ADHD have an important genetic basis and are "moderately heritable" or "highly heritable."[2] Researchers frequently refer to these conditions as "multifactorial complex disorders," which means that they view them as being caused by the effects of multiple genes in combination with multiple environmental factors. This idea is based on the earlier predisposition-stress (diathesis-stress) theory of psychiatric disorders.

The predisposition-stress/multifactorial complex disorder position has been very successful in establishing the idea that psychiatric disorders have an important genetic basis. Psychologist Mary Boyle observed that it has been effective in part because of its seeming inclusiveness and reasonableness in the sense that "who could deny that biological and psychological or social factors interact?" At the same time, she pointed out that the model "firmly maintains the primacy of biology, not least through word order, and potentially de-emphasizes the environment by making it look as if the 'stress' part of the vulnerability-stress model consists of ordinary stresses which most of us would cope with, but which overwhelm only 'vulnerable' people" (Boyle, 2002a). Boyle noted that by "inserting an unspecified innate vulnerability between the person and their environment, the claimed vulnerability and not the environment becomes the focus of concern" (Boyle, 2007, p. 291).

The psychiatric genetics field was founded in Germany by Ernst Rüdin and others in the early twentieth century. Genetic studies of psychiatric disorders have been the main focus of the field (Joseph, 2004; Joseph & Wetzel, 2013; Weiss, 2010). The first psychiatric twin study was a 1928 schizophrenia investigation published by Rüdin's associate Hans Luxenburger (Luxenburger, 1928). Although they recognize a role for environmental factors, psychiatric genetic researchers and popularizers of their work emphasize the centrality of perceived genetic factors, and focus their research in this area while promoting the use of genetic counseling for prospective parents, which may lead to reducing the births of children seen as being predisposed to develop mental disorders (Faraone, Tsuang, & Tsuang, 1999, pp. 160–188; Hoge & Appelbaum, 2008).

Psychiatric genetic research and theories are integrated into mainstream psychiatric thinking, and the search for genetic variants predisposing for psychiatric disorders has been underway since the 1960s and earlier (Joseph, 2013b; McGuffin & Sturt, 1986). False-positive reports date back to the 1960s, when researchers attempting to uncover genes for "manic-depressive disease" (now known as bipolar disorder) concluded that "affective disorder in which mania occurs is probably linked to the X chromosome . . . . This finding clarifies some aspects of transmission. It also *proves* a genetic factor in manic-depressive disease" (Reich, Clayton, & Winokur, 1969, p. 1367, italics added). Subsequently non-replicated gene-finding claims have been a central feature of psychiatry for decades, and continue into the current period.

Psychiatry and psychiatric genetics have been shaken by the fact that decades of gene-finding attempts have failed to produce the genes presumed to underlie the major psychiatric disorders—genes that they were expecting to find by the late 1980s (a point discussed in more detail in

Chapters 9 and 10). The following statement is taken from an official American Psychiatric Association (APA) press release by the DSM-5 Task Force. The DSM (*Diagnostic and Statistical Manual of the American Psychiatric Association*) is the official APA publication listing psychiatric disorders and the criteria needed to diagnose them. The Fifth Edition (DSM-5) was released in the spring of 2013 after years of delay (APA, 2013b).[3] In the press release, Task Force head David Kupfer stated,

> In the future, we hope to be able to identify disorders using biological and genetic markers that provide precise diagnoses that can be delivered with complete reliability and validity. Yet this promise, which we have anticipated since the 1970s, remains disappointingly distant. We've been telling patients for several decades that we are waiting for biomarkers. We're still waiting.
> (APA, 2013a)

From another perspective, psychiatry has been telling patients and the public for decades that people carrying psychiatric diagnoses have "chemical imbalances" caused by faulty genes. Yet here we have an official communication from the APA in effect admitting that, as Mary Boyle once put it, such claims were based on "smoke and mirrors" (Boyle, 2002a). Kupfer and the APA wrote that psychiatry has been "anticipating" the identification of biological and genetic markers "since the 1970s," yet they refuse to consider the possibility that previously held genetic theories in psychiatry are simply wrong. The question then becomes: How many more decades must psychiatry wait until it decides to reexamine these theories?

Kupfer and the APA admitted that they have no genes for psychiatric disorders, only the inference of genes based largely on genetic interpretations of the results of psychiatric twin studies. This has been the case for decades, yet psychiatry has steadfastly refused to critically examine the twin and adoption studies upon which expected gene discoveries are based. It is a telling point that American psychiatry, which since 1970 has created over 30 "task forces" to examine various issues, has never created a task force charged with undertaking an in-depth critical evaluation of the assumptions of psychiatric twin studies.[4]

Stephen Faraone, Ming Tsuang, and their psychiatric genetic colleagues admitted in 2008, "It is no secret that our field has published thousands of candidate gene association studies but few replicated findings" (Faraone, Smoller, Pato, Sullivan, & Tsuang, 2008, p. 1). This statement is as true today as it was in 2008, and in 2013 Faraone complained about the decades-old "nonreplication curse" in psychiatric molecular genetic research (Faraone, 2013, p. 1007). But in a sense non-replication *is* a secret because the general public has been told a very different story. Almost every month, it seems, yet another (subsequently non-replicated) "gene discovery" for depression, bipolar disorder, schizophrenia, anorexia nervosa, and other disorders is announced with great fanfare in the media. The most recent claims (for example, see Arehart-Treichel, 2014; Schizophrenia Working Group of the Psychiatric Genomics Consortium, 2014; Wright, 2014) are likely to suffer the same fate as similar non-replicated claims we have heard about for decades, easily found in Google searches for terms such as "schizophrenia gene discovery," "ADHD gene discovery," "autism gene discovery," "bipolar gene discovery," and in the online archives of scientific journals that have published these "thousands" of subsequently non-replicated gene-finding claims (for example, *The American Journal of Psychiatry*, *American Journal of Medical Genetics Part B*, and *Molecular Psychiatry*).

Science writer John Horgan wrote in 2013 about decades of well-publicized claims announcing the discovery of "genes for" behaviors such as "high IQ, gambling, attention-deficit disorder, obsessive-compulsive disorder, bipolar disorder, schizophrenia, autism, dyslexia, alcoholism, heroin addiction, extroversion, introversion, anxiety, anorexia nervosa, seasonal affective disorder, violent aggression—and so on." Horgan took note of the fact that "so far, not one of these claims has been consistently confirmed by follow-up studies" (Horgan, 2013). Given the decades-long track record of these and other highly publicized yet non-replicated claims, *we must assume that all gene discovery claims in psychiatry are false-positive findings until proven otherwise.*

In this chapter I will discuss twin research in psychiatry from a critical perspective, using as little technical jargon as possible. I will therefore largely steer clear of tables, figures, and statistics. My purpose here is to show, as simply as possible, how reliance on twin research and the mistaken acceptance of its underlying assumptions has misled psychiatry and psychiatric genetics in much the same way as behavioral genetics and other behavioral and social science fields have been misled.

The Equal Environment Assumption in Psychiatric Twin Research

Apart from a MISTRA study of substance abuse/dependence and antisocial personality (Grove et al., 1990), all psychiatric twin studies assessing genetic influences are based on twin method comparisons of MZT versus same-sex DZT pairs reared together in the same home. This means that the validity (or non-validity) of the MZT–DZT EEA is the crucial factor in assessing the results of psychiatric twin studies, even though many people unfamiliar with twin research in psychiatry assume that twins are reared apart. They are not. We saw in Chapter 7 that MZTs in fact grow up experiencing much more similar environments than DZTs, and that attempts by twin researchers to redefine or qualify the EEA do not hold up to critical examination.

After defining the disorder in question and obtaining a twin sample, psychiatric twin researchers calculate MZT and same-sex DZT concordance rates. Concordance rates are used instead of correlations when a disorder or a characteristic is categorical or binary (affected, or not affected), as opposed to "continuously distributed" characteristics such as IQ and personality, where people and their scores are seen as falling on a continuum. When both members of a twin pair are similarly diagnosed they are counted as a *concordant* pair; when one is diagnosed and the other is not, they are *discordant*. For example, after identifying 100 MZT twin pairs where one is diagnosed with schizophrenia, if in 30 of these pairs the second twin is also diagnosed with schizophrenia, concordance would be 30 percent (and discordance would be 70 percent). Assuming that the schizophrenia rate in the general population is roughly 1 percent, in this example the co-twin of a member of an MZT pair is diagnosed with schizophrenia at a rate roughly 30 times greater than a chance 1 percent finding. A similar procedure is performed with DZT pairs, and MZT and DZT concordance rates are then compared.[5] If researchers find that the MZT concordance rate is significantly higher than the DZT rate, based on the validity of the EEA they conclude that the disorder is influenced by genetic factors, and then calculate heritability estimates based on the difference between MZT and DZT concordance, or based on the results of biometrical model-fitting techniques (see Chapter 4). They conclude that most psychiatric disorders are moderately or highly heritable.

We saw in Chapter 7 that, until the mid-1960s, twin researchers used the traditional definition of the EEA, which states without qualification that MZT and DZT childhood and adult environments are roughly equal. Since that time, the vast majority of psychiatric genetic researchers have upheld the EEA on the basis of *Argument A* and/or *Argument B* (also discussed in Chapter 7), while in some cases researchers do not discuss the EEA at all, thereby tacitly accepting its validity. As seen in Appendix C, leading psychiatric twin researchers past and present attempting to uphold the EEA on the basis of *Argument A* include Avshalom Caspi, Lindon Eaves, Jonathan Flint, Irving Gottesman, Kenneth Kendler, Einar Kringlen, Franz Kallmann, Michael Lyons, Nicholas Martin, Robert Plomin, Carol Prescott, David Rowe, Michael Rutter, James Shields, and Ming Tsuang.

It is beyond question that MZT pairs resemble each other more (are more concordant) than DZT pairs for most psychiatric disorders and behavioral characteristics. Critics usually do not dispute this, but have instead focused on the validity of the EEA and therefore disagree with psychiatric genetic and mainstream psychiatric *interpretations* of this pervasive finding. Although critics have documented numerous methodological flaws and biases in psychiatric twin research, the fundamental question is how we should interpret the results.

Psychiatric Genetic Defenses of the EEA

Kendler

Psychiatric genetic researchers usually cite the body of "EEA-test" studies in support of the validity of the EEA, and conclude that the assumption, and genetic interpretations of psychiatric twin studies, are valid or are at least "reasonable." Although recognizing that MZTs experience more similar environments than DZTs, Kenneth Kendler of the Virginia Institute for Psychiatric and Behavioral Genetics has been the strongest and most widely published supporter of this position in psychiatry (for example, see Kendler, 1983, 1993, 2000; Kendler & Prescott, 2006). Kendler has defended genetic interpretations of psychiatric twin studies on the basis of *Argument A*, writing in 1983 that "studies have shown that the similarity of the social environment of monozygotic twins is the result and not the cause of their behavioral similarity" (Kendler, 1983, p. 1422).

In 1987, Kendler wrote, "Although the similarity in environment might make MZ twins more similar, the similarity in behavior of MZ twins might *create* for themselves more similar environments. As recently reviewed . . . these two alternative hypotheses have been subject to empirical test in at least nine different studies." Kendler concluded that "these studies suggest that the environmental similarity of MZ twins is the *result* and not the cause of their behavioral similarity," and that "current evidence supports the general validity of the equal environment assumption of twin studies" (Kendler, 1987, p. 706, italics in original). In this passage, Kendler recognized that MZT pairs experience more similar environments than DZT pairs, but again upheld the EEA on the basis of the *Argument A* position that MZTs create more similar environments for themselves because they are more similar genetically—an untenable argument, as seen in Chapter 7. We saw in Chapter 7 that Kendler also invoked the *Argument B* "trait-relevant" position in defense of psychiatric twin studies.

Kendler has written since 1983 that the EEA has been tested and upheld in several different ways (Kendler, 1983; Kendler & Prescott, 2006). In a highly qualified and somewhat tortuous fashion, in a 1993 article he concluded, "With some uniformity, the available evidence suggests that the EEA is probably at least approximately correct for the normative traits and psychiatric disorders studied" (Kendler, 1993, p. 907). It appears that even the EEA's leading defender had at least some doubts about the assumption, and this conclusion, which appeared in a leading psychiatric journal (*Archives of General Psychiatry*, now *JAMA Psychiatry*) once again is hardly a ringing endorsement of the twin method and the EEA.

Although Kendler and others cite the EEA-test literature in their defenses of psychiatric twin studies, these EEA-test researchers concentrate only on particular issues they choose to focus on, while overlooking abundant evidence, both statistical and from the actual lives of twins and non-twins, that argues strongly against the validity of the EEA. For example, they usually ignore the evidence, seen in Table 7.1, that MZTs experience much higher levels of identity confusion and attachment than experienced by DZT pairs.

In addition to the findings reported in Table 7.1, an example of evidence running counter to the EEA that is largely ignored by twin researchers is that the pooled schizophrenia concordance rate across all studies that compiled such figures is 11.3 percent for *same-sex* DZTs (59/523), but only 4.7 percent for *opposite-sex* DZTs (20/422; Joseph, 2006, p. 129). An additional 2007 study of 29,602 Swedish twin pairs, which recorded hospitalization rates for psychosis and other psychiatric disorders, revealed that same-sex DZT psychosis correlations were two to three times higher than the opposite-sex DZT correlations (Prescott, Kuhn, & Pedersen, 2007, p. 553). Because both types of DZT pairs share the same genetic relationship to each other (50 percent on average), according to genetic theory same- and opposite-sex DZT concordance rates should be similar (see Joseph, 2004, pp. 176–178). However, the results show that the more similar treatment, closeness, and psychological association experienced by same-sex DZTs lead them to resemble each other more for schizophrenia or psychosis at a rate two to three times greater than the rate among opposite-sex DZT pairs. Even though psychiatric geneticists have been aware of the same-sex versus opposite-sex DZT concordance rate difference for over half a century, I am not aware of any genetic researcher attempting to explain these differences in terms of genetics (see Gottesman & Shields, 1966a; Jackson, 1960; Rosenthal, 1962). For Kendler and others, this remarkable finding in the schizophrenia twin literature does not count as "available evidence" in their evaluations of the EEA, because they choose not to count it as such.

If non-genetic factors cause same-sex DZTs to be concordant for schizophrenia two to three times more often than opposite-sex DZT pairs, similar factors could completely explain observed concordance rate differences between MZTs and DZTs for schizophrenia and other psychiatric disorders.

As I showed in *The Gene Illusion*, many leading psychiatric twin researchers of the post World War II era recognized that environmental factors explain part—but in their opinion only part—of higher MZT concordance rates (Joseph, 2004, pp. 171–175). For example, in the process of arguing that twin studies are "still our best method," Kringlen wrote in 1976, "The total difference in concordance rate between MZ and DZ twins cannot be ascribed to genetic factors only. A series of studies of both normal and abnormal twins show that the environment of the MZ twin pair is more similar than the environment of the DZ twin pair" (Kringlen, 1976, p. 431). And according to founding behavioral geneticists Fuller and Thompson, "Perhaps the best judgment is that part of the greater similarity between MZ cotwins comes from the fact that they are treated more alike by parents and associates" (Fuller & Thompson, 1960, p. 113). Contemporary defenders of psychiatric twin research usually fail to acknowledge that most of their predecessors believed that some portion of MZT–DZT concordance rate differences are caused by environmental factors.

Returning to the "EEA-test" studies, let's imagine that several teams of researchers decide to conduct a series of studies to test their counterintuitive yet strongly held belief that the sun never shines on New York City. Let us also imagine that their academic careers, research funding, and affiliations are based on this belief. If these researchers decide to perform their studies only between the hours of 11:00 p.m. and 3:00 a.m., they would unanimously conclude that the "available evidence" suggests that the sun never shines on New York City! Studies carried out by twin researchers testing the "validity of the EEA" hypothesis do pretty much the same thing, and, carrying the analogy further, they sometimes unexpectedly find sunshine and attribute it to darkness (usually by invoking *Argument A*). In an EEA-test study cited by Kendler in several publications (e.g., Kendler, 1993; Kendler & Prescott, 2006), for example, a team of Australian researchers led by A. Morris-Yates found that MZTs experience more similar environments than DZTs, and also correlate more similarly on personality tests. These researchers could have concluded that the EEA is false, but instead reasoned,

> On the basis of several indicators of environmental similarity, the equal environments assumption appears to be invalid. This appearance is deceptive, however. Closer analysis suggests that a large component of the greater similarity of MZs environment during childhood and early adolescence is a consequence of their genetic identity.

Therefore, they concluded "for the purposes of most analyses, the equal environments assumption is valid" (Morris-Yates, Andrews, Howie, & Henderson, 1990, p. 325).

Morris-Yates and colleagues concluded that the EEA "appears to be invalid," but in the very next sentence decided that this conclusion is "deceptive" by invoking *Argument A*, allowing them to conclude that "the equal environments assumption is valid." This represents yet another example of genetically oriented researchers' biases compelling them to conclude in favor of genetics when the data suggest otherwise.

We have seen that almost everyone (twin researchers and their critics alike) agrees that MZTs resemble each other more than DZTs for psychiatric disorders, and almost everyone also agrees that MZTs experience more similar environments than same-sex DZTs experience. Therefore, although completely overlooked by Kendler and his fellow psychiatric geneticists and behavioral geneticists, the best-replicated and longest-running test of the EEA ever undertaken consists merely of all the psychiatric twin studies ever performed. Nine decades of psychiatric twin studies have shown, with almost complete uniformity, that pairs experiencing similar environments and high levels of identity confusion and attachment—MZTs—resemble each other more for psychiatric disorders than do pairs experiencing less similar environments and much lower levels of identity confusion and attachment—DZTs. The results of *these* EEA-test studies strongly suggest that the assumption is false.

Flint, Greenspan, and Kendler

A subsequent defense of the EEA and psychiatric twin research is found in a 2010 chapter on schizophrenia in *How Genes Influence Behavior*, which Kendler co-authored (Flint, Greenspan, & Kendler, 2010, pp. 26–31). Here, Jonathan Flint, head of the Psychiatric Genetics Group at the Wellcome Trust Centre for Human Genetics, neurobiologist Ralph Greenspan, and Kendler ignored several publications by critics of psychiatric twin research, instead choosing to focus on Leon Kamin's 1974 critique of IQ twin studies in *The Science and Politics of I.Q.* (see Chapter 3).[6] Flint and colleagues described Kamin as someone "who thinks that twin studies are not worth the paper they are printed on," who argues "in full blood" and "lambasts" twin researchers with his "diatribe," while aiming his "barbs" at the IQ tests themselves. In addition to attacking a critic of research that is only tangentially related to psychiatry, the authors apparently missed the irony that Kamin's decades-old critique finds additional support each passing year as two decades of sustained research have failed to uncover genes that contribute to the normal range of IQ (Bouchard, 2014; Kirkpatrick et al., 2014; see also Chapters 9 and 10). The ongoing failure to find genes for IQ suggests, more than ever, that Kamin was right and that the behavioral geneticists and IQ hereditarians were, and are, wrong.

As Flint and colleagues saw it, the main problem with people like Kamin and his "scorn" for the twin method and the EEA is the "mixing of politics with science that always seem to accompany these studies" (p. 26). Although psychiatric twin researchers more often choose to ignore all of the critics, Flint, Greenspan, and Kendler ignored most of them while pinning their version of the timeworn "politically-motivated ideologue" tag on the author of a decades-old critique of IQ twin studies.[7] This has been a common theme of such writings for decades, and has served as a convenient method to ignore or dismiss the arguments of critics without having to answer them directly. Flint and colleagues thereby continued the long-running practice, described in 1981 by Stephen Jay Gould in *The Mismeasure of Man*, in which genetically oriented researchers and commentators "have often invoked the traditional prestige of science as objective knowledge, free from social and political taint. They portray themselves as purveyors of harsh truth and their opponents as sentimentalists, ideologues, and wishful thinkers" (Gould, 1981, p. 20).

Like other twin researchers, Flint and colleagues cited the body of EEA-test studies in support of the twin method. The only EEA-test study they referred to by name was a 1977 investigation by Canadian psychologist Hugh Lytton (1921–2002), who observed parents and twins interacting in their homes (Lytton, 1977). Flint and colleagues designated this "influential and sophisticated" study as a "Key Paper" in support of the EEA (p. 30). The authors approvingly cited Lytton's *Argument A* conclusion that "parents respond to, rather than create, differences between the twins," after which they concluded, in a similarly circular fashion, "In measuring similarity of treatment or social environments in twin studies, it is important to consider that MZ twins, because of their more similar behavior, can elicit more similar treatment" (Flint et al., 2010, p. 31). Nevertheless, the only relevant question that EEA-test studies can answer is *whether*, not why, MZT pairs experience more similar environments than those experienced by DZT pairs.

Other problem areas in Lytton's frequently cited 1977 EEA-test study include: (a) the small and very young twin sample; (b) potential bias because the raters were not blind to the status of the families; (c) poor inter-rater reliability; and (d) the unsupported claim that one can make a distinction between "child-initiated parental responses" and "parent-initiated actions" (Pam, Kemker, Ross, & Golden, 1996). The raters observed twins and parents interacting in their homes, and in an earlier publication that Lytton referenced as a description of his methods, he wrote, "It is obvious that the introduction of an observer in a home must affect relationships to some extent and produce some distortion of the 'normal' interaction." Lytton also recognized that some parental behavior "may have been staged" (Lytton, 1973, p. 8; for more details on problems in Lytton's frequently cited EEA-test study, see Joseph, 2006, pp. 183–185).

In addition to these major problems with Lytton's study, and his conclusion based on *Argument A*, this "influential and sophisticated" "Key Paper" Flint, Greenspan, and Kendler put forward in support of the EEA and psychiatric twin studies was based on observing parental behavior that, in Lytton's own words, "may have been staged."

In an era when twin researchers wrote much more cautiously about their discipline, Gerald McClearn, a longtime leading behavioral genetic researcher and co-author of the popular multi-edition textbook *Behavioral Genetics*, wrote in 1964 that environmental biases in twin research potentially "vanish" genetic interpretations of MZT–DZT comparisons:

> With these complicating features of the role of environment, the apparent ease of weighing the relative effects of nature and nurture by twin study *vanishes*. The greater disparity observed between fraternals than between identicals may be interpreted as due to heredity or environment or to some indeterminable combination of the two, depending on the predilections of the person making the interpretation.
>
> (McClearn, 1964, p. 196, italics added)

It is indeed the "predilection" of many critics to interpret twin method results solely in terms of the environmental differences distinguishing the two types of twin pairs. Advocates of a purely environmental (non-genetic) understanding of psychiatric disorders therefore predict that psychiatric genetic research will find: (a) familial clustering of the disorder; (b) higher MZT versus same-sex DZT concordance for the disorder; and (c) no replicated gene discoveries for the disorder (Joseph, 2005b, 2006). The past 45 years of psychiatric genetic research have decisively confirmed these predictions.

Problems with Psychiatric Diagnoses

Reliability and Validity

Establishing the reliability and validity of a psychiatric disorder is a prerequisite for any twin study attempting to assess the role of genetic influences. Reliability in psychiatry refers to the ability of psychiatrists to consistently agree on a diagnosis. In the context of psychiatric genetic research, if reliability is low it would follow that many of the participants (subjects) in a study were misdiagnosed. This finding alone would call into question any conclusions in favor of genetics.

A disorder must be valid in addition to being reliable. Validity refers to whether the construct actually exists as a true disorder. In psychiatry, this means that the disorder is assumed to be familial and to have a biological basis (see Feighner et al., 1972). As critics frequently point out, being gay ("homosexuality") used to be counted as an official DSM mental disorder. Now it isn't, because under public pressure in the 1970s the APA voted to remove it from its list of mental disorders. In other words, under social pressure, the APA decided that being gay is not a valid mental disorder (see Greenberg, 2013; Kirk, Gomory, & Cohen, 2013).

In psychiatry, twin studies and accompanying genetic theories play a big role in support of the claim that its diagnoses are valid mental disorders. Although a condition must be reliable in order to be valid, merely being able to reliably identify something does not make it valid. For example, people could agree (and did agree during the sixteenth and seventeenth centuries) on criteria that reliably identify witches, but the concept of "witch" would remain invalid given the lack of evidence that witches exist. Many critics of psychiatry have argued that psychiatric disorders are not reliable or valid discrete illnesses, but rather describe people's varying psychological responses to having experienced adverse events and environments, or are simply disapproved behavior that psychiatry labels as a mental disorder (for example, the DSM's "oppositional-defiant disorder").

Professors of social work Stuart Kirk, Tomy Gomory, and David Cohen showed that there are serious reliability and validity problems in psychiatry, suggesting that research is impaired when it relies on the DSM to diagnose patients with similar problems:

> If their diagnoses are unreliable or invalid, the patients selected for the study would be too heterogeneous in general and in their responses to the same treatment, undermining the conclusions that the researchers may reach. There is emerging evidence that this, in fact, has happened.
>
> (Kirk et al., 2013, p. 197)

These authors were more focused on a lack of reliability and validity as it relates to psychiatric drug trials, but these problems also have important implications for psychiatric twin (and family and adoption) studies because many people diagnosed in these studies may not actually "have" the condition at all.[8] According to the psychologist John Read, co-editor of and contributor to the 2013 Second Edition of *Models of Madness*, "without reliability investigating validity is meaningless. If researchers can't agree on who has 'schizophrenia,' then the supposed properties of 'schizophrenia' cannot be evaluated. The people one researcher studies differ from those studied by other researchers" (Read, 2013b, p. 51).

The APA's admission in its official 2013 press release that psychiatry is "still waiting" for the discovery of biomarkers also relieves critics of the necessity of refuting the purported "smoke and mirrors" evidence in support of psychiatric "brain disease" theories, since the APA has officially done this itself (while continuing to vaguely speculate about alleged "chemical imbalances" and brain "circuitry problems"). Psychiatry and psychiatric genetics use medical terminology and concepts to depict psychiatric disorders as similar to medical conditions, yet there is little evidence that they are medical conditions at all. Psychiatry is where one finds *claimed* brain diseases; neurology is where one finds *real* brain diseases (Kirk et al., 2013; Szasz, 1987).

The failure to demonstrate the reliability, validity, biological basis, and genetic basis of its diagnoses, in addition to its cozy relationship with the makers of highly profitable psychotropic drugs (dubbed "Big Pharma" by the critics), led Kirk and colleagues to view American psychiatry as being based on

> unverified concepts, the invention of new forms of coercion, unremitting disease mongering, the widespread use of treatments with poorly tested and misleading claims of effectiveness, and rampant conflicts of interest that have completely blurred science and marketing. This is the "madness" of American psychiatry, and of psychiatry in much of the world.
>
> (Kirk et al., 2013, p. ix)

Psychiatric labels may have some use in helping clinicians understand and work with clients, as well as to facilitate communication with each other, but their status as discrete, valid medical conditions that can be reliably identified for scientific study, including genetic research, is very questionable.

Moreover, psychiatric labels often have a harmful and stigmatizing effect and can dehumanize people and obscure the meaning of their behavior. The behaviors listed in DSM psychiatric disorder criteria become more understandable when viewed in the context of people's lives and experiences. DSM diagnoses are based on a checklist of behavioral symptoms that usually fail to take the context of the behavior into account. In the words of family therapist Norbert Wetzel,

> DSM 5 categories hardly reflect the often very difficult social and environmental contexts profoundly determining people's lives, such as poverty, social oppression, insufficient housing, violence, racism and sexism, isolation and hunger, lack of job opportunities, visible and subtle forms of injustice, and individual and collective traumatization, particularly in early childhood.
>
> (Wetzel, 2013)

The use of DSM diagnoses in psychiatry, psychology and their allied fields often serves to obscure or even deny the impact of these environmental contexts, while locating the source of illness within the bodies, brains, and genes of those who experience psychological harm caused by these environmental factors.

The DSM-5 and Genetics

In 2002, the developers of DSM-5 published *A Research Agenda for DSM-V*, at a time when gene discoveries appeared imminent to the leaders of psychiatry. This publication, edited by DSM-5 architects David Kupfer, Michael First, and Darrel Regier, consisted of six "white papers" related to the development of the DSM-5 (Kupfer, First, & Regier, 2002). The authors expected that, in the near future, psychiatric diagnoses would be based on neurobiological and genetic discoveries. According to Dennis Charney and colleagues, the authors of one of the white papers, "The field is getting closer" to gene discoveries, "and new advances in genetics (including the availability of the human genome sequence) portend rapid progress" (Charney et al., 2002, p. 34). Like many in psychiatry, including especially its subfield of psychiatric genetics, the Human Genome Project's sequencing of the human genome was expected to lead to the rapid identification of the genes these authors believed underlie psychiatric disorders (see Chapters 9 and 10).

Charney and colleagues put forward a 2002 "speculative outline," which envisioned a future DSM-5 practice of classifying disorders on the basis of a revised Axis I that would be "set aside for recording the patient's *genotype*, identifying symptom- or disease-related genes, resiliency genes, and genes related to therapeutic responses and side effects to specific psychotropic drugs" (p. 71, italics in original). The authors speculated that the future DSM-5, with a projected publication date of 2010, would be based on a revised five-axis diagnostic system based on expected gene discoveries. Charney and colleagues' 2002 "outline for a possible future multiaxial system" read as follows:

- **Axis I: Genotype.** Identification of disease- /symptom-related genes. Identification of resiliency/protective genes. Identification of genes related to therapeutic responses to and side effects of specific psychotropic drugs.
- **Axis II: Neurobiological phenotype.** Identification of intermediate phenotypes (neuroimaging, cognitive function, emotional regulation) related to genotype. Relates to targeted pharmacotherapy.
- **Axis III: Behavioral phenotype.** Range and frequency of expressed behaviors associated with genotype, neurobiological phenotype, and environment. Relates to targeted therapies.
- **Axis IV: Environmental modifiers or precipitants.** Environmental factors that alter the behavioral and neurobiological phenotype.
- **Axis V: Therapeutic targets and response.**

(Charney et al., 2002, pp. 71–72)

This 2002 outline of a future DSM-5 diagnostic scheme leaned heavily on genetics, neurobiology, and psychopharmacological interventions. People's complex life experiences, relationships, and traumas, in addition to their social and political environments, were now reduced to "modifiers or precipitants" of the actions of the expected identification of genes that underlie their psychiatric disorders.

In 2002, at least some of the DSM-5 architects believed that genes would at long last be identified and would be integrated into the next version of the DSM. But this did not happen. The DSM-5 was finally published in 2013, and the multiaxial diagnostic system, used in DSM III through DSM-IV-TR (1980–2013), was abandoned. A major reason appears to be psychiatry's unexpected failure to uncover genes for its disorders, a failure that critics have argued for decades is the result not of illusive genes or "missing heritability," but rather of psychiatry's misplaced faith in the results of previous twin and adoption studies.

Schizophrenia: The Classic Psychiatric Diagnosis

Schizophrenia is psychiatry's paradigmatic disorder, often associated with the term "madness" and "psychosis." As a mainstream psychiatrist put it, "The psychiatrist that knows schizophrenia knows psychiatry" (Lewis, 2006, p. xv). Schizophrenia has been the subject of more genetic investigation than any other diagnosis, and has been described in very different ways by various people and groups. For mainstream psychiatry and psychiatric genetics, schizophrenia is "a severe mental disorder with a lifetime risk of about 1%, characterized by hallucinations, delusions and cognitive deficits, with heritability estimated at up to 80%" (International Schizophrenia Consortium, 2009, p. 748), a "highly heritable neuropsychiatric disorder of complex genetic etiology" (Szatkiewicz et al., 2014, p. 762), a "brain disease" (Torrey, 1995, p. 142), and a "disease" that can be "reliably diagnosed" (Flint et al., 2010, p. 15). For critics of the concept, on the other hand, schizophrenia is psychiatry's "sacred symbol—the largest grab bag of all the misbehaviors which psychiatrists . . . are now ready to diagnose, prognose, and therapize" (Szasz, 1976, p. 18), a "scientific delusion" (Boyle, 2002b), a "moral verdict" (Sarbin & Mancuso, 1980), or a "scientifically meaningless and socially devastating label" (Read, 2013c, p. 32).

Allen Frances, the former Chair of the DSM-IV Task Force turned DSM-5 critic, wrote in 2011 that

> schizophrenia is admittedly a flawed construct with limited descriptive and explanatory power. It is wildly heterogeneous with dozens of different presentations and probably hundreds of different causes (none of them known) . . . . There is no available biological test available for its diagnosis and none is on the horizon.
> (Frances, 2011)

The behaviors may be disturbing, difficult, and heartbreaking for family members, but disturbing behavior does not constitute a disease. The APA's DSM-5 confirmed this: "Currently, there are no radiological, laboratory, or psychometric tests for the disorder" (APA, 2013b, p. 101).

As psychiatry critic Thomas Szasz once asked, "if schizophrenia is a brain disease, why do the scientists at the National Institute of *Mental Health*, rather than those at the National Institute of *Neurological Diseases*, tell us that?" (Szasz, 1987, p. 50, italics in original).

The APA's position on whether schizophrenia genes have been discovered appeared in two versions in the spring of 2013. As we saw, the May 3rd APA press release admitted that psychiatry is "still waiting" for the identification of "genetic markers" for its disorders. In the schizophrenia section of DSM-5, however, the APA wrote that schizophrenia "liability is conferred by a spectrum of risk alleles, common and rare, with each allele contributing only a small fraction to the total population variance. The risk alleles identified to date are also associated with other mental disorders" (APA, 2013b, p.103). The main difference between these two conflicting documents is that hardly anyone knows about (or has read) the press release, whereas entire fields over a number of years will be misinformed by the DSM-5 claim that a "spectrum" of schizophrenia "risk alleles" has been identified.

The criteria for diagnosing schizophrenia are so vague that two people could be diagnosed with it without sharing any symptoms. As Read has shown, there are 15 ways in which two people can meet the DSM criteria for a schizophrenia diagnosis without having any symptoms in common (Read, 2013b). Schizophrenia is a "highly heritable disorder" in which, as the DSM-5 reported, "most individuals who have been diagnosed with schizophrenia have no family history of psychosis" (APA, 2013b, p. 103). It is difficult to imagine a "strongly genetic disorder" where most of the people diagnosed with it have no family history of the disorder.

In the 16 schizophrenia twin studies published between 1928 and 1999, the pooled MZT concordance rate is 40 percent, while the pooled DZT rate is 7.5 percent. Looking at the ten methodologically superior studies published between 1963 and 1999, pooled rates fall to 23 percent MZT versus 5 percent DZT, meaning that in these better-performed studies the MZT co-twin of a person diagnosed with schizophrenia is not so diagnosed over 75 percent of the time (Joseph, 2013b, p. 74). Although twin researchers continue to interpret these results in favor of genetics and have calculated schizophrenia heritability in the 80% range on the basis of twin studies (Sullivan, Kendler, & Neale, 2003), schizophrenia twin research appears to have recorded little more than MZTs' more similar childhood and adult environments, their higher levels of identity confusion and attachment to each other (Table 7.1), and their greater tendency to experience *folie à deux* (shared psychotic disorder) than DZT pairs (Jackson, 1960; Joseph, 2004).

Environmental Factors that Contribute to Schizophrenia and Psychosis

The psychiatric genetic literature contains few references to specific environmental factors that play a causative role, and while researchers acknowledge a role for the environment, they usually write that the environmental causes of schizophrenia and psychotic disorders are mysterious or unknown. But research suggests otherwise. As superbly reviewed by John Read (Read, 2013a, 2013d), since the turn of the twenty-first century many studies have linked schizophrenia and other psychotic conditions to childhood adversities such as having experienced bullying, emotional abuse, incest, neglect, parental loss, physical abuse, sexual abuse—findings that are well known to clinicians who work with people diagnosed with psychotic disorders.

Read reviewed research linking schizophrenia and other psychotic disorders to social environments such as poverty, racism, migratory stress, and urbanicity. He concluded, "There is ample evidence that inequality, deprivation and discrimination, filtered through their social and personal meanings, are key causal factors in psychosis" (Read, 2013d, p. 205). Psychological processes through which childhood adversities may lead to symptoms of psychosis later in life include attachment, dissociation, dysfunctional cognitive processes, psychodynamic defenses, problematic coping responses, impaired access to social support, behavioral sensitization and revictimization (Read, Fosse, Moscowitz, & Perry, 2014, p. 66)

A biologically oriented commentator might object that even if these factors play a role in causing schizophrenia and psychosis, only people who are genetically predisposed will develop them, and it is therefore important to understand and study hereditary factors. Aside from the fact that the evidence in support of genetics is weak, a clear understanding of the environmental causes of a condition frequently renders potential genetic factors irrelevant. For example, 33 miners were trapped underground for 69 days in a copper mine near Copiapó, Chile in 2010. Although the miners were finally rescued and were treated as heroes, and in some cases as celebrities, many subsequently developed severe psychological symptoms caused by their ordeal, such as depression, anxiety, nightmares, and avoidant behavior (Franklin, 2011). Because the causes of these symptoms are obvious and recognized, no one to my knowledge has suggested that the miners have genetically based brain disorders or "chemical imbalances." It is clear that the miners' experiences caused their symptoms, and the symptoms of most psychiatric conditions can also be seen in this way, even if genetic factors come into play.

Adverse childhood and adult experiences and environments play a role comparable to the Copiapó mine experience of the 33 trapped Chilean miners. The main difference is that the causes of psychological distress are more obvious, and therefore more recognized, in the Chilean miners' case.

It could also be argued that many of the Chilean miners were diagnosed with PTSD, a psychiatric diagnosis recognizing that trauma plays a role in causing the symptoms. However, although in the case of PTSD psychiatry chooses to recognize trauma as a causative factor, one could argue that schizophrenia and many other psychiatric disorders are also the result of having experienced trauma and other adverse environmental events.[9]

An Implicit Assumption of Genetic Theories in Psychiatry

An unstated assumption of psychiatric genetic research is that, although the family environment can have a negative impact, the society in which it is undertaken is basically healthy and does not systematically cause people to suffer psychological distress or manifest psychiatric disorders. In other words, the implicit assumption is: "Healthy society—containing some unhealthy family environments and some unhealthy genes and brains."

But what if psychological theories, in addition to research findings, are correct in pointing to the childhood environment as playing a major role in a person's potential for healthy or unhealthy psychological functioning? There is also the larger social perspective, impacting these family environments both directly and indirectly, which emphasizes the psychologically harmful effects of racism, chronic stress, living in poverty, the oppression of women, social class status, discrimination against sexual minorities, diminished social networks and greater levels of social isolation, social inequality, corporate greed, advertising industry marketing campaigns, unemployment, and the consumer-driven individualist culture promoted in advanced industrial societies. Psychologist George Albee (1921–2006) discussed the "strong possibility that many mental disorders are socially acquired maladjustments, learned patterns of undesirable behavior that result from a pathological social environment" (Albee, 1996, p. 1130).

As the psychologist Philip Cushman put it in 1995, the quest for corporate profit in the post World War II era transformed the predominant American self into an "empty self," which is "striving for self-liberation through the compulsive purchase and consumption of goods, experiences, and celebrities" (Cushman, 1995, p. 211). Clearly, an empty self is not an emotionally healthy self.

From these perspectives, in the words of sociologist Allan Horwitz, "many of the fifty million Americans who meet the criteria for a mental disorder [each year] in community studies do not have valid disorders but suffer from distress that is rooted in stressful social arrangements and that will disappear when these situations improve" (Horwitz, 2002, p. 222).

An alternative to genetically oriented researchers' implied "Healthy society—containing some unhealthy family environments and some unhealthy genes and brains" position could be characterized as "Unhealthy society—containing unhealthy families impacted by the unhealthy society—healthy genes and brains." From this perspective any possible genetic predisposition would be of little interest, and society would focus on improving social and family conditions, creating free universal healthcare, promoting equality, eradicating racism and other forms of oppression, greatly improving education, creating full employment, and so on.

If psychologically unhealthy family, social, and political arrangements are indeed the main factors underlying emotional problems and psychiatric disorders, then focusing on genetics and the brain are monumental diversions, in much the same way as the tobacco industry has preferred to focus on an alleged genetic predisposition to develop lung cancer and not on the carcinogenic effects of using tobacco (Chaufan, 2007; Proctor, 1995; Wallace, 2009). Steven Rose spoke of the "urgent pressure to find explanations for the scale of social and personal distress in advanced industrial societies . . . explanations which shift the 'blame' for the problem away from the political realm and onto the individual" (Rose, 1997, p. 296). Indeed, genetic explanations of social and personal distress, which are based largely on twin research, are one of the major ways that this shift has been accomplished.

The ultimate expression of the use of psychiatric labels in the service of social control, accompanied by claims of biological and genetic causation, was described by David Hill in *The Politics of Schizophrenia*:

> The social control implemented by the mental health movement of the 20th century seems to involve four components. First, there are the essential ingredients of any social control process; the establishment of certain norms by either the majority or the powerful, and the breaking of those norms by a relatively powerless minority. Second, an exaggeration of the difference between the "in group" and the "out group" is accomplished, in this case, by the application of the medical dichotomy "sick–healthy" to behaviors, followed by ignoring the context of those behaviors, thereby rendering them even more bizarre. Third, the control aspect is presented as benevolent concern; accomplished by the portrayal of those exhibiting the strange behaviors as not being responsible for them; this in turn being explained by some supposed physiological or hereditary etiology or by some disorder of volition or will. These first three ingredients prepare the way for the fourth, the implementation of sanction called, in this particular case, "psychiatric treatment."
>
> (Hill, 1983, p. 104)

As Hill described it, the established powers have succeeded in medicalizing behaviors that fall outside the norms they have created, and then approach these behaviors (disorders) on the basis of their alleged medical (i.e., biological and genetic) basis. Psychiatry is charged with carrying out this role, although most of the evidence it cites in support of this position is based on largely "ignoring the context" of behavior, and on dubious genetic theories with twin studies at the forefront.

While mainstream psychiatric researchers and others worry about the "societal burden of mental disorders" (Kessler, Chiu, Demler, & Walters, 2005, p. 601), from another perspective much psychological distress could be characterized as the *mental burden of societal disorders*.[10]

An Article Emblematic of the Failures of Psychiatric Genetics

Psychiatric genetic researchers James Hudziak and Stephen Faraone published an article in a 2010 edition of the prestigious *Journal of the American Academy of Child and Adolescent Psychiatry* that captured some of the biases and fallacies of twin research-based contemporary psychiatric genetic thought (Hudziak & Faraone, 2010).[11]

Child and adolescent psychiatrists, according to Hudziak and Faraone, must be able to grasp the "'new genetics' of complex disorders," which are "influenced by multiple or even thousands of genes interacting with environmental factors." They continued, "Almost daily in newspapers, general magazines, and online, new genetic discoveries are announced" (p. 730). However, media reports of "new genetic discoveries" almost always turn out to be false-positive findings. As we have seen, Faraone and colleagues recognized in 2008, "It is no secret that our field has published thousands of candidate gene association studies but few replicated findings" (Faraone et al., 2008, p. 1). The newspaper, magazine, and online accounts of these thousands of subsequently non-replicated molecular genetic studies have served mainly to mislead the public and even the scientific community to believe that genes have been discovered. This clearly is not a positive development, as the authors seemed to imply.

Hudziak and Faraone wrote that "twin studies report that ADHD is influenced 60% to 90% by genes" (p. 731). Twin studies, in fact, report nothing of the kind—twin *researchers* report that ADHD is influenced 60–90 percent by genes. This merely reflects their interpretations of the results of twin studies, based on their acceptance of the validity of the EEA and the heritability concept. Studies do not find and estimate heritability; *people* find and estimate heritability. Other people have interpreted these studies very differently, and have questioned the reliability and validity of ADHD and other psychiatric conditions (Furman, 2009; Kirk et al., 2013; Kirk & Kutchins, 1992; Read & Dillon, 2013).

For Hudziak and Faraone, although "no causal DNA variant has been discovered using" genetic linkage analysis, "this has led to the important discovery that, if common variants exist, their genetic effect sizes must be very small" (p. 731). Thus, in rhetoric but not in reality, gene-finding *failures* are transformed into an "important discovery." An alternative interpretation, unmentioned by the authors, is that researchers have discovered that no such genes exist.

The authors went on to discuss candidate gene studies that have helped us understand "the role of the environment in a child's outcome" (p. 731). As evidence, they cited a study (Sugden et al., 2010) whose authors claimed to have shown that, when victimized by bullies, children with a particular genetic variant, when compared with children who do not have the variant, "were at greater risk to have emotional problems at age 12 years" (Hudziak & Faraone, 2010, p. 732). Hudziak and Faraone believed that candidate gene studies such as this one "could lead to public health interventions," such as "greater efforts to decrease bullying" (p. 732). But didn't we already know, long before candidate gene studies, that bullying harmed children and that interventions aimed at reducing or preventing bullying would help alleviate the suffering of the victims and help prevent "childhood psychopathology"?

Simply put, we do not need molecular genetic research to teach us that bullying harms children any more than we need it to demonstrate the harmful psychological effects of other obvious environmental adversities. As a group of mainstream psychiatric researchers found, in a study spanning 21 countries, "childhood adversities have strong associations with all classes of [psychiatric] disorders at all life-course stages in all groups of WMH [World Mental Health] countries" (Kessler et al., 2010, p. 378).

But focusing on genes does serve as a diversion from noticing the harmful psychological effects of these and countless other adverse environmental conditions and events. It actually helps these harmful conditions to persist, which is the exact opposite result that Hudziak and Faraone claimed for molecular genetic research.

Although Hudziak and Faraone recognized the "failure of candidate gene studies to easily explain the heritability of childhood-onset disorders" (p. 732), we have seen them argue that these studies did provide useful information on where to focus public health interventions, such as an anti-bullying program. Paradoxically, it seems that the main finding of childhood and adolescent psychiatric molecular genetic research has been the identification of the environmental conditions—but not the presumed genes—that cause emotional damage and the appearance of psychiatric disorders.

Instead of studying brains and genes, societal and research attention should instead focus on the familial, social, political, and physical circumstances that cause children and adolescents to act out, harm themselves and others, suffer low self-esteem, and experience sadness, loss, fear, heartache, loneliness, aggression, insecurity, and other negative emotions—behaviors and emotions that psychiatric genetics and mainstream psychiatry decontextualize and subsume under the medical designation "child and adolescent psychopathology."

According to Hudziak and Faraone, ten years after "the first draft of the human genome was reported . . . genetic research on developmental psychopathology has grown exponentially, as reflected not only in the number of published papers but also in the power of molecular genetic and statistical technologies." They believed that "although we are only in the infancy of our field, the pathway to discovery is clear. One can only imagine the incredible progress that will be made in the next decades (Hudziak & Faraone, 2010, p., 734). The authors therefore implied that the "number of published papers" constitutes scientific progress, instead of emphasizing that the findings of these published papers—literally thousands of them as Faraone and colleagues had written in 2008—were not replicated.

They also implied that failures are to be expected because "developmental psychopathology" molecular genetic research is only in its "infancy." Ten years earlier, Faraone and Biederman, in a reply to my publication on genetics and ADHD (Joseph, 2000), had also characterized ADHD molecular genetic research as being in its "infancy" while claiming, wrongly as it turned out, that "molecular genetic studies have already implicated several genes as mediating the susceptibility to ADHD" (Faraone & Biederman, 2000, p. 572).

Finally, Hudziak and Faraone, again choosing to de-emphasize years of failure, claimed that the "pathway to discovery is clear," and that "incredible progress . . . will be made in the next decades." However, psychiatric geneticists have been saying this for over four decades. Rather than being in its infancy, 15–20 years of molecular genetic studies of childhood and adolescent psychiatric disorders have produced an important finding: The genetic basis of these disorders appears to have been refuted, and it is imperative that the scientific community reexamine genetic interpretations of the twin (and adoption) studies that compelled researchers to look for genes in the first place.

Is Psychiatric Genetics Moving Toward the Status of a "Null Field"?

Future historians will assess the current stage of psychiatric genetic research in one of three main ways. The first would be that scientists were able to improve their methods and uncover genes playing an important role in causing mental disorders. The second would be that some genes are eventually identified, but society did not consider this an important discovery and chose to focus on improving social, family, and other environmental conditions. The third outcome would be that no genes are ever found, most likely because they do not exist, and psychiatric genetics was declared a "null field" and was disbanded.

As the epidemiologist John Ioannidis defined it, a "null field" is an area of research "with absolutely no yield of true scientific information" (Ioannidis, 2005, p. 700). For example, a branch of psychological research dedicated to studying parenting techniques that cause Huntington's disease would eventually turn out to be a null field. Ioannidis recognized that researchers working in such a discipline "are likely to resist accepting that the whole field in which they have spent their careers is a 'null field.'" However, additional evidence or lack of evidence "may lead eventually to the dismantling of a scientific field" (Ioannidis, 2005, p. 700). In what may turn out to be a stage in this process, an open letter endorsed by 96 leading psychiatric genetic researchers urged potential funding sources not to "give up" on financially supporting molecular genetic studies of "psychiatric diseases" (Sullivan et al., 2012).

A set of converging factors leads to the distinct possibility that psychiatric genetics will one day be designated as a null field. These include: (a) the likelihood that genes for the major psychiatric disorders do not exist, and were merely an illusion created by incorrect interpretations of twin studies; (b) the mistaken interpretation of (typically enormously flawed) psychiatric adoption studies in favor of genetics; (c) the questionable reliability and validity of psychiatric disorders; and (d) the critical and dominant role of environmental causes of psychiatric disorders.

Conclusions

Psychiatric twin studies have played a major role in misleading the field of psychiatry and its subfield of psychiatric genetics into believing that the major psychiatric disorders have an underlying genetic component. Moreover, the reliability and validity of psychiatric diagnoses as discrete medical disorders are highly questionable. At bottom, psychiatric disorders are names for groups of behaviors, not diseases, and are diagnosed on the basis of behavior and self-report.

The historical crimes committed by the "racial hygienist" founders of psychiatric genetics such as Ernst Rüdin in Nazi Germany have been documented (Baron, 1998; Joseph, 2004, 2006; Joseph & Wetzel, 2013; Lerner, 1992; Müller-Hill, 1998; Roelcke, 2006, 2010, 2012; Weiss, 2010; see also note 7). The massively flawed research produced by this field has also been documented (see note 1).

This leads to the following question: Has the field of psychiatric genetics contributed anything positive to the human condition in its roughly 100 years of existence? A leading group of psychiatric genetic researchers supplied a partial answer to this question in 2008. According to Glatt, Faraone, and Tsuang, although they believed that their field possesses "a powerful toolbox of methods," the "major contributions of psychiatric genetic research to the diagnoses, treatment, prediction, and prevention of psychiatric disorders have yet to be realized" (Glatt, Faraone, & Tsuang, 2008, pp. 24–25). This statement is as true today as when it was written.

Another answer to this question comes from the psychologist Richard Bentall, in his 2009 book *Doctoring the Mind*. Bentall wrote, "From the point of view of patients, there can be few other areas of medical research that have yielded such a dismal return for effort expended" than psychiatric genetic research:

> No patient, not a single one, has ever benefited from genetic research into mental illness, although many have been indirectly harmed by it (because it has discouraged the development of adequate services for patients and, during one shameful period, was used to justify their slaughter). No effective treatments have so far been devised on the basis of genetic information and, given what we now know, it seems very unlikely that further research into the genetics of psychosis will lead to important therapeutic advances in the future.
>
> (Bentall, 2009, p. 145)

The time has come to suspend psychiatric molecular genetic research and to undertake a thorough public reassessment of the original twin (and adoption) studies that inspired the fruitless search for genes in the first place. At the same time, the familial, social, and political causes of human distress (psychiatric disorders) must become the focus of attention.

Ironically, the only positive contribution that the field of psychiatric genetics has ever made to the human condition is its finding that genes for the major psychiatric disorders do not appear to exist. Future historians may well view the current "missing heritability" stage (see Chapter 9) of psychiatric genetics as a station on the road to its eventual destination alongside other abandoned "null fields" in the history of science—a status that will be based largely on the mistaken belief that twin studies prove something about genetic influences on psychiatric disorders. The field of psychiatry as a whole will be forced to reevaluate the evidence it has accepted as providing conclusive proof of the genetic basis of its disorders, and the validity of the twin method and its critical EEA will come under increasing scrutiny.

Notes

1 For more on the major problems in psychiatric adoption research, see Joseph, 2004, 2006, 2010a, 2013b, and the references therein.
2 I use the terms "condition," "disorder," and "diagnosis" interchangeably in this chapter. In doing so I do not endorse the position that these are valid or discrete categories similar to real medical conditions or diseases, nor does the use of these terms here imply that they have a biological or genetic basis.
3 The APA had originally planned to continue its practice of using roman numerals for the DSM, and in the early stages of research the Fifth Edition was called "DSM-V." It was later decided to use Arabic numbers, leading to the current

DSM-5. Apart from quotations or titles, I will use "DSM-5" throughout this chapter.
4 For a list of previous APA Task Forces, see http://www.psych.org/learn/library--archives/task-force-reports.
5 In this example I use the "pairwise" concordance method. Some researchers promote the use of the "probandwise" concordance method, which double-counts the first identified twin and produces higher concordance rates.
6 Critical analyses of psychiatric twin research include Don Jackson's seminal and never-refuted 1960 description of the numerous environmental confounds in schizophrenia twin research (Jackson, 1960), Lewontin and colleagues' 1984 *Not in Our Genes* (Lewontin, Rose, & Kamin, 1984), Ross and Pam's 1995 *Pseudoscience in Biological Psychiatry: Blaming the Body* (Ross & Pam, 1995), Mary Boyle's *Schizophrenia: A Scientific Delusion?* (Boyle, 2002b), and two books I have published (Joseph, 2004, 2006).
7 Flint, Greenspan, and Kendler cited the rise of the eugenics movement in the first half of the twentieth century as another example of the supposed hazard of mixing science and politics, inappropriately linking the "politics" of this steadfast opponent of eugenics (Kamin) to the politics of the eugenics movement and Nazism. "The ultimate embodiment of eugenics," wrote Flint and colleagues, "came under the National Socialist (Nazi) program in Germany, starting with the compulsory sterilization of mental patients (modeled after US statutes) and ending with the Final Solution" (Flint, Greenspan, & Kendler, 2010, p. 27). Flint and colleagues failed to mention the fact that German psychiatric genetic researchers, such as the founder of their discipline Ernst Rüdin, were instrumental in creating the conditions for and providing a scientific stamp of approval to the atrocities of the Third Reich. In fact, Rüdin personified the "ultimate embodiment of eugenics" in Hitler's Germany, and was involved in the killing of mental patients and children as part of the Nazi's T4 "Euthanasia" program (see Joseph & Wetzel, 2013; Roelcke, 2006, 2012; Weiss, 2010).
8 I placed the word "have" in quotation marks because, lacking a proven biological basis, one cannot "have" psychiatric disorders in the same way as people have real biologically based medical conditions.
9 In a mocking jab at critics of psychiatry such as R. D. Laing and Thomas Szasz, Seymour Kety, the lead researcher of the influential yet severely flawed Danish schizophrenia adoption studies, famously wrote in 1974: "If schizophrenia is a myth, it is a myth with a strong genetic component!" (Kety, 1974, p. 961). Schizophrenia molecular genetic research was relatively new in those days, but the results of decades of molecular genetic research are now in: there appear to be no genes for schizophrenia. We could therefore revise Kety's position to bring it in line with current scientific results: "If schizophrenia is a genetic disorder, it is a genetic disorder without any genes."
10 As Richard Lewontin once put it, "Problems of health and disease have been located within the individual so that the individual becomes a problem for society to cope with rather than society becoming a problem for the individual" (Lewontin, 1991, p. 16).
11 For a more detailed review of this article, see Joseph (2012).

Part III

APPROACHING A POST-BEHAVIORAL-GENETICS ERA?

9

MOLECULAR GENETIC RESEARCH

The Ultimate Test of Genetic Interpretations of Twin Studies

> Progress has been slow in finding genes associated with behavior.
> — Robert Plomin, 2013 (Plomin, 2013a, p. 104)

> In human behavior genetics ... powerful new methods have failed to reveal even one bona fide, replicable gene effect pertinent to the normal range of variation in intelligence and personality.
> — Critical Behavioral Genetic Researcher Douglas Wahlsten, 2012 (Wahlsten, 2012, p. 475)

> [An] immediate social consequence of reductionist ideology is that attention and funding is diverted from the social to the molecular.
> — Biologist Steven Rose, 1997 (Rose, 1997, p. 297)

Given the widespread acceptance of behavioral genetic and psychiatric genetic positions, coupled with tremendous technological advances, several decades of molecular genetic research should by now have uncovered the genes that are believed to underlie behavioral differences and psychiatric disorders. Researchers have failed to uncover them, however, which provides an additional powerful counterargument against genetic interpretations of twin method MZT–DZT comparisons and TRA studies. We saw in the previous chapter that a 2013 statement by the APA officially admitted that five decades of gene searches in psychiatry have turned up nothing (APA, 2013a). Although gene discovery claims continue to appear on a regular basis in original studies, in review articles and textbooks, and in the media, recent history suggests that these claims, like decades of similar claims before them, will not stand up.

Current Status

The following quotations from leading genetically oriented researchers and others make it clear that, despite well-funded international efforts and cutting-edge technologies and innovations, the search for genes underlying IQ, personality, and psychiatric disorders has been a stunning failure:

Cognitive Ability (IQ)

Dozens of candidate genes have been reported as being associated with intelligence . . . almost none of them has been replicated . . . . We, as yet, know nothing about the genes that influence intelligence differences. Candidate gene studies of intelligence differences have been disappointing.

(Deary, 2012, p. 463)

Most reported genetic associations with general intelligence are probably false positives.

(Chabris et al., 2012, p. 1314)

Results from twin, family and adoption studies are consistent with general intelligence being highly heritable and genetically stable throughout the life course. No robustly associated genetic loci or variants for childhood intelligence have been reported.

(Benyamin et al., 2014, p. 253)

The high heritability of g has made it a popular target in the search for genes that influence behavior. In spite of numerous studies with sufficient power to detect rather small effects, the results to date have been dismal in comparison with expectation.

(Bouchard, 2014)

Although twin, family, and adoption studies have shown that general cognitive ability (GCA) is substantially heritable, GWAS [genomewide association study] has not uncovered a genetic polymorphism replicably associated with this phenotype.

(Kirkpatrick et al., 2014, p. 98)

Personality and Behavior

It was widely thought that the Human Genome Project would deliver the vindication of [behavioral] quantitative genetics . . . Everyone assumed that once the human genome was sequenced the "genes for" the phenomena

that had been demonstrated to be heritable would be just around the corner, but it hasn't happened.
(Turkheimer, 2011b, p. 231)

QTL [quantitative trait loci] associations have been reported for several candidate genes and personality traits. However, similar to research on psychopathology, replication of associations has been difficult in part because effect sizes are much smaller than originally anticipated. Genomewide association studies have also not yet yielded consistent results.
(Plomin, DeFries, et al., 2013, p. 296)

There have been a handful of "candidate gene" studies proposing a link between specific genetic variants and specific political traits.... However, similar to the study of other complex human traits, these candidate gene studies have found only nominally significant results and have not withstood long-term replication.
(Hatemi et al., 2014)

Psychiatric Disorders

It is no secret that our field has published thousands of candidate gene association studies but few replicated findings.
(Faraone, Smoller, Pato, Sullivan, & Tsuang, 2008, p. 1)

In the future, we hope to be able to identify disorders using biological and genetic markers.... Yet this promise, which we have anticipated since the 1970s, remains disappointingly distant. We've been telling patients for several decades that we are waiting for biomarkers. We're still waiting.
(American Psychiatric Association, 2013a)

Childhood behavior problems have become the target of genome-wide association (GWA) studies that attempt to identify the genes responsible for their heritability. As in other life sciences, these GWA expeditions have come up largely empty-handed.
(Trzaskowski, Dale, & Plomin, 2013, p. 1048)

Although genetic analysis has identified risk loci for many other common medical diseases ... success has yet to visit MD [major depression].
(Flint & Kendler, 2014, p. 484)

Something is clearly wrong here—behavioral genetic and psychiatric genetic researchers and the popularizers of their work have argued that family, twin, and adoption studies have conclusively shown that important genetic factors underlie most aspects of human behavior and psychology, yet they have been unable to identify genes at the molecular level. As Turkheimer and colleagues put it in 2014, molecular genetic research of personality is experiencing "an extended period of frustration as most of the reported discoveries either turned out to be very small or failed to replicate at all" (Turkheimer, Pettersson, & Horn, 2014, p. 534).

The "Missing Heritability" Explanation

Since 2008, many leading molecular genetic researchers in behavioral genetics and psychiatric genetics have adopted the position of "missing heritability" as an explanation for their failure to discover genes (Chaufan & Joseph, 2013; Faraone, 2013; Joseph, 2012; Maher, 2008; Manolio et al., 2009; Plomin, 2013a). The "missing heritability" interpretation of negative results was developed in the context of the failure to uncover most of the genes presumed to underlie common non-Mendelian medical conditions, and, with possible rare exceptions, all of the genes presumed to underlie behavioral differences and the major psychiatric disorders. In the words of Francis Collins, Director of the U.S. National Institutes of Health, and former Director of the National Center for Human Genome Research, in 2008 missing heritability was "the big topic in the genetics of common disease right now" (quoted in Maher, 2008, p. 18). Since then, the topic had grown much bigger.

According to a group of prominent researchers, heritability is "missing" due to the finding that molecular genetic "genomewide association" (GWA) studies "have explained relatively little of the heritability of most complex traits, and the variants identified through these studies have small effects" (Eichler et al., 2010, p. 446). GWA studies, which have been used extensively since 2005, involve rapidly scanning markers across the genomes of affected and non-affected people to find common genetic variants associated with particular diseases or behaviors. GWA studies are "hypothesis free" and attempt to identify single-nucleotide polymorphisms (commonly known as "SNPs") associated with the condition or characteristic under study.

In the popular literature the word "gene" is shorthand for genetic variant, which refers to differing variations of a gene found among individuals or populations. SNPs are a type of genetic variation (polymorphism) occurring between different people. GWA studies focus on common variants, which refer to variants found in 5 percent or more of the population. The dominant view in human genetics, and the rationale for GWA studies, has been that common variants underlie common diseases and other behavioral differences, which is known as the "common disease, common variant hypothesis." Given the lack of findings from GWA studies, some have proposed that research attention should focus on identifying rare variants which might underlie medical and psychiatric disorders.

Rare variants are defined as variants found in less than 0.5 percent of the population (Manolio et al., 2009). Another type of genetic variant that researchers look for are copy-number variants (CNVs). It is important to remember that, even if a variant is associated with a behavior or disease, it does not necessarily mean that the variant *causes* it (Meaney, 2010). "Association" and "correlation" are synonymous concepts in this context, and it is axiomatic in science that correlation does not equal cause.

A large group of genetic researchers headed by Teri Manolio of the National Human Genome Research Institute, which included Francis Collins and other prominent investigators, published a 2009 article in *Nature* entitled, "Finding the Missing Heritability" (Manolio et al., 2009). This article has served as a reference point for molecular genetic researchers, including those in psychology and psychiatry, who have attempted to come to terms with years of negative results. Manolio and colleagues recognized that "the identification of genetic variants contributing to . . . 'complex diseases' has been slow and arduous" (p. 747), and they saw the few positive findings of variants for non-psychiatric medical conditions as explaining "only a small proportion of the estimated heritability" (p. 748). Turning to psychiatric disorders, the authors recognized "the lack of variants detected so far for some neuropsychiatric conditions" (p. 748). They had no doubt that the problem is missing heritability, as opposed to non-existent heritability, because "a substantial proportion of individual differences in disease susceptibility is known to be due to genetic factors." Finding missing heritability is important, they wrote, in order to aid in "better prevention, diagnosis, and treatment of disease" (p. 748). Manolio and colleagues saw missing heritability as the "'dark matter' of GWA in the sense that one is sure it exists, can detect its influence, but simply cannot 'see' it (yet)" (p. 748).

Manolio and colleagues' position that they are "sure" that genes exist and await discovery was based largely on the results of family studies, which, at least as they pertain to psychiatric disorders and variation in behavioral characteristics such as IQ and personality, are widely recognized as being unable to disentangle the potential roles of genes and environment (see Chapters 1 and 7). Strikingly, the authors did not mention twin studies, which *are* widely seen as being able to disentangle these influences—a claim that is examined in detail in this book. Manolio and colleagues believed that heritability estimates are roughly accurate, and suggested several research strategies to uncover the genetic "dark matter" they are sure exists. They saw this as an important task that will "illuminate the genetics of complex diseases and enhance its potential to enable effective disease prevention or treatment" (p. 747). From the "missing heritability" standpoint, genetic variants that cause behaviors and disorders have found good hiding places that require better methods and larger sample sizes to flush them out.

Two years prior to the appearance of "missing heritability," I published a book entitled *The Missing Gene* (Joseph, 2006). My use of the word "missing" in 2006, however, differed from the way genetic researchers have used it from 2008 to the present. For me, it was (and remains) very possible that genes underlying variation in behavior and psychiatric disorders do not exist, due largely to researchers' misinterpretation of twin and adoption data. For people convinced that twin studies have provided indisputable evidence in support of genetics, genes are "missing" because researchers have not yet been able to identify them, or possibly because heritability estimates are inflated (Zuk, Hechter, Sunyaev, & Lander, 2012).

Challenging the Missing Heritability Position

The missing heritability interpretation of GWA results was challenged in 2010 by Jonathan Latham and Allison Wilson of the Bioscience Resource Project, who concluded that the "genetics revolution ... is in big trouble" due to the inability of GWA studies, with a few notable exceptions, to find important disease genes. "Instead of invoking missing genes," wrote Latham and Wilson, if "we take the GWA studies at face value, then apart from the exceptions ... genetic predispositions as significant factors in the prevalence of common diseases are refuted" (Latham & Wilson, 2010). They concluded, "The dearth of disease-causing genes is without question a scientific discovery of tremendous significance."

Latham and Wilson pointed to the "plentiful evidence" that environmental factors cause many common diseases, even as the popular press and science journals continue to focus on genetics and the need to keep looking for genes. Manolio and colleagues' position, as Latham and Wilson described it, was that "since heritability measurements suggest that genes for disease must exist, they must be hiding under some as-yet-unturned genetic rock."

Addressing the larger picture, Latham and Wilson wrote that, although the "evidence for genetic causation has always been weak" because it is based mainly on "disputed" studies of twins and other relatives, it is "necessary to understand the role that genetic determinism plays in consolidating the social order." Writing mainly about genetic research in medicine, but with much relevance to the social and behavioral sciences, they identified groups in society with an interest in promoting genetic determinist theories of disease causation. Among these they included politicians and corporations, "because it substantially reduces their responsibility for people's ill health," and medical researchers, who in turn "can raise research dollars with relative ease" with the help of these politicians and corporations. "The history of scientific refutation," wrote Latham and Wilson, "is that adherents of established theories construct ever more elaborate or unlikely explanations to fend off their critics."

Missing Heritability and the Human Genome Project

The missing heritability position has provided behavioral genetic and psychiatric genetic researchers with a ready-made explanation for their continuing failure to discover genes. Although disappointment goes back to the 1980s and earlier, by the 1990s many researchers placed their hopes on the completion of the sequencing of the human genome, performed by the Human Genome Project (HGP), which was then nearing completion. Psychiatric geneticists Stephen Faraone, Ming Tsuang, and Debby Tsuang wrote in 1999, for example, "From the perspective of psychiatric genetics, the Human Genome Project is an immense factory producing and refining the tools we will need to discover the genes that cause mental illness" (Faraone, Tsuang, & Tsuang, 1999, p. 198).

In his widely cited 2000 article "Three Laws of Behavior Genetics and What They Mean," Turkheimer concluded, largely on the basis of twin studies, that "all human behavioral traits are heritable" (Turkheimer, 2000, p. 160). He also believed that the completion of the HGP would lead to gene discovery, writing that "behavior geneticists anticipate vindication" by the discovery of genes causing behavioral variation. On the other hand, wrote Turkheimer,

> Critics of behavior genetics expect the opposite, pointing to the repeated failures to replicate associations between genes and behavior as evidence of the shaky theoretical underpinnings of which they have so long complained.
> (Turkheimer, 2000, p. 163)

That was an accurate description of many critics' expectations at that time and earlier. A decade and a half later, it appears that the critics have indeed been vindicated. While continuing to support behavioral genetic theories and research, Turkheimer wrote in 2011, "to the great surprise of almost everyone, the molecular genetic project has foundered on the . . . shoals of developmental complexity" (Turkheimer, 2011a, p. 600). Three years later, he still could not point to any subsequent gene discoveries (Turkheimer, Pettersson, & Horn, 2014). Decades of negative results suggest that the problem is, indeed, the "shaky theoretical underpinnings" of twin research.

In Chapter 10 I will examine over 35 years of gene-finding excitement, claims, predictions, and disappointment in the writings of Robert Plomin, who also placed great hope in the HGP. In 2003, Plomin wrote that the HGP "continues to shower the [behavioral genetics] field with new information and new technologies" (Plomin, 2003a, p. 196).

Four Key Problems with the Missing Heritability Argument

Four major problems with the missing heritability concept as it is used in the evaluation of molecular genetic studies of behavioral characteristics are listed here. These four points have been critically assessed throughout this book:[1]

1. It is based on the reductionist position that we must identify genes in order to understand human behavior and human behavioral differences, or to be able to treat and prevent psychiatric disorders (as opposed to simply removing symptoms).
2. Although the claim that human behavioral differences and psychiatric disorders have an important genetic component is based largely on twin studies (and to a lesser degree, family and adoption studies), unsupported assumptions and obvious environmental confounds in twin research are usually denied or overlooked.
3. It is based on the misused and frequently misunderstood concept of heritability. Heritability estimates were designed to predict the outcome of selective breeding programs. They are *not* an indicator of the relative influences of genes and environment (see Chapter 4).
4. Researchers rarely give serious consideration to the possibility that years of negative gene-finding results indicate that genes for behavioral differences and psychiatric disorders do not exist.

Although most supporters of the missing heritability position fail to recognize it, a very plausible interpretation of the current state of affairs is that genes for behavior have not been found because they do not exist. As we have seen Latham and Wilson conclude, "The dearth of disease-causing genes is without question a scientific discovery of tremendous significance." Indeed, it is.

The real issue confronting researchers is not missing heritability, but missing *genes*, and there is good reason to believe that these "missing" genes are actually non-existent genes. "Where are the genes?" asked Richard Lewontin in 2009, and this question is even more relevant today (Lewontin, 2009).

Missing Heritability and the MISTRA

The MISTRA researchers also believed that the HGP would help identify numerous genes for the behaviors they studied, with Bouchard and McGue writing in 2003: "Despite the failure to find confirmed [gene] associations, the search for specific genes in personality is likely only to intensify as additional behaviorally relevant genes are identified through the Human Genome Project" (Bouchard & McGue, 2003, p. 26). In 2009, 30 years after initiating the MISTRA, Bouchard continued to write about gene discovery as something that would occur in the future: "The coming of the age of molecular genetics, genomics and the study of genetic network architecture will add dramatically to our understanding of how genes influence the phenotype of IQ" (Bouchard, 2009, p. 540). In his 2013 discussion of the status of behavioral- and public health-related molecular genetic research, McGue could not name a gene discovery for any MISTRA-studied behavior, believing that "most of the heritability remains missing" (McGue, 2013, p. S7). A year later, he and his colleagues published the results of their (negative) IQ gene-finding study, and recognized that other researchers had also failed to uncover genes for "general cognitive ability" (Kirkpatrick et al., 2014).

Believing that the "heritabilities of most traits have been established," in *Born Together—Reared Apart* Segal wrote that "interest in uncovering the underlying molecular and environmental mechanisms is paramount" (2012, p. 265), and that "molecular genetic advances have largely changed the complexion of human behavioral-genetic research and reordered its agenda" (p. 323). While deciding to endorse the "missing heritability" perspective (as opposed to deciding to reassess the MISTRA findings), she claimed that several "common gene variants" have been found for schizophrenia, and that many genes of small effect had been found to underlie general intelligence (p. 324). Segal stressed the "focus on specific genes," and the use of "new techniques" that "promise to bring us closer to the answers" (p. 323).

Faced with the reality of failed gene-finding attempts, approaching retirement in 2008, Bouchard cited the example of corn oil production as a characteristic that is known to be "heritable," yet has yielded few actual genetic variants. Noting that "corn is the world's largest crop in metric tons grown," he asked, "What do we know about corn oil? For one thing, we know it is 'heritable.' The longest-running selection experiment in the history of genetics (100 years) involves corn oil. Lines have been selected systematically for high and low oil content" (Bouchard, 2008, p. 26).

Bouchard used corn oil as an example of the difficulty of finding genes for characteristics that have a presumed important genetic component. He observed that "genes for corn oil have not been identified even though powerful breeding experiments have been available for a long time," concluding that "the argument that no one has discovered genes for behavior, as an argument against behavior genetic research, is both wrong (such genes are known) and premature (we know it is a difficult problem)"

(p. 27). Bouchard did not identify these "known" genes for behavior, or explain why gene discovery is "difficult."

The use of heritability estimates to predict the results of a selective breeding program for corn oil production, where many environmental factors can be controlled, is a proper use of such estimates. As Wendy Johnson recognized, "Heritability estimation was originally developed to measure the response to selection that could be expected from agricultural breeding experiments" (Johnson, 2010, p. 179). We saw in Chapter 4 that some critics have argued that predicting the results of a selective breeding program is the only valid use of such estimates (Wahlsten, 1990). At the same time, the use of heritability estimates as an indicator of the strength of genetic influences on behavioral differences is an *im*proper and misleading use of the heritability concept. The heritability of corn oil production may indeed be a valid indicator of the "missing heritability" molecular genetic researchers in this area should expect to find, whereas heritability estimates for human behavior have completely misled behavioral geneticists and molecular genetic researchers in their futile attempts to identify genes.

Still, by 2008 researchers could find only a small fraction of the genes responsible for corn oil variation, which may have provided some support to Bouchard's argument that it is difficult to identify genes that behavioral geneticists argue must exist. By 2013, however, researchers using the GWA approach identified 26 genetic variants associated with corn oil concentration, which they concluded "could explain up to 83% of the phenotypic variation" (Li et al., 2013, p. 43). At the same time, the fruitless search for genes in the social and behavioral sciences continues, based largely on the mistaken belief that twin studies have established beyond any doubt that human behavioral variation, like corn oil variation, has an important genetic component. In a 2014 publication, Bouchard recognized that the search for genes presumed to underlie general intelligence (*g*) has produced "results [that] to date have been dismal in comparison with expectation" (Bouchard, 2014).

McGue and Bouchard wrote in 1998 that a possible (although in their opinion an unlikely) explanation for the failure to discover genes for "specific human behavioral phenotypes" is "that we have been misled by the twin and adoption study findings" (McGue & Bouchard, 1998, p. 18). A central argument of this book is that the continuing failure to discover genes for behavior characteristics most likely is the result of researchers having been misled by twin studies.

A New Approach

In the context of the ongoing "missing heritability" problem, researchers developed a new molecular genetic method in 2010, sometimes referred to as "genomewide complex trait analysis," or GCTA (Yang et al., 2010). As described by Plomin and colleagues, the GCTA method "compares chance genetic similarity across hundreds of thousands of SNPs for each pair of individuals in a matrix of thousands of unrelated individuals.... the large sample size makes it possible to estimate heritability directly from DNA markers measured on the microarray." However, "it does not identify which SNPs are responsible for the heritability of a trait" (Plomin, DeFries, et al., 2013, pp. 90–91). The method does not identify causal genetic variants, but rather estimates total genetic variance on the basis of comparing the genetic profiles of a large group of people. In other words, it can produce a "finding" of genes even when no specific genes are identified. As the GCTA developers put it, "we estimate the total variance explained by the SNPs without focusing on individual SNPs" (Visscher, Yang, & Goddard, 2010, p. 517).

The original study, published in 2010 by Yang and colleagues, assessed the genetic basis of human height variation (Yang et al., 2010). Previous researchers had estimated the heritability of height at 80 percent, yet GWA studies had identified only 5 percent of the genetic variants responsible. Using the new GCTA method, Yang and colleagues estimated that the proportion of height variance "explained by the SNPs" is 45 percent (p. 566). Genetic researchers sometimes refer to variation in human height as an example of a characteristic that we "know" is "highly heritable," but where gene-finding efforts have encountered difficulty. However, instead of arguing that the "missing heritability" of human height variation suggests that causal genes must exist for behavioral variation, attention should be refocused on the many problems with the concept of heritability itself, even as it applies to human height.

Although the GCTA method was developed as a means of solving the missing heritability problem, like GWA studies and other methods, it is based on assuming the validity of heritability estimates for human behavioral characteristics, as well as assuming that twin studies have established the genetic basis of these characteristics. The validity of each of these assumptions, as we have seen, is very questionable. And yet, leading behavioral geneticists such as Plomin and Turkheimer embraced GCTA and saw it as a way out of the missing heritability conundrum (Plomin, DeFries et al., 2013; Turkheimer, 2011a). Turkheimer even saw it as the ultimate refutation of the arguments of twin research critics, writing that "the new paradigm" has put criticism of the assumptions of family and twin studies "to rest" (Turkheimer, 2011b, p. 235). He believed that the GCTA method "should drive a stake through the heart of a classical line of argument against classical behavioral genetics and its attendant statistical assumptions" (p. 236).

Negative Results, Once Again

Cracks in the GCTA method already began appearing in 2012 and 2013, when researchers using the method found that heritability accounted for by GCTA estimates was similar to previous GWA studies, and was far below estimates based on twin studies. In a 2012 study of the theorized personality dimensions of neuroticism and extraversion, Vinkhuyzen and colleagues used the GCTA method and found that the proportion of variance explained by variants in linkage disequilibrium with common SNPs was 12 percent for extraversion, and only 6 percent for neuroticism (Vinkhuyzen et al., 2012). This contrasted with much higher heritability estimates based on previous twin studies. In 2013, Trzaskowski, Plomin and colleagues conducted a study on anxiety-related behaviors in childhood, finding GCTA variance estimates of 1–19 percent (none reaching statistical significance), whereas twin method MZT–DZT comparisons had produced heritability estimates of 50–61 percent (Trzaskowski, Eley, et al., 2013). In another 2013 publication, Essi Viding, Plomin and their colleagues performed a GCTA study of "callous-unemotional (CU) behavior in children." Although the authors of previous CU twin studies had estimated heritability ranging from 45 percent to 67 percent, the GCTA results showed that "estimates of heritability were near zero" (Viding et al., 2013, p. 1). Viding and colleagues even coined a new term for this discrepancy, the "missing GCTA heritability" (p. 6).

In an October, 2013 study, Trzaskowski, Dale, and Plomin compared GCTA results with twin method results in a study of "childhood behavior problems" which included autistic, depressive, hyperactive, anxiety, and conduct symptoms. The title of their article was clear: "No Genetic Influence for Childhood Behavior Problems from DNA Analysis" (Trzaskowski, Dale, & Plomin, 2013). The researchers used a large sample of over 2,000 twin pairs, and over 2,000 individuals for the GCTA analysis, and were confronted with a large difference between twin method results and the GCTA results. The twin study findings reflected the usual behavioral genetic conclusions based on MZT–DZT comparisons and the acceptance of its EEA, with the researchers calculating heritabilities in the 40–60 percent range. The GCTA estimates, however, "are nonsignificant and mostly zero for self-report and parent measures of behavior problems" (p. 1051). They again referred to this discrepancy as the "missing GCTA heritability," which they contrasted with the previous "missing GWA heritability."

Trzaskowski, Dale, and Plomin asked why GCTA results

> show no significant genetic influence for diverse childhood behavior problems as rated by parents, teachers, or children themselves, even though twin study estimates of heritability are significant and substantial in the same sample using the same measures, and even though GCTA estimates for cognitive traits are significant and substantial?
>
> (Trzaskowski, Dale, & Plomin, 2013, p. 1052).

The researchers then attempted to explain their contradictory findings, describing unexpected results in ways that did not challenge the genetic theories upon which gene searches are based. In doing so, they rejected the possibility that invalidating false assumptions and other major problems underlie both the GCTA method *and* twin studies.

In an accompanying article, Faraone recognized that the 2013 Trzaskowski, Dale, and Plomin GCTA study contradicted the findings of the "Cross-Disorder Group of the Psychiatric Genomics Consortium" study published online in February, 2013. In that study, the investigators concluded, "Our findings show that specific SNPs are associated with a range of psychiatric disorders of childhood onset or adult onset" (Cross-Disorder Group of the Psychiatric Genomics Consortium, 2013, p. 1371). The results of the Cross-Disorder Group study were reported with great fanfare in the media as constituting important new gene discoveries in psychiatry. As Faraone candidly posed the question, "Nonreplication had been the curse of molecular psychiatric genetics for decades. Has it returned in a new guise?" (Faraone, 2013, p. 1007).

The answer to Faraone's question probably is yes, because, due to major problems and false assumptions underlying previous family, twin, and adoption studies, in addition to the questionable validity and reliability of psychiatric disorders in general, the "curse" Faraone referred to is merely the scientific likelihood that genes for the major psychiatric disorders do not exist. This is a cause for celebration, not despair, as society can now part ways with genetic diversions and focus on environmental causes, interventions, and prevention.

A Faltering Paradigm?

In other GCTA studies showing positive results, it is likely that the method produces false-positive findings based on systematic errors and a reliance on questionable assumptions and concepts, similar to those found in GWA studies and other types of molecular genetic research methods that have failed to uncover genes for behavioral characteristics. Evan Charney listed several potential biases in GCTA studies, including the failure to adequately account for genetic differences based on variation found among differing populations (population stratification), which introduces a potential environmental confound into GCTA studies. Charney concluded that the GCTA search for thousands of genetic variants of tiny effect "is the last gasp of a failed paradigm" (Charney, 2013b). Commenting on a 2011 GCTA study of IQ, critical geneticist Mae-Wan Ho wrote, "This exercise sounds more like a counsel of despair than a solution to the problem, and the result certainly does not offer any useful predictive information" (Ho, 2013, p. 76).

Most likely, these will become the final appraisals of the GCTA method once it runs its course in behavioral genetics and psychiatry, which recent history tells us will be followed by yet another molecular genetic technique promising to deliver the long-lost "missing heritability," "missing GCTA heritability," "hidden heritability" (Gibson, 2010), "phantom heritability" (Zuk et al., 2012), or some other future "[fill-in-the-blank] heritability." Therefore, although the GCTA approach does appear to be a "gasp of a failed paradigm," it is probably not the last gasp. What actually *is* "missing" is an independent commission charged with the task of thoroughly examining behavioral genetic and psychiatric genetic family, twin, and adoption studies—including related theories, assumptions, original publications, and the works of the critics—in order to determine whether or not these studies prove anything about genetics.

Conclusions

Although it is rarely framed as such, molecular genetic research is the ultimate test of genetic interpretations of twin studies, which include twin method MZT–DZT comparisons and TRA studies. The results of decades of molecular genetic research are now in, and they suggest that, with possible rare exceptions, there are no genetic variants underlying normal variation in human cognitive ability (IQ), personality, criminality, schizophrenia and other psychiatric disorders, and behavioral differences in general.[2] Of course, a future finding that they *do* exist would not necessarily support the continuing use of genetic approaches in these areas, as society could decide to focus on the importance of environmental factors, most of which are changeable.[3]

The fields of behavioral genetics and psychiatric genetics appear to have painted themselves into a corner by going "all in" with molecular genetic research that has failed to produce the causative genetic variants that they have been claiming for decades must exist. As they attempt to extricate themselves from this corner, the glaring problems and environmental confounds of twin research will be further illuminated. The leaders of these fields are free to interpret the results of twin and adoption studies any way they wish, and to ignore or dismiss the arguments of the critics, but they will never be able to produce "IQ genes," "personality genes," or genes for psychiatric disorders if they do not exist.

Rather than give serious consideration to the possibility that they have found no genes because there are no genes, the past few decades have shown that researchers downplay the implications of negative findings at the same time that they claim that some new or future technology or technique will finally deliver the promised genes. A far better approach would begin with the recognition that the best explanation for a genetically "positive" twin study finding, in combination with negative molecular genetic results, is not that "heritability is missing," but that something is wrong with previous genetic interpretations of twin data.

Notes

1 Versions of points 1–4 were discussed in previous publications (Chaufan & Joseph, 2013; Joseph, 2012).
2 As an example of a possible rare exception, Flint, Greenspan, and Kendler mentioned the ALDH2 gene, which appears to influence the risk for alcoholism. They cited this example to counter what they saw as the mistaken argument by critics "that 'science has not yet found a gene that conclusively influences risk for psychiatric disorder'" (Flint, Greenspan, & Kendler, 2010, p. 58).
3 In 2014, Kendler concluded that all humans carry genes predisposing them to schizophrenia: "The genetic risk for schizophrenia is widely distributed in human populations so that we all carry some degree of risk" (Kendler, 2014, p. 1).

10
THE CRUMBLING PILLARS OF BEHAVIORAL GENETICS

> Molecular genetics has come on center stage in behavioral genetics much faster than anyone anticipated.
> — Behavioral genetic researchers Robert Plomin, John DeFries, Ian Craig, & Peter McGuffin, 2003 (Plomin, DeFries, Craig, & McGuffin, 2003, p. 531)

> The truth is that next to nothing is determined by the genes, and our environments are hugely powerful.
> — Behavioral genetic researchers Kathryn Asbury and Robert Plomin, 2014 (Asbury & Plomin, 2014, p. 96)

Schizophrenia researcher Timothy Crow wrote in 2008 that molecular genetic researchers investigating disorders such as schizophrenia had previously thought that "success was inevitable—one would 'drain the pond dry' and there would be the genes!"[1] But as Crow concluded, "The pond is empty" (Crow, 2008, p. 1682). Several years later, the psychiatric genetic and behavioral genetic "gene ponds" appear to have been completely drained, and there are few, if any, genes to be found.

A generation earlier, leading genetic researchers in psychiatry and behavioral genetics were preparing for the discovery of the genes they believed caused psychiatric disorders such as schizophrenia and bipolar disorder, in an era that Robert Plomin and colleagues later referred to as being characterized by the "euphoria of the 1980s" (Plomin, DeFries, Knopik, & Neiderhiser, 2013, p. 240). Also looking back, Faraone wrote, "In the 1970s and 1980s, hope ran high as new methods in molecular genetics promised quick discoveries and answers to basic questions of etiology and pathophysiology" (Faraone, 2013, p. 1006). In this book I have attempted to show that the behavioral genetic and psychiatric genetic pillars of twin research and molecular genetic research are crumbling together at the same time, and that there are few other pillars strong enough to hold up the theoretical structures these fields rest upon.

We have seen that leading behavioral genetic researchers of the early 1990s attempted to shift the field's focus away from twin and adoption studies and towards gene-finding efforts. After all, they reasoned, "quantitative genetic" studies of families, twins, and adoptees had established beyond question that variation in "normally distributed" psychological characteristics such as personality and IQ had an important genetic component. As Plomin recalled in 2002, "In 1990, I decided that quantitative genetic research had gone about as far as it could in documenting genetic influence on g . . . . The most exciting prospect was to try to identify some of the QTLs responsible for the heritability of g. This led to a project called the IQ QTL Project" (Plomin, 2002, p. 217). QTLs, or quantitative trait loci, are presumed genetic variants of varying effect sizes that underlie presumed quantitative (continuous) characteristics, such as IQ and personality.

The 1990s did in fact witness an explosion of molecular genetic research attempting to pinpoint the genes believed to underlie human behavioral differences. This was followed by the publication of the initial working draft of the human genome sequence in 2001, which many researchers believed would lead to rapid gene discoveries in psychiatry and psychology. According to prominent researchers Kathleen Merikangas and Neil Risch, writing in 2003, "Completion of the human genome project has provided an unprecedented opportunity to identify the effect of gene variants on complex phenotypes, such as psychiatric disorders" (Merikangas & Risch, 2003, p. 626).

In light of the ongoing failure to discover genes, it is worth looking back at behavioral geneticists' numerous claims and predictions published in textbooks and leading scientific journals. Here I focus mainly on the writings of Robert Plomin, who we have seen is one of the world's leading and most influential behavioral geneticists, and is the lead author of *Behavioral Genetics* (Sixth Edition; Plomin, DeFries, et al., 2013).

Three and a Half Decades of Claims and Predictions

1978–1990

As far back as 1978, DeFries and Plomin claimed that "evidence has accumulated to indicate that inheritance of bipolar depression involves X-linkage in some instances" (DeFries & Plomin, 1978, p. 479). Although these and other claims were not replicated, psychiatric molecular genetic research took off in the 1980s, a decade that witnessed many more highly publicized yet subsequently unsubstantiated gene-finding claims. In 1983, Plomin wrote that developmental behavioral genetics will "profit from the spectacular advances made in molecular genetics during the past few years," which "hold the promise of directly assessing genetic variability among individuals." However, he believed that the "successful application of these techniques to the study of multifactorial characters is not likely to happen in this century" (Plomin, 1983, p. 255).

Another group of prominent behavioral genetic researchers wrote in a 1988 *Annual Review of Psychology* contribution, "We are witnessing major breakthroughs in identifying genes coding for some mental disorders" (Loehlin, Willerman, & Horn, 1988, p. 124). The late 1980s saw the publication of two widely reported, yet subsequently non-replicated, "gene discoveries" for bipolar disorder (Egeland, Gerhard, Pauls, Sussex, & Kidd, 1987) and schizophrenia (Sherrington et al., 1988).

Plomin discussed psychiatric molecular genetic research in a 1989 article written for *American Psychologist* (Plomin, 1989). He noted the then-recent schizophrenia and manic depression gene-finding claims and subsequent failures to replicate, yet concluded that the linkage findings probably were valid in each of the populations used in the original Egeland and Sherrington studies.

In the 1990 Second Edition of *Behavioral Genetics*, Plomin and colleagues wrote, "During the past decade, advances in molecular genetics have led to the dawn of a new era for behavioral genetic research." They believed that "these techniques are already beginning to revolutionize behavioral genetic research in some areas, especially psychopathology" (Plomin, DeFries, & McClearn, 1990, p. 151). However, these "revolutionary advances" were not actual replicated gene findings. Also in 1990, Plomin wrote in *Science* that "behavior is a new frontier for molecular biology" (Plomin, 1990, p. 183), and predicted that "the use of molecular biology techniques will revolutionize behavioral genetics" (p. 188).

1991–1995

In their 1991 *Annual Review of Psychology* contribution, Plomin and Rende wrote that the "pace of developments" in the molecular genetics field "is breathtaking," and that the future completion of the HGP "will lead to the identification of many more genetic markers" (Plomin & Rende, 1991, p. 176). They asked us to "imagine being able to identify behavior-relevant DNA variation directly in individuals rather than resorting to indirect estimates of a genetic component of variance derived from twin and adoption studies," and concluded that "advances in molecular biology are on the way to making this fantasy a reality" (p. 176). Plomin and Rende made the following forecast:

> We predict that in less than ten years—perhaps by the time of the *Annual Review of Psychology* chapter on human behavioral genetics scheduled for the year 2000—molecular-genetic techniques will have revolutionized human behavioral genetics.
>
> (Plomin & Rende, 1991, p. 176)

No chapter on human behavioral genetics appeared in the 2000 edition of the *Annual Review*, but had there been one the authors would have had no revolutionary molecular genetic findings to report. Plomin and Bergeman wrote similarly in another 1991 publication: "We predict that 10 years from now, at the turn of the century, molecular genetic techniques will have revolutionized human behavioral genetics" (Plomin & Bergeman, 1991a, p. 424).

In a 1991 article by McClearn, Plomin and colleagues, entitled "The Gene Chase in Behavioral Science," the authors described several gene discoveries in agriculture. They predicted that similar success would occur in behavioral research: "It is clear that attempts to associate marker loci with quantitative variation have been very successful in these organisms and for these traits. There is little reason to expect that we will have less success in dealing with behavioral variables" (McClearn, Plomin, Gora-Maslak, & Crabbe, 1991, p. 224).

Plomin and his colleagues reported the first results of the IQ QTL Project in a 1994 publication (Plomin et al., 1994), and Plomin participated in a 1999 molecular genetic study in which the researchers believed they had found QTLs associated with IQ (Fisher et al., 1999). However, this study, as well as subsequent molecular genetic IQ studies, was not replicated. In a 1994 article written for *Science*, Plomin and colleagues reported genetic linkages and associations for reading disability, sexual orientation, alcoholism, drug use, violence, paranoid schizophrenia, and hyperactivity (Plomin, Owen, & McGuffin, 1994, p. 1737).

In a 1995 publication Plomin wrote, "I predict that by the turn of the century, psychologists will routinely use DNA markers of genetic risk in their research in the same way many psychologists now use biological markers, such as hormones and evoked potentials" (Plomin, 1995, p. 114). In the same article, he sought to "introduce psychologists to recent molecular genetics research that has begun to identify specific genes associated with behavior" (p. 114).

1996–1999

In the Third Edition of *Behavioral Genetics*, published in 1997, Plomin and colleagues continued their theme that "Psychology is at the dawn of a new era," and that "many genes responsible for the widespread genetic influence on behavior will be identified and routinely used to assess genetic risk within the next decade" (Plomin, DeFries, McClearn, & Rutter, 1997, p. 107). In the same year, Rutter and Plomin wrote that, although gene discoveries had not yet been made in psychiatry, "it is obvious that these are likely to be forthcoming very soon as findings with respect to schizophrenia, affective disorder and dyslexia all show" (Rutter & Plomin, 1997, p. 214). Plomin contributed a 1997 chapter on cognitive ability gene searches, writing that "revolutionary genetic research" will identify "specific genes that contribute to genetic influence" (Plomin, 1997, p. 90). He began this chapter by writing, "I predict that the next generation of psychologists will wonder what all the nature–nurture fuss was about" (p. 89).

Plomin and Rutter co-authored a 1998 article for *Child Development*, where they informed developmental psychologists, "Genes associated with behavioral dimensions and disorders are beginning to be identified" (Plomin & Rutter, 1998, p. 1223). They added, "As associations between genes and complex behavioral traits are found, they are beginning to revolutionize research" (p. 1225). The authors were attempting to prepare psychologists for gene discoveries in the making, which they believed would soon revolutionize their field. In another 1998 publication, Plomin and colleagues wrote that a pair of 1996 studies finding an association between the D4DR gene and the personality trait of "novelty seeking" constituted a "watershed" event for the field (Plomin, Corley, Caspi, Fulker, & DeFries, 1998, p. 218).[2] In another 1998 article, Plomin and Caspi wrote of "new genetic approaches that are beginning to identify genes for personality" (Plomin & Caspi, 1998, p. 387), and claimed that "specific genes associated with personality are being discovered" (p. 388). In still another 1998 article, Plomin advised health psychologists that "DNA is coming to a neighborhood near you," and predicted that in a couple of years, "psychologists will routinely use DNA in research and perhaps even in clinical practice" (Plomin, 1998, p. 53).

2000–2002

At the dawn of the new millennium, Plomin and Crabbe predicted that "within a few years, many areas of psychology will be awash with specific genes responsible for the widespread influence of genetics on behavior" (Plomin & Crabbe, 2000, p. 806). They also predicted that, in the future, the collection of DNA samples would aid clinical psychologists "in diagnosis and to plan treatment programs" (p. 823). Elsewhere in 2000, Plomin wrote that genetic variants "are being found for personality; reading disability, and *g*, in addition to the main area of research in psychopathology" (Plomin, 2000, p. 32). In 2001, at the time of the publication of the first draft of the sequence of the human genome, McGuffin, Riley, and Plomin published an article in *Science* entitled "Toward Behavioral

Genomics," repeating the 1994 claim that gene linkages and associations had been discovered for behaviors such as aggression, schizophrenia, ADHD, male homosexuality, and dyslexia (McGuffin, Riley, & Plomin, 2001). In another 2001 publication, Plomin wrote, "Research has begun to identify QTLs responsible for the heritability of g" (Plomin, 2001, p. 138)

In the same year, Plomin and colleagues published the Fourth Edition of *Behavioral Genetics*. Here, they claimed that "ADHD is one of the first behavioral areas in which specific genes have been identified" (Plomin, DeFries, McClearn, & McGuffin, 2001, p. 1). They continued the theme that "within the next decade" genes will be identified and will be "used in psychological research and clinics to assess genetic risk" (p. 115). In 2002, Plomin and colleagues reported, "During the past decade, quantitative genetics and molecular genetics have begun to come together to identify genes that contribute to complex, quantitative traits" (Plomin, Happé, & Caspi, 2002, p. 99).

2003–2004

In the period 2003–2004, Plomin began to write more about gene discoveries as something that had not yet occurred, and less about discoveries that had been made or were in the process of being made. Having entered the "postgenomic era," in 2003 Plomin and McGuffin acknowledged that progress in identifying genes that influence behavior has "been slower than some experts expected" (Plomin & McGuffin, 2003, p. 205). They wrote that the identification of genes for schizophrenia "remains elusive" (p. 213), and the "story for major depression and bipolar depression is similar to schizophrenia" (p. 214). Nevertheless, they continued to believe that the future of molecular genetic research in psychiatry "looks bright because complex traits like psychopathology will be the major beneficiaries of postgenomic developments" (p. 223).

In his 2003 chapter in *Behavioral Genetics in the Postgenomic Era*, Plomin again placed great hope in the HGP, which "continues to shower the [behavioral genetics] field with new information and new technologies" (Plomin, 2003a, p. 196). In his chapter in a 2003 book paying tribute to Arthur Jensen (Plomin, 2003b), Plomin saw the HGP as the "crowning glory" of the twentieth century (p. 111), although he noted the "slow progress so far" in identifying genes (p. 113). A year later, McGuffin and Plomin wrote that, although "genetics is entering the golden postgenomic era," researchers would need "very large samples" to uncover genes (McGuffin & Plomin, 2004, pp. 281–282).

"The future of genetic research in developmental psychology," Plomin wrote in 2004, "lies in molecular genetic studies of DNA that will eventually identify specific DNA variants responsible for the widespread influence of genes in psychological development" (Plomin, 2004, p. 347). Elsewhere, Plomin recognized that "no solid" gene associations for IQ "have yet emerged" (Plomin & Spinath, 2004, p. 121), and that "the road ahead will be much more difficult than generally assumed" (p. 124).

2005–2011

Plomin and Asbury wrote in a 2005 article that the "future of genetic research on behavior lies in molecular genetic studies of DNA that will eventually identify specific DNA variants responsible for the widespread influence of genes in behavioral development" (Plomin & Asbury, 2005, p. 93). While claiming that "some genes have been identified" for "behavioral disorders such as schizophrenia, affective disorders, dementia, autism, reading disability, alcoholism, and hyperactivity," they recognized that the "process of identifying genes for complex traits in behavioral science as well as in medicine has been slower and more difficult than anticipated" (p. 95).

Plomin's frustration became more apparent later in 2005, when he asked, in relation to gene-finding attempts, "When are we going to be there?" He answered, "Being an optimist, my response is 'soon.'" Referring to his "Child Development, Molecular Genetics, and What to Do With Genes Once They are Found" 1998 publication he co-authored with Michael Rutter, Plomin recognized that his readers might be "skeptical, because they have heard this before" (Plomin, 2005, p. 1030). Although he claimed as always that the field was moving toward gene discoveries, he believed that behavioral genetics remained only "on the cusp of a new post-genomic era." He and his colleagues had decided not to produce a new edition of *Behavioral Genetics*, he wrote, "until we had some solid DNA results to present" (p. 1030).

Plomin and colleagues published the Fifth Edition of *Behavioral Genetics* in 2008 (Plomin, DeFries, McClearn, & McGuffin, 2008). The behavioral sciences, they wrote, remained "at the dawn of a new era" of forthcoming gene discoveries (p. 90), and again predicted, "Many genes responsible for the widespread genetic influence on behavior will be identified and used in research and clinics to assess genetic risk within the next decade" (p. 118). They repeated their previous claim that researchers had discovered genes contributing to ADHD (p. 1).

Plomin and Davis wrote very positively in 2009 about the then relatively new GWA method, placing great hope in future discoveries based on these studies, which have "revolutionized attempts to find DNA variation responsible for the high heritability of many common disorders" (Plomin & Davis, 2009, p. 66). They believed that the "future of genetics belongs to molecular genetics" (p. 64), and with much enthusiasm wrote that "the speed of discovery in genetics is now so great that it would be impossible to predict what will happen in the next five years, let alone the next 50 years." They went on to predict that, in the future, "we will each have an electronic chip with our DNA sequence," and that "individual DNA chips will herald a revolution in personalised medicine in which treatment is individually tailored rather than one-size-fits-all" (Plomin & Davis, 2009, p. 68).

In a 2010 publication, Haworth and Plomin appeared to give up hope that GWA studies would uncover genes any time soon, writing that "it seems highly unlikely that most of the genes responsible for the heritability for any complex trait will be identified in the foreseeable future" (Haworth & Plomin, 2010, pp. 783–784). They added, "We hope that our prediction about GWA research is wrong" (p. 784). In the process, they fell back on the "missing heritability" theory to explain GWA failures (see Chapter 9). Indeed, they recognized that GWA studies "are struggling to identify a few of the many genes responsible for the ubiquitous heritability of common disorders" and psychological traits (p. 791). In the face of the unexpected and disappointing failures of GWA studies and previous molecular genetic research methods, Haworth and Plomin believed that the field should return its focus to quantitative genetic studies of families, twins, and adoptees, which have a "bright future" (p. 785). In calling for a retreat to previous kinship research, Plomin apparently did not consider the possibility that the critics had been right all along that the massive flaws and untenable theoretical assumptions of twin and adoption studies explain these failures.

Plomin could not name any replicated behavioral gene findings in a 2011 publication, and continued to explain negative results on the basis of "missing heritability." According to Plomin, "The big question now in molecular genetics is how to identify the 'missing' heritability; the big question for non-shared environment is how to identify the 'missing' non-shared environment" (Plomin, 2011, p. 585). As critics have argued, both are "missing" because leading behavioral geneticists continue to place total faith in twin research, and continue to ignore the implications of other evidence, which includes Plomin's own 1998 longitudinal adoption study that found no personality correlation between birthparents and their 240 adopted-away biological offspring (Joseph, 2013a; Plomin et al., 1998; see Appendix B).

2012–2014

Plomin published an article on child development and molecular genetic research in a 2013 edition of *Child Development* (Plomin, 2013a). He admitted, "Progress has been slow in finding genes associated with behavior," recognizing that it "has been much more difficult than expected to identify genes responsible for the heritability of complex traits and common disorders" (p. 104). Despite this "slow progress," he continued to hold to the position that "family, adoption and twin designs generally converge on similar estimates of heritability" (p. 110).

Referring to his 1998 "What to Do with Genes Once They are Found" article he co-authored with Michael Rutter, Plomin recognized that the

> 1998 article was overly optimistic, especially in the use of the word "soon" in the following quote: "Although gene–behavior associations are currently available in only a few domains, the intensity of the research effort to find genes associated with behavior makes it likely that such associations will soon be widespread."
>
> (Plomin, 2013a, p. 104)

He devoted much of this 2013 article to the missing heritability issue, and spoke of gene discoveries as something that he still believed would occur in the future: "I continue to believe that once genes are found they will transform the ability of developmental research to address questions about developmental continuities, about psychopathological patterns, and about environmental risk mechanisms" (p. 114).

In the same year, Plomin and colleagues published the 2013 Sixth Edition of *Behavioral Genetics* (Plomin, DeFries, et al., 2013). This volume stood in striking contrast to Plomin's concurrent *Child Development* article in that the tone was very optimistic, extolling the "exciting" achievements of molecular genetic research, accompanied by the implication that many genes had been identified for several behavioral characteristics. Themes of Plomin's 2013 edition of *Behavioral Genetics*, written for a general audience and for students, included validation, "exciting" developments and an exciting future for the field, and gene discovery (or imminent discovery). Themes of Plomin's 2013 *Child Development* article, written for developmental psychologists, included failure, disappointment, a recognition that previous publications were overly optimistic, tempered by continued optimism that genes would eventually be discovered by using better methods.

Plomin and colleagues continued their 1990 "dawn of a new era" theme in the 2013 edition of *Behavioral Genetics*, as if more than two decades of gene-finding failures, and accompanying disappointment, had not occurred:

> It is clear that we are at the dawn of a new era in which behavioral genetic research is moving beyond the demonstration of the importance of heredity to the identification of specific genes. In clinics and research laboratories, behavioral scientists of the future will routinely collect saliva or blood and send the samples to a laboratory for DNA extraction.... Trait-specific sets

of hundreds of genes will be available on microarrays that can genotype even large samples at modest cost; these "gene set" data will be incorporated into behavioral research as genetic risk indicators.

(Plomin, DeFries, et al., 2013, p. 327)

He therefore continued the same optimistic themes he had put forward since at least 1991, when he spoke of the "breathtaking" pace of molecular genetic research. Such optimism was perhaps understandable during the "euphoria of the 1980s," but decades of failure have led to molecular genetic researchers' *dys*phoria of the 2010s. Yet the 2013 edition of Plomin's textbook gave little indication of this change.

The section on schizophrenia molecular genetic research in this Sixth Edition of *Behavioral Genetics* (Plomin, DeFries, et al., 2013, pp. 239–241) ended on an optimistic note, and implied that genes have been discovered in the past few years. Plomin and colleagues claimed that studies have "detected new possible loci," that the International Schizophrenia Consortium "has found that hundreds of genes, each with small individual effects, contribute to the risk for developing the disorder," and that "rare and large CNVs associated with schizophrenia have been found on several chromosomes" (pp. 240–241). Similar claims based on subsequently non-replicated schizophrenia gene associations were made in previous editions of *Behavioral Genetics* (for example, see Plomin, DeFries, et al., 1997, p. 177; Plomin et al., 2001, pp. 215–216; Plomin et al., 2008, p. 207). To repeat: given the established track record, all gene-finding claims in the behavioral and social sciences should be assumed to be false positive until proven otherwise.

The 2013 edition of *Behavioral Genetics* concluded with a chapter entitled "The Future of Behavioral Genetics," which was "reviewed by 30 of the world's top behavioral geneticists and represents a consensus statement about the future of the field" (p. xviii). In this concluding chapter, Plomin and colleagues again wrote of the "breathtaking pace of molecular genetics," which led them "to predict that behavior scientists will increasingly use DNA markers as a tool in their research to identify the relevant genetic differences among individuals" (p. 352). From a current critical vantage point, however, the most "breathtaking" development in behavioral genetics has been its apparent discovery that genes underlying human behavioral variation do not exist.

Optimism and excitement were again the theme of a 2013 article by Plomin and Simpson, who began by writing, "The momentum of genomic science will carry it far into the future and into the heart of research on typical and atypical behavioral development" (Plomin & Simpson, 2013, p. 1263). Again writing as if decades of molecular genetic failures had not happened, they wrote, "A momentous shift is underway; these two worlds of genetics [molecular genetics and quantitative genetics] are merging as genomic technology makes it possible to identify the polygenic origins of individual differences in complex traits and common disorders" (p. 1264). They predicted that complete genome sequencing would become part of newborn screening in the future: "Our long-term prediction for the future of genomics for developmentalists is the routine use of polygenic scores derived from DNA sequence data" (p. 1274).

Plomin and colleagues published an IQ molecular genetic study in 2013 based on the "new approach" of GCTA, which was discussed in Chapter 9. They concluded that they found DNA markers that "accounted for .66 of the estimated heritability" of cognitive abilities (Plomin, Haworth, et al., 2013, p. 562). They believed that the heritability estimates they derived using the GCTA method help to validate twin studies, from which researchers derive similar estimates. However, we saw in Chapter 9 that it is very likely that the GCTA approach yields false-positive results in ways similar to the previous failed approaches, such as GWA studies. Another major potential bias in this study was that IQ tests were given over the Internet, and therefore were outside of the researchers' control.

We also saw in Chapter 9 that a combined GCTA/twin method study published by Plomin and colleagues in 2013, based on thousands of participants, found no significant GCTA findings for any of the several "childhood behavior problems" they studied, while simultaneously finding "substantial genetic influence" in the twin method data (Trzaskowski, Dale, & Plomin, 2013). According to the investigators, behavioral "problems in childhood—whether rated by parents, teachers, or children themselves—show no significant genetic influence using GCTA, even though twin study estimates of heritability are substantial in the same sample, and even though both GCTA and twin study estimates of genetic influence are substantial for cognitive and anthropometric traits" (p. 1048). As we saw, they explained the results on the basis of the new "missing GCTA heritability" position.

A more realistic interpretation of these results, however, is the very plausible one that I have proposed in this book—that the best explanation for a "positive" twin study finding in combination with negative molecular genetic results is not that "heritability is missing," but that something is wrong with genetic interpretations of twin data. From a critical perspective, what Plomin and colleagues saw as contradictory results are consistent with the position that the equal environment of the twin method is false, and that TRA studies are flawed on several critical dimensions.

We saw in Chapter 9 that Turkheimer believed that the GCTA method would "drive a stake through the heart of" criticism of behavioral genetic theories and methods, and finally put criticism of twin studies "to rest." The opposite scenario appears to be playing out before us, however, as leading behavioral genetic researchers struggle to prevent negative GCTA findings, and the obvious false assumptions underlying twin research, from driving a stake through the heart of twin studies.

In yet another 2013 article published for an academic audience, Plomin recognized that "DNA research has not yet delivered the genes that developmentalists are eager to incorporate in their research" (Plomin, 2013b, p. 1147). He again referred to the "missing heritability problem" that "plagues not just behavioral research but all genomic research in the life sciences" (p. 1147). In an article published in the fall of 2013 in *Nature*, Plomin was quoted as saying, in relation to finding a genetic contribution to IQ at the molecular genetic level, "I'm optimistic that we will find it.... I'm not going to quit until we do" (Hayden, 2013, p. 27). And in an interview published the following year Plomin admitted, in relation to cognitive ability, "I've been looking for these genes for 15 years and I don't have any" (Wilby, 2014).

In 2014 Plomin published a book on genetic influences in education and achievement, co-authored by fellow behavioral geneticist Kathryn Asbury, entitled *G is for Genes: The Impact of Genetics on Education and Achievement* (Asbury & Plomin, 2014). The authors argued that genetic factors should be integrated into the educational process based on twin method data produced by Plomin's UK-based Twins' Early Development Study (TEDS) and other twin method data. Undeterred by decades of gene-finding failures and unfulfilled predictions, the book was published as Plomin and others attempted to change education policies in the United Kingdom to reflect findings from a TEDS twin study published in the fall of 2013, where he and his co-authors concluded, as always based on the validity of the twin method's EEA, that genetic factors play a substantial role in educational achievement. Plomin and his colleagues recommended the creation of "a model of education that recognizes the important role of genetics" (Shakeshaft et al., 2013, p. 1). Ten years earlier, Plomin had written that fears that genetic information would be used "to select individuals for education or employment" were based "on misunderstandings about how genes affect complex traits" (Plomin, 2003b, p. 119).

The beginning sections of *G is for Genes* were intended for readers new to behavioral genetics and followed the Plomin textbook themes of exciting times and research, punctuated by exciting discoveries, and discoveries to come. Asbury and Plomin believed that it is "time for geneticists to sit down with educationalists and policy makers," and that "we... need to be prepared for the genetic advances that are just around the corner," which will include "DNA chips" (Asbury & Plomin, 2014, p. 12).

We saw that a year earlier, writing for an academic audience, Plomin recognized that his earlier predictions had been "overly optimistic" because he had predicted that widespread gene associations would occur "soon." Yet in *G is for Genes*, an easy-reading popular work intended to effect changes in educational policies in the United Kingdom and elsewhere, Plomin was again claiming that gene discoveries "are just around the corner."

The fact that Plomin and his colleagues had been making unfulfilled predictions of this type for decades was not mentioned in this book.

Conclusions

Over 20 years ago, science writer John Horgan published a critical appraisal of behavioral genetics in *Scientific American* (Horgan, 1993). He wrote that, although there were many gene-finding claims for behavioral characteristics such as crime, bipolar disorder, schizophrenia, alcoholism, intelligence, and sexual orientation, none of these claims had been replicated. He presented the results under the heading, "Behavioral Genetics: A Lack-of Progress Report." We can now update Horgan's "progress report" and issue the field of behavioral genetics its apparent final report card: The evidence suggests that genes for the major psychiatric disorders, as well as for IQ and personality differences, do not exist. Horgan continues to follow the field, writing in a blog dated October 4th, 2013, "Ever since I first hammered behavioral genetics in my 1993 *Scientific American* article 'Eugenics Revisited,' critics have faulted me for treating the field so harshly. But over the last 20 years, the field has performed even more poorly than I expected" (Horgan, 2013).

Simply put, the gene-finding claims and predictions by Plomin and other leading behavioral geneticists turned out to be wrong. The best explanation for why this occurred is not that "heritability is missing" but that—regardless of whether twins were reared together or reared apart—previous and current claims that twin studies of behavior prove something about genetics are also wrong.

Genes (genetic variants) either exist or they do not exist. Genes do not decide that the more similar environments experienced by MZT versus DZT pairs can be transformed into a genetic effect. Genes do not decide that a 0.01 birthparent/adopted-away biological offspring correlation supports the "moderate heritability" of personality (see Appendix B). Genes do not decide that genetically identical siblings separated for the first time at age 10 can be counted as "reared-apart MZ twins" (see Pedersen, Plomin, Nesselroade, & McClearn, 1992). Genes also do not decide to explain negative findings on the basis of "missing heritability," or "missing GCTA heritability." People can and do make these decisions, but people cannot discover genes that do not exist. The numerous assumptions, decisions, predictions, and claims made by Plomin and leading behavioral genetic and psychiatric genetic researchers have been put to the ultimate test under the microscope of molecular genetic research—and the results are now in.

We cannot expect the leaders of behavioral genetics to recognize that the historical positions of their field are mistaken, that their prized research methods and "landmark" studies are massively flawed and environmentally confounded, and that family, social, cultural, economic, and political environments—and not genetics—are the main causes of psychiatric disorders and variation in human behavior. Because most leaders of the field will not allow themselves to see this, it is left to others to show that the pillars of behavioral genetics are crumbling before our very eyes.

We are indeed at the "dawn of a new era," but it will be an era very different than the one that Plomin and his colleagues envisioned.

Notes

1 This chapter is based on an updated, expanded, and revised version of an article that first appeared in *GeneWatch* (Joseph, 2011a).

2 Prominent genetic researcher C. Robert Cloninger and his colleagues wrote in 1996 about these studies, published in the same year, linking a genetic variant to "novelty seeking." They concluded that the second constituted a "quick and clear replication of the D4DR association with novelty seeking." At the same time, they recognized that the search for genes underlying schizophrenia "has been elusive" (Cloninger, Adolfsson, & Svrakic, 1996, p. 4). Six years later, in an article entitled "The Discovery of Susceptibility Genes for Mental Disorders," Cloninger announced that genes for schizophrenia had been discovered by three research teams: "Research on the genetic basis of mental disorders crossed a major watershed this summer. For the first time, specific genes have been discovered that influence susceptibility to schizophrenia" (Cloninger, 2002, p. 13365). Like virtually all such claims in behavioral genetics and psychiatric genetics, these studies were not replicated. In *The Gene Illusion*, I wrote that Cloninger's 2002 claim "is more the result of wishful thinking than objective scientific evaluation" (Joseph, 2004, p. 324). In a 1997 publication, Bouchard wrote that if the novelty-seeking results held up, "it will constitute a dramatic paradigm shift in behavior genetics" (Bouchard, 1997a, p. 289).

11
A HUMAN GENETICS PARABLE

Introduction

In the United States and other contemporary western societies, various groups have an interest in emphasizing the alleged importance of heredity, and de-emphasizing environmental causes of psychiatric disorders, common medical conditions, and the abysmal social conditions experienced by large segments of the world's population.[1] A decision to emphasize environmental causes of medical conditions would cut into profits by forcing corporations, for example, to reduce the emission of known environmental toxins. Emphasizing environmental causes of mental distress and dysfunction would reduce the enormous profits of companies that produce and market psychotropic drugs such as antidepressants, and would compel governments to reduce economic inequality and to divert the large sums of money they now spend on the military towards a dramatic improvement in social, health, and educational conditions, the elimination of poverty, the creation of jobs, investment in community programs, and so on. It therefore is not surprising that institutions and groups with political and economic interests in promoting genetic theories would attempt to steer public thinking, and research agendas, in the genetic direction.

That much current research attention remains focused on genetics, despite decades of fruitless gene-finding efforts in areas such as, for example, schizophrenia, bipolar disorder, autism, ADHD, cognitive ability (IQ), personality, and political behavior is based on the ideology of genetic determinism (sometimes referred to as hereditarianism). According to Richard Lewontin, genetic determinism is the "assumption that all-important variations in basic physiological and developmental processes are the direct result of genetic variation" (Lewontin, 2009). Genetic determinists usually recognize that environmental factors play a role, but their main focus is always on genetics (Duster, 2003).

The various eugenics textbooks appearing in the first half of the twentieth century in the United States can be understood not only as "bad science" produced by individual authors, but also as pseudoscientific statements of the views of the American upper class. An example is found in

Paul Popenoe and Roswell Johnson's 1933 Revised Edition of *Applied Eugenics*, whose 1918 edition had, according to the authors, "found widespread use as a college textbook" (Popenoe & Johnson, 1933, p. v). Major positions put forward in this book included the genetic superiority of the "Nordic race" and the accompanying genetic inferiority of "non-Nordic" and dark-skinned peoples; the hereditary nature of criminality; the need for compulsory eugenic sterilization to prevent "racial deterioration"; the mental superiority of men over women; that economic inequality is due to biological differences between social classes, and that egalitarian socialism is therefore incompatible with biological reality; that policies and institutions such as trade unions, the minimum wage, interracial marriage, feminism, and old age pensions have "dysgenic" effects and are therefore undesirable; that mental disorders are the result of poor heredity; and that in general, the leaders of society should strive to encourage the reproduction and immigration of the genetically "fit" at the same time as they attempt to prevent the reproduction and immigration of the genetically "unfit." Due to historical events, and subsequent changes in society based in large part on decades of social struggles, few contemporary authors continue to write this way.

Nevertheless, there is little reason to believe that the views of the American upper class have changed dramatically since Popenoe and Johnson's time, and it continues to exert its economic and political influence in attempts to convince the rest of us to evaluate human beings, the country, and the world as they do. Gould wrote that, despite the lack of evidence in support of genetic determinism, it is needed by "those who benefit most from the status quo":

> We live with several unpleasant biological truths, death being the most undeniable and ineluctable. If genetic determinism is true, we will learn to live with it as well. But I reiterate my statement that no evidence exists to support it, that the crude versions of past centuries have been conclusively disproved, and that its continued popularity is a function of social prejudice among those who benefit most from the status quo.
>
> (Gould, 1977, p. 258)

According to philosophy professor Phil Gasper, "biological determinism" has two main goals. The first is to try "to convince us that the social order is a consequence of unchanging human biology, so that inequality and injustice cannot be eliminated." The second, according to Gasper, is that

> in the case of problems that are impossible to ignore, it tells us to look for the solution at the level of the individual and not at the level of social institutions. The problems lie not in the structure of

society, but in some of the individuals who make up society. The solution is thus to change—or even eliminate—the individuals, not to challenge existing social structures.

(Gasper, 2004)

An extreme form of genetic determinism holds that behavioral characteristics are hereditarily set for us at birth; in other words, that people are "born that way." According to genetic researcher Dean Hamer, "People are different because they have different genes that created different brains that formed different personalities" (Hamer & Copeland, 1998, p. 25). Personality researchers Robert McCrea and Paul Costa, leading proponents of the "Five Factor" theory of personality, wrote that "personality traits are endogenous dispositions, influenced not at all by the environment" (McCrea et al., 2000, p. 175).[2] And the Nobel Laureate James Watson wrote in his forward to a major behavioral genetics textbook that "children come into the world with fixed personalities that are hard to ascribe to specific home or school environmental influences. Particularly happy children almost seem to be born that way" (Watson, 2003, p. xxii). Some early eugenicists even argued that a person's "inability to cope with the disease germ" is the "real cause of death" in medical conditions caused by known environmental pathogens (see Davenport, 1911, pp. 253–254).

Most contemporary genetic researchers believe that both genetic and environmental factors are necessary for the development of behavioral characteristics, psychiatric disorders, and common medical conditions, and many believe that environmental factors are important. Nevertheless, they continue to frame the causes in terms of genetics, with the built-in incentive that the lion's share of research dollars is directed in the genetic and biological direction. Even in the case of medical disorders such as type 2 diabetes, for which social and dietary causes are well known, a great deal of research attention continues to be focused on genetics (Chaufan, 2007).

We have seen that a key question relating to the understanding, treatment, and prevention of psychiatric disorders and common medical conditions is how society should approach them, even if genetic factors play a role. Should society focus on people's genes, or on their environments? Current approaches in behavioral genetics, psychiatric genetics, and medical genetics continue to focus on an individual's alleged "inability to cope" with environmental adversities and pathogens, as opposed to the approach of focusing on reducing, eliminating, or mitigating such environmental adversities and pathogens. I have used the word "approach" in this book to emphasize the fact that the leaders of society and science *choose* whether to focus on heredity or on the environment. The behavioral genetic argument that society and science should focus on the "complex interplay" of genes and environment is sometimes used to alleviate fears of genetic determinism. Although the importance of the environment is usually acknowledged, the focus remains squarely on genetics.

The following story illustrates the differences between environmental and genetic approaches in relation to human behavioral differences, and as they relate to the understanding and prevention of psychiatric disorders and some common medical conditions. I am confident that informed readers will recognize the analogous ideas, research strategies, interest groups, publications, and historical controversies that encompass every aspect of this story.

A Human Genetics Parable

There was once a city of 500,000 inhabitants named Genomia. The city had been victimized by a group of arsonists, calling themselves the "House Burning Crew," who had begun a campaign of setting fire to five of Genomia's 50,000 single-family homes each week. Before these attacks began, it was a rare occurrence for a house to burn down in Genomia.

The citizens became incensed and fearful, and decided to dedicate a portion of the city finances to stop the arson attacks. A group led by Mayor Ellen Geewas argued that, although everyone recognized that people were involved in setting the fires, the main problem was the variation among Genomia's houses in their ability to withstand arson attacks. She pointed out that some houses did not burn down when the arsonists attacked, whereas other houses did. Although all of Genomia's houses had been built of wood, various types were used in their construction. These included the less flammable hardwoods such as oak, mahogany, teak, walnut, and maple, and the more flammable softwoods such as cedar, Douglas fir and pine. It was known that each type of wood burned at different rates and varied in its degree of flammability.

Mayor Geewas therefore proposed allocating a portion of Genomia's budget to hire a company to scan the wood cells of the city's 50,000 houses and to determine which houses were most likely to burn. She argued that after the company completed its work, citizens would finally be able to understand and prevent arson in their city. Genomia's newspapers and Internet sites spoke in a virtually unanimous voice that, while it was still necessary to keep an eye out for the people setting the fires, this wood cell scan was the best way to prevent further arson from occurring. Meanwhile, houses continued to burn down at the rate of five per week.

Although there was some grumbling about the Mayor's approach, she repeatedly justified her strategy on, as she called it, a "splendid natural experiment" that had occurred in the community. It seemed that around 3 percent of Genomia's houses had been built in *pairs* at the same time. These houses, which were built on adjacent lots, were popularly known as "The Twin House-Pairs of Genomia." Moreover, two types of house-pairs had been built. The first type was built with the identical kind of wood and with identical plans, and was known as a "monomaterial house-pair" (usually referred to as "MM"). The second type of pair consisted of houses that had been built with somewhat differing plans and kinds of wood. These pairs were known as "dimaterial house-pairs" (usually referred to as "DM"). The method used to compare them was known as the "house-pair method."

Mayor Geewas believed that by applying the house-pair method of comparing the flammability of MM house-pairs versus that of the DM house-pairs, the city would be able to assess how much of the variation of arson was due to the materials used to build the houses, and how much was due to arsonists. She believed that it was important to quantify this variation, and she cited the concept of "arsonability," which was presented as a number ranging from 0.0 to 1.0. Zero arsonability meant that the type of wood used to build the houses played no role in the arson attacks and that people are the main culprits; an arsonability estimate approaching 1.0 meant that the variation of wood type explained virtually all of the arson variability among the city's 50,000 houses, and that arsonists played little, if any, role. (Although most people knew that the House Burning Crew was involved in the arson attacks, the Mayor and her allies continued to argue that the people involved could not be easily identified, and were therefore "mysterious.")

The Mayor hired a team of "house-pair researchers" to study the flammability of each pair of houses. Using the house-pair method, they started with house-pairs in which one house was burned by arsonists. Then they assessed whether the second house also burned in the attack. (The House Burning Crew usually attempted to burn down both houses in a house-pair.) The researchers obtained the following house-pair method results. Among the MM pairs, which had been built identically, when one house burned, the second house also burned roughly 85 percent of the time. Among the DM pairs, which were built differently, the second house burned only 40 percent of the time. The arsonability statistic is calculated by doubling the difference between the MM versus DM pair burn rate, or by feeding these figures into more complex "arson model-fitting" procedures. This yielded an arsonability coefficient of 0.9 (or 90 percent), and the researchers concluded that about 90 percent of the arson variation among Genomia's houses was due to wood cell variation. Meanwhile, houses continued to burn down at the rate of five per week.

To bolster her case, the Mayor pointed to a few rare cases where house-pairs had been built identically on adjacent lots, but where one of the houses had been removed within the first few years of construction and had been relocated to a different (yet very similar) part of the city, often only a few blocks away. Because research showed that both of these "separated MM" house-pairs were similarly disposed to burn with the same effort, she claimed that this finding supported her argument in favor of the high arsonability of Genomia's houses, and that identifying and arresting the arsonists would do little to prevent houses from burning. Meanwhile, houses continued to burn down at the rate of five per week.

Several of Genomia's journalists and scientists published widely distributed and influential books, where they wrote that house-pair research had established: (1) the primary importance of the houses' differing susceptibilities to burning down after an arson attack, which was based on the type of wood cells the houses were made of; (2) that the house-pair method, and especially studies of separated MM houses, had forever changed the way we understand and approach arson; and (3) the obsolescence of the "sentimental" idea that arsonists were the main factor in intentional fire setting.

In one of these books, entitled *The Blank House*, the author argued that house-pair research showed that arson susceptibility is built into houses from the first day of construction, which refuted previous theorists who, he claimed, argued that all houses had been built identically and that all arson susceptibility variation was caused by events that took place after the houses had been completed. Other books supporting the Mayor's arson prevention strategy included *The Agile Wood Cell*, *The Arsonist Assumption*, *Built Like That*, *Entwined Houses*, *House Pairs: And What They Tell Us About What Houses Are*, *The Limits of Arresting Arsonists*, *Living With Our Wood Cells*, *Mean Wood Cells*, *No Two Houses Alike*, *The Selfish Wood Cell*, and *Wood Cells and Destiny*.

By far the most controversial of these books was entitled *The Wooden Curve*. In it, the authors argued that houses made out of darker-color wood were inherently more flammable than houses made out of lighter wood, and that no amount of wood treatment or arson prevention measures could eliminate the gap. The authors suggested that the owners of expensive lighter-wood houses would be compelled to build high fire-resistant walls, and hire their own police force, to separate their houses from the potential harm caused by the more arson-vulnerable houses made from darker wood. The authors were inspired by an earlier controversial Arson Science investigator at Genomia State University, who began his widely discussed article on the importance of arsonability estimates by writing, "Stopping arsonists has been tried and it apparently has failed." Meanwhile, houses continued to burn down at the rate of five per week.

One laboratory-based wood scientist at Genomia State University came out with another provocative tract called *The Wood Cell Bomb*, whose cover featured a photograph of an entire city set aflame by arsonists. In it, she attempted to revive the long-discredited doctrine of "woodgenics," which warned of the dangers that the most flammable houses posed to all other houses in the community. Early woodgenists had theorized that construction company foremen would see less-expensive "feeble-wooded" flammable houses and would be encouraged to reproduce many more of their kind, which eventually would lead to fire destroying the entire community and its people unless society intervened with "woodgenic foresight."

The father of the discipline, Sir Wellbourne Francis, had coined the term "woodgenics" and was the first to propose using house-pairs to assess for arsonability. Francis initiated the field with his nineteenth-century classic work *Hereditary Arson-Resistant Houses*, where he made the seminal discovery that the houses of the offspring of wealthy British aristocrats were as well constructed and arson-resistant as those of their parents, and were much more arson-resistant than the houses of the offspring of working-class parents. Sir Wellbourne proposed two main strategies. The first was "positive woodgenics," which advocated paying bonuses to construction companies to build houses of less flammable wood. The second strategy he called "negative woodgenics," which involved rescinding the licenses of companies building houses of more flammable wood, and seizing the tools of construction workers working on such projects. Some of his German and American followers even called for the immediate destruction of what they believed were the most flammable houses as the fastest and most efficient way to create an arson-free society in the future.

Although the arson attacks continued just as before, the Mayor and the press continued to urge citizens to have faith that their strategy would soon pay dividends. They frequently stated that the arsonability of Genomia's homes was 90 percent, which meant that attention needed to be focused on the types of wood used to build the houses.

One day, a tenured Genomia State University professor by the name of Samuel Eugene "Gene" Skeptic stepped up to the podium of a Genomia city council meeting. Although he recognized that, in a few rare cases, houses were built so poorly that they burned down even without House Burning Crew attacks, he openly disagreed with the Mayor's position. Dr. Skeptic reasoned as follows: "While it may or may not be true that some of Genomia's houses burn more easily than others, the best strategy to stop the arson attacks would be to devote most of the city's resources and funds toward tracking down and arresting the House Burning Crew. By concentrating on the houses, we are allowing the arsonists to continue to commit their crimes. If we catch them, the houses would be safe regardless of what type of wood was used to build them." He pointed out that the identity of the House Burning Crew membership was not mysterious at all, since when committing their crimes they proudly wore Crew tee-shirts with their last names emblazoned on the back.

Mayor Geewas vehemently objected. "We cannot understand or prevent these arson attacks," she thundered, "until we understand the wood cell architecture of the houses of this community." She again cited house-pair studies and the 90 percent arsonability figure. She accused

Dr. Skeptic of being a politically motivated anti-science ideologue who did not even reside in Genomia, knows little about wood science or the house-pair method, and who repeats long-discredited "arrest the arsonists," "arsonogenic homeowner," "refrigerator-like homeowner," or even "spontaneous combustion" theories of arson prevention. Meanwhile, houses continued to burn down at the rate of five per week.

Although Dr. Skeptic questioned the validity of the arsonability concept, he argued that, even if the 90 percent arsonability figure were correct, or even if it were 100 percent, it would still make much more sense to focus attention on arresting members of the House Burning Crew. Furthermore, he had uncovered a fatal flaw with the house-pair method of comparing MM versus DM house-pairs. It seemed that the house-pair method was based on a little-mentioned theoretical assumption that arsonists would attempt to burn both houses in a pair the same way. This was known as the "equal arson assumption." However, decades of research had shown that, although arsonists usually approached the burning of an MM pair in the same way because they were constructed the same way, they approached DM house-pairs somewhat differently. The researchers discovered that, although the DM houses made of flammable wood burned easily, the second house was sometimes more difficult to set ablaze because it was built of less flammable wood. The arsonists frequently left the scene of the crime rather than taking the extra time necessary to set the second house on fire, which would increase their chances of being caught.

Dr. Skeptic argued, therefore, that the equal arson assumption of the house-pair method was not valid, and that the House Burning Crew treated MM and DM house pairs differently. Thus, it was likely that the house-pair method recorded little more than differing ways that the House Burning Crew approached the burning of MM and DM house-pairs. In addition, he pointed out that even the separated MM pairs tended to be placed close by to each other in neighborhoods frequently targeted by the Crew, and that the Crew usually targeted both separated MM houses at the same time. In truth, it was obvious to Dr. Skeptic that focusing on the House Burning Crew was the best strategy to prevent arson, even if house-pair research were valid. But because the method was widely used by the Mayor and others to justify doing little to stop the Crew, he felt it was important to show that the house-pair method was based on false assumptions.

The Mayor responded by conceding that arsonists usually approach MM and DM house-pairs somewhat differently, but that in numerous studies house-pair researchers had tested and upheld the equal arson assumption, and that the house-pair method was therefore valid. She said that house-pair researchers had arrived at that conclusion because they had discovered that the houses themselves had "created" or "elicited" arsonists' differing house-burning approaches. Most of the politicians and citizens attending the meeting agreed with the Mayor, and Dr. Skeptic was forced to leave by an angry mob of the Mayor's supporters. Meanwhile, houses continued to burn down at the rate of five per week.

Dr. Skeptic came out with a book entitled *Not in the Wood Cells*, where he made a strong case that arsonability studies, which included the house-pair method, contained numerous flaws and implausible assumptions. In his concluding chapter he urged the community to pay much less attention to wood and to make a concerted effort to arrest the House Burning Crew. Dr. Skeptic's book, however, was not widely discussed, and was rarely mentioned in the media or by the authors of the popular books that supported the Mayor's position. House-pair researchers usually ignored his arguments too, and when they did address his views they often presented them in a distorted way, or made personal attacks against him. Meanwhile, houses continued to burn down at the rate of five per week.

Over at Genomia State University, arson prevention research focused mainly on arsonability studies and the flammability of differing wood types. The University had established the Arson Science department to coordinate this research. The department was heavily funded by the giant "Profitsus Corporation," which had large holdings in lumber, roofing material, and an arson-resistant chemical used to treat wood, which the company marketed under the trade name "Arzonax." In addition, the Profitsus Corporation was the parent company of Ignite-a-Fire LLC, which produced a very expensive fire-starting kit that was frequently used by the House Burning Crew. Although some of its other products helped Genomia's residents repair and prevent different (non-fire-related) types of damage done to their houses, much of Profitsus' advertising and promotion focused on Arzonax.

Dr. Skeptic issued frequent press releases pointing out the obvious conflict of interest that the Profitsus Corporation, which made money from arson and therefore had a financial interest in not preventing it, funded and played a major role in dictating the research agenda. He stressed that it was in the company's interest to divert attention from the House Burning Crew and to promote sales of its lumber and roofing material, and the use of its highly profitable Arzonax wood treatment product.

Dr. Skeptic showed that Arzonax was enormously successful not only because of Genomia's potential market of 50,000 houses, but also because Arzonax would need to be administered weekly for the entire life of the house. In their television and online advertisements, as well as in frequent ads appearing in building contractor journals, Profitsus stressed that flammability was a house characteristic just like any other house characteristic, and required lifelong wood treatment with Arzonax in the same way that lawns needed watering several times a week. Their television ads even attempted to convince the owners of the less flammable houses that they may be in danger, and therefore needed to use Arzonax to ease their worries. The treatments were expensive, and every ten years or so, after the patent ran out and the wood treatment formula became "generic" and inexpensive, the company came out with a "new and improved" expensive wood treatment product which it marketed by telling everyone that their old product was potentially dangerous, could cause wood rot, and might not be very good at preventing arson after all. Dr. Skeptic's press releases continued to criticize this state of affairs, but the media continued to ignore him. Around town, it was whispered that the Profitsus Corporation held a 70 percent stake in Genomia's main newspapers, Internet sites, and television and radio stations.

Genomia State University researchers friendly to Dr. Skeptic, who wanted to focus on the people who set fires as the main task of arson prevention, were also frustrated. It seemed that when they applied for grants from the Genomia Institute of House Health (GIHH) to investigate ways to arrest arsonists, they would frequently be turned down on the grounds that arsonability studies were the Institute's top priority. These researchers decided to channel their frustration into investigating the GIHH itself. They discovered the existence of a "very cozy relationship" between the Profitsus Corporation and the GIHH, and that the company provided 63 percent of the GIHH's operating budget. Many of the GIHH directors and researchers had previously worked for Profitsus, and many others were given high-paying positions in the company after they left the GIHH. Dr. Skeptic did his best to publicize these practices too, but few paid attention. Meanwhile, houses continued to burn down at the rate of five per week.

The city press was dominated by reports that great progress had been made in identifying the houses made of easily burning wood, and that a program would soon be undertaken to provide city-subsidized Arzonax treatments to the most "at-risk" houses. Mayor Geewas also proposed the creation of a research program to develop a new cutting-edge treatment: "wood cell therapy." However, she acknowledged that this type of therapy might be years or even decades away, despite the fact that the multi-billion dollar internationally conducted "House Wood Cell Project" (HWCP) had been completed nearly a decade earlier. The scientists leading and promoting the HWCP had promised at its inception that, once the DNA of wood cells had been sequenced and mapped, we would finally be able to understand and prevent arson. The most well-known of these scientists went so far as to state that for the first time in history, the HWCP would "allow us to understand what a house really is." The Mayor continued to make regular announcements on progress, and experts were writing that Genomia was witnessing the "dawn of a new era of arson prevention." Meanwhile, houses continued to burn down at the rate of five per week.

Later, an outside investigation discovered that Mayor Geewas had for years received lavish consulting fees and gifts from the Profitsus Corporation, as well as from other home-building material and wood-treating companies. The city decided to pass a law requiring politicians to disclose this type of income in all subsequent official documents, which the Mayor reluctantly did. But she denied that there was any conflict of interest, and few of her colleagues seemed to pay much attention. A footnote in one of the newer city documents, printed in small type, read: "Mayor Geewas has served on the Advisory Board and receives consulting and speaking fees from the Profitsus Corporation. In addition, she has received support and consulting fees from Genomia Roofing Products Inc., The National Wood Treatment Association, Genomia Lumber, and the Genomia Institute of House Health."

A journalist visited Genomia 8 years later. She reported that the House Burning Crew continued to burn five houses per week, and that Mayor Geewas was finding it difficult to develop an effective method of treating the wood of Genomia's most vulnerable houses. (It turned out that Arzonax did not work most of the time, even though sales and marketing remained strong. The Profitsus Corporation was in the process of patenting a new wood treatment product chemically similar to Arzonax, which it planned to market as "Burnzarest.") Still, the Mayor promised that better treatment methods were being developed, which would lead to the prevention of arson attacks in the near future. For Mayor Geewas, a major issue was the "missing arsonability" problem of identifying the wood cells that predisposed houses to burn after arson attacks. Once this problem was resolved, she said, better arson treatment and prevention could be developed.

Meanwhile, houses continued to burn down at the rate of five per week.

Notes

1 This chapter is adapted from an article that first appeared in *The Journal of Mind and Behavior* (Joseph, 2011b).
2 McCrea and colleagues qualified their position that personality traits are influenced "not at all by the environment" by writing that this "assertion is, of course, an oversimplification," used to counter theories that stressed the importance of the environment (McCrea et al., 2000, p. 175).

12

SUMMARY AND CONCLUSIONS

In this book I have argued that twin studies, whether based on twins reared together or twins said to have been reared apart, are based on a set of explicit and implicit theoretical assumptions that range from plausible, to questionable, to outright false. In addition, twin research has been subject to many other types of biases and methodological issues. In the context of this argument I will review and summarize each chapter, after which I will arrive at a final evaluation of twin research.

Chapter 1 introduced twin research and the main fields that carry it out in the social and behavioral sciences. I provided a brief history of behavioral genetics, and the basic positions of the "nature–nurture debate" were discussed. I also provided a brief history of twin research based on a summary of the account provided previously in *The Gene Illusion*, and briefly discussed other types of behavioral genetic and psychiatric genetic research methods, such as family and adoption studies. Most genetic researchers and their critics agree that a behavior "running in the family" can be entirely explained by non-genetic factors. Adoption studies are much rarer, and have their own set of methodological issues and questionable assumptions. In light of gene discovery failures, twin research has constituted, and continues to constitute, the main evidence put forward by the "nature" (genetic) side of the nature–nurture debate.

Chapter 2 began a five-chapter analysis of TRA studies, with a special emphasis on the classical studies performed by Newman and colleagues, Shields, and Juel-Nielsen. The MISTRA was introduced, and I discussed the researchers' reporting of individual pairs whose stories were selectively released to the media. Researchers and the media have tended to sensationalize these stories as "eerie" examples of the power of genetics. Regarding the earlier classical studies, the information provided by the original investigators in their detailed case histories showed that few pairs were "reared apart" in the commonly understood meaning of the term, even though most contemporary accounts of these studies fail to acknowledge this. Other topics discussed in Chapter 2 included the Cyril Burt scandal and fraud in the social and behavioral sciences in general, and the controversy surrounding Arthur Jensen's theories of genetic influences on racial differences in IQ.

In *Chapter 3* I discussed the works and ideas of previous TRA study critics, with a section devoted to each of the main publications and their authors. The chapter closed with a table (Table 3.1) summarizing 22 potentially invalidating flaws and biases discussed by these critics. These authors paved the way for subsequent reviewers, and laid the groundwork for much of the analysis in Part I of this book.

In *Chapter 4* I covered the controversies surrounding many key concepts and assumptions used in both reared-together and reared-apart twin studies. The validity of concepts such as IQ, personality, heritability, and biometrical model fitting were explored, and were questioned. Many potential flaws, biases, and environmental confounds in TRA research were also explored, including how behavioral similarity can result from the fact that twin pairs are the same age, are the same sex, are very similar in physical appearance, and usually grow up in very similar cultural and socioeconomic environments at the same time. The concept of epigenetics was also introduced.

Chapter 5 began a two-chapter focus on the MISTRA, based in part on an analysis of MISTRA researcher Nancy Segal's 2012 book describing the study, *Born Together—Reared Apart: The Landmark Minnesota Twin Study*. In this chapter I described the logic and methods of the study in greater detail, and focused on problem areas such as the similarity of the twins' social and cultural environments, the researchers' failure to make their data available for inspection by independent reviewers, the questionable assumptions underlying the researchers' model-fitting procedures, sample size issues, recruitment bias, the researchers' decision to bypass the step of determining that the MZA correlation is significantly higher than the DZA correlation, a reliance on twins' potentially unreliable accounts of their degree of separation and behavioral similarity, and issues related to the control group. An important question is whether the MISTRA twin sample achieved a higher level of separation and environmental dissimilarity when compared with the earlier studies. We saw that the evidence, though closely guarded and inadequately reported by the investigators, suggests that it did not.

Chapter 6 focused on the MISTRA studies of IQ and personality. We saw that these studies contained methodological problems and were based on many questionable assumptions (in addition to those discussed in Chapters 4 and 5). A major issue was the failure of the Minnesota researchers to publish their full-sample DZA IQ correlations. This occurred despite the fact that IQ (cognitive ability) was the main focus area of the study, and that the researchers had designated DZA twins as the MISTRA control group they would compare with MZAs. In the 1990 MISTRA study published in *Science*, DZA control group IQ and personality correlations were not reported, even though full-sample DZA special mental abilities and personality correlations were reported in other concurrently appearing MISTRA publications. The study took place between 1979 and 2000, yet the researchers still have not published the results for all tests completed by the full sample of twin pairs they studied, while continuing to deny independent reviewers access to the raw data. Nevertheless, based on the incomplete data that have been published, there does not appear to be a statistically significant Wechsler (WAIS) IQ difference between the MISTRA MZA and DZA groups, which also appears to be the case with the MISTRA Raven Progressive Matrices MZA and DZA IQ correlations. These results by themselves would invalidate the researchers' conclusion that genetic factors (strongly) influence IQ since, as Segal recognized, a determination that the MZA correlation is (significantly) higher than the DZA correlation is a preliminary "first step" in TRA study genetic analysis. Contrary to the way they are usually written about, the MISTRA studies produced no scientifically acceptable evidence that genetic factors influence intelligence, personality, and other types of behavior, which is consistent with the ongoing failure to uncover genes for these behavioral characteristics.

Chapter 7 focused on the much more common "twin method" studies comparing MZT and DZT pairs. I showed that the controversial MZT–DZT "equal environment assumption" (EEA) is not supported by the evidence, and that MZT twin pairs grow up experiencing much more similar environments, and greater levels of identity confusion and attachment, than experienced by DZTs. I examined the two main arguments twin researchers have made in support of the equal environment assumption and the twin method. These are the *Argument A* "twins create their own environments because they are more similar genetically" position, and the *Argument B* "environments must be shown to differ on trait-relevant dimensions" position. I showed that both arguments are faulty, and that MZT–DZT comparisons can be completely explained by environmental factors. This does not mean that the twin method merely "overestimates heritability," or that researchers should assess the EEA on a study-by-study basis, but rather that genetic interpretations of all past, present, and future studies using the twin method in the social and behavioral sciences must be rejected outright.

In *Chapter 8* I evaluated twin research in psychiatry in the context of over four decades of gene search failures in that field. Psychiatric twin studies are based on twin method MZT–DZT comparisons, and constitute the most frequently cited evidence that the major psychiatric disorders have an important genetic component. I examined problems in psychiatric twin research, including how the untenable MZT–DZT EEA is applied and defended in psychiatry. I also examined mainstream psychiatry's position that psychiatric disorders are valid medical conditions that can be reliably diagnosed. Schizophrenia provides an example of how these issues play out in contemporary psychiatry, and I used this diagnosis to illustrate many questionable claims and assumptions psychiatry makes about its disorders. I argued that the current emphasis on biology and genetics in psychiatry causes the field to overlook or de-emphasize many environmental factors that have been shown to play an important role in causing various disorders. Paradoxically, it is becoming clearer every day that the main finding of the field of psychiatric genetics is that genes for the major psychiatric disorders do not appear to exist. In the future, mainstream psychiatry will be forced to reevaluate the genetic evidence, and the validity of the twin method and its critical EEA will come under increasing scrutiny.

In *Chapter 9* I documented the ongoing decades-long failure of molecular genetic researchers to identify genes for the behaviors studied in the social and behavioral sciences, and examined some new methods that have been developed in the past few years. I devoted a chapter to molecular genetic research in both of my previous books, and here I performed a fresh and updated analysis in the context of what genetic researchers have referred to since 2008 as the "missing heritability problem." I proposed an alternative understanding of these negative molecular genetic results—that the best explanation for "positive" twin study findings in combination with negative molecular genetic results is not that "heritability is missing," but that something is wrong with genetic interpretations of twin data. From a critical perspective, what behavioral geneticists and others see as contradictory results are consistent with the position that the EEA of the twin method is false, and that reared-apart twin studies are flawed on several critical dimensions. The numerous assumptions, decisions, and claims made by leading behavioral genetic and psychiatric genetic researchers have been tested under the microscope of molecular genetic research—and the (negative) results are now in.

Chapter 10 examined over 35 years of gene-finding claims and predictions by Robert Plomin, one of the world's leading behavioral genetic researchers and authors. This chapter surveyed Plomin's writings from 1978 to 2014, where until about 2003 he consistently wrote that gene discoveries for various behaviors and behavioral disorders had already been made, were in the process of being made, or would be made in the very near future. I again argued that the ongoing failure to discover genes, as well as Plomin's misplaced optimism, has been based largely on the mistaken interpretation of twin studies in favor of genetics.

Chapter 11 consisted of a parable illustrating the potential folly of approaching the causes of behavioral differences, psychiatric disorders, and common medical conditions from the genetic perspective, even when genetic factors or predispositions may be present. In the introduction, I discussed how institutions and groups with political and economic interests in promoting genetic theories attempt to steer public thinking, and research agendas, in the genetic direction.

A Final Evaluation of Twin Research

I have attempted to show in this book that twin studies are based on several questionable and outright false theoretical assumptions, and that genetic interpretations of these studies depend on the validity of these assumptions. Twin studies have also been subject to several other major methodological issues. Therefore, studies of twins—regardless of whether pairs were reared together or "reared apart"—have failed to provide scientifically acceptable evidence in support of genetic influences on human behavioral differences. As Richard Lerner once wrote in relation to behavioral genetic research, there simply is "nothing there" (Lerner, 2002, p. 249). It follows that traditionally understood social, political, cultural, class, religious, and familial environmental influences remain the best explanation for differences in human behavior, as well as for the behaviors grouped in various "psychiatric disorder" categories.

We have seen that a theme of this book has been that the best explanation for a "positive" twin study finding in combination with negative molecular genetic results is that something is wrong with genetic interpretations of twin data. Once the invalidating flaws of twin research are recognized, the apparent contradiction between these findings disappears. Genetic researchers and their supporters, however, continue to resist arriving at this obvious conclusion. For example, in political scientist Peter Hatemi and colleagues' 2014 combined twin and GWA study of political ideology (Hatemi et al., 2014), they concluded that their "first stage" twin data provided "evidence that genetic factors play a role in the formation of political ideology" (p. 282). In the accompanying "second stage" GWA study, however, Hatemi and colleagues failed to detect "any definitive evidence of a specific genetic marker being related to [political] ideology" (p. 292). Instead of questioning their twin study results, they wrote that "the failure to identify significant SNPs should not be surprising," and continued to believe that there are "thousands of genetic variants of very small effects" that eventually will be uncovered by obtaining "large enough samples" and by utilizing "improved techniques" (p. 292).

This book has attempted to answer the crucial question of whether twin research is good science, uncertain science, or pseudoscience. In *The Missing Gene* I concluded that the twin method shares several characteristics with pseudoscience, and showed how several arguments and methods utilized by twin researchers are consistent with pseudoscientific practices (Joseph, 2006). Today, it is even more clear that the twin method, when it is used to assess genetic influences on human behavioral differences, belongs in the pseudoscience category.

In 2005 I published (Joseph, 2005b) a brief critique of Kendler's attempt to reconcile the failure of "gene finding methods" with the results of family, twin, and adoption studies, which Kendler viewed as demonstrating the importance of "genetic risk factors . . . for nearly all psychiatric and drug abuse disorders examined to date" (Kendler, 2005b, p. 6). In his response to my critique, Kendler wrote, "It is one thing to criticize the methodology of specific studies. It is quite another to suggest, as Dr. Joseph does, that we reject the results of an entire field of scientific inquiry." Although "this might have been warranted for some pseudoscientific systems, such as astrology, alchemy, and the Ptolemaic astronomic system," Kendler believed that "it is highly unlikely that modern psychiatric genetics will be judged by future historians of science to be in such company" (Kendler, 2005a, p. 1986). Whether or not it is premature to "reject the results of an entire field of scientific inquiry," an extensive and critical review of these results is long overdue.

Despite the major problems that I have discussed in detail in this book, twin research remains a widely used and accepted research method. This leads to the obvious question of why this is so. As discussed in previous chapters, despite its obviously massive flaws, twin research is needed by various groups and fields in support of their positions. It is needed by psychiatry and the psychopharmaceutical industry to legitimize their claims that psychiatric disorders are valid medical conditions in need of medication; it is needed by behavioral genetics and psychiatric genetics in support each field's theories; it is needed by medical genetics in support of its emphasis on genetic approaches to many common medical conditions, such as cancer and type 2 diabetes; and it is needed by proponents of scientific racism and the remaining proponents of eugenic policies (e.g., Lynn, 2001). It is also needed by the political and economic elites in support of their policies and worldviews. Wahlsten pointed to the "long tradition, exemplified by Malthus, of basing recommendations for government social policies on claims about limitations imposed by human psychology and biology" (Wahlsten, 1997, p. 71; see also Chase, 1980). Twin research continues to provide the main evidence put forward in support of these alleged limitations.

TRA studies published to date have failed to provide scientifically acceptable evidence that genetic factors influence human behavioral differences. Turning to the use of the classical twin method in the social and behavioral sciences, the world will get along fine without the confusion, diversions, and false claims it has produced, as well as the social and political policies it has influenced. The human race will survive without twin method behavioral research just as it has survived, or will survive, without alchemy, astrology, channeling, cold fusion, craniometry, creation science, crystal healing, dowsing, faith healing, levitation, mesmerism, numerology, palmistry, phrenology, psychic surgery, and the Ptolemaic astronomy system. There is no doubt that the twin method will join this list. The only question is when.

APPENDIX A
THE FUNDING OF MISTRA

In previous publications covering the MISTRA and other TRA studies, I chose to bypass the controversies surrounding how these studies were funded, and focused instead on the faulty science of this area of research. In *Born Together—Reared Apart*, however, Nancy Segal dedicated a portion of her final chapter to defending her colleagues' decision to accept funding from controversial sources. The MISTRA received a total of $2,330,720, of which $1,420,551 (61 percent, or over $3,000,000 in 2014 dollars) was awarded by the Pioneer Fund, an organization described below (Segal, 2012, p. 329). The Fund thus contributed the bulk of MISTRA's expenses, and in Bouchard's opinion, "If not for Pioneer we would have folded long ago" (Segal, 2012, p, 317).

The Pioneer Fund

The Pioneer Fund was a little-known, low-profile organization until the publication of *The Bell Curve* in 1994, where some critics of the genetic race-differences in IQ aspect of that book pointed to the authors' citation of several Pioneer-funded researchers. In their acknowledgement section, *Bell Curve* authors Herrnstein and Murray wrote that they "benefitted especially from the advice of" (among others) Pioneer grantee Richard Lynn (Herrnstein & Murray, 1994, p. xxv).

The Pioneer Fund was established in the United States in 1937 by Wickliffe Draper (1891–1972), leading American eugenicist Harry Laughlin (1880–1943), and others. As the author of a 2013 publication put it, the Fund "has been the only major foundation devoted to subsidizing race science and eugenics research, areas of science that are now fully discredited" (Beirich, 2013).

At the time of its founding, eugenic programs of selective breeding and compulsory sterilization were widely supported in both American and German academic and political circles (Black, 2003; Chase, 1980; Proctor; 1988; Reilly, 1991). This was an era in which Harvard anthropologist Ernest Hooton did not feel inhibited to write, and the prestigious journal *Science* apparently did not feel inhibited to publish, a 1936 article

APPENDIX A

calling for a "biological purge" in the United States that would "cast into the fire" the "growing numbers of the physically inferior, the mentally ineffective and the anti-social" people (Hooton, 1936, p. 513).

In Germany, with the rise to power of Hitler in 1933, eugenics and "racial hygiene" became state policy and contributed to the persecution of the Jews and other targeted groups, the killing of hundreds of thousands of mental patients, and ultimately the Holocaust (Joseph & Wetzel, 2013; Müller-Hill, 1998; Proctor, 1988; Weindling, 1989).

The question of whether "defective" American children should be put to death for eugenic and other purposes in a "euthanasia" program similar to Hitler's was openly debated by two doctors in a 1942 edition of the *American Journal of Psychiatry*. This was followed by an unsigned editorial more or less supporting the proposed killing program, which advised psychiatrists to focus on overcoming parental resistance to the "disposal by euthanasia of their idiot offspring" (Anonymous, 1942, p. 142).[1] Draper created the Pioneer Fund during this period using millions of dollars he had inherited, and sought to promote the policies of German racial hygiene as a model for eugenic programs in the United States (Lombardo, 2002a, 2002b; Mehler, 1983; Tucker, 2002b). As noted by the German historian Stefan Kühl in 1994, "A Fund that was founded by supporters of Hitler's policies against ethnic minorities and handicapped people and that provided money for introducing Nazi race propaganda into the United States still sponsors research that has striking similarities to earlier studies that provided the scientific basis for Nazi measures" (Kühl, 1994, p. 106).

After World War II and the defeat of Nazi Germany and the revelations of the Holocaust and other massive Nazi atrocities, Draper and the Pioneer Fund continued to finance and promote eugenic research, and especially research allegedly showing that American black people are genetically inferior to white people for intelligence and other characteristics (see Lane, 1995; Miller, 1995). The mission continued following Draper's death in 1972, and continues to this day. As documented by William Tucker in his 2002 book about the Pioneer Fund, *The Funding of Scientific Racism* (Tucker, 2002b), the Fund was involved for decades in financing and promoting the work of scientific supporters of Nazism and fascism, which of course includes the genocidal anti-Semitic admirers of Hitler (see also Sedgwick, 1995; Tucker, 2002a; Winston, 1998). As one of numerous examples documented by Tucker, Draper and the Fund provided financial support to the International Association of for the Advancement of Ethnology and Eugenics (IAAEE), established in 1959. The IAAEE was a "scientific" meeting point of Nazi supporters and other supporters of Nordic supremacy. It opposed the 1954 U.S. Brown vs. Board of Education decision, which ruled that racially segregated schools were unconstitutional, while proving assistance to the White Citizens' Counsels of the American south as well as other opponents of civil rights.

APPENDIX A

Another example of a Pioneer grantee was the British anthropologist Roger Pearson, who according to Tucker,

> founded the Northern League in Britain as a postwar gathering point for Nazis; dedicated to Teutonic unity and preservation of the superior Nordics from the threat of "infection" by "healthy stock".... The league published the journal *Northern World*, based largely on the writing of the Third Reich's most important expert on "race science," Hans F. K. Günther, a founding member of the league.
>
> (Tucker, 2002b, p. 80)

In his 1966 book *Eugenics and Race*, in the context of favorably reviewing the ideas of an earlier anthropologist, Pearson offered the following call to a genetically "superior" nation to avoid committing "racial suicide," which might include "exterminating" the "inferior tribe":

> If a nation with a more advanced, more specialized, or in any way superior set of genes mingles with, instead of exterminating, an inferior tribe, then it commits racial suicide, and destroys the work of thousands of years of biological isolation and natural selection.
>
> (Pearson, 1966, p. 26)

Pearson published articles in the Swastika-festooned newspaper *White Power* while he was a Pioneer grantee (e.g., Pearson, 1974). According to Tucker, Pearson received more than $1 million in grant money (over $3 million in 2014 dollars) from the Pioneer Fund (Tucker, 2002b, p. 80).

While continuing to financially support racist and Nordic supremacist ideologues, due to the changing political atmosphere and the rejection of openly eugenic programs by the 1970s, the Fund's leaders decided to support genetic research not directly investigating racial differences, such as the MISTRA and the Texas Adoption Project (both focused on IQ and personality). This did not mean that the goals and objectives of the Fund had changed, but indicated only a shift in tactics in a changing social and political climate. The goal was to aid theories of white racial superiority by supporting research whose authors concluded in favor of the "high heritability" of behavioral characteristics such as intelligence and personality without necessarily discussing, or believing that there were, racial implications of their research. As Tucker concluded:

> Whatever projects of scientific interest Pioneer may have supported—and there certainly are a few—it is also indisputable that the fund has continued to fill the role once played by its

founder: to subsidize the creation and distribution of literature that could be used to support racial superiority and racial purity. Pioneer has indeed been scientific racism's keeper of the flame.

(Tucker, 2002b, p. 196)

Segal on the Pioneer Fund

According to Segal's account in *Born Together—Reared Apart*, the Pioneer Fund was founded in 1937 by Wickliffe Draper, who was "interested in the genetic basis of intelligence and in eugenics" (Segal, 2012, p. 314). Although she recognized that the Fund had a "reputation for funding race-related research," and that in the 1970s some critics "discovered that the fund had supported previous research on race differences in intelligence" (p. 315), the MISTRA researchers decided to accept Pioneer money and were not influenced by its possible racial agenda. Lykken reasoned that "we could take bad money and do good things with it" (p. 316). At the same time, Segal raised doubts that the Fund even had a racial/racist agenda by favorably quoting non-MISTRA psychologist Tony Vernon, who "believes that racist allegations against the Pioneer Fund were 'questionable' at best, given that there has been 'no solid evidence'" (p. 317). In addition to the utter falseness of this claim, as Segal acknowledged, Tony Vernon was himself a Pioneer grantee.

Segal's position was that, while the Pioneer Fund may or may not have financed racial or racist research, the MISTRA investigators made the correct decision to accept its money. She insisted that the researchers were not influenced by Pioneer's agenda, and that the Fund did not tell the researchers what to write or conclude. She favorably quoted MISTRA researcher Matt McGue, who claimed that "the Pioneer Fund never influenced the study," and that what Pioneer "got out of" the MISTRA research "was minimal" (p. 316). In a revealing passage earlier in her book that appears to contradict this claim, Segal wrote that an early-1980s attempt to publish the MISTRA IQ data in *Science* "was based on pressure from one of our funding sources, which wanted to see how the scientific community responded to the findings" (p. 104). Apparently, this unnamed funding source (the Pioneer Fund?) did indeed "pressure" the researchers in relation to when and where they should publish their findings. He who pays the piper calls the tune.

We have seen that Segal recognized that the Pioneer Fund had a "reputation for supporting research with a racial bent" (p. 310). In addition to the fact that the term "racial bent" grossly understates the actions and goals of the Fund, Segal failed to mention the Fund's documented support to racial research, and to racist organizations and people with ties to fascism. By writing about its "reputation," she avoided the need to state clearly whether or not the Pioneer Fund financially supported such research, organizations, and people. Segal ignored the facts, and presented the issue as if it remained an open question—in the process citing whitewash accounts written by Pioneer Fund leaders such as Richard Lynn and Harry Weyher (the latter succeeded eugenicist Frederick Osborn as Fund director from 1958 until his death in 2002).

Everyone Segal quoted in support of the MISTRA researchers' decision to accept Pioneer Fund money was a MISTRA researcher or supporter, and all had participated in studies financially supported by the Fund (see Segal, 2012, pp. 314–317). At the same time, she failed to discuss the findings of Tucker, Paul Lombardo, Barry Mehler and other critics of the Fund. If the facts presented in Tucker's book about the Pioneer Fund's support to racist and fascist individuals and groups were wrong, Segal missed an excellent opportunity to refute them. Regrettably, Segal's account overlooked the Pioneer Fund's decades of financial support to open racists, segregationists, fascists, and proponents and defenders of genocide against the Jewish people.

Although McGue, Segal, and other MISTRA researchers may believe that the benefit the Pioneer Fund received from their research "was minimal," the Fund was in fact richly rewarded through the strengthening of the (albeit false) position that inherited factors play a predominant role in shaping human intelligence and behavior. The MISTRA has had an important impact, virtually rewriting dozens of behavioral and social science textbooks with a stronger genetic emphasis in its wake. In turn, the Fund gained greater legitimacy as the sponsor of widely cited scientific research (Tucker, 2013). The Fund directors could hardly have imagined the return that their investment would bring, as its backers are well aware that the acceptance of the view that behavior and IQ are "highly heritable" makes it easier to convince people that differences between racial groups are also largely the result of genetic differences. In journalist William Wright's 1998 *Born That Way*, a book whose content and tone were equally admiring of the MISTRA as it was hostile to its critics, the author conceded that in the "worst-case," the people running the Pioneer Fund "operate on the conviction that genetic differences between races do exist; therefore *any* research into genetic influence on personality and behavior will advance this assumption" (Wright, 1998, p. 47, italics in original).

Although it is unlikely that the Pioneer Fund leaders told the researchers what they should write or what they should conclude, there is little reason to do this when funding behavioral genetic researchers, who are very likely to conclude in favor of important genetic influences and produce heritability estimates. Promoting the (alleged) importance of genetics, by definition, is what behavioral geneticists do.

Rushton and Lynn

The psychologist J. Philippe Rushton was the Director of the Pioneer Fund from 2002 until his death in 2012. Rushton was well known for his belief (which he alleged was backed by scientific research) that black people are genetically inferior to whites in measured IQ and other characteristics (and that East Asians are superior to both). Rushton first published his book *Race, Evolution, and Behavior: A Life History Perspective* in 1995 (Rushton, 1995), which was followed by several revised editions (e.g., Rushton, 2000b). He also published abridged editions of this book (e.g., Rushton, 2000a), which were subsequently mailed out unsolicited to tens of thousands of social scientists using Pioneer Fund money (Lombardo, 2002a; Tucker, 2002a).

In the 2000 abridged edition of *Race, Evolution, and Behavior*, Rushton recounted the "shocked" observations of early European "explorers" in Africa (actually, in many cases colonial plunderers and conquerors attempting to justify murder, plunder, and conquest), while approvingly listing some of the crudest racial stereotypes imaginable, such as comparing Africans' behavior to "wild animals," their having a "natural sense of rhythm," and their being prone to cannibalism (Rushton, 2000a, p. 8). Rushton implied that people of the African diaspora currently continue to harbor similar allegedly inherited tendencies.

As of 2013 and continuing into 2014, Richard Lynn has been listed as the Pioneer Fund "contact" person on the organization's website. Lynn has also supported genetic theories of IQ racial differences. In 2001 Lynn published *Eugenics: A Reassessment*, where he provided a detailed argument in support of instituting eugenic breeding plans to improve human "health, intelligence, and moral character," and called for the restoration of compulsory eugenic sterilization and other negative eugenic measures (Lynn, 2001, p. 53). Lynn supported the compulsorily eugenic sterilization of "criminals" and others, writing that "eugenics does not require the extermination of undesirables. It is sufficient for eugenics that the mentally retarded and recidivist criminals should be sterilized" (Lynn, 2001, p. 239). Lynn discussed the possibility of injecting a virus into the bodies of low-IQ scorers and "psychopaths" at age 12 as a means of "temporary sterilization," in the same way this method has been used for "the sterilization of rabbits, kangaroos, and other pests" (p. 213).[2]

Rushton and Lynn were leading figures of the Pioneer Fund following Weyher's death in 2002, and their views were consistent with the Fund's history and mission.

Notes

1. See also Joseph, 2005a, 2006. For the original articles for and against "euthanasia," see Kanner, 1942 (against), and Kennedy, 1942 (for). For the unsigned editorial, see Anonymous, 1942.
2. In 2004, MISTRA researcher David Lykken published a very positive review of Lynn's *Eugenics: A Reassessment* (Lykken, 2004).

APPENDIX B

A LITTLE-KNOWN BEHAVIORAL GENETIC ADOPTION STUDY WHOSE RESULTS CONTRAST WITH THE MISTRA PERSONALITY FINDINGS

A behavioral genetic (non-twin) adoption study, methodologically far superior to the MISTRA, was published in 1998.[1] This study's results showed no genetic influences on human personality differences. Nancy Segal did not mention or cite this study in *Born Together—Reared Apart* even though, apart from IQ, personality has been the main area of TRA study focus. While the results of this adoption study point to a lack of genetic influences on personality, we will soon see that the leading behavioral genetic investigators who performed and published it reached a very different set of conclusions.

This story is not as much about a specific adoption study as it is an example of how the genetic biases of behavioral genetic researchers influence their investigations, including most importantly the assumptions they accept and the conclusions they reach. We saw in Chapters 2 through 6 that these biases were in evidence in the MISTRA and the classical TRA studies.

In reviewing this study, it should be kept in mind that the psychometric and behavioral genetic concept of "personality" as a stable set of enduring "traits" that are seen across various settings, and can be measured with personality tests, remains questionable and controversial (see Chapter 4). Like TRA studies, adoption studies are subject to several methodological problems and biases discussed briefly in Chapter 1, and to the confounding influence of *non-familial* environmental influences. We saw in Chapter 4 that these include common national, regional, ethnic, religious, economic class, and in some cases gender influences. Behavioral genetic adoption researchers, like the MISTRA researchers, typically overlook these major environmental influences and focus mainly on the role of family influences.

APPENDIX B

Overview of the Study

In 1998, Robert Plomin and his behavioral genetic colleagues published an adoption study of personality (Plomin, Corley, Caspi, Fulker, & DeFries, 1998) based on their work in the longitudinal Colorado Adoption Project (CAP; Plomin & DeFries, 1985). Plomin was also involved in the Swedish TRA study (SATSA; Pedersen, Plomin, Nesselroade, & McClearn, 1992). This adoption study of personality, which from this point forward I will call the "1998 CAP study," has all but disappeared in a tidal wave of claims by the authors of textbooks, popular works, scientific articles, and press reports that the MISTRA results have shown that genetic differences play a major role in human behavioral and psychological development.

The CAP was initiated by Plomin and DeFries in the mid-1970s (Plomin & DeFries, 1985). Because it was a longitudinal study, the researchers were able to track and assess the families since the birth of the children. The sample consisted of 287 birthparents, 240 children (adoptees) they put up for adoption at birth, and 469 adoptive (rearing) parents of these adoptees. The researchers also established a control group consisting of 245 non-adopted children and their biological parents. Adoptees were placed with their adoptive parents at an average age of 29 days. Over 90 percent of the parents in each group were of European ancestry. Birthparents and adoptive parents had completed an EASI self-report personality questionnaire around the time of the children's birth. The EASI was designed to assess "emotionality," "activity," "sociability," and "impulsivity," which, according to the investigators, are "thought to be the most heritable personality traits" (Plomin et al., 1998, p. 212).

The children were assessed between the ages of 9 and 16 using the Colorado Childhood Temperament Inventory (CCTI), a self-report measure that is an extension of the EASI questionnaire for children. At age 16, the children were administered the EASI. Because of its unique status as a longitudinal adoption study following children from birth, at age 16 the children "completed the same EASI questionnaire that their parents had completed 16 years earlier" (Plomin et al., 1998, p. 212). The researchers saw their study as unique because it was the first adoption study to test for genetic influences on self-reported normal personality (Plomin et al., 1998, p. 211).

Plomin and colleagues found a near-zero average 0.01 personality test score correlation between birthparents and their 240 adopted-away biological offspring, based on eight yearly test score correlations from ages 9 through 16 (Plomin et al., 1998, p. 214).[2] In other words, the results showed no genetic influence on personality. Plomin and colleagues' preliminary conclusions were that these results suggest "little effect of nature or nurture" (p. 212), and that "genetic factors correlated with parents' self-reported personality have little effect" (p. 212). "On the face of it," they wrote, "these results from CAP suggest that neither nature nor nurture contributes importantly to individual differences in self-reported personality." As an example, they pointed to "a direct test of genetic influence [that] comes from the resemblance between biological parents and their adopted-away offspring, who correlated only .01 averaged across the 8 years of assessment of the offspring and across the four EASI traits" (p. 215). According to the researchers, the birthparent/adopted-away biological offspring correlation "directly indexes genetic influence, unlike the indirect comparisons between nonadoptive and adoptive relatives or between identical and fraternal twins" (p. 211).

The investigators could have stopped at this point and simply concluded that the study found no genetic influence on personality, accompanied by a discussion of the implications of this finding. However, they decided to interpret the results on the basis of (a) model-fitting analysis, and (b) the results of previous twin studies. Using model-fitting analysis (see Chapter 4), the researchers calculated an average heritability estimate for personality of 14 percent, which was not significantly different from previous adoption studies, although it was "lower than the average estimates from twin studies" (p. 215). They assumed that there was no selective placement in their sample (see the note in Plomin and colleagues' Table 4, p. 215).

Plomin and colleagues noted that the authors of previous twin studies of personality had estimated heritability at roughly 40 percent, and argued that the "most obvious implication of these results is that other family and adoption studies are needed to triangulate with twin studies on the estimation of genetic influence for personality as assessed by self-reported personality questionnaires" (p. 215). They speculated that the discrepancy between the results of their adoption study and those of previous twin studies was due to adoption studies' reduced ability to detect non-additive genetic factors: "The most interesting hypothesis to explain lower heritability estimates from adoption studies as compared to twin studies is nonadditive genetic variance" (p. 217).

The researchers argued that studies based on first-degree relatives, such as their 1998 CAP study, "will not detect nonadditive genetic variance" (p. 217), and chose to conclude that their results can be explained by "nonadditive genetic influence, which can be detected by twin studies but not by adoption studies" (p. 211; for a critical review of the CAP, see Richardson & Norgate, 2006).

Alternative Explanations of the Results

The Converging Evidence Argument

According to psychiatric geneticists Faraone, Tsuang, and Tsuang,

> We cannot rely on either a single study or class of studies to draw conclusions about the effects of genes and environment on mental illness. Instead, from an examination of many studies we seek a

pattern of converging evidence that consistently confirms genetic and/or environmental hypotheses about the familial transmission of the disorder.

(Faraone, Tsuang, & Tsuang, 1999, p. 45)

However, it has been pointed out that proponents of "converging evidence" arguments in support of such claims "typically maintain that scientific claims can be evaluated only within the context of broader claims and therefore cannot be judged in isolation." This enables such proponents to "readily avoid subjecting their claims to the risk of falsification" (Lilienfeld, Lynn, & Lohr, 2003, p. 9).

Plomin and colleagues chose to "triangulate" the 1998 CAP study findings with the results of family and twin studies, and argued that the results should be interpreted in the context of twin studies' supposed ability to detect non-additive genetic influence.[3] Indeed, the opening paragraph of their publication was about twin studies and the 40 percent heritability estimate that researchers had derived from their results. In other words, they argued that their results should not be evaluated in isolation, and should be viewed in the context of broader "converging evidence" claims about genetics.

Heritability and Model Fitting

We saw in Chapter 4 that the heritability concept is a controversial one, and that the use of heritability estimates in the social and behavioral sciences has been criticized by many reviewers over the past four decades. Many critics of the concept have argued that heritability estimates are misleading, meaningless, or even harmful. We also examined the questionable assumptions underlying model-fitting procedures (which produce heritability estimates), and saw that several leading behavioral genetic investigators recognized that these assumptions are questionable, or do not hold.

In the 1998 CAP study, Plomin and colleagues used model-fitting analysis to convert the failure to find a personality test score correlation between birthparents and their adopted-away biological offspring into a genetic finding: "At 16 years, the average model-fitting estimate of heritability was 14% for the four [EASI] traits using data from the three types of parents and their adopted and nonadopted children" (p. 215). In other words, through statistical transformation, the researchers turned a finding that genes play no role in personality formation into a finding that genes *do* play a role in personality formation. They went on to write that this 14 percent heritability estimate was not significantly lower than the handful of earlier adoption studies (p. 215), implying that the 1998 CAP study results were comparable to these earlier studies.

As seen in Chapter 4, however, in their 1990 "Behavioral Genetics and Personality" chapter in Pervin's *Handbook of Personality: Theory and Research*, Plomin, Chipuer, and Loehlin had cautioned that model fitting "has the disadvantage of being complex and sometimes seems to be a black box from which parameter estimates magically appear." Furthermore, they wrote that "if the MZ correlation does not exceed the DZ correlation for a particular trait, there is no genetic influence (unless assortative mating approaches unity), and model-fitting analyses *must come to that conclusion or there is something wrong with the model*" (Plomin, Chipuer, & Loehlin, 1990, p. 235, italics added). Here, Plomin and colleagues argued that if a correlation indicates no genetic influence on a characteristic, but that subsequent model-fitting analyses find such influence, "there is something wrong with the model." Several years later in the 1998 CAP study, however, Plomin and colleagues found no average genetic influence on personality, and then used "the model" to find such influence. After collecting the data, Plomin stood his previous position on its head and concluded, in effect, that there is something wrong with the *correlation*.

In the subsequent 1999 revised edition of Plomin's chapter in *Handbook of Personality: Theory and Research* (Plomin & Caspi, 1999), the previous edition's section on model fitting was removed. Turning to the various editions of Plomin and colleagues' textbook *Behavioral Genetics*, the 1990 Second Edition contained the above-quoted "black box/something wrong with the model" caution about model fitting (Plomin, DeFries, & McClearn, 1990, p. 246), as did the 1997 Third Edition (Plomin, DeFries, McClearn, & Rutter, 1997, p. 310). In the 2001, 2008, and 2013 editions, however, this section was removed (for these later *Behavioral Genetics* discussions of model fitting, see Plomin, DeFries, McClearn, & McGuffin, 2001, pp. 351–371; Plomin, DeFries, McClearn, & McGuffin, 2008, pp. 379–402; Plomin, DeFries, Knopik, & Neiderhiser, 2013, pp. 383–392).

The 1998 CAP Study and the Twin Method

As far back as 1976, Plomin and DeFries wrote in *Science*, "We believe that well-designed adoption studies can provide the best information about the relative importance of heredity as a cause of individual differences in human behavior" (Plomin & DeFries, 1976, p. 12). In a frequently cited 1977 publication, Plomin and colleagues favored adoption studies over the twin method because the latter was subject to genotype–environment correlations, which "may complicate the interpretation of results from the classical twin design" (Plomin, DeFries, & Loehlin, 1977, p. 318).

In their 1978 *Annual Review of Psychology* contribution, DeFries and Plomin wrote, comparing adoption studies to family studies and twin studies, "It is our opinion that adoption studies provide a more convincing demonstration of genetic influence upon human behavioral characters" (DeFries & Plomin, 1978, p. 481). In 1985 they wrote, "The adoption study is generally considered to be the most powerful method in human behavioral genetics" (Plomin & DeFries, 1985, p. 17).

Clearly, Plomin and colleagues were in the camp of those seeing adoption studies as providing a better method of disentangling genetic and environmental factors than that provided by twin method MZT–DZT comparisons. It follows that they should have concluded that the results of the 1998 CAP study indicated that there is something wrong with twin studies of personality, and that previous interpretations of twin data in favor of genetics should be reevaluated. Instead, they wrote that "tests of the equal environments assumption of the twin method generally support the reasonableness of the assumption" (Plomin et al., 1998, p. 216). The arguments put forward in support of this position were examined in Chapters 7 and 8, and were rejected.

The 1998 CAP Study and the MISTRA

As we have seen, the results of the 1998 CAP study of normal personality stand in direct contrast to the widely cited MISTRA studies discussed in Part I. The MISTRA researchers reported a personality correlation of 0.50 for 44 MZA pairs (Bouchard, Lykken, McGue, Segal, & Tellegen, 1990), whereas the 1998 CAP study found no biological parent/adoptee personality correlation. As we saw in Chapter 6, Bouchard wrote in a leading scientific journal that "the similarity we see in personality between biological relatives is almost entirely genetic in origin." The results of the 1998 CAP study did not lead Bouchard to revise this position, and, like Plomin and colleagues, he speculated about non-additive genetic effects and was of the opinion that, in the 1998 CAP study, "a variety of methodological and measurement problems (age at measurement, comparability of measures, sampling, etc.) cannot be ruled out" (Bouchard & McGue, 2003, p. 23). As often seen in human behavioral genetics, studies finding little or no genetic effects are downplayed or are seen as having "methodological and measurement problems," whereas massively flawed studies based on implausible assumptions are cited uncritically and become "landmark studies."

The 1998 CAP Study's Lack of Impact

In their discussions of the "genetics of personality" topic, the authors of many influential psychology textbooks and works discussing behavioral genetic research, including texts focusing specifically on personality research, did not cite or discuss the 1998 CAP study. This also holds true for several works popularizing behavioral genetic research and theories (e.g., Barondes, 2012; Harris, 2006; Pinker, 2002; Ridley, 2003; Rutter, 2006). As I have shown elsewhere (Joseph, 2013a), influential academic texts, introductory psychology textbooks, and popular works discussing the genetics of personality topic frequently fail to mention or reference the 1998 CAP study. The few authors citing the study usually report that its results are generally consistent with behavioral genetic positions that genetic factors play an important role in personality development. Only one of the 48 publications citing the 1998 CAP study found in a July 2nd, 2012 PsycINFO database search reported the 0.01 EASI birthparent/adopted-away offspring correlation (see Joseph, 2013a, for more details on how the study has been cited and discussed).

Rather than "triangulate" the 1998 CAP zero birthparent/biological offspring personality correlation with the results of twin studies, as Plomin and colleagues did in 1998, we could plausibly "triangulate": (a) the 1998 CAP study zero correlation finding; (b) the biases and untenable assumptions of twin research; and (c) the negative results of molecular genetic research (see Chapters 8–10). We could then conclude that genes for personality variation do not appear to exist.

Conclusions

Plomin and colleagues' 1998 CAP study, with a much larger sample than any TRA study, found no personality test score correlation between biological mothers and their 240 adopted-away biological offspring—a finding that completely contradicts the MISTRA results. The main difference between these studies is how they have been reported in both the scientific literature and in the media. The 1998 CAP study finding is largely unknown. In contrast, in the media and in authoritative secondary sources such as psychology textbooks, claims of important genetic influences on the basis of TRA studies such as the MISTRA are widely reported, often accompanied by photographs of reunited twin pairs and a list of their supposed similarities. And yet a plausible interpretation of the 1998 CAP study is that, in the context of the current "missing heritability" stage of molecular genetic research, it provides additional evidence that twin studies of personality and behavior—including the MISTRA, other TRA studies, and studies using reared-together pairs—have recorded nothing more than the impact of environmental influences and research bias. This conclusion is consistent with the position that family, social, cultural, economic, religious, and political environments, and not genetics, are the main factors underlying variation in human behavior.

Notes

1 Appendix B is based on a condensed and updated version of a previous publication that appeared in *Advances in Child Development and Behavior* (Joseph, 2013a). Please see this publication for a complete analysis of the issues raised in Appendix B.
2 Although the researchers studied 245 adoptees, by age 16 only 240 were available for testing.
3 The words "twin" or "twins" appeared no fewer than 70 times in the eight-page 1998 CAP study publication (roughly three pages consisted of references and tables).

APPENDIX C

LIST OF QUOTATIONS FROM TWIN RESEARCHERS AND OTHERS INVOKING THE "TWINS CREATE THEIR OWN ENVIRONMENT" *ARGUMENT A* IN DEFENSE OF THE MZT–DZT EQUAL ENVIRONMENT ASSUMPTION OF THE TWIN METHOD: 1954–2014

(All quotations refer to twins reared together: MZTs and DZTs)

In so far as binovular [DZT] twins are treated differently from one another and more differently than uniovular [MZT] twins, this is likely to be due, not so much to causes outside the twins as to innate differences in the needs of the binovular twins themselves, manifested by different patterns of behaviour.

(Shields, 1954, p. 240)

The popular notion that the behavior patterns of one-egg [MZT] twins are alike chiefly because of unusual similarity in their early environments has yet to be substantiated. If confirmed, the argument would only strengthen rather than weaken any correctly formulated genetic theory. Psychodynamic concepts, too, are built on the premise that man is selective in respect to important aspects of his life experiences and so can be thought of as "creating his own environment."

(Kallmann, 1958, p. 543)

APPENDIX C

The assumption [has been] confirmed that the environment in which twins are brought up is generally much more alike for monozygotic than for dizygotic twins. By reason of their outward striking resemblance, monozygotic twins will from a very early stage influence those in their surroundings and also each other in a very uniform fashion, while nothing equivalent should be characteristic for dizygotic twins. This similarity in the environment of monozygotic twins must naturally ultimately be due to their identical genotype.
(Juel-Nielsen, 1965/1980, Part I, p. 26)

Greater early differences in fraternal twins than in identical pairs due to hereditary factors will usually elicit more differential behavior toward each individual on the part of the parents, sibs, and friends.
(Vandenberg, 1966, p. 330)

Differences in the parental treatment that twins receive are much more a function of the degree of the twins' genetic relatedness than of parental beliefs about "identicalness" and "fraternalness."
(Scarr, 1968, p. 40)

It has been argued that the environmental difference of monozygotic twins is reduced because they tend to seek similar environments; however, in so far as they do this because of their genetic similarity rather than just to copy one another, their behaviour is a reflection of their genotype and must be regarded as influencing their genetic rather than their environmental variance.
(Bulmer, 1970, p. 144)

Most probably, identical twins are treated more alike because they look and act more alike.
(Loehlin & Nichols, 1976, p. 87)

Although MZ twins experience more similar environments than DZ twins, the assumption that these unequal environments *cause* greater personality similarity in MZ twins is not warranted. It is possible that the unequal environmental treatment is an effect rather than a cause of the greater similarity of the identical twins.
(Plomin, Willerman, & Loehlin, 1976, pp. 44–45, italics in original)

Much of the greater similarity of MZ over DZ environments seems to be a consequence, rather than a cause, of the behavior of the twins.
(Loehlin, 1978a, p. 431)

APPENDIX C

Although MZ twins generally experience more similar environments, this fact seems to result from their genetic similarities and not to be a cause of exaggerated phenotypic resemblance.

(Scarr & Carter-Saltzman, 1979, p. 541)

The behavioral similarity of monozygotic twins appears not to result from the similarity in social environment of the twins. Rather, the available evidence suggests that the similarity of the social environment of monozygotic twins is the result of the behavioral similarity of the twins.

(Kendler, 1983, p. 1416)

Twins tend to elicit, select, seek out, or create very similar effective environments and, to that extent, the impact of these experiences is counted as a genetic influence.

(Bouchard, Lykken, McGue, Segal, & Tellegen, 1990, pp. 227–228)

For example, the question can be asked whether parents create or respond to differences in their twins . . . . The answer to the question is that when parents treat identical twins more similarly than they would fraternal twins, parents are responding to differences in their children's behavior.

(Plomin, DeFries, & McClearn, 1990, p. 317)

A number of studies that examined nonpsychiatric phenotypes have concluded that, to the extent that MZ twins have more similar environments than same-sex DZ twins, the greater MZ environmental similarity is the result of the greater phenotypic similarity of MZ twins rather than the cause of it.

(Lyons, Kendler, Provet, & Tsuang, 1991, p. 126)

Although it is apparent that the social environment of MZ twins is more similar than that of DZ twins, such evidence as is available suggests that, for the most part, the similarity is the result (and not the cause) of their behavioral similarity.

(Rutter, Simonoff, & Silberg, 1993, p. 180).

Do parental treatments mold twins' traits alike? Or do twins' similar genetic traits provoke a search for similar, mutually reinforcing environmental opportunities? In the tendency of MZ twins to receive similar treatments, or to seek them out, the arrow of causality is certainly bidirectional.

(Rowe, 1994, p. 45)

APPENDIX C

As for adult MZ co-twins, they are indeed more similar than DZ co-twins in terms of having the same friends, studying together, etc., but it is questionable whether this is due to parental behavior and/or other environmental influences, or whether it results from individual tendencies of a genetic nature.

(Parisi, 1995, p. 13)

A series of ingenious studies . . . have all pointed to the conclusion that, for the most part, the more similar treatment of MZs is not the cause of their greater phenotypic similarity but, rather, a consequence of their genetic identity and the more similar responses this elicits from the environment.

(Martin, Boomsma, & Machin, 1997, p. 390)

Why are identical twins closer than fraternal twins? There is evidence that parents and caretakers do not bear the primary responsibility for twins' similarities or how they relate to one another. Instead, many studies demonstrate that parents respond to, rather than create, behaviors expressed by identical twins.

(Segal, 1999, p. 101)

Environmental bias [in twin studies] is highly unlikely, because most studies show that the similarity of the social environment of MZ is the result and not the cause of similar behavior.

(Kringlen, 2000, p. 5)

The more similar parental treatment of MZ vs. DZ twins occurs *in response to* the greater similarity of actions initiated by MZ pairs . . . . It seems . . . likely that the increased similarity in treatment of MZ twins is a consequence of their genetic identity and the more similar responses this elicits from the environment.

(Evans & Martin, 2000, p. 78, italics in original)

Twin resemblance for ND [nicotine dependence] was predicted by frequency of adult contact, which could be a violation of the equal environment assumption. However, that would assume that frequent contact "causes" resemblance for ND which may be less likely than twins with similar smoking habits choosing to be in closer contact.

(Maes et al., 2004, p. 10)

Violations of the equal environment assumption (EEA) would be suggested by greater similarity of alcoholism-relevant environments among MZ than DZ pairs . . . . We cannot rule this out, but . . . pair similarity for alcohol-related behaviors may be a cause (not a consequence) of within-pair contact and environmental similarity, which would not bias genetic estimates.

(Prescott et al., 2005, p. 54)

MZ and DZ twins are not perfectly equal on some environmental experiences. However, some part of the greater MZ than DZ twin similarity in treatment arises because MZ twins' genetically influenced similar behavior evokes similar treatment.

(Caspi & Shiner, 2006, p. 331)

The EEA will not be violated if that [MZTs eliciting more similar environments] is all that is occurring. That is because if the environments are being entirely driven by genes, it is reasonable to attribute the effects to genes provided, and only provided, that the environments that differ between MZ and DZ pairs do not have an effect on the trait being studied.

(Rutter, 2006, pp. 41–42)

Where MZ twins elicit more similar experiences from their environments than DZ twins due to the greater genetic similarity of the MZ twins, however, this is generally considered to be an expression of their genetically influenced characteristics rather than an unmeasured shared environmental influence.

(Johnson et al., 2007, p. 548)

Although MZ twins are sometimes in more frequent contact with each other than DZ twins, it appears that twin similarity (e.g., in attitudes and personality) may cause greater contact rather than vice versa.

(Fowler, Baker, & Dawes, 2008, p. 235)

It is important to emphasize that even if MZ twins are treated more similarly, this does not in and of itself constitute a violation of the assumption; greater similarity in environment may be caused by the greater similarity in genotypes.

(Cesarini, Johannesson, Wallace, & Lichtenstein, 2009, p. 621)

There is little argument that MZ twins are treated more similarly than DZ twins in certain aspects. . . . However, the central questions of the equal environment assumption (EEA) are whether these differences influence the specific trait under analysis and if these environmental differences are manifestations of the genetic similarity of MZ twins.

(Medland & Hatemi, 2009, pp. 198–199)

It is important to note that if MZ twins are treated more alike than DZ twins, it is most likely associated with their genetically based behavioral similarities.

(Segal & Johnson, 2009, p. 82)

APPENDIX C

In measuring similarity of treatment or social environments in twin studies, it is important to consider that MZ twins, because of their more similar behavior, can elicit more similar treatment.

(Flint, Greenspan, & Kendler, 2010, p. 31)

If MZ twins are treated more similarly because they are biologically more alike, this can hardly be considered a violation of the EEA. For the reason that MZ environments are more similar than DZ environments (if indeed they are) is *because of the initial difference in genetic predispositions.*

(Sturgis et al., 2010, p. 222, italics in original)

If, as twin studies suggest, there is a genetic predisposition toward ideology, this in turn raises the possibility that there is a genetic component underlying the environmental variation reported by twins. This latter view already has considerable empirical support.

(Smith et al., 2012, p. 28)

A subtle, but important, issue is that identical twins might have more similar experiences than fraternal twins because identical twins are more similar genetically. Such differences between identical and fraternal twins in experience are not a violation of the equal environments assumption because the differences are not caused environmentally.

(Plomin, DeFries, Knopik, & Neiderhiser, 2013, p. 82)

The results of our study alone cannot decisively reveal if MZ–DZ twin differences in peer network overlap are violations of the EEA because genetic similarity may lead MZ twins to choose more similar peers compared to other dyads.

(McGuire & Segal, 2013, p. 508).

This is not to say parents do not treat children differently in other [non-political ideology] domains. This occurs, for example, when parents react differently to different children depending on the children's personality. However, this would be a type of reactive heritability and not a violation of the equal environment assumption.

(Hatemi et al., 2014, p. 284)

GLOSSARY

ADHD "Attention-deficit hyperactivity disorder." A psychiatric diagnosis given most often to children exhibiting poor concentration, distractibility, hyperactivity, and impulsiveness.

adoption study A study that attempts to disentangle the potential influences of genes and environment by studying children who are given up by their biological (birth) parent(s), who are then adopted by another family with whom they share no genetic relationship.

allele Different forms of the same gene. Different alleles produce variations in inherited characteristics such as eye color or blood type.

assortative mating A non-random pattern of mating in which individuals with similar genotypes and/or phenotypes mate with each other more frequently than expected by chance.

assumption Something taken for granted or accepted as true without proof. The project or investigation then treats it, and researchers arrive at conclusions, as if it were true.

attention-deficit hyperactivity disorder See **ADHD**.

autism A developmental disorder appearing by age 3 years, and diagnosed on the basis of: (a) marked communication abnormalities; (b) impairment in the ability to communicate with others; and (c) an excess of stereotyped, ritualistic, and repetitive behaviors.

behavioral genetics See **human behavioral genetics**.

bipolar disorder (manic depression) A psychiatric disorder characterized by moods that alternate between mania and depression.

chromosome A threadlike structure in cells that carries genes (DNA).

circular reasoning An illogical argument used to support a statement by repeating the statement in different or stronger terms. In a circular argument, the conclusion is based on an assumption whose validity is dependent on the conclusion. For example, "X is true because Y is true; Y is true because X is true."

cohort effects Similarities in people's behavior, preferences, physical condition, and other attributes that arise from the characteristics of the historical periods and cultural milieu in which they experience stages of life at the same time.

concordance When both members of a twin pair are diagnosed with the same disorder.

confound An unforeseen or uncontrolled-for factor that threatens the validity of conclusions researchers draw from their studies. Confounding occurs when the association between two variables is caused by a third variable that influences both.

control group A group used in scientific experiments where the factor being tested is not present or applied, so that it may serve as a standard for comparison against another group where the factor is present or applied.

correlation A statistical measure of association that ranges from +1.0 (completely positive correlation), through 0.0 (no correlation), to −1.0 (completely negative correlation). Correlation coefficients measure how characteristics vary together, but do not indicate what causes the association.

co-twin control study A little-used twin study method in which researchers assess the impact of environmental interventions or factors on MZ twins, compared with their MZ co-twins who did not experience the intervention or factor.

***Diagnostic and Statistical Manual of Mental Disorders* (DSM)** A book produced by the American Psychiatric Association and revised periodically. It attempts to define, describe, and standardize psychiatric diagnostic categories. The categories used in the DSM are accepted by most official organizations, including hospitals, insurance companies, and other institutions. The most recent edition, *DSM-5*, was published in 2013.

discordance One member of a twin pair is diagnosed with a disorder, while the other twin is not.

dizygotic (DZ, fraternal) twins Twins who develop from two separately fertilized eggs. Like ordinary siblings, these twins are said to share a 50 percent average genetic resemblance.

DNA (deoxyribonucleic acid) The material that in most cells is localized on chromosomes, and that carries genetic information.

dysgenic Human mating patterns that eugenicists and others believe exert a detrimental effect on later generations through the presumed inheritance of undesirable characteristics.

EEA-test study A study designed to test the validity of the MZT–DZT equal environment assumption of the twin method. See Equal environment assumption.

emergenesis A concept put forward by David Lykken in 1982. According to Segal, "Emergenesis refers to genetically influenced traits that do not run in families. Emergenic traits are thought to emerge out of complex configurations of polymorphic genes that come together by chance in an individual."

empirically keyed test A self-report psychological test based on items (questions) that are said to discriminate between normal individuals

GLOSSARY

and individuals with various diagnoses or psychological characteristics. The items are not necessarily theoretically relevant to the diagnosis or characteristic in question.

environment   All non-genetic factors that potentially contribute to or cause diseases, psychiatric disorders, or differences in behavior.

epigenetics   The study of how the expression of genetic characteristics is modified by environmental influences or other mechanisms without a change to the DNA sequence.

equal environment assumption (EEA)   The most important, and most controversial, assumption of the twin method. It holds that MZT and same-sex DZT twins grow up experiencing roughly the same environments. All conclusions in favor of genetics derived from twin method data depend on the validity of this assumption.

eugenics   A doctrine holding that humans can be "improved" by selective breeding to increase the reproduction of people seen carrying "desirable" genetic traits, and by reducing or preventing the reproduction of people seen as carrying "undesirable" genetic traits. Early eugenicists argued that low IQ, many social problems, and psychiatric disorders are caused by heredity, which can and should be bred out of the population for the benefit of future generations.

family study   A study assessing the behavioral resemblance or diagnostic status of biological relatives. Family resemblance is usually compared to a control group or to the general population.

favism   A disease marked by the development of hemolytic anemia. It is caused by an inherited deficiency of glucose-6-phosphate located on the X chromosome, combined with the consumption of fava (broad) beans or the inhalation of fava bean pollen.

fraternal twins   See **dizygotic twins**.

gene   Components of chromosomes composed of segments of DNA that are the basic functional units of heredity.

general intelligence (g)   The psychometric theory of intelligence. It holds that there exists a singular pervasive mental (cognitive) ability that is biologically based and has an important genetic basis, and can be reliably measured by IQ tests.

generalizability   In the twin research context, refers to the ability to apply the findings from twin studies to the much larger non-twin population.

genetic counseling   The act of providing advice to prospective parents concerning the chances of genetic disorders appearing in their future child.

genetic determinism   The belief that differences in basic physiological, developmental, and behavioral processes are mainly the result of genetic variation.

genetic marker   A segment of DNA with an identifiable physical location on a chromosome and whose inheritance can be followed.

genetic predisposition   See **Predisposition-stress theory**.

GLOSSARY

genetics The study of the patterns of inheritance of specific characteristics.
genome The total genetic material of an organism or species.
genomics The branch of molecular biology concerned with the structure, function, evolution, and mapping of genomes.
genomewide association (GWA) study A molecular genetic method that involves rapidly scanning markers across the genomes of affected and non-affected people to find common genetic variants associated with particular diseases or characteristics. GWA studies attempt to identify single-nucleotide polymorphisms (commonly known as "SNPs") associated with the characteristic or condition under study.
genomewide complex-trait analysis (GCTA) A molecular genetic technique used since 2010 that estimates the extent to which the variance of a characteristic can be "explained by" genetic variation (SNPs, or single-nucleotide polymorphisms). See **SNP**.
genotype An organism's individual genetic composition at a specified chromosomal location.
heritability According to genetic researchers in the social and behavioral sciences, the proportion of behavioral differences among individuals in a population that can be attributed to genetic factors. Heritability estimates range from 0.0 to 1.0 (0 percent to 100 percent).
human behavioral genetics A discipline, rooted in the field of psychology, that uses family, twin, adoption, and molecular genetic studies to assess the role of genetic influences on characteristics such as IQ, personality, psychiatric disorders, and other aspects of behavior.
Human Genome Project An international research effort established to determine the DNA sequence of the entire human genome. The first draft of the human genome was published in 2001.
identical twins See **monozygotic twins**.
intraclass correlation A correlational method used to measure the association of pairs of values when the order in each pair is arbitrary.
kinship research The study of relatives sharing various genetic relationships, for the purpose of assessing possible familial or genetic transmission. Examples of kinship research include family, twin, and adoption studies.
Mendelian inheritance Inheritance of characters specifically transmitted by genes in accord with Mendel's laws.
missing heritability A concept developed in 2008–2009 to explain the large discrepancy between heritability estimates based on the results of family, twin, and adoption studies, versus the results of molecular genetic studies.
model fitting A technique used frequently in behavioral genetics for testing the fit between models of genetic and environmental relatedness against the observed data.

molecular genetics The study of the structure and function of genes at the molecular level.

monozygotic (MZ, identical) twins Twins produced by the division of a single fertilized egg. Both are born with identical genotypes (100 percent genetic resemblance).

multifactorial complex disorder A disorder or syndrome believed to be caused by an interacting combination of multiple genes and multiple environmental risk factors.

pedigree A record of one's ancestors, offspring, and siblings through several generations. Usually presented in graphic form through the use of standard symbols.

phenotype An observable trait or characteristic of an organism. For example, eye color, weight, or the presence or absence of a disease.

PKU (phenylketonuria) An inherited metabolic disorder in which the body cannot metabolize an amino acid called phenylalanine. It can result in intellectual disability (mental retardation) and other neurological problems. If detected early enough, the condition can be prevented by means of a special diet.

polygenic disorder A disorder believed to result from the combined action of more than one gene.

polymorphism Multiple forms of a single gene that can exist in a population.

predisposition-stress (diathesis-stress) theory The theory that a given disorder is caused by an inherited biological (genetic) predisposition in combination with environmental conditions or events.

pseudoscience A set of ideas or claims based on theories purporting to be scientific, but that are not scientific.

psychiatric genetics A field founded by Ernst Rüdin and his German colleagues in the early part of the twentieth century. German psychiatric geneticists used family and twin studies in an attempt to establish the genetic basis of psychiatric disorders. Their primary goal was to promote the eugenic program (called "racial hygiene" in Germany) of curbing the reproduction of people they viewed as carrying the "hereditary taint of mental illness," by sterilization or other means. Contemporary psychiatric geneticists perform family, twin, adoption, and molecular genetic research in an attempt to assess the influence of genetic factors on mental disorders in order to better treat and prevent them, while promoting the use of genetic counseling programs.

psychiatry The branch of medicine dealing with the diagnosis and treatment of mental disorders.

psychometrics A branch of psychology that deals with the design, administration, and interpretation of quantitative tests for the measurement of psychological characteristics such as intelligence, aptitude, and personality traits. It is concerned with individual differences in

GLOSSARY

the population for these characteristics, and with the causes of these differences.

quantitative genetics The study of the inheritance of continuously distributed characteristics and their mechanisms.

quantitative trait loci (QTLs) Stretches of DNA containing, or linked to, the genes that underlie a presumed quantitative characteristic (meaning a characteristic believed to be caused by the action of many genes of varying effect size).

reductionism The tendency to view complex systems, including humans and human societies, as the sum of their parts.

selective placement Adoption agencies' practice of intentionally placing adoptees into homes matching the socioeconomic and perceived genetic status of the birth (biological) parents.

self-report personality test A psychological test assessing a person's own report of his or her symptoms, behaviors, beliefs, attitudes, and other psychological characteristics. It is often presented in a paper-and-pencil format, or may be administered on a computer.

separated twin study See **twins reared-apart (TRA) study**.

SNP (single-nucleotide polymorphism) A type of genetic variation (polymorphism) occurring between different people.

special mental abilities Non-IQ mental abilities including verbal, perceptual, spatial, and memory tasks.

twin method (classical twin method) A research method developed in the 1920s that compares the resemblance of reared-together monozygotic (MZT; believed to share 100 percent of their segregating genes) versus the resemblance of reared-together same-sex dizygotic twin pairs (DZT; believed to share on average 50 percent of their segregating genes). If MZT pairs resemble each other more than same-sex DZT pairs for the characteristic or condition in question (on the basis of correlations or concordance rates), twin researchers conclude that it has a genetic component and then calculate heritability estimates based on the magnitude of the difference, or based on more complex statistical methods. See **equal environment assumption**.

twins reared apart (TRA) study A research method that studies twins who were separated at some point during the first few years of childhood, and were reared apart in different homes. Also known as a "separated twin study."

variance A numerical value used to indicate how widely individuals in a group (sample or population) vary in relation to the group mean.

zygosity In twin research, the genetic status of twin pairs, such as whether the pair is monozygotic (MZT or MZA) or dizygotic (DZT or DZA).

zygosity determination The method used by twin researchers to determine a twin pair's zygosity. See **zygosity**.

REFERENCES

Agrawal, A. (2013). Minutes of the annual business meeting of the members of the Behavior Genetics Association. *Behavior Genetics, 43,* 551–553.

Ainslie, R. C. (1997). *The psychology of twinship.* Northvale, New Jersey: Jason Aronson.

Albee, G. W. (1996). Revolutions and counterrevolutions in prevention. *American Psychologist, 51,* 1130–1133.

Alford, J. R., Funk, C. L., & Hibbing, J. R. (2005). Are political orientations genetically transmitted? *American Political Science Review, 99,* 153–167.

Alford, J. R., Funk, C. L., & Hibbing, J. R. (2008). Beyond liberals and conservatives to political genotypes and phenotypes. *Perspectives on Politics, 6,* 321–328.

Allport, G. W. (1961). *Pattern and growth in personality.* New York: Holt, Rinehart, and Winston.

American Psychiatric Association. (2013a, May 3rd). Chair of DSM-5 task force discusses future of mental health research; Statement by David Kupfer, M.D. American Psychiatric Association [press release].

American Psychiatric Association. (2013b). *Diagnostic and statistical manual of mental disorders* (5th ed.). Arlington, VA: American Psychiatric Association.

Anonymous. (1942). Euthanasia. *American Journal of Psychiatry, 99,* 141–143.

Anonymous. (2014). Gold Medal Award for Life Achievement in the Science of Psychology: Thomas J. Bouchard, Jr. *American Psychologist, 69,* 477–479.

Anum, E. A., Silberg, J., & Retchin, S. M. (2014). Heritability of DUI convictions: A twin study of driving under the influence of alcohol. *Twin Research and Human Genetics, 17,* 10–15.

Arehart-Treichel, J. (2014, March 20th). Psychiatric genetics holds great promise. *Psychiatric News.* DOI: 10.1176/appi.pn.2014.3a1.

Arvey, R. D., et al. (1994, December 13th). Mainstream science on intelligence. *Wall Street Journal,* p. A18.

Asbury, K., & Plomin, R. (2014). *G is for genes: The impact of genetics on education and achievement.* Chichester, UK: Wiley Blackwell.

Bailey, A., Le Couteur, A., Gottesman, I., Bolton, P., Simonoff, E., Yuzda, E., & Rutter, M. (1995). Autism as a strongly genetic disorder: Evidence from a British twin study. *Psychological Medicine, 25,* 63–77.

Baron, M. (1998). Psychiatric genetics and prejudice: Can the science be separated from the scientist? *Molecular Psychiatry, 3,* 96–100.

Barondes, S. H. (2012). *Making sense of people: Decoding the mysteries of personality.* Upper Saddle River, NJ: FT Press.

Bartels, M., & Boomsma, D. I. (2009). Born to be happy? The etiology of subjective well-being. *Behavior Genetics, 39,* 605–615.

Beckwith, J., Geller, L., & Sarkar, S. (1991). IQ and heredity [letter to the editor]. *Science, 252,* 191.

Beckwith, J., & Morris, C. A. (2008). Twin studies of political behavior: Untenable assumptions? *Perspectives on Politics, 6,* 785–791.

Begley, S. (1987, November 23rd). All about twins. *Newsweek, 58*–69.

Beirich, H. (2013, October). Pioneer fund assets divided; New leadership appointed. *Hatewatch.* Southern Poverty Law Center. Retrieved 2/15/2014 from http://www.splcenter.org/blog/2013/10/22/pioneer-fund-assets-divided-new-leadership-appointed/.

Bentall, R. P. (2009). *Doctoring the mind: Is our current treatment of mental illness really any good?* New York: New York University Press.

Benyamin, B., Pourcain, B., Davis, O. S., Davies, G., Hansell, N. K., Brion, M. J., . . . Visscher, P. M. (2014). Childhood intelligence is heritable, highly polygenic and associated with FNBP1L. *Molecular Psychiatry, 19,* 253–258.

Black, E. (2003). *War against the weak: Eugenics and America's campaign to create a master race.* New York: Four Walls Eight Windows.

Bleuler, M. (1978). *The schizophrenic disorders: Long-term patient and family disorders.* New Haven, CT: Yale University Press.

Blinkhorn, S., & Johnson, C. (1990). The insignificance of personality testing. *Nature, 348,* 671–672.

Block, N. J., & Dworkin, G. (Eds.). (1976). *The IQ controversy.* New York: Pantheon.

Boomsma, D. I., Willemsen, G., Dolan, C. V., Hawkley, L. C., & Cacioppo, J. T. (2005). Genetic and environmental contributions to loneliness in adults: The Netherlands Twin Register Study. *Behavior Genetics, 35,* 745–752.

Bouchard, T. J., Jr. (1976). Genetic factors in intelligence. In A. Kaplan (Ed.), *Human behavior genetics* (pp. 164–197). Springfield, IL: Charles C. Thomas.

Bouchard, T. J., Jr. (1981). The study of mental ability using twin and adoption designs. In L. Gedda, P. Parisi, & W. Nance (Eds.), *Twin research 3: Part B. Intelligence, personality, and development* (pp. 21-23). New York: Alan R. Liss.

Bouchard, T. J., Jr. (1982a). [Review of the book *The intelligence controversy,* by H. Eysenck versus L. Kamin]. *American Journal of Psychology, 95,* 346-349.

Bouchard, T. J., Jr. (1982b). Identical twins reared apart: Reanalysis or pseudo-analysis? [Review of the book *Identical twins reared apart: A reanalysis,* by S. L. Farber]. *Contemporary Psychology, 27,* 190-191.

Bouchard, T. J., Jr. (1983). Do environmental similarities explain the similarity in intelligence of identical twins reared apart? *Intelligence, 7,* 175–184.

Bouchard, T. J., Jr. (1984). Twins reared together and apart: What they tell us about human diversity. In S. Fox (Ed.), *Individuality and determinism: Chemical and biological bases* (pp. 147–184). New York: Plenum Press.

Bouchard, T. J., Jr. (1987). The hereditarian research program: Triumphs and tribulations. In S. Modgil & C. Modgil (Eds.), *Arthur Jensen: Consensus and controversy* (pp. 55–75). New York: Falmer Press.

Bouchard, T. J., Jr. (1991). A twice told tale: Twins reared apart. In W. Grove & D. Ciccehetti (Eds.), *Thinking clearly about psychology: Essays in honor of Paul Everett Meehl, personality and psychopathology* (Vol. 2; pp. 188–215). Minneapolis: University of Minnesota Press.

REFERENCES

Bouchard, T. J., Jr. (1993a). The genetic architecture of human intelligence. In P. Vernon (Ed.), *Biological approaches to the study of human intelligence* (pp. 33–93). Norwood, NJ: Ablex Publishing Corporation.

Bouchard, T. J., Jr. (1993b). Genetic and environmental influences on adult personality: Evaluating the evidence. In J. Hettema & I. Deary (Eds.), *Basic issues in personality* (pp. 15–44). Dordrecht, The Netherlands: Kluwer Academic Publishers.

Bouchard, T. J., Jr. (1994a). Genes, environment, and personality. *Science, 264,* 1700–1701.

Bouchard, T. J., Jr. (1994b). Twin studies of intelligence. In R. Sternberg (Ed.), *Encyclopedia of intelligence* (pp. 1091–1095). New York: Macmillan.

Bouchard, T. J., Jr. (1995). Breaking the last taboo. [Review of the book *The Bell Curve,* by R. J. Herrnstein & C. Murray]. *Contemporary Psychology, 40,* 415–421.

Bouchard, T. J., Jr. (1996). Behaviour genetic studies of intelligence, yesterday and today: The long journey from plausibility to proof. *Journal of Biosocial Science, 28,* 527–555.

Bouchard, T. J., Jr. (1997a). The genetics of personality. In K. Blum & E. Noble (Eds.), *Handbook of psychiatric genetics* (pp. 273–296). Boca Raton, FL: CRC Press.

Bouchard, T. J., Jr. (1997b). IQ similarity in twins reared apart: Findings and responses to critics. In R. Sternberg & E. Grigorenko (Eds.), *Intelligence, heredity, and environment* (pp. 126–160). New York: Cambridge University Press.

Bouchard, T. J., Jr. (1997c, September/October). Whenever twain shall meet. *The Sciences, 37,* 52–57.

Bouchard, T. J., Jr. (1998). Genetic and environmental influences on adult intelligence and special mental abilities. *Human Biology, 70,* 257–279.

Bouchard, T. J., Jr. (1999). Foreword. In N. Segal, *Entwined lives: Twins and what they tell us about human behavior* (pp. ix–x). New York: Dutton.

Bouchard, T. J., Jr. (Interviewee). (2004). Distinguished contributor interview: Thomas Bouchard, Jr. International Society for Intelligence Research (ISIR) Conference 2004 (Parts 1 & 2). Retrieved 8/21/2014 from https://www.youtube.com/watch?v=ycdDxTnpeTU.

Bouchard, T. J., Jr. (2008). Genes and human psychological traits. In P. Carruthers, S. Laurence, & S. Stich (Eds.), *The innate mind: Foundations and the future* (Vol. 3). doi: 10.1093/acprof:oso/9780195332834.001.0001.

Bouchard, T. J., Jr. (2009). Genetic influence on human intelligence (Spearman's g): How much? *Annals of Human Biology, 36,* 527–544.

Bouchard, T. J., Jr., (2013). The Wilson effect: The increase in heritability of IQ with age. *Twin Research and Human Genetics, 16,* 923–930.

Bouchard, T. J., Jr., (2014). Genes, evolution and intelligence. *Behavior Genetics.* Published online March 7, 2014. DOI 10.1007/s10519-014-9646-x.

Bouchard, T. J., Jr., & Loehlin, J. C. (2001). Genes, evolution, and personality. *Behavior Genetics, 31,* 243–273.

Bouchard, T. J., Jr., Lykken, D. T., McGue, M., Segal, N. L., & Tellegen, A. (1990). Sources of human psychological differences: The Minnesota Study of Twins Reared Apart. *Science, 250,* 223–228.

REFERENCES

Bouchard, T. J., Jr., Lykken, D. T., McGue, M., Segal, N. L., & Tellegen, A. (1991). Response [letter to the editor]. *Science, 252,* 191–192.

Bouchard, T. J., Jr., Lykken, D. T., Segal, N. L., & Wilcox, K. J. (1986). Development in twins reared apart: A test of the chronogenetic hypothesis. In A. Demirjian (Ed.), *Human growth: A multidisciplinary review* (pp. 299–310). London: Taylor & Francis.

Bouchard, T. J., Jr., Lykken, D. T., Tellegen, A., & McGue, M. (1996). Genes, drives, environment, and experience: EPD theory revisited. In C. Persson Benbow & D. Lubinski (Eds.), *Intellectual talent* (pp. 5–43). Baltimore: Johns Hopkins University Press.

Bouchard, T. J., Jr., & McGue, M. (1981). Familial studies of intelligence: A review. *Science, 212,* 1055–1059.

Bouchard, T. J., Jr., & McGue, M. (1990). Genetic and rearing environmental influences on adult personality: An analysis of adopted twins reared apart. *Journal of Personality, 58,* 263–292.

Bouchard, T. J., Jr., & McGue, M. (2003). Genetic and environmental influences on human psychological differences. *Journal of Neurobiology, 54,* 4–45.

Bouchard, T. J., Jr., McGue, M., Hur, Y., & Horn, J. M. (1998). A genetic and environmental analysis of the California Psychological Inventory using adult twins reared together and apart. *European Journal of Personality, 12,* 307–320.

Bouchard, T. J., Jr., & Pedersen, N. (1999). Twins reared apart: Nature's double experiment. In M. LaBuda & E. Grigorenko (Eds.), *On the way to individuality: Methodological issues in behavioral genetics* (pp. 71–93). Commack, NY: Nova Science.

Bouchard, T. J., Jr., & Segal, N. (1985). Environment and IQ. In B. Wolman (Ed.), *Handbook of intelligence* (pp. 391–464). New York: Wiley.

Bouchard, T. J., Jr., Segal, N. L., & Lykken, D. T. (1990). Genetic and environmental influences on special mental abilities in a sample of twins reared apart. *Acta Geneticae Medicae et Gemellologiae, 39,* 193–206.

Bouchard, T. J., Jr., Segal, N. L., Tellegen, A., McGue, M., Keyes, M., & Krueger, R. (2004). Genetic influence on social attitudes: Another challenge to psychology from behavior genetics. In L. DiLalla (Ed.), *Behavior genetics principles* (pp. 89–104). Washington, DC: American Psychological Association Press.

Boyle, M. (2002a). It's all done with smoke and mirrors. Or, how to create the illusion of a schizophrenic brain disease. *Clinical Psychology, 12,* 9–16.

Boyle, M. (2002b). *Schizophrenia: A scientific delusion?* (2nd ed.). Hove, UK: Routledge.

Boyle, M. (2007). The problem with diagnosis. *The Psychologist, 20,* 290–292.

Bradshaw, M., & Ellison, C. G. (2008). Do genetic factors influence religious life? Findings from a behavior genetic analysis of twin siblings. *Journal for the Scientific Study of Religion, 47,* 529–544.

Bulmer, M. G. (1970). *The biology of twinning in man.* Oxford: Clarendon Press.

Burt, C. (1966). The genetic determination of differences in intelligence: A study of monozygotic twins reared together and apart. *British Journal of Psychology, 57,* 137–153.

Buss, A. H., Plomin, R., & Willerman, L. (1973). The inheritance of temperaments. *Journal of Personality, 41,* 513–524.

REFERENCES

Carey, B. (2011, November 2nd). Fraud case seen as a red flag for psychology research. *New York Times*, Retrieved from http://www.nytimes.com/2011/11/03/health/research/noted-dutch-psychologist-stapel-accused-of-research-fraud.html

Carter, H. D. (1940). Ten years of research on twins: Contributions to the nature–nurture problem. In G. Whipple (Ed.), *National society for the study of education yearbook* (pp. 235–255; Vol. 39, No. 1). Bloomington, IL: Public School Publishing.

Caspi, A., & Shiner, R. L. (2006). Personality development. In N. Eisenberg, W. Damon, & R. Lerner (Eds.), *Handbook of child psychology: Social, emotional, and personality development* (Vol. 3, 6th ed.; pp. 300–365). Hoboken, NJ: John Wiley & Sons.

Cassill, K. (1982). *Twins: Nature's amazing mystery*. New York: Atheneum.

Cassou, B., Schiff, M., & Stewart, J. (1980). Génétique et schizophrénie: Réévaluation d'un consensus [Genetics and schizophrenia: Reevaluation of a consensus]. *Psychiatrie de l'Enfant, 23,* 87–201.

Ceci, S. J., Rosenbaum, T., de Bruyn, E., & Yee, D. K. (1997). A bio-ecological model of intellectual development: Moving beyond h^2. In R. Sternberg & E. Grigorenko (Eds.), *Intelligence, heredity, and environment* (pp. 303–322). New York: Cambridge University Press.

Cederlöf, R., Friberg, L., Jonsson, E., & Kaij, L. (1961). The diagnosis of twin zygosity. *Acta Genetica et Statistica Medica, 11,* 338–362.

Cesarini, D., Johannesson, M., Wallace, B., & Lichtenstein, P. (2009). Heritability of overconfidence. *Journal of the European Economic Association, 7,* 617–627.

Chabris, C. F., Hebert, B. M., Benjamin, D. J., Beauchamp, J. P., Cesarini, D., van der Loos, M., . . . Laibson, D. (2012). Most reported genetic associations with general intelligence are probably false positives. *Psychological Science, 23,* 1314–1323.

Charney, D. S., Barlow, D. H., Botteron, K., Cohen, J. D., Goldman, D., Gur, R. E., . . . Zalcman, S. J. (2002). Neuroscience research agenda to guide development of a pathophysiologically based classification system. In D. Kupfer, M. First, & D. Regier (Eds.), *A research agenda for DSM-V* (pp. 31–83). Washington, DC: American Psychiatric Association.

Charney, E. (2008a). Genes and ideologies. *Perspectives on Politics, 6,* 292–319.

Charney, E. (2008b). Politics, genetics, and "greedy reductionism." *Perspectives on Politics, 6,* 337–343.

Charney, E. (2012). Behavior genetics and post genomics. *Behavioral and Brain Sciences, 35,* 331–358.

Charney, E. (2013a). Nature and nurture. *Perspectives on Politics, 11,* 558–561.

Charney, E. (2013b, September 19th). Still chasing ghosts: A new genetic methodology will not find the "missing heritability." *Independent Science News*. Retrieved from http://www.independentsciencenews.org/health/still-chasing-ghosts-a-new-genetic-methodology-will-not-find-the-missing-heritability/.

Charney, E., & English, W. (2012). Candidate genes and political behavior. *American Political Science Review, 106,* 1–34.

Chase, A. (1980). *The legacy of Malthus: The social costs of the new scientific racism*. Urbana, IL/Chicago: University of Illinois Press. (Originally published in 1977.)

Chaufan, C. (2007). How much can a large population study on genes, environments, their interactions and common diseases contribute to the health of the American people? *Social Science and Medicine, 65*, 1730–1741.

Chaufan, C., & Joseph, J. (2013). The heritability of common disorders is "missing": Should health researchers care? *International Journal of Health Services, 43*, 281–303.

Cloninger, C. R. (2002). The discovery of susceptibility genes for mental disorders. *Proceedings of the National Academy of Sciences, 99*, 13365–13367.

Cloninger, C. R., Adolfsson, R., & Svrakic, N. M. (1996). Mapping genes for human personality. *Nature Genetics, 12*, 3–4.

Cohen, D. J., Dibble, E., Grawe, J. M., & Pollin, W. (1973). Separating identical from fraternal twins. *Archives of General Psychiatry, 29*, 465–469.

Cohen, D. J., Dibble, E., Grawe, J., & Pollin, W. (1975). Reliably separating identical from fraternal twins. *Archives of General Psychiatry, 32*, 1371–1375.

Cohen, R. J., Swerdlik, M. E., & Smith, D. K. (1992). *Psychological testing and assessment* (2nd ed.). Mountain View, CA: Mayfield.

Coop, G., Eisen, M. B., Nielsen, R., Przeworski, M., & Rosenberg, N. (2014, August 8th, Sunday Book Review). "A Troublesome Inheritance." Retrieved online from http://www.nytimes.com/2014/08/10/books/review/letters-a-troublesome-inheritance.html?_r=1

Cropanzano, R., & James, K. (1990). Some methodological considerations for the behavioral genetic analysis of work attitudes. *Journal of Applied Psychology, 75*, 433–439.

Cross-Disorder Group of the Psychiatric Genomics Consortium. (2013). Identification of risk loci with shared effects on five major psychiatric disorders: A genome-wide analysis. *Lancet, 381*, 1371–1379.

Crow, T. J. (2008). The emperors of the schizophrenia polygene have no clothes. *Psychological Medicine, 38*, 1681–1685.

Cushman, P. (1995). *Constructing the self, constructing America*. Reading, MA: Addison-Wesley.

Dalgard, O. S., & Kringlen, E. (1976). A Norwegian twin study of criminality. *British Journal of Criminology, 16*, 213–232.

Davenport, C. B. (1911). *Heredity in relation to eugenics*. New York: Henry Holt.

Davis, J. O., Phelps, J. A., & Bracha, H. S. (1995). Prenatal development of monozygotic twins and concordance for schizophrenia. *Schizophrenia Bulletin, 21*, 357–366.

Dawood, K., Kirk, K. M., Bailey, J. M., Andrews, P. W., & Martin, N. G. (2005). Genetic and environmental influences on the frequency of orgasm in women. *Twin Research and Human Genetics, 8*, 27–33.

Deary, I. J. (2012). Intelligence. *Annual Review of Psychology, 63*, 453–482.

DeFries, J. C. (1967). Quantitative genetics and behavior: Overview and perspective. In J. Hirsch (Ed.), *Behavior-genetic analysis* (pp. 322–339). New York: McGraw-Hill.

DeFries, J. C., & Plomin, R. (1978). Behavioral genetics. *Annual Review of Psychology, 29*, 473–515.

Derks, E. M., Dolan, C. V., & Boomsma, D. I. (2006). A test of the equal environment assumption (EEA) in multivariate twin studies. *Twin Research and Human Genetics, 9*, 403–411.

REFERENCES

Dibble, E., Cohen, D. J., & Grawe, J. M. (1978). Methodological issues in twin research: The assumption of environmental equivalence. In W. Nance (Ed.), *Twin research: Psychology and methodology* (pp. 245–251). New York: Alan R. Liss.

DiLalla, D. L., Gottesman, I. I., Carey, G., & Bouchard, T. J., Jr. (1996). Heritability of MMPI personality indicators of psychopathology in twins reared apart. *Journal of Abnormal Psychology, 105,* 491–499.

Dorfman, D. D. (1995). Soft science with a neoconservative agenda. [Review of the book *The Bell Curve,* by R. J. Herrnstein & C. Murray]. *Contemporary Psychology, 40,* 418–421.

Dudley, R. M. (1991). IQ and heredity [letter to the editor]. *Science, 252,* 191.

Dusek, V. (1987). Bewitching science. *Science for the People, 19,* (6) 19–22.

Duster, T. (2003). *Backdoor to eugenics* (2nd ed.). New York: Routledge.

Eaves, L. J., Eysenck, H. J., & Martin, N. G. (1989). *Genes, culture, and personality: An empirical approach.* London: Academic Press.

Eaves, L., Foley, D., & Silberg, J. (2003). Has the "equal environments" assumption been tested in twin studies? *Twin Research, 6,* 486–489.

Eckert, E. D., Bouchard, T. J., Jr., Bohlen, J., & Heston, L. L. (1986). Homosexuality in monozygotic twins reared apart. *British Journal of Psychiatry, 148,* 421–425.

Eckert, E. D., Heston, L. L., & Bouchard, T. J., Jr. (1981). MZ twins reared apart: Preliminary findings of psychiatric disturbances and traits. In L. Gedda, P. Parisi, & W. Nance (Eds.), *Twin research 3: Part B. Intelligence, personality, and development* (pp. 179-188). New York: Alan R. Liss.

Egeland, J. A., Gerhard, D. S., Pauls, D. L., Sussex, J. N., & Kidd, K. K. (1987). Bipolar affective disorders linked to DNA markers on chromosome 11. *Nature, 325,* 783–787.

Eichler, E. E., Flint, J., Gibson, G., Kong, A., Leal, S. M., Moore, J. H., & Nadeau, J. H. (2010). Missing heritability and strategies for finding the underlying causes of complex disease. *Nature Reviews Genetics,11,* 446–450.

Evans, D. M., & Martin, N. G. (2000). The validity of twin research. *GeneScreen, 1,* 77–79.

Eysenck, H. J. (1967). *The biological basis of personality.* Springfield, IL: Charles Thomas.

Eysenck, H. J., vs. Kamin, L. J. (1981). *The intelligence controversy.* New York: John Wiley.

Eysenck, H. J., & Prell, D. B. (1951). The inheritance of neuroticism: An experimental study. *Journal of Mental Science, 97,* 441–465.

Fanelli, D. (2009). How many scientists fabricate and falsify research? A systematic review and meta-analysis of survey data. *PLoS One, 4, (5),* 1–11.

Faraone, S. V. (2013). Real progress in molecular psychiatric genetics. *Journal of the American Academy of Child and Adolescent Psychiatry, 52,* 1006–1008.

Faraone, S. V., & Biederman, J. (2000). Nature, nurture, and attention deficit hyperactivity disorder. *Developmental Review, 20,* 568–581.

Faraone, S. V., Smoller, J. W., Pato, C. N., Sullivan, P., & Tsuang, M. T. (2008). The new neuropsychiatric genetics. *American Journal of Medical Genetics Part B (Neuropsychiatric Genetics) 147B,* 1–2.

Faraone, S. V., Tsuang, M. T., & Tsuang, D. W. (1999). *Genetics of mental disorders.* New York: Guilford Press.

Farber, S. L. (1981). *Identical twins reared apart: A reanalysis*. New York: Basic Books.

Feighner, J. P., Robins, E., Guze, S. B., Woodruff, R. A., Winokur, G., & Munoz, R. (1972). Diagnostic criteria for use in psychiatric research. *Archives of General Psychiatry, 26*, 57–63.

Felson, J. (2014). What can we learn from twin studies? A comprehensive evaluation of the equal environments assumption. *Social Science Research, 43*,184–199.

Fischer, C. S., Hout, M., Sánchez Jankowski, M., Lucas, S. R., Swidler, A., & Voss, K. (1996). *Inequality by design: Cracking the bell curve myth*. Princeton, NJ: Princeton University Press.

Fisher, P. J., Turic, D., Williams, N. M., McGuffin, P., Asherson, P., Ball, D., . . . Owen, M. J. (1999). DNA pooling identifies QTLs on chromosome 4 for general cognitive ability in children. *Human Molecular Genetics, 8*, 915–922.

Fletcher, R. (1991). *Science, ideology, and the media: The Cyril Burt scandal*. New Brunswick, NJ: Transaction Publishers.

Flint, J., Greenspan, R. J., & Kendler, K. S. (2010). *How genes influence behavior*. Oxford, UK: Oxford University Press.

Flint, J., & Kendler, K. S. (2014). The genetics of major depression. *Neuron, 81*, 484–503.

Flynn, J. R. (1984). The mean IQ of Americans: Massive gains 1932 to 1978. *Psychological Bulletin, 95*, 29–51.

Flynn, J. R. (1999). Searching for justice: The discovery of IQ gains over time. *American Psychologist, 54*, 5–20.

Folstein, S., & Rutter, M. (1977). Genetic influences on infantile autism. *Nature, 265*, 726–728.

Ford, B. D. (1993). Emergenesis: An alternative and a confound [letter to the editor]. *American Psychologist, 48*, 1294.

Fowler, J. H., Baker, L. A., & Dawes, C. T. (2008). Genetic variation in political participation. *American Political Science Review, 102*, 233–248.

Frances, A. (2011, July 27). The British Psychological Society condemns DSM 5 [Web log post, *Psychology Today* "DSM5 in Distress"]. Retrieved from http://www.psychologytoday.com/blog/dsm5-in-distress/201107/the-british-psychological-society-condemns-dsm-5.

Franklin, J. (2011, October 9th). Chilean miners fight their demons. *The Daily Beast*. Retrieved from http://www.thedailybeast.com/articles/2011/10/09/chilean-miners-fight-their-demons.html.

Fuller, J. L., & Thompson, W. R. (1960). *Behavior genetics*. New York: John Wiley.

Furman, L. (2009). ADHD: What do we really know? In S. Timimi & J. Leo (Eds.), *Rethinking ADHD: From brain to culture* (pp. 21–57). London: Palgrave MacMillan.

Galton, F. (1876). The history of twins as a criterion of the relative powers of nature and nurture. *Journal of the Anthropological Institute of Great Britain and Ireland, 5*, 391–406.

Gardner, I. C., & Newman, H. H. (1940). Mental and physical traits of identical twins reared apart. *Journal of Heredity, 31*, 119–126.

Gasper, P. (2004). Is biology destiny? *International Socialist Review, 38*. Retrieved from http://www.isreview.org/issues/38/genes.shtml.

REFERENCES

Gibson, G. (2010). Hints of hidden heritability in GWAS. *Nature Genetics, 42,* 558–560.

Gillie, O. (1976, October 24th). Crucial data was faked by eminent scientist. *The Sunday Times,* London.

Glatt, S. J., Faraone, S. V., & Tsuang, M. T. (2008). Psychiatric genetics: A primer. In J. Smoller, B. Sheidley, & M. Tsuang (Eds.). *Psychiatric genetics: Applications in clinical practice* (pp. 3–26). Washington, DC: American Psychiatric Publishing.

Goldberger, A. S. (1978). Pitfalls in the resolution of IQ inheritance. In N. Morton & C. Chung (Eds.), *Genetic epidemiology* (pp. 195–221). New York: Academic Press.

Goldberger, A. S. (1979). Heritability. *Economica, 46,* 327–347.

Gottesman, I. I. (1963). Heritability of personality: A demonstration. *Psychological Monographs, 77, (9, whole volume 572),* 1–21.

Gottesman, I. I. (1966). Genetic variance in adaptive personality traits. *Journal of Child Psychology and Psychiatry, 7,* 199–208.

Gottesman, I. I. (1982). [Review of the book *Identical twins reared apart: A reanalysis,* by S. Farber]. *American Journal of Psychology, 95,* 350-352.

Gottesman, I. I., & Hanson, D. R. (2005). Human development: Biological and genetic processes. *Annual Review of Psychology, 56,* 263–286.

Gottesman, I. I., & Shields, J. (1966a). Contributions of twin studies to perspectives on schizophrenia. In B. Maher (Ed.), *Progress in experimental personality research* (Vol. 3, pp. 1–84). New York: Academic Press.

Gottesman, I. I., & Shields, J. (1966b). Schizophrenia in twins: 16 years' consecutive admissions to a psychiatric clinic. *British Journal of Psychiatry, 112,* 809–818.

Gottesman, I. I., & Shields, J. (1972). *Schizophrenia and genetics: A twin study vantage point.* New York: Academic Press.

Gottlieb, G. (2003). On making behavioral genetics truly developmental. *Human Development, 46,* 337–355.

Gough, H. G., & Bradley, P. (1996). *CPI manual* (3rd ed.). Palo Alto, CA: Consulting Psychologists Press.

Gould, S. J. (1974/1999). Racist arguments and IQ. In A. Montagu (Ed.), *Race and IQ* (expanded ed.; pp. 184–189). Oxford: Oxford University Press. (Originally published in 1974.)

Gould, S. J. (1977). *Ever since Darwin.* New York: W. W. Norton.

Gould, S. J. (1981). *The mismeasure of man.* New York: W. W. Norton.

Graham, J. R. (1987). *The MMPI: A practical guide* (2nd ed.). New York: Oxford University Press.

Greenberg, G. (2013). *The book of woe: The DSM and the unmaking of psychiatry.* New York: Blue Rider Press.

Grove, W. M., Eckert, E. D., Heston, L. L., Bouchard, T. J., Jr., Segal, N. L., & Lykken, D. T. (1990). Heritability of substance abuse and antisocial behavior: A study of monozygotic twins reared apart. *Biological Psychiatry, 27,* 1293–1304.

Hadjivassiliou, M., Sanders, D. S., Grünewald, R. A., Woodroofe, N., Boscolo, S., & Aeschlimann, D. (2010). Gluten sensitivity: From gut to brain. *Lancet Neurology, 9,* 318–330.

Hamer, D., & Copeland, P. (1998). *Living with our genes*. New York: Anchor Books.

Harris, J. R. (1998). *The nurture assumption: Why children turn out the way they do*. New York: The Free Press.

Harris, J. R. (2006). *No two alike: Human nature and human individuality*. New York: Norton.

Hatemi, P. K., & McDermott, R. (2012). The genetics of politics: Discovery, challenges, and progress. *Trends in Genetics, 28*, 525–533.

Hatemi, P. K., Medland, S. E., Klemmensen, R., Oskarsson, S., Littvay, L., Dawes, C., ... Martin, N. G. (2014). Genetic influences on political ideologies: Twin analyses of 19 measures of political ideologies from five democracies and genome-wide findings from three populations. *Behavior Genetics, 44*, 282–294.

Haworth, C. M. A., & Plomin, R. (2010). Quantitative genetics in the era of molecular genetics: Learning abilities and disabilities as an example. *Journal of the American Academy of Child and Adolescent Psychiatry, 49*, 783–793.

Hayden, E. C. (2013). Taboo genetics. *Nature, 502*, 26–28.

Hearnshaw, L. S. (1979). *Cyril Burt: Psychologist*. Ithaca, NY: Cornell University Press.

Hemani, G., Shakhbazov, K., Westra, H. J., Esko, T., Henders, A. K., McRae, A. F., & Powell, J. E. (2014). Detection and replication of epistasis influencing transcription in humans. *Nature, 508*, 249–253.

Herrnstein, R. J., & Murray, C. (1994). *The bell curve*. New York: The Free Press.

Hibbing, J. R. (2013). Ten misconceptions concerning neurobiology and politics. *Perspectives on Politics, 11*, 475–489.

Hill, D. (1983). *The politics of schizophrenia: Psychiatric oppression in the United States*. Lanham, MD: University Press of America.

Hirsch, J. (1975). Jensenism: The bankruptcy of "science" without scholarship. *Educational Theory, 25*, 3–26.

Hirsch, J. (1981). To "unfrock the charlatans." *SAGE Race Relations Abstracts, 6* (2), 1–65. London: Sage Publications.

Hirsch, J. (1983). [Review of the book *The IQ game: A methodological inquiry into the heredity-environment controversy*, by H. F. Taylor]. *Social Biology, 30*, 116–118.

Hirsch, J. (1997). Some history of heredity-vs-environment, genetic inferiority at Harvard (?), and The (incredible) Bell Curve. *Genetica, 99*, 207–224.

Ho, M. W. (2013). No genes for intelligence in the fluid genome. In R. Lerner & J. Benson (Eds.), *Advances in Child Development and Behavior, 45*, 67–92. San Diego: Elsevier.

Hogben, L. (1933). *Nature and nurture*. London: George Allen & Unwin.

Hoge, S. K., & Appelbaum, P. S. (2008). Ethical, legal, and social implications of psychiatric genetics and genetic counseling. In J. Smoller, B. Sheidley, & M. Tsuang (Eds.). *Psychiatric genetics: Applications in clinical practice* (pp. 255–276). Washington, DC: American Psychiatric Publishing.

Holden, C. (1980). Identical twins reared apart. *Science, 207*, 1323–1328.

Holzinger, K. J. (1929). The relative effect of nature and nurture influences on twin differences. *Journal of Educational Psychology, 20*, 241–248.

Hooton, E. A. (1936). Plain statements about race. *Science, 83*, 511–513.

Horgan, J. (1993). Eugenics revisited. *Scientific American, 268* (6), 122–131.

REFERENCES

Horgan, J. (2013, October 4th). My problem with "taboo" behavioral genetics? The science stinks! *Scientific American* [Web log post]. Retrieved from http://blogs.scientificamerican.com/cross-check/2013/10/04/my-problem-with-taboo-behavioral-genetics-the-science-stinks/.

Horn, J. M., & Loehlin, J. C. (2010). *Heredity and environment in 300 adoptive families: The Texas Adoption Project.* New Brunswick, NJ: Aldine Transaction.

Horn, J. M., Loehlin, J. C., & Willerman, L. (1979). Intellectual resemblance among adoptive and biological relatives: The Texas Adoption Project. *Behavior Genetics, 9,* 177–207.

Horwitz, A. V. (2002). *Creating mental illness.* Chicago: University of Chicago Press.

Hudziak, J. J., & Faraone, S. V. (2010). New genetics in child psychiatry. *Journal of the American Academy of Child and Adolescent Psychiatry, 49,* 729–735.

Hur, Y. M., Bouchard, T. J., Jr., & Eckert, E. (1998). Genetic and environmental influences on self-reported diet: A reared-apart twin study. *Physiology & Behavior, 64,* 629–636.

Hur, Y. M., & Craig, J. M. (2103). Twin registries worldwide: An important resource for scientific research. *Twin Research and Human Genetics, 16,* 1–12.

Husén, T. (1959). *Psychological twin research: A methodological study.* Stockholm: Almqvist & Wiksell.

International Schizophrenia Consortium. (2009). Common polygenic variation contributes to risk of schizophrenia and bipolar disorder. *Nature, 460,* 748–752.

Ioannidis, J. P. A. (2005). Why most published research findings are false. *PLoS Medicine, 2,* 696–701.

Ioannidis, J. P. A. (2014). Research accomplishments that are too good to be true. *Intensive Care Medicine, 40,* 99–101.

Jackson, D. (1980, October). Reunion of identical twins, raised apart, reveals some astonishing similarities. *Smithsonian,* pp. 48–56.

Jackson, D. D. (1960). A critique of the literature on the genetics of schizophrenia. In D. Jackson (Ed.), *The etiology of schizophrenia* (pp. 37–87). New York: Basic Books.

Jackson, G. E. (2003). Rethinking the Finnish adoption studies of schizophrenia: A challenge to genetic determinism. *Journal of Critical Psychology, Counselling and Psychotherapy, 3,* 129–138.

Jacoby, R., & Glauberman, N. (Eds.). (1995). *The Bell Curve debate.* New York: Times Books.

Jensen, A. R. (1969). How much can we boost IQ and scholastic achievement? *Harvard Educational Review, 39,* 1–123.

Jensen, A. R. (1970). IQs of identical twins reared apart. *Behavior Genetics, 1,* 133–148.

Jensen, A. R. (1974). Kinship correlations reported by Sir Cyril Burt. *Behavior Genetics, 4,* 1–28.

Jensen, A. R. (1980). *Bias in mental testing.* New York: Free Press.

Jensen, A. R. (1998). *The g factor.* Westport, CT: Praeger.

Jinks, J. L., & Fulker, D. W. (1970). Comparison of the biometrical genetic, MAVA, and classical approaches to the analysis of human behavior. *Psychological Bulletin, 73,* 311–349.

John, L. K., Loewenstein, G., & Prelec, D. (2012). Measuring the prevalence of questionable research practices with incentives for truth telling. *Psychological Science, 23*, 524–532.

Johnson, W. (2010). Understanding the genetics of intelligence: Can height help? Can corn oil? *Current Directions in Psychological Science, 19*, 177–182.

Johnson, W., & Bouchard, T. J., Jr. (2011). The MISTRA data: Forty-two mental ability tests in three batteries. *Intelligence, 39*, 82–88.

Johnson, W., Bouchard, T. J., Jr., McGue, M., Segal, N. L., Tellegen, A., Keyes, M., & Gottesman, I. I. (2007). Genetic and environmental influences on the Verbal-Perceptual-Image Rotation (VPR) model of the structure of mental abilities in the Minnesota Study of Twins Reared Apart. *Intelligence, 35*, 542–562.

Johnson, W., Penke, L., & Spinath, F. M. (2011). Heritability in the era of molecular genetics: Some thoughts for understanding genetic influences on behavioral traits. *European Journal of Personality, 25*, 254–266.

Johnson, W., Turkheimer, E., Gottesman, I. I., & Bouchard, T. J., Jr. (2009). Beyond heritability: Twin studies in behavioral research. *Current Directions in Psychological Science, 18*, 217–220.

Jones, H. E. (1955). Perceived differences among twins. *Eugenics Quarterly, 2*, 98–102.

Joseph, J. (1998). The equal environment assumption of the classical twin method: A critical analysis. *Journal of Mind and Behavior, 19*, 325–358.

Joseph, J. (2000). Not in their genes: A critical view of the genetics of attention-deficit hyperactivity disorder. *Developmental Review, 20*, 539–567.

Joseph, J. (2001). Separated twins and the genetics of personality differences: A critique. *American Journal of Psychology, 114*, 1–30.

Joseph, J. (2004). *The gene illusion: Genetic research in psychiatry and psychology under the microscope.* New York: Algora. (2003 United Kingdom Edition by PCCS Books.)

Joseph, J. (2005a). The 1942 "euthanasia" debate in the American Journal of Psychiatry. *History of Psychiatry, 16*, 171–179.

Joseph, J. (2005b). Research paradigms of psychiatric genetics [letter to the editor]. *American Journal of Psychiatry, 162*, 1985.

Joseph, J. (2006). *The missing gene: Psychiatry, heredity, and the fruitless search for genes.* New York: Algora.

Joseph, J. (2010a). Genetic research in psychiatry and psychology: A critical overview. In K. Hood, C. Tucker Halpern, G. Greenberg, & R. Lerner (Eds.), *Handbook of developmental science, behavior, and genetics* (pp. 557–625). Malden, MA: Wiley-Blackwell.

Joseph, J. (2010b). The genetics of political attitudes and behavior: Claims and refutations. *Ethical Human Psychology and Psychiatry, 12*, 200–217.

Joseph, J. (2011a). The crumbling pillars of behavioral genetics. *GeneWatch, 24* (6), 4–7.

Joseph, J. (2011b). A human genetics parable. *Journal of Mind and Behavior, 32*, 209–221.

Joseph, J. (2012). The "missing heritability" of psychiatric disorders: Elusive genes or non-existent genes? *Applied Developmental Science, 16*, 65–83.

Joseph, J. (2013a). The lost study: A 1998 adoption study of personality that found no genetic relationship between birthparents and their 240 adopted-away biological offspring. In R. Lerner & J. Benson (Eds.), *Advances in Child Development and Behavior, 45,* 93–124. San Diego: Elsevier.

Joseph, J. (2013b). "Schizophrenia" and heredity: Why the emperor (still) has no genes. In J. Read & J. Dillon (Eds.), *Models of madness: Psychological, social and biological approaches to psychosis* (2nd ed.; pp. 72–90). London: Routledge.

Joseph, J. (2013c). The use of the classical twin method in the behavioral sciences: The fallacy continues. *Journal of Mind and Behavior, 34,* 1–39.

Joseph, J., & Ratner, C. (2013). The fruitless search for genes in psychiatry and psychology: Time to re-examine a paradigm. In S. Krimsky & J. Gruber (Eds.), *Genetic explanations: Sense and nonsense* (pp. 94–106). Cambridge, MA: Harvard University Press.

Joseph, J., & Wetzel, N. (2013). Ernst Rüdin: Hitler's racial hygiene mastermind. *Journal of the History of Biology, 46,* 1–30.

Joynson, R. B. (1989). *The Burt affair.* London: RKP.

Juel-Nielsen, N. (1965/1980). *Individual and environment: Monozygotic twins reared apart* (rev. ed.). New York: International Universities Press.

Kallmann, F. J. (1958). The uses of genetics in psychiatry. *Journal of Mental Science, 104,* 542–552.

Kamin, L. J. (1974). *The science and politics of I.Q.* Potomac, MD: Lawrence Erlbaum Associates.

Kamin, L. J, in Eysenck, H. J., vs. Kamin, L. J. (1981). *The intelligence controversy.* New York: John Wiley.

Kamin, L. J., & Goldberger, A. S. (2002). Twin studies in behavioral research: A skeptical view. *Theoretical Population Biology, 61,* 83–95.

Kanner, L. (1942). Exoneration of the feebleminded. *American Journal of Psychiatry, 99,* 17–22.

Kasriel, J., & Eaves, L. (1976). The zygosity of twins: Further evidence on the agreement between diagnosis by blood groups and written questionnaires. *Journal of Biosocial Science, 8,* 263–266.

Keller, E. F. (2010). *The mirage of a space between nature and nurture.* Durham, NC: Duke University Press.

Keller, L. M., Arvey, R. D., Bouchard, T. J., Jr., Segal, N. L., & Dawis, R. V. (1992). Work values: Genetic and environmental influences. *Journal of Applied Psychology, 77,* 79–88.

Kendler, K. S. (1983). Overview: A current perspective on twin studies of schizophrenia. *American Journal of Psychiatry, 140,* 1413–1425.

Kendler, K. S. (1987). The genetics of schizophrenia: A current perspective. In H. Meltzer (Ed.), *Psychopharmacology: The third generation of progress* (pp. 705–713). New York: Raven Press.

Kendler, K. S. (1993). Twin studies of psychiatric illness: Current status and future directions. *Archives of General Psychiatry, 50,* 905–915.

Kendler, K. S. (2000). Schizophrenia: Genetics. In B. Sadock & V. Sadock (Eds.), *Kaplan & Sadock's comprehensive textbook of psychiatry* (7th ed., Vol. 1, pp. 1147–1158). Philadelphia: Lippincott, Williams, & Wilkins.

Kendler, K. S. (2005a). Dr. Kendler responds [letter to the editor]. *American Journal of Psychiatry, 162,* 1985–1986.

Kendler, K. S. (2005b). Psychiatric genetics: A methodologic critique. *American Journal of Psychiatry, 162,* 3–11.

Kendler, K. S. (2014). A joint history of the nature of genetic variation and the nature of schizophrenia. *Molecular Psychiatry*. Published online August 19th, 2014. DOI:10.1038/mp.2014.94

Kendler, K. S., Neale, M. C., Kessler, R. C., Heath, A. C., & Eaves, L. J. (1993). A test of the equal-environment assumption in twin studies of psychiatric illness. *Behavior Genetics, 23*, 21–27.

Kendler, K. S., & Prescott, C. A. (2006). *Genes, environment, and psychopathology*. New York: Guilford.

Kennedy, F. (1942). The problem of social control of the congenital defective: Education, sterilization, euthanasia. *American Journal of Psychiatry, 99*, 13–16.

Keski-Rahkonen, A., Viken, R. J., Kaprio, J., Rissanen, A., & Rose, R. J. (2004). Genetic and environmental factors in breakfast eating patterns. *Behavior Genetics, 34*, 503–514.

Kessler, R. C., Chiu, W. T., Demler, O., & Walters, E. E. (2005). Prevalence, severity, and comorbidity of 12-month DSM-IV disorders in the National Comorbidity Survey replication. *Archives of General Psychiatry, 62*, 617–627.

Kessler, R. C., McLaughlin, K. A., Green, J. G., Gruber, M. J., Sampson, N. A., Zaslavsky, . . . Williams, D. R. (2010). Childhood adversities and adult psychopathology in the WHO World Mental Health Surveys. *British Journal of Psychiatry, 197*, 378–385.

Kety, S. S. (1974). From rationalization to reason. *American Journal of Psychiatry, 131*, 957–963.

Kety, S. S. (1978). Heredity and environment. In J. Shershow (Ed.), *Schizophrenia: Science and practice* (pp. 47–68). Cambridge, MA: Harvard University Press.

Kety, S. S., Rosenthal, D., Wender, P. H., & Schulsinger, F. (1968). The types and prevalence of mental illness in the biological and adoptive families of adopted schizophrenics. In D. Rosenthal & S. Kety (Eds.), *The transmission of schizophrenia* (pp. 345–362). New York: Pergamon Press.

Kety, S. S., Wender, P. H., Jacobsen, B., Ingraham, L. J., Jansson, L., Faber, B., & Kinney, D. K. (1994). Mental illness in the biological and adoptive relatives of schizophrenic adoptees: Replication of the Copenhagen study to the rest of Denmark. *Archives of General Psychiatry, 51*, 442–455.

Kirk, S. A., Gomory, T., & Cohen, D. (2013). *Mad science: Psychiatric coercion, diagnosis, and drugs*. New Brunswick, NJ: Transaction.

Kirk, S. A., & Kutchins, H. (1992). *The selling of DSM: The rhetoric of science in psychiatry*. New York: Aldine De Gruyter.

Kirkpatrick, R. M., McGue, M., Iacono, W. G., Miller, M. B., Basu, S., & Pankratz, N. (2014). Low-frequency copy-number variants and general cognitive ability: No evidence of association. *Intelligence, 42*, 98–106.

Kline, P. (1993). *The handbook of psychological testing*. London: Routledge.

Kline, P. (1995). A critical review of the measurement of personality and intelligence. In D. Saklofske & M. Zeidner (Eds.), *International handbook of personality and intelligence* (pp. 505–524). New York: Cambridge University Press.

Koch, H. L. (1966). *Twins and twin relations*. Chicago: The University of Chicago Press.

Kringlen, E. (1967). *Heredity and environment in the functional psychoses: An epidemiological-clinical study*. Oslo: Universitetsforlaget.

REFERENCES

Kringlen, E. (1976). Twins—still our best method. *Schizophrenia Bulletin, 2,* 429–433.

Kringlen, E. (2000). Twin studies in schizophrenia with special emphasis on concordance figures. *American Journal of Medical Genetics (Semin. Med. Genet), 97,* 4–11.

Kühl, K. (1994). *The Nazi connection: Eugenics, American racism, and German National Socialism.* New York: Oxford University Press.

Kupfer, D. J., First, M. B., & Regier, D. A. (2002). *A research agenda for DSM-V.* Washington, DC: American Psychiatric Association.

Lane, C. (1995). Tainted sources. In R. Jacoby & N. Glauberman (Eds.), *The Bell Curve debate* (pp. 125–139). New York: Times Books. (Originally published in 1994.)

Lang, J. S. (1987, April 13th). How genes shape personality. *U.S. News and World Report,* pp. 58–66.

Lange, J. (1931). *Crime as destiny.* London: George Allen & Unwin.

Langinvainio, H., Koskenvuo, M., Kaprio, J., Lönnqvist, J., & Tarkkonen, L. (1981). Finnish twins reared apart: Preliminary characterization of rearing environment. In L. Gedda, P. Parisi, & W. Nance (Eds.), *Twin research 3: Part B. Intelligence, personality, and development* (pp. 189–198). New York: Alan R. Liss.

Langinvainio, H., Koskenvuo, M., Kaprio, J., & Sistonen, P. (1984). Finnish twins reared apart II: Validation of zygosity, environmental dissimilarity and weight and height. *Acta Geneticae Medicae et Gemellologiae, 33,* 251–258.

Långström N., Grann M., & Lichtenstein P. (2002). Genetic and environmental influences on problematic masturbatory behavior in children: A study of same-sex twins. *Archives of Sexual Behavior, 31,* 343–350.

Latham, J., & Wilson, A. (2010). The great DNA data deficit: Are genes for disease a mirage? *The Bioscience Research Project.* Retrieved from http://independentsciencenews.org/health/the-great-dna-data-deficit/.

Layzer, D. (1974). Heritability analysis of IQ scores: Science or numerology? *Science, 183,* 1259–1266.

Lerner, R. M. (1992). *Final solutions: Biology, prejudice, and genocide.* University Park, PA: Pennsylvania State University Press.

Lerner, R. M. (2002). *Concepts and theories of human development* (3rd ed.). Mahwah, NJ: Erlbaum.

Levelt Committee, Noort Committee, Drenth Committee. (2012). *Flawed science: The fraudulent research practices of social psychologist Diederik Stapel.* Retrieved from https://www.commissielevelt.nl/.

Lewis, D. A. (2006). Forward. In J. Lieberman, T. Stroup, & D. Perkins (Eds.), *Textbook of schizophrenia* (p. xv). Washington, DC: American Psychiatric Publishing.

Lewontin, R. C. (1974). The analysis of variance and the analysis of causes. *American Journal of Human Genetics, 26,* 400–411.

Lewontin, R. C. (1991). *Biology as ideology.* New York: Harper Perennial.

Lewontin, R. C. (2009, May). Where are the genes? *GeneWatch.* Retrieved from http://www.councilforresponsiblegenetics.org/GeneWatch/GeneWatchPage.aspx?pageId=183&archive=yes.

Lewontin, R. C., Rose, S., & Kamin, L. J. (1984). *Not in our genes.* New York: Pantheon.

Li, H., Peng, Z., Yang, X., Wang, W., Fu, J., Wang, J., ... Yan, J. (2013). Genome-wide association study dissects the genetic architecture of oil biosynthesis in maize kernels. *Nature Genetics, 45,* 43–50.

Lidz, T. (1976). Commentary on a critical review of recent adoption, twin, and family studies of schizophrenia: Behavioral genetics perspectives. *Schizophrenia Bulletin, 2,* 402–412.

Lidz, T., & Blatt, S. (1983). Critique of the Danish-American studies of the biological and adoptive relatives of adoptees who became schizophrenic. *American Journal of Psychiatry, 140,* 426–435.

Lidz, T., Blatt, S., & Cook, B. (1981). Critique of the Danish-American studies of the adopted-away offspring of schizophrenic parents. *American Journal of Psychiatry, 138,* 1063–1068.

Lifton, R. J. (1986). *The Nazi doctors.* New York: Basic Books.

Lilienfeld, S. O., Lynn, S. J., & Lohr, J. M. (2003). Science and pseudoscience in clinical psychology: Initial thoughts, reflections, and considerations. In S. Lilienfeld, S. Lynn, & J. Lohr (Eds.), *Science and pseudoscience in clinical psychology* (pp. 1–14). New York: Guilford.

Loehlin, J. C. (1978a). Heredity–environment analyses of Jencks's IQ correlations. *Behavior Genetics, 8,* 415–436.

Loehlin, J. C. (1978b). Identical twins reared apart and other routes to the same direction. In W. Nance, G. Allen, & P. Parisi (Eds.), *Twin research, Part A: Psychology and methodology* (pp. 69–77). New York: Alan R. Liss.

Loehlin, J. C., & Nichols, R. C. (1976). *Heredity, environment, and personality.* Austin: University of Texas Press.

Loehlin, J. C., Willerman, L., & Horn, J. M. (1988). Human behavior genetics. *Annual Review of Psychology, 39,* 101–133.

Loewen, P. J., & Dawes, C. T. (2012). The heritability of duty and voter turnout. *Political Psychology, 33,* 363–373.

Lombardo, P. A. (2002a). "The American Breed": Nazi eugenics and the origins of the Pioneer Fund. *Albany Law Review, 65,* 743–830.

Lombardo, P. A. (2002b). Pioneer's big lie. *Albany Law Review, 66,* 1125–1144.

Luciano M., Kirk, K. M., Heath, A. C., & Martin, N. G. (2005). The genetics of tea and coffee drinking and preference for source of caffeine in a large community sample of Australian twins. *Addiction, 100,* 1510–1517.

Luxenburger, H. (1928). Vorläufiger Bericht über psychiatrische Serienuntersuchungen an Zwillingen [provisional report on a series of psychiatric investigations of twins]. *Zeitschrift fur die Gesamte Neurologie und Psychiatrie, 116,* 297–347.

Lykken, D. T. (1978). Volunteer bias in twin research: The rule of two-thirds. *Social Biology, 25,* 1–9.

Lykken, D. T. (1982). Research with twins: The concept of emergenesis. *Psychophysiology, 19,* 361–373.

Lykken, D. T. (1995). *The antisocial personalities.* Hillsdale, NJ: Lawrence Erlbaum Associates.

Lykken, D. T. (1999). *Happiness: The nature and nurture of joy and contentment.* New York: St. Martin's Griffin.

Lykken, D. T. (2000). The causes and costs of crime and a controversial cure. *Journal of Personality, 68,* 559–605.

Lykken, D. T. (2004). The new eugenics. *Contemporary Psychology, 49*, 670–672.

Lykken, D. T. (2006). The mechanism of emergenesis. *Genes, Brain, and Behavior, 5*, 306–310.

Lykken, D. T., McGue, M., Tellegen, A., & Bouchard, T. J., Jr. (1992). Emergenesis: Genetic traits that may not run in families. *American Psychologist, 47*, 1565–1577.

Lynn, R. (2001). *Eugenics: A reassessment*. Westport, CT: Praeger.

Lyons, M. J., Kendler, K. S., Provet, A., & Tsuang, M. T. (1991). The genetics of schizophrenia. In M. Tsuang, K. Kendler, & M. Lyons (Eds.), *Genetic issues in psychosocial epidemiology* (pp. 119–152). New Brunswick, NJ: Rutgers University Press.

Lytton, H. (1973). Three approaches to the study of parent–child interaction: Ethological, interview and experimental. *Journal of Child Psychology and Psychiatry, 14*, 1–17.

Lytton, H. (1977). Do parents create, or respond to, differences in twins? *Developmental Psychology, 13*, 456–459.

Maes, H. H., Sullivan, P. F., Bulik, C. M., Neale, M. C., Prescott, C. A., Eaves, L. J., & Kendler, K. S. (2004). A twin study of genetic and environmental influences on tobacco initiation, regular tobacco use and nicotine dependence. *Psychological Medicine, 34*, 1–11.

Maher, B. (2008). The case of the missing heritability. *Nature, 456*, 18–21.

Manolio, T. A., Collins, F. S., Cox, N. J., Goldstein, D. B., Hindorff, L. A., Hunter, D. J., . . . Visscher, P. M. (2009). Finding the missing heritability of complex diseases. *Nature, 461*, 747–753.

Martin, N., Boomsma, D., & Machin, G. (1997). A twin-pronged attack on complex traits. *Nature Genetics, 17*, 387–392.

Martin, N. G., Eaves, L. J., Heath, A. C., Jardine, R., Feingold, L. M., & Eysenck, H. J. (1986). Transmission of social attitudes. *Proceedings of the National Academy of Science, 83*, 4364–4368.

Martinson, B. C., Anderson, M. S., & de Vries, M. (2005). Scientists behaving badly. *Nature, 435*, 737–738.

McClearn, G. E. (1964). The inheritance of behavior. In L. Postman (Ed.), *Psychology in the making* (pp. 144–252). New York: Alfred A. Knopf.

McClearn, G. E., Plomin, R., Gora-Maslak, G., & Crabbe, J. C. (1991). The gene chase in behavioral science. *Psychological Science, 2*, 222–229.

McCourt, K., Bouchard, T. J., Jr., Lykken, D. T., Tellegen, A., & Keyes, M. (1999). Authoritarianism revisited: Genetic and environmental influences in twins reared apart and together. *Personality and Individual Differences, 27*, 985–1014.

McCrea, R. R., Costa, P. T., Ostendorf, F., Angleitner, A., Hřebíčková, M., Avia, M. D., Sanz, J., & Sanchez-Bernardos, M. L. (2000). Nature over nurture: Temperament, personality, and life span development. *Journal of Personality and Social Psychology, 78*, 173–186.

McGue, M. (2013). Genomics and the nature of behavioral and social risk. *American Journal of Public Health, 103 (Supplement 1)*, S7–S9.

McGue, M., & Bouchard, T. J., Jr. (1984). Adjustment of twin data for the effects of age and sex. *Behavior Genetics, 14*, 325–343.

McGue, M., & Bouchard, T. J., Jr. (1989). Genetic and environmental determinants of information processing and special mental abilities: A twin analysis. In R. Sternberg (Ed.), *Advances in the psychology of human intelligence* (Vol. 5, pp. 7–45). Hillsdale, NJ: Lawrence Erlbaum.

McGue, M., & Bouchard, T. J., Jr. (1998). Genetic and environmental influences on human behavioral differences. *Annual Review of Neuroscience, 21,* 1–24.

McGue, M., Bouchard, T. J., Jr., Iacono, W. G., & Lykken, D. T. (1993). Behavioral genetics of cognitive ability: A life-span perspective. In R. Plomin & G. McClearn (Eds.), *Nature, nurture, and psychology* (pp. 59–76). Washington, DC: American Psychological Association.

McGue, M., Bouchard, T. J., Jr., Lykken, D. T., & Feuer, D. (1984). Information processing abilities in twins reared apart. *Intelligence, 8,* 239–258.

McGuffin, P., & Plomin, R. (2004). A decade of the Social, Genetic and Developmental Psychiatry Centre at the Institute of Psychiatry. *British Journal of Psychiatry, 185,* 280–282.

McGuffin, P., Riley, B., & Plomin, R. (2001). Towards behavioral genomics. *Science, 291,* 1232–1249.

McGuffin, P., & Sturt, E. (1986). Genetic markers in schizophrenia. *Human Heredity, 36,* 65–88.

McGuire, T. R., & Hirsch, J. (1977). General intelligence (*g*) and heritability (H^2, h^2). In I. Uzgiris & F. Weitzmann (Eds.), *The structuring of experience* (pp. 25–72). New York: Plenum Press.

McGuire, S., & Segal, N. L. (2013). Peer network overlap in twin, sibling, and friend dyads. *Child Development, 84,* 500–511.

McMahon, R. C. (1980). Genetic etiology in the hyperactive child syndrome: A critical review. *American Journal of Orthopsychiatry, 50,* 145–150.

Meaney, M. J. (2010). Epigenetics and the biological definition of gene × environment interactions. *Child Development, 81,* 41–79.

Medland, S. E., & Hatemi, P. K. (2009). Political science, biometric theory, and twin studies: A methodological introduction. *Political Analysis, 17,* 191–214.

Mehler, B. (1983). The new eugenics: Academic racism in the U.S. today. *Science For The People, 15 (3),* 18–23.

Mensh, E., & Mensh, H. (1991). *The IQ mythology: Class, race, gender, and inequality.* Carbondale, IL: Southern Illinois Press.

Merikangas, K. R., & Risch, N. (2003). Will the genomics revolution revolutionize psychiatry? *American Journal of Psychiatry, 160,* 625–635.

Miller, A. (1995). Professors of hate. In R. Jacoby & N. Glauberman (Eds.), *The Bell Curve debate* (pp. 162–178). New York: Times Books. (Originally published in 1994.)

Miller, P. (2012, January). A thing or two about twins. *National Geographic,* pp. 38–65.

Miller, G., Zhu, G., Wright, M. J., Hansell, N. K., & Martin, N. G. (2012). The heritability and genetic correlates of mobile phone use: A twin study of consumer behavior. *Twin Research and Human Genetics, 15,* 97–106.

Mischel, W. (1968). *Personality and assessment.* New York: Wiley.

Montagu, A. (Ed.). (1999). *Race and IQ* (expanded ed.). Oxford, UK: Oxford University Press.

REFERENCES

Moore, D. S. (2013). Current thinking about nature and nurture. In K. Kampourakis (Ed.), *The philosophy of biology: A companion for educators* (pp. 629–652). Dordrecht: Springer.

Morgeson, F. P., Campion, M. A., Dipboye, R. L., Hollenbeck, J. R., Murphy, K., & Schmitt, N. (2007a). Are we getting fooled again? Coming to terms with limitations in the use of personality tests for personnel selection. *Personnel Psychology, 60,* 1029–1049.

Morgeson, F. P., Campion, M. A., Dipboye, R. L., Hollenbeck, J. R., Murphy, K., & Schmitt, N. (2007b). Reconsidering the use of personality tests in personnel selection contexts. *Personnel Psychology, 60,* 683–729.

Morris-Yates, A., Andrews, G., Howie, P., & Henderson, S. (1990). Twins: A test of the equal environments assumption. *Acta Psychiatrica Scandinavica, 81,* 322–326.

Mosher, L. R., Pollin, W., & Stabenau, J. R. (1971). Families with identical twins discordant for schizophrenia: Some relationships between identification, thinking styles, psychopathology and dominance-submissiveness. *British Journal of Psychiatry, 118,* 29–42.

Mowrer, E. R. (1954). Some factors in the affectional adjustment of twins. *American Sociological Review, 19,* 468–471.

Muller, H. J. (1925). Mental traits and heredity. *Journal of Heredity, 16,* 433–448.

Muller, H. J. (1933, July). The dominance of economics over eugenics. *The Scientific Monthly, 37* (1), 40–47.

Müller-Hill, B. (1998). *Murderous science.* Plainview, NY: Cold Spring Harbor Laboratory Press. (Original English version published in 1988.)

Munsinger, H. (1975). The adopted child's IQ: A critical review. *Psychological Bulletin, 82,* 623–659.

Mustelin, L., Joutsi, J., Latvala, A., Pietilainen, K. H., Rissanen, A., & Kaprio, J. (2012). Genetic influences on physical activity in young adults. *Medicine & Science in Sports & Exercise, 44,* 1293–1301.

Neel, J. V., & Schull, W. J. (1954). *Human heredity.* Chicago: University of Chicago Press.

Newman, D. L., Tellegen, A., & Bouchard, T. J., Jr. (1998). Individual differences in adult ego development: Sources of influences in twins reared apart. *Journal of Personality and Social Psychology, 74,* 985–995.

Newman, H. H., Freeman, F. N., & Holzinger, K. J. (1937). *Twins: A study of heredity and environment.* Chicago: The University of Chicago Press.

Nichols, R. C., & Bilbro, W. C. (1966). The diagnosis of twin zygosity. *Acta Genetica et Statistica Medica, 16,* 265–275.

Ooki, S. (2005). Genetic and environmental influences on finger-sucking and nail-biting in Japanese twin children. *Twin Research and Human Genetics, 8,* 320–327.

Orey, B. D., & Park, H. (2012). Nature, nurture, and ethnocentrism in the Minnesota twin study. *Twin Research and Human Genetics, 15,* 71–73.

Pam, A. (1995). Biological psychiatry: Science or pseudoscience? In C. Ross & A. Pam (Eds.), *Pseudoscience in biological psychiatry: Blaming the body* (pp. 7–84). New York: John Wiley.

Pam, A., Kemker, S. S., Ross, C. A., & Golden, R. (1996). The "equal environment assumption" in MZ–DZ comparisons: An untenable premise of psychiatric genetics? *Acta Geneticae Medicae et Gemellologiae, 45,* 349–360.

Parisi, P. (1995). The twin method. In L. Keith, E. Papiernik, D. Keith, & B. Luke (Eds.), *Multiple pregnancy: Epidemiology, gestation, and perinatal outcome* (pp. 9–20). New York: Parthenon.

Parisi, P. (2004). Twin research, and its multiple births and expressions: A short, personal voyage through its scope, history, and organization. *Twin Research, 7,* 309–317.

Pearson, R. (1966). *Eugenics and race* (2nd ed.). London: The Clair Press.

Pearson, R. (1974). The fall of Rome. *White Power, 54* (6), 8.

Pedersen, N. L., Plomin, R., McClearn, G. E., & Friberg, L. (1985). Separated fraternal twins: Resemblance for cognitive abilities. *Behavior Genetics, 15,* 407–419.

Pedersen, N. L., Plomin, R., McClearn, G. E., & Friberg, L. (1988). Neuroticism, extraversion, and related traits in adult twins reared apart and reared together. *Journal of Personality and Social Psychology, 55,* 950–957.

Pedersen, N. L., Plomin, R., Nesselroade, J. R., & McClearn, G. E. (1992). A quantitative genetic analysis of cognitive abilities during the second half of the life span. *Psychological Science, 3,* 346–353.

Penrose, L. S. (1973). *Outline of human genetics* (3rd ed.). New York: Crane, Russak.

Pinker, S. (2002). *The blank slate.* New York: Viking.

Pirie, M. (2006). *How to win every argument: The use and abuse of logic.* London: Continuum.

Plomin, R. (1983). Developmental behavioral genetics. *Child Development, 54,* 253–259.

Plomin, R. (1989). Environments and genes: Determinants of behavior. *American Psychologist, 44,* 105–111.

Plomin, R. (1990). The role of inheritance in behavior. *Science, 248,* 183–188.

Plomin, R. (1995). Molecular genetics and psychology. *Current Directions in Psychological Science, 4,* 114–117.

Plomin, R. (1997). Identifying genes for cognitive abilities and disabilities. In R. Sternberg & E. Grigorenko (Eds.), *Intelligence, heredity, and environment* (pp. 89–104). New York: Cambridge University Press.

Plomin, R. (1998). Using DNA in health psychology. *Health Psychology, 17,* 53–55.

Plomin, R. (2000). Behavioural genetics in the 21st century. *International Journal of Behavioral Development, 24,* 30–34.

Plomin, R. (2001). The genetics of g in human and mouse. *Nature Reviews Neuroscience, 2,* 136–141.

Plomin, R. (2002). Quantitative trait loci and general cognitive ability. In J. Benjamin, R. Ebstein, & R. Belmaker (Eds.), *Molecular genetics and the human personality* (pp. 211–230). Washington, DC: American Psychiatric Press.

Plomin, R. (2003a). General cognitive ability. In R. Plomin, J. DeFries, I. Craig, & P. McGuffin (Eds.), *Behavioral genetics in the postgenomic era* (pp. 183–201). Washington, DC: American Psychological Association Press.

Plomin, R. (2003b). Molecular genetics and g. In H. Nyborg (Ed.), *The scientific study of general intelligence: Tribute to Arthur R. Jensen* (pp. 107–122). Amsterdam: Pergamon.

Plomin, R. (2004). Genetics and developmental psychology. *Merrill-Palmer Quarterly, 50,* 341–352.

Plomin, R. (2005). Finding genes in child psychology and psychiatry: When are we going to be there? *Journal of Child Psychology and Psychiatry, 46,* 1030–1038.

Plomin, R. (2011). Commentary: Why are children in the same family so different? Non-shared environment three decades later. *International Journal of Epidemiology, 40,* 582–592.

Plomin, R. (2013a). Child development and molecular genetics: 14 years later. *Child Development, 84,* 104–120.

Plomin, R. (2013b). Commentary: Missing heritability, polygenic scores, and gene–environment correlation. *Journal of Child Psychology and Psychiatry, 54,* 1147–1149.

Plomin, R., & Asbury, K. (2005). Nature and nurture: Genetic and environmental influences on behavior. *The Annals of the American Academy of Political and Social Science, 600,* 86–98.

Plomin, R., & Bergeman, C. S. (1991a). Author response: The nature of nurture: Genetic influence on "environmental" measures. *Behavioral and Brain Sciences, 14,* 414–427.

Plomin, R., & Bergeman, C. S. (1991b). The nature of nurture: Genetic influence on "environmental" measures. *Behavioral and Brain Sciences, 14,* 373–386.

Plomin, R., & Caspi, A. (1998). DNA and personality. *European Journal of Personality, 12,* 387–407.

Plomin, R., & Caspi, A. (1999). Behavioral genetics and personality. In L. Pervin & O. John (Eds.), *Handbook of personality: Theory and research* (2nd ed., pp. 251–276). New York: Guilford.

Plomin, R., Chipuer, H. M., & Loehlin, J. C. (1990). Behavioral genetics and personality. In L. Pervin (Ed.), *Handbook of personality: Theory and research* (pp. 225–243). New York: Guilford.

Plomin, R., Corley, R., Caspi, A., Fulker, D. W., & DeFries, J. C. (1998). Adoption results for self-reported personality: Evidence for nonadditive genetic effects? *Journal of Personality and Social Psychology, 75,* 211–218.

Plomin, R., & Crabbe, J. (2000). DNA. *Psychological Bulletin, 126,* 806–828.

Plomin, R., & Daniels, D. (1987). Why are children in the same family so different from one another? *Behavioral and Brain Science, 10,* 1–16.

Plomin, R., & Davis, O. S. P. (2009).The future of genetics in psychology and psychiatry: Microarrays, genome-wide association, and non-coding RNA. *Journal of Child Psychology and Psychiatry, 50,* 63–71.

Plomin, R., & DeFries, J. C. (1976). Letter to the editor in response to "The Heritability Hang-up" by Feldman and Lewontin. *Science, 194,* 10–12.

Plomin, R., & DeFries, J. C. (1985). *Origins of individual differences in infancy: The Colorado Adoption Project.* Orlando, FL: Academic Press.

Plomin, R., DeFries, J. C., Craig, I. W., & McGuffin, P. (2003). Behavioral genomics. In R. Plomin, J. DeFries, I. Craig, & P. McGuffin (Eds.), *Behavioral genetics in the postgenomic era* (pp. 531–540). Washington, DC: American Psychological Association Press.

Plomin, R., DeFries, J. C., Knopik, V. S., & Neiderhiser, J. M. (2013). *Behavioral genetics* (6th ed.). New York: Worth Publishers.

Plomin, R., DeFries, J. C., & Loehlin, J. C. (1977). Genotype–environment interaction and correlation in the analysis of human behavior. *Psychological Bulletin, 84,* 309–322.

Plomin, R., DeFries, J. C., & McClearn, G. E. (1990). *Behavioral genetics: A primer* (2nd ed.). New York: W. H. Freeman.

Plomin, R., DeFries, J. C., McClearn, G. E., & McGuffin, P. (2001). *Behavioral genetics* (4th ed.). New York: Worth Publishers.

Plomin, R., DeFries, J. C., McClearn, G. E., & McGuffin, P. (2008). *Behavioral genetics* (5th ed.). New York: Worth Publishers.

Plomin, R., DeFries, J. C., McClearn, G. E., & Rutter, M. (1997). *Behavioral genetics* (3rd ed.). New York: W. H. Freeman.

Plomin, R., Happé, F., & Caspi, A. (2002). Personality and cognitive abilities. In P. McGuffin, M. Owen, & I. Gottesman (Eds.), *Psychiatric genetics and genomics* (pp. 77–112). Oxford: Oxford University Press.

Plomin, R., Haworth, C. M. A., Meaburn, E. L., Price, T. S., Wellcome Trust Case Control Consortium 2, & Davis, O. S. P. (2013). Common DNA markers can account for more than half of the genetic influence on cognitive abilities. *Psychological Science, 24,* 562–568.

Plomin, R., McClearn, G. E., Smith, D. L., Vignetti, S., Chorney, M. J., Chorney, K., . . . McGuffin, P. (1994). DNA markers associated with high versus low IQ: The IQ Quantitative Trait Loci (QTL) project. *Behavior Genetics, 24,* 107–118.

Plomin, R., & McGuffin, P. (2003). Psychopathology in the postgenomic era. *Annual Review of Psychology, 54,* 205–228.

Plomin, R., Owen, M. J., & McGuffin, P. (1994). The genetic basis of complex behaviors. *Science, 264,* 1733–1739.

Plomin, R., & Rende, R. (1991). Human behavioral genetics. *Annual Review of Psychology, 42,* 161–190.

Plomin, R., & Rutter, M. (1998). Child development, molecular genetics, and what to do with genes once they are found. *Child Development, 69,* 1223–1242.

Plomin, R., & Simpson, M. A. (2013). The future of genomics for developmentalists. *Development and Psychopathology, 25,* 1263–1278.

Plomin, R., & Spinath, F. M. (2004). Intelligence: Genetics, genes, and genomics. *Journal of Personality and Social Psychology, 86,* 112–129.

Plomin, R., Willerman, L., & Loehlin, J. C. (1976). Resemblance in appearance and the equal environments assumption in twin studies of personality traits. *Behavior Genetics, 6,* 43–52.

Popenoe, P. (1922). Twins reared apart. *Journal of Heredity, 13,* 142–144.

Popenoe, P., & Johnson, R. (1918). *Applied eugenics.* New York: Macmillan.

Popenoe, P., & Johnson, R. (1933). *Applied eugenics* (rev. ed.). New York: Macmillan.

Preacher, K. J. (2002, May). Calculation for the test of the difference between two independent correlation coefficients [computer software]. Available from http://quantpsy.org.

Prescott, C. A., Caldwell, C. B., Carey, G., Vogler, G. P., Trumbetta, S. L., & Gottesman, I. I. (2005). The Washington University Twin Study of Alcoholism.

REFERENCES

American Journal of Medical Genetics Part B (Neuropsychiatric Genetics), 134B, 48–55.

Prescott, C. A., Kuhn, J. W., & Pedersen, N. L. (2007). Twin pair resemblance for psychiatric hospitalization in the Swedish Twin Registry: A 32-year follow-up study of 29,602 twin pairs. *Behavior Genetics, 37,* 547–558.

Prinz, J. J. (2012). *Beyond human nature: How culture and experience shape the human mind.* New York: W. W. Norton.

Proctor, R. N. (1988). *Racial hygiene: Medicine under the Nazis.* Cambridge, MA: Harvard University Press.

Proctor, R. N. (1995). *Cancer wars: How politics shapes what we know and don't know about cancer.* New York: Basic Books.

Purcell, S. (2013). Statistical methods in behavioral genetics. Appendix in R. Plomin, J. DeFries, V. Knopik, & J. Neiderhiser (Eds.), *Behavioral genetics* (6th ed.; pp. 357–411). New York: Worth Publishers.

Ratner, C., & El-Badwi, E. (2011). A cultural psychological theory of mental illness, supported by research in Saudi Arabia. *Journal of Social Distress and the Homeless, 20,* 217–274.

Read, J. (2013a). Childhood adversity and psychosis. In J. Read & J. Dillon (Eds.), *Models of madness: Psychological, social and biological approaches to psychosis* (2nd ed.; pp. 249–275). London: Routledge.

Read, J. (2013b). Does "schizophrenia" exist? In J. Read & J. Dillon (Eds.), *Models of madness: Psychological, social and biological approaches to psychosis* (2nd ed.; pp. 47–61). London: Routledge.

Read, J. (2013c). The invention of schizophrenia. In J. Read & J. Dillon (Eds.), *Models of madness: Psychological, social and biological approaches to psychosis* (2nd ed.; pp. 20–33). London: Routledge.

Read, J. (2013d). Psychosis, poverty, and ethnicity. In J. Read & J. Dillon (Eds.), *Models of madness: Psychological, social and biological approaches to psychosis* (2nd ed.; pp. 191–209). London: Routledge.

Read, J., Bentall, R. P., & Fosse, R. (2009). Time to abandon the bio-bio-bio model of psychosis: Exploring the epigenetic and psychological mechanisms by which adverse life events lead to psychotic symptoms. *Epidemiologia e Psichiatria Sociale, 18,* 299–310.

Read J., & Dillon, J. (Eds.). (2013). *Models of madness: Psychological, social and biological approaches to psychosis* (2nd ed.). London: Routledge.

Read, J., Fosse, R., Moscowitz, A., & Perry, B. (2014). The traumagenic neurodevelopmental model of psychosis revisited. *Neuropsychiatry, 4,* 65–79.

Reber, A. S. (1985). *The Penguin dictionary of psychology.* London: Penguin Books.

Reich, T., Clayton, P. J., & Winokur, G. (1969). Family history studies: V. The genetics of mania. *American Journal of Psychiatry, 125,* 1358–1369.

Reilly, P. R. (1991). *The surgical solution: A history of involuntary sterilization in the United States.* Baltimore: The Johns Hopkins University Press.

Richardson, K. (1998). *The origins of human potential.* London: Routledge.

Richardson, K. (2000). *The making of intelligence.* New York: Columbia University Press.

Richardson, K., & Norgate, S. (2005). The equal environment assumption of classical twin studies may not hold. *British Journal of Educational Psychology, 75,* 339–350.

Richardson, K., & Norgate, S. (2006). A critical analysis of IQ studies of adopted children. *Human Development, 49*, 319–335.

Ridley, M. (2003). *The agile gene: How nature turns on nurture*. New York: Perennial.

Rips, L. J. (2002). Circular reasoning. *Cognitive Science, 26*, 767–795

Roelcke, V. (2006). Funding the scientific foundations of race policies: Ernst Rüdin and the impact of career resources on psychiatric genetics, ca 1910–1945. In W. Eckart (Ed.), *Man, medicine, and the state: The human body as an object of government sponsored medical research in the 20th century* (pp. 73–87). Stuttgart: Steiner.

Roelcke, V. (2010). Medicine during the Nazi period: Historical facts and some implications for teaching medical ethics and professionalism. In S. Rubenfeld (Ed.), *Medicine after the Holocaust: From the master race to the human genome and beyond* (pp. 18–27). New York: Palgrave Macmillan.

Roelcke, V. (2012). Ernst Rüdin—renommierter Wissenschaftler, radikaler Rassenhygieniker [Ernst Rüdin—Distinguished scientist, radical racial hygienist.] *Der Nervenarzt, 83*, 303–310.

Rose, R. J. (1982). Separated twins: Data and their limits. [Review of the book *Identical twins reared apart: A reanalysis*, by S. L. Farber]. *Science, 215*, 959–960.

Rose, S. (1997). *Lifelines: Life beyond the genes*. New York: Oxford University Press.

Rosenthal, D. (1962). Familial concordance by sex with respect to schizophrenia. *Psychological Bulletin, 59*, 401–421.

Rosenthal, R., & Rosnow, R. L. (1975). *The volunteer subject*. New York: John Wiley.

Rosenthal, D., Wender, P. H., Kety, S. S., Welner, J., & Schulsinger, F. (1971). The adopted-away offspring of schizophrenics. *American Journal of Psychiatry, 128*, 307–311.

Ross, C. A., & Pam, A. (Eds.). (1995). *Pseudoscience in biological psychiatry: Blaming the body*. New York: John Wiley.

Rossi, M. (2013). Consider Jack and Oskar. [Review of the book *Born together—reared apart: The landmark Minnesota twin study*, by N. L. Segal]. *London Review of Books, 35 (3)*, 346–349.

Rowe, D. C. (1994). *The limits of family influence: Genes, experience, and behavior*. New York: The Guilford Press.

Rowe, D. C., & Jacobson, K. C. (1999). In the mainstream. In R. Carson & M. Rothstein (Eds.), *Behavioral genetics: The clash of culture and biology* (pp. 12–34). Baltimore: The Johns Hopkins University Press.

Rushton, J. P. (1995). *Race, evolution, and behavior: A life history perspective*. New Brunswick, NJ: Transaction.

Rushton, J. P. (2000a). *Race, evolution, and behavior: A life history perspective* (2nd special abridged ed.). Port Huron, MI: Charles Darwin Research Institute.

Rushton, J. P. (2000b). *Race, evolution, and behavior: A life history perspective* (3rd ed.). Port Huron, MI: Charles Darwin Research Institute.

Rushton, J. P., & Jensen, A. R. (2008). James Watson's most inconvenient truth: Race realism and the moralistic fallacy. *Medical Hypotheses, 71*, 629–640.

Rushton, J. P., & Jensen, A. R. (2010). The rise and fall of the Flynn effect as a reason to expect a narrowing of the Black–White IQ gap. *Intelligence, 38*, 213–219.

Rutter, M. (2006). *Genes and behavior: Nature–nurture interplay explained.* Malden, MA: Blackwell.

Rutter, M., & Plomin, R. (1997). Opportunities for psychiatry from genetic findings. *British Journal of Psychiatry, 171,* 209–219.

Rutter, M., Silberg, J., & Simonoff, E. (1993). Whither behavioral genetics?—A developmental psychopathological perspective. In R. Plomin & G. McClearn (Eds.), *Nature, nurture, and psychology* (pp. 433–456). Washington, DC: American Psychological Association.

Rutter, M., Simonoff, E., & Silberg, J. (1993). How informative are twin studies of child psychopathology? In T. Bouchard & P. Propping (Eds.), *Twins as a tool of behavioral genetics* (pp. 179–194). New York: John Wiley.

Sapone, A., Bai, J. C., Ciacci, C., Dolinsek, J., Green, P. H., Hadjivassiliou, M., . . . Fasano, A. (2012). Spectrum of gluten-related disorders: Consensus on new nomenclature and classification. *BMC Medicine, 10* (1), 13. doi:10.1186/1741-7015-10-13.

Sarbin, T. R., & Mancuso, J. C. (1980). *Schizophrenia: Medical diagnosis or moral verdict?* New York: Pergamon Press.

Scarr, S. (1968). Environmental bias in twin studies. *Eugenics Quarterly, 15,* 34–40.

Scarr, S. (1987). Three cheers for behavior genetics: Winning the war and losing our identity. *Behavior Genetics, 17,* 219–228.

Scarr, S. (1998). On Arthur Jensen's integrity. *Intelligence, 26,* 227–232.

Scarr, S., & Carter-Saltzman, L. (1979). Twin method: Defense of a critical assumption. *Behavior Genetics, 9,* 527–542.

Scarr, S., & Carter-Saltzman, L. (1982). Genetics and intelligence. In R. Sternberg (Ed.), *Handbook of human intelligence* (pp. 792–896). New York: Cambridge University Press.

Schiff, M., Duyme, M., Dumaret, A., & Tomkiewicz, S. (1982). How much *could* we boost scholastic achievement and IQ scores? A direct answer from a French adoption study. *Cognition, 12,* 165–196.

Schiff, M., & Lewontin, R. C. (1986). *Education and class: The irrelevance of IQ genetic studies.* Oxford: Clarendon Press.

Schizophrenia Working Group of the Psychiatric Genomics Consortium. (2014). Biological insights from 108 schizophrenia-associated genetic loci. *Nature, 511,* 421–427.

Sedgwick, J. (1995). Inside the Pioneer Fund. In R. Jacoby & N. Glauberman (Eds.), *The Bell Curve debate* (pp. 144–161). New York: Times Books. (Originally published in 1994.)

Segal, N. L. (1993). Twin, sibling, and adoption methods: Tests of evolutionary hypotheses. *American Psychologist, 48,* 943–956.

Segal, N. L. (1999). *Entwined lives: Twins and what they tell us about human behavior.* New York: Dutton.

Segal, N. L. (2003). News, views, and comments: Spotlights; research samplings; literature, politics, photography and athletics. *Twin Research and Human Genetics, 6,* 72–81.

Segal, N. L. (2012). *Born together—reared apart: The landmark Minnesota twin study.* Cambridge, MA: Harvard University Press.

Segal, N. L. (2013). Personality similarity in unrelated look-alike pairs: Addressing a twin study challenge. *Personality and Individual Differences, 54,* 23–28.

Segal, N. L., & Johnson, W. (2009). Twin studies of general mental ability. In Y. Kim (Ed.), *Handbook of behavior genetics* (pp. 81–99). New York: Springer.

Sesardic, N. (2005). *Making sense of heritability*. Cambridge: Cambridge University Press.

Shakeshaft, N. G., Trzaskowski, M., McMillan, A., Rimfeld, K., Krapohl, E., Haworth, . . . Plomin, R. (2013). Strong genetic influence on a UK nationwide test of educational achievement at the end of compulsory education at age 16. *PLoS ONE, 8 (12)*, 1–10.

Shao, H., Burrage, L. C., Sinasac, D. S., Hill, A. E., Ernest, S. R., O'Brien, W., . . . Nadeau, J. H. (2008). Genetic architecture of complex traits: Large phenotypic effects and pervasive epistasis. *Proceedings of the National Academy of Sciences, 105*, 19910–19914.

Sherrington, R., Brynjolfsson, J., Petursson, H., Potter, M., Duddleston, K., Barraclough, B., Wasmuth, J., Dobbs, M., & Gurling, H. (1988). Localization of a susceptibility locus for schizophrenia on chromosome 5. *Nature, 336*, 164–167.

Shields, J. (1954). Personality differences and neurotic traits in normal twin schoolchildren. *Eugenics Review, 45*, 213–246.

Shields, J. (1962). *Monozygotic twins brought up apart and brought up together*. London: Oxford University Press.

Shields, J. (1978). MZA twins: Their use and abuse. In W. Nance, G. Allen, & P. Parisi (Eds.), *Twin research: Psychology and methodology, Part A*, (pp. 79–93). New York: Alan R. Liss.

Siemens, H. W. (1924). *Die zwillingspathologie* [Twin pathology]. Berlin: Springer Verlag.

Simon, J. L. (1997). Four comments on The Bell Curve. *Genetica, 99*, 199–205.

Slife, B. D., & Williams, R. N. (1995). *What's behind the research? Discovering hidden assumptions in the behavioral sciences*. Thousand Oaks, CA: Sage.

Smith, K., Alford, J. R., Hatemi, P. K., Eaves, L. J., Funk, C., & Hibbing, J. R. (2012). Biology, ideology, and epistemology: How do we know political attitudes are inherited and why should we care? *American Journal of Political Science, 56*, 17–33.

Sternberg, R. J. (2007). Critical thinking in psychology is really critical. In R. Sternberg, H. Roediger III, & D. Halpern (Eds.), *Critical thinking in psychology* (pp. 289–296). New York: Cambridge University Press.

Stocks, P. (1930). A biometric investigation of twins and their brothers and sisters. *Annals of Eugenics, 4*, 49–108.

Stoltenberg, S. F. (1997). Coming to terms with heritability. *Genetica, 99*, 89–96.

Stoolmiller, M. (1999). Implications of the restricted range of family environments for estimates of heritability and nonshared environment in behavior–genetic adoption studies. *Psychological Bulletin, 125*, 392–409.

Sturgis, P., Read, S., Hatemi, P. K., Zhu, G., Trull, T., Wright, M. J., & Martin, N. G. (2010). A genetic basis for social trust? *Political Behavior, 32*, 205–230.

Sugden, K., Arseneault, L., Harrington, H., Moffitt, T., Williams, B., & Caspi, A. (2010). Serotonin transporter gene moderates the development of emotional problems among children following bullying victimization. *Journal of the American Academy of Child and Adolescent Psychiatry, 49*, 830–840.

REFERENCES

Suhay, E., Kalmoe, N., & McDermott, C. (2007). Why twin studies are problematic for the study of political ideology: Rethinking "Are Political Orientations Genetically Transmitted?" Presented at the International Society of Political Psychology. Retrieved from http://sitemaker.umich.edu/suhay/files/critique_of_twin_studies_--_suhay__kalmoe__mcdermott_101007.pdf.

Sullivan, P. et al. (2012). Don't give up on GWAS. *Molecular Psychiatry, 17,* 2–3.

Sullivan, P. F., Kendler, K. S., & Neale, M. C. (2003). Schizophrenia as a complex trait: Evidence from a meta-analysis of twin studies. *Archives of General Psychiatry, 60,* 1187–1192.

Szasz, T. S. (1976). *Schizophrenia: The sacred symbol of psychiatry.* New York: Basic Books.

Szasz, T. S. (1987). *Insanity: The idea and its consequences.* Syracuse, NY: Syracuse University Press.

Szatkiewicz, J. P., O'Dushlaine, C., Chen, G., Chambert, K., Moran, J. L., Neale, B. M., ... Sullivan, P. F. (2014). Copy number variation in schizophrenia in Sweden. *Molecular Psychiatry, 19,* 762–773.

Tabery, J., & Griffiths, P. E. (2010). Historical and philosophical perspectives on behavioral genetics and developmental science. In K. Hood, C. Tucker Halpern, G. Greenberg, & R. Lerner (Eds.), *Handbook of developmental science, behavior, and genetics* (pp. 41–60). Malden, MA: Wiley-Blackwell.

Taylor, H. F. (1980). *The IQ game: A methodological inquiry into the heredity–environment controversy.* New Brunswick, NJ: Rutgers University Press.

Tellegen, A., Lykken, D. T., Bouchard, T. J., Jr., Wilcox, K. J., Segal, N. L., & Rich, S. (1988). Personality similarity in twins reared apart and together. *Journal of Personality and Social Psychology, 54,* 1031–1039.

Tienari, P. (1963). *Psychiatric illnesses in identical twins.* Copenhagen: Munksgaard.

Torgersen, S. (1979). The determination of zygosity by means of a mailed questionnaire. *Acta Geneticae Medicae et Gemellologiae, 28,* 225–236.

Torrey, E. F. (1995). *Surviving schizophrenia* (3rd ed.). New York: Harper Perennial.

True, W. R., Rice, J., Eisen, S. A., Heath, A. C., Goldberg, J., Lyons, M. J., & Nowak, J. (1993). A twin study of genetic and environmental contributions to liability for posttraumatic stress symptoms. *Archives of General Psychiatry, 50,* 257–264.

Trzaskowski, M., Dale, P. S., & Plomin, R. (2013). No genetic influence for childhood behavior problems from DNA analysis. *Journal of the American Academy of Child and Adolescent Psychiatry, 52,* 1048–1056.

Trzaskowski, M., Eley, T. C., Davis, O. S. P., Doherty, S. J., Hanscombe, K. B., Meaburn, E. L., ... Plomin, R. (2013). First genome-wide association study on anxiety-related behaviours in childhood. *PLoS ONE, 8 (4),* 1–7.

Tucker, W. H. (1994). *The science and politics of racial research.* Urbana, IL: University of Illinois Press.

Tucker, W. H. (2002a). A closer look at the Pioneer Fund: Response to Rushton. *Albany Law Review, 66,* 1145–1159.

Tucker, W. H. (2002b). *The funding of scientific racism: Wickliffe Draper and the Pioneer Fund.* Urbana: University of Illinois Press.

Tucker, W. H. (2009). *The Cattell controversy: Race, science, and ideology.* Urbana: University of Illinois Press.

REFERENCES

Tucker, W. H. (2013). [Review of the book *Born together—reared apart: The landmark Minnesota twin study*, by N. L. Segal]. *Journal of the History of the Behavioral Sciences, 49*, 337–341.

Turkheimer, E. (2000). Three laws of behavior genetics and what they mean. *Current Directions in Psychological Science, 9*, 160–164.

Turkheimer, E. (2011a). Commentary: Variation and causation in the environment and genome. *International Journal of Epidemiology, 40*, 598–601.

Turkheimer, E. (2011b). Still missing. *Research in Human Development, 8*, 227–241.

Turkheimer, E., Pettersson, E., & Horn, E. E. (2014). A phenotypic null hypothesis for the genetics of personality. *Annual Review of Psychology, 65*, 515–540.

Vandenberg, S. V. (1966). Contributions of twin research to psychology. *Psychological Bulletin, 66*, 327–352.

Viding, E., Price, T. S., Jaffee, S. R., Trzaskowski, M., Davis, O. S. P., Meaburn, E. L., ... Plomin, R. (2103). Genetics of callous-unemotional behavior in children. *PLoS ONE, 8 (7)*, 1–9.

Vinkhuyzen, A. A. E., Pedersen, N. L., Yang, J., Lee, S. H., Magnusson, P. K. E., Iacono, ... Wray, N. R. (2012). Common SNPs explain some of the variation in the personality dimensions of neuroticism and extraversion. *Translational Psychiatry, 2*, e102.

Visscher, P. M., Yang, J., & Goddard, M. E. (2010). A commentary on "Common SNPs Explain a Large Proportion of the Heritability for Human Height" by Yang et al. (2010). *Twin Research and Human Genetics, 13*, 517–524.

von Bracken, H. (1934). Mutual intimacy in twins. *Character and Personality, 2*, 293–309.

Wade, C., & Tavris, C. (2006). *Psychology* (8th ed.). Upper Saddle River, NJ: Pearson Prentice Hall.

Wade, N. (2014). *A troublesome inheritance: Genes, race, and human history*. New York: Penguin.

Wahlsten, D. (1990). Insensitivity of the analysis of variance to heredity-environment interaction. *Behavioral and Brain Sciences, 13*, 109–120.

Wahlsten, D. (1994). The intelligence of heritability. *Canadian Psychology, 35*, 244–259.

Wahlsten, D. (1997). The malleability of intelligence is not constrained by heritability. In B. Devlin, S. Fienberg, D. Resnick, & K. Roeder (Eds.), *Intelligence, genes, and success* (pp. 71–87). New York: Springer.

Wahlsten, D. (2012). The hunt for gene effects pertinent to behavioral traits and psychiatric disorders: From mouse to human. *Developmental Psychobiology, 54*, 475–492.

Wallace, H. (2009). Big tobacco and the human genome: Driving the scientific bandwagon? *Genomics, Society and Policy, 5*, 1–54.

Walton, D. (1999). The appeal to ignorance, or *argumentum ad ignorantiam*. *Argumentation, 13*, 367–377.

Watson, J. D. (2003). A molecular genetics perspective. In R. Plomin, J. DeFries, I. Craig, & P. McGuffin (Eds.), *Behavioral genetics in the postgenomic era* (pp. xxi–xxii). Washington, DC: American Psychological Association Press.

Watson, P. (1981). *Twins: An investigation into the strange coincidences in the lives of separated twins*. London: Hutchinson.

REFERENCES

Weber, M. M. (1996). Ernst Rüdin, 1874–1952. *American Journal of Medical Genetics (Neuropsychiatric Genetics), 67,* 323–331.

Weindling, P. (1989). *Health, race, and German politics between national unification and Nazism, 1870–1945.* Cambridge: Cambridge University Press.

Weiss, S. F. (2010). *The Nazi symbiosis: Human genetics and politics in the Third Reich.* Chicago: University of Chicago Press.

Wetzel, N. A. (2013, July 18). Categories for human anguish? DSM 5: The new inventory of "mental illnesses" [Web log post]. Retrieved from http://www.princetonfamily.com/blog/post.php?s=2013-07-18-categories-for-human-anguish-dsm-5-the-new-inventory-of-mental-illnesses.

Wilby, P. (2014, February 17th). Psychologist on a mission to give every child a learning chip. *The Guardian.* Retrieved from http://www.theguardian.com/education/2014/feb/18/psychologist-robert-plomin-says-genes-crucial-education.

Willerman, L. (1979). *The psychology of individual and group differences.* San Francisco: W. H. Freeman.

Wilson, G. D., & Patterson, J. R. (1968). A new measure of conservatism. *British Journal of Social and Clinical Psychology, 7,* 264–269.

Wilson, P. T. (1934). A study of twins with special reference to heredity as a factor determining differences in environment. *Human Biology, 6,* 324–354.

Winston, A. S. (1998). Science in the service of the far right: Henry E. Garrett, the IAAEE, and the Liberty Lobby. *Journal of Social Sciences, 54,* 179–210.

Winter, D. G. (1996). *Personality: Analysis and interpretation of lives.* New York: McGraw-Hill.

Woodworth, R. S. (1941). *Heredity and environment: A critical survey of recently published material on twins and foster children.* New York: Social Science Research Center.

Wright, J. (2014). Unravelling complexity. *Nature, 508,* S6–S7.

Wright, L. (1997). *Twins: And what they tell us about who we are.* New York: John Wiley.

Wright, W. (1998). *Born that way.* New York: Alfred A. Knopf.

Yang, J., Benyamin, B., McEvoy, B. P., Gordon, S., Henders, A. K., Nyholt, . . . Visscher, P. M. (2010). Common SNPs explain a large proportion of the heritability for human height. *Nature Genetics, 42,* 565–569.

Zuk, O., Hechter, E., Sunyaev, S. R., & Lander, E. S. (2012). The mystery of missing heritability: Genetic interactions create phantom heritability. *PNAS, 109,* 1193–1198.

INDEX

ability, and genes/environments 3
ACE Model 82, 162
Acta Geneticae Medicae et Gemellologiae article 133
ADHD 198, 200, 227, 228, 273
adopted twin studies *see* TRA studies
adoption, selective placement 13–14, 106, 278
adoption studies 13–14, 97, 99, 149n.9, 179, 259, 263–4, 273
adoptive rearing environments, and behavioral similarity 106
adults, environment-creating behavior of 160
age/sex confounds, MISTRA 117–18
Agile Gene, The 54–5
Ainslie, Ricardo 155
Albee, George 196
Alford et al. 154, 171
alleles 194, 273
Allport, Gordon 93
American eugenics movement 18
American Psychiatric Association (APA) 190, 193, 194, 207, 209
American Psychological Foundation 114
American Psychologist 224
Annual Review of Neuroscience 136
Annual Review of Psychology 224, 263
appearance, similarity of influencing treatment 94–5
Applied Eugenics 237
Arvey, Richard 53
Asbury, K. and Plomin, R. 233
Asbury, Kathryn 233
ascertainment bias 65, 104
assortative mating 83, 113, 138, 142, 273

assumptions: about inheritance 99; and bias 41–3; equal environment assumption (EEA) *see* equal environment assumption (EEA); of genetic theories in psychiatry 196–8; IQ tests matching 90; MISTRA 86, 107, 108, 113–15, 130, 142, 147; model-fitting 138; questionable 84–6; term 6, 273; twin method (twins reared together) 154; underlying conclusions 64
attachment, MZT–DZT twins 164–8, 185
attention-deficit hyperactivity disorder *see* ADHD
autism 80, 273

Bailey et al. 80
Beckwith, Jonathan 124
behavior: and environments 3, 11, 95, 235, 265; genetic factors 3, 5, 56, 107, 154, 175–6, 208–9, 234; heritability estimates for 216, 217; and molecular biology 224; non-genetic influences 177; running in families 12
behavioral development, and genes 228
behavioral differences, MISTRA study 147
behavioral disorders, genes for 228
behavioral genetic research, psychopathology 224, 227
Behavioral Genetics 100n.3, 188, 223, 224, 225, 227, 228, 230, 231, 263
behavioral genetics: adoption studies 13–14; criticisms of 79–80; failure

INDEX

to produce causative genes 220; family studies 11–12; family studies v. twin method 170; molecular genetic research 15–16; psychometric approach to 76; reared-apart twin studies 15; term 276; twin method (twins reared together) 12–13
"Behavioral Genetics: A Lack-of Progress Report" 234
Behavioral Genetics in the Postgenomic Era 227
behavioral resemblances: and adoptive rearing environments 106; genetic factors 107; non-genetic factors 109, 177
behavioral science 6, 103–4
Behavior Genetics 9, 141, 164
Behavior Genetics Association (BGA) 10
Behavior Genetics (journal) 10
behavior shaping cohort effects 96
behavior-shaping environments 42–3
Bell Curve, The 51, 53, 253
bell-shaped curve 76, 77
Bentall, Richard 99, 202
Benyamin et al. 208
bias: in adoption studies 14; ascertainment 65, 104; and assumptions 41–3; confirmation bias 120–2; environmental in twin research 188; in GCTA studies 219; MISTRA 115–17, 126, 127; in recruiting twins 22–4, 70, 115–17; sampling 21–4, 29, 62, 65, 66, 72, 104; sources of 44, 48; TRA studies 68, 116; unconscious experimenter bias 62
biological causes, and environmental causes 174
biological determinism 237
biological factors, and genetic factors 174
biology, and genetics 177–8n.7
biometrical model fitting 82–7
Bioscience Resource Project 212
bipolar disorder 180, 224, 227, 273
Birmingham School 85
birth defects 175
black people *see also* racism: and eugenics 52; as genetically inferior 51, 254, 258
Born That Way 257

Born Together—Reared Apart 102–3, 107, 115, 121–2, 129, 132, 139, 143, 146, 215, 248, 259
Bouchard et al. (1986) 111
Bouchard et al. (1990) 104, 112, 129, 131, 269
Bouchard et al. (1991) 124
Bouchard et al. (1996) 135
Bouchard, Thomas Jr.: and after-the-fact analyses of trends 74n.1; and assumptions 86; and CAP study 264; and circular arguments 114–15; cohort effects 117; and degree of separation of twins 127n.2; and difficulty of gene discovery 215–16; Gold Medal Award for Life Achievement in the Science of Psychology 53; and heritability 77; and heritability estimates 81, 112; and heritability of g/genes for behavior 208; and Howard Taylor 64; multiple measure approach 130; publicity quotes 54–5; and quantitative analytical techniques 67; and random assignment 88; refusal of access to data 125; sample size 120–1; selective reporting of data 134, 135, 136, 141, 143–4
Bouchard, T. J. Jr. and Loehlin, J. C. 145
Bouchard, T. J. Jr. and McGue, M. 137, 141, 145, 161, 214–15
Bouchard, T. J. Jr. and Pederson, N. 137
Boyle, Mary 180
breeding plans, eugenics 258
British Royal Commission on the Distribution of Income and Wealth 5
broad heritability 77
Bulmer, M. G. 268
Burlingham, Dorothy 164
Burt, Cyril 48–50, 68, 123

California Psychological Inventory (CPI) 93, 143, 145
callous-unemotional (CU) behavior 218
candidate gene studies 199
Carey, Benedict 49
Carter, H. D. 155

INDEX

Caspi, A. and Shiner, R. L. 271
cause, and variation 78–80
central registry for TRA data 66
Cesarini et al. 271
Chabris et al. 208
Charney et al. 192
Charney, Evan 99, 100, 174, 176, 219
Child Development 226, 229, 230
"Child Development, Molecular Genetics, and What to Do With Genes Once They are Found" 228, 230
childhood adversities, and psychiatric disorders 199
childhood behavior problems 218, 232
childhood environment, and psychological functioning 196
child psychopathology *see* psychopathology
children, euthanasia of defective 254
chromosome 273
circular reasoning 42, 65, 86–7, 159–60, 186; MISTRA 113, 114, 160; term 273
class difference *see* social classes
class elites, power of 237 *see also* elites
Cloninger et al. 235n.2
cognitive ability *see* intelligence; IQ
Cohen et al 165, 168
cohort effects 66, 69, 70–1; MZA pairs 95–7, 103, 110; term 273; TRA IQ correlations 117
Collins, Francis 210
Colorado Adoption Project (CAP) 143, 260–5
Colorado Childhood Temperament Inventory (CCTI) 260
common disease, common variant hypothesis 210
common variants 210
Comprehensive Ability Battery (CAB) 130
concordance 274
concordance rates: MZT and same-sex DZT 183; MZT–DZT/environmental factors 186; pooled/schizophrenia 185
confirmation bias, MISTRA 120–2
confounds 14, 168, 274
conservatism, genetic influences on 177n.6

contact time formula, twin separation 104–5
control groups: MISTRA 107–9, 130, 131, 132, 139, 146; need for in TRA studies 69, 72, 74; term 274; unrelated people 43
converging evidence argument, Colorado Adoption Project (CAP) 261–2
copy-number variants (CNVs) 211
corn oil production, heritability of 216
corporations, and genetic determinism 212
correlations 274
Costa, Paul 238
co-twin control method 7, 274
craniometry 89
criminal behavior: environmentalist/hereditarian position 4–5; hereditary nature of 237
critical kinship relationships 135
Cropanzano, R. and James, K. 94
Cross-Disorder Group of the Psychiatric Genomics Consortium study 219
Crow, Timothy 222
cultural influences: MZA pairs 110; personality differences 92–3
Cushman, Philip 196

Daphne and Barbara (the Giggle Twins) 119
data: and dialogue 103; failure to make available/MISTRA 71, 122–6, 127, 132–3, 134, 141, 143, 146, 248–9; mandatory access to 122–3
Deary, I. J. 208
deceptions, by twins 22, 56–7, 118–19 *see also* lies
DeFries, J. C. and Plomin, R. 223
depression 227
Derks et al. 163–4
developmental psychology, genetic research in 227–8
developmental psychopathology 199–200
Diagnostic and Statistical Manual of Mental Disorders (DSM) *see* DSM
dialogue, and data 103
Digit Span Forward 83
discordance 274

"Discovery of Susceptibility Genes for Mental Disorders, The" 235n.2
disorders, running in families 12
dizygotic (DZ, fraternal) twins 274
DNA (deoxyribonucleic acid) 274
Doctoring the Mind 202
Dominoes Intelligence Test 29
Dorfman, Donald 119
Draper, Wickliffe 253, 254
drug companies, and genetic research 236, 252
DSM 190, 191, 274
DSM-5 181, 191–3, 274
DSM-IV Task Force 193
Dudley, Richard 124
Duke, David 125
Dusek, Val 57
dysgenic 274
DZA control group, MISTRA 107–9, 130, 131, 132, 139, 146
DZA correlations, v. MZA correlations 108–9, 110–11
DZ pairs reared together *see* DZT
DZTs 15, 278
DZ twins reared apart *see* DZA

EASI self-report personality questionnaire 260
Eaves et al. 154
Eaves, Lindon 85
Eckert et al. 122
economic inequality: and biological differences in social class 237; and illness 236
economic interests, promoting genetic theories 236
educational achievement, and genetic factors 233
EEA-test studies 157, 162, 184, 185, 186, 188, 274
ego development, WAIS scores 136
elites, political/economic 237, 252
emergenesis 148n.7, 274
emotional closeness, of twins 165, 168
empirical genetic prognosis 11–12
empirically keyed test 274
empty self 196
Encyclopedia of Intelligence 135
Entwined Lives 121, 137, 168
environmental approaches, v. genetic approaches 239–46

environmental bias, in twin research 188
environmental causes, and biological causes 174
environmental confounds 14, 168
environmental factors: causing common diseases 212; and medical conditions 236, 250; MZT concordance rates 185; and MZT–DZT comparisons 249; MZT–DZT concordance rates 186; psychiatric disorders 235, 236; and schizophrenia/psychosis 194–6
environmentalist position, criminal behavior 4
environmental similarity measures 164
environmental similarity questionnaire, MISTRA 106
environment-creating behavior, of adults 160
environments: and ability 3; and behavior 3, 11, 95, 235, 265; childhood/and psychological functioning 196; and childrens' outcomes 199; dissimilarity of 166–7; and genes 238–9; and MZA pairs 96–8; MZT–DZT 155, 156, 160, 164, 176, 249; and political temperament 173; prenatal 174–5; and psychiatric disorders 235, 236; shared and genetics 147; term 275; twins creating their own 267; uncorrelated 95
epigenetics 99–100, 275
epistasis 114
equal environment assumption (EEA): 2012 test of 169, 171–6; arguments in defense of 158–64, 184–9; definitions of 155–6; MZT–DZT 154, 162, 175, 182–9, 249, 267–72; psychiatric twin research 182–9; term 275; trait-relevant argument of 160–1; twin method 278; validity of 13, 173
eugenics: American movement 18, 254; breeding plans 258; and criminal behavior 4–5; eugenic programs 253–4; Jensen 52; legislation 12; politics of 203n.7; and reproduction 7; term 275; textbooks 236–7; and twin research 7, 252

INDEX

Eugenics and Race 255
Eugenics: A Reassessment 258
'Eugenics Revisited' 234
euthanasia programs 254
evaluation: of MISTRA cognitive ability studies 141–2; of MISTRA personality studies 145; of twin research 251–2
Evans, D. M. and Martin, N. G. 270
exaggeration, by twins 22, 56–7, 118–19 *see also* lies
experiences, similar/MZT pairs 172–3
Eysenck, Hans 5, 20, 67–8, 85
Eysenck, H. J. and Prell, D. B. 156

facism, scientific supporters of 254
familiality, and heritability 12
family resemblance 11
family studies: and behavioral/psychiatric genetics 11–12, 170; term 275; and twin method 168–9, 170
Faraone et al. 181, 209, 213, 261
Faraone, S. V. 219, 222
Farber, Susan 65–7, 68, 122–3
favism 79, 275
Figure Logic 83
"Finding the Missing Heritability" 211
Fireman Twins 121–2
Fischer, Claude 76
Five Factor theory, of personality 238
Flint et al. 187–8, 272
Flint, Jonathan 187
Flynn, James 90
Ford, B. Douglas 95
Fosse, Roar 99
Fowler et al. 271
Frances, Allen 193
fraternal twins 275
fraud/misconduct, Stapel 123
Fuller, J. & Thompson, W. 9, 164, 186
Funding of Scientific Racism, The 254

Galton, Francis 7–8, 9–10, 76
Gardner, Iva 116
Gasper, Phil 237
"Gene Chase in Behavioral Science, The" 225
gene discovery claims, in psychiatry 182
gene–environment correlation 86
gene–environment interactions 85

Gene Illusion, The 7, 72, 116, 121, 124, 185, 235n.2
general intelligence (g) 52, 76, 89, 129, 131, 275
generalizability 275
genes: and ability 3; for ADHD 227, 228; for behavior 3, 208–9, 234; and behavioral development/disorders 228; and criminal behavior 4–5; and the environment 238–9; failure to discover 210–16, 223–34; gene-finding claims/predictions 234; for IQ 3, 208, 220, 228, 233, 234; for personality 3, 208–9, 226, 234; for pinkie finger curling 121–2; for psychiatric disorders 3, 209, 234, 250; for schizophrenia 224, 227, 235n.2; and socially disapproved behavior 3; term 275
Genes and Behavior 85
genetic approaches: to medical conditions 238, 252; v. environmental approaches 239–46
genetic counselling 275
genetic determinism 212, 236, 237–8, 275
genetic differences, racial groups 52, 53, 257
genetic explanations, social/personal distress 197
genetic factors: behavior 3, 5, 56, 75–6, 107, 154, 208–9, 234; and biological factors 174; and educational achievement 233; general intelligence (g) 131; MZA correlations 126, 133, 144; and personality 30, 41, 54, 55, 143–6, 265; and political ideology 171, 251; psychiatric disorders 180, 181–2; psychological traits 145; race difference 125
genetic heritability, of IQ 75
genetic inferiority, of black people 51, 254, 258
genetic influences: on behavior 3, 5, 56, 154, 175–6, 208–9, 234; on conservatism 177n.6; on IQ 54, 140; on personality 30, 41, 54, 55, 143–6, 265
genetic interpretations: of family studies 169; MZT–DZT twin method 177; of twin data 251

INDEX

genetic markers 275
genetic predisposition *see* predisposition-stress theory
genetic research: critical analysis of 63; in developmental psychology 227–8; and drug companies 236, 252; and political science 157, 169, 171–6, 177; reliability/validity of psychiatric 189–91
genetic risk factors 252
genetics: and biology 177–8n.7; and DSM-5 191–3; and medical disorders 238, 252; and race 125; and shared environments 147; term 276
genetic superiority, of races 237
genetic theories: of IQ 64; and political/economic interests 236
genetic variants 210–11
genoeconomics 157
genomes 276
genome sequencing, newborn screening 232
genome-wide association (GWA) studies 209, 210, 212, 228, 229, 232, 276
genomewide complex trait analysis (GCTA) 216–20, 232, 276
genomics 276
genopolitics 157
genotype 276
genotype–environment correlation 85
Germany: eugenics program 254; twin research 8
Gillie, Oliver 48
G is for Genes: The Impact of Genetics on Education and Achievement 233
Glatt et al. 12, 201
gluten sensitivity 80–1
Goldberger, Arthur 5, 87
Gottesman, I. I. and Hanson, D. R. 174
Gottesman, Irving 29, 81, 147, 161–2
Gottlieb, Gilbert 79–80
Gould, Stephen J. 89, 142, 188, 237
Günther, Hans F. K. 255

Hamer, Dean 238
Handbook of Behavior Genetics 139
Handbook of Developmental Science, Behavior, and Genetics 72
Handbook of Personality: Theory and Research 263

Hatemi et al. 209, 251, 272
Hawaii Family Study of Cognition 130
Haworth, C. M. A. and Plomin, R. 229
Hearnshaw, Leslie 48–9
hereditarianism *see* genetic determinism
hereditary traits, selective breeding for 7
heredity: and IQ 121; of mental disorders 237
heredity–environment question 5, 85
heritability: of corn oil production 216; of criminal behavior 4; defined 77–82; and familiality 12; and inherited 78, 82; of IQ 29, 51, 52–3, 63, 64, 68, 90, 121; missing heritability explanation 210–16, 229, 230, 233, 250, 276; and model-fitting 262–3; and psychiatric conditions 80–1; special mental abilities 133; term 276; of traits/validity of 68
heritability estimates: for behavior 216, 217; criticisms of 72, 77–8, 87, 262; IQ 232; MISTRA 110, 145; and MZA correlations 111–12, 126, 127n.1, 131, 139; original purpose of 214, 216; validity of 62–3, 68, 70
heritable, and inherited 78
Herrnstein, R. J. and Murray, C. 51, 253
Hibbing, John 177n.7
Hill, David 197
Hirsch, Jerry 78
Holden, Constance 54
Holzinger, K. J. 155
Ho, Mae-Wan 219
homosexuality 189
Hooton, Ernest 253
Horgan, John 182, 234
Horwitz, Allan 196
How Genes Influence Behavior 187
Hudziak, J. J. and Faraone, S. V. 198–200
human ability *see* ability
human behavior *see* behavior
human behavioral genetics *see* behavioral genetics
Human Development 136
Human Genome Project (HGP) 192, 208, 212, 215, 223, 224, 227, 276

Human Heredity 156
Husén, Torsten 165

identical twins *see* monozygotic twins
Identical Twins Reared Apart: A Reanalysis in Science 65, 68, 122–3
identity, and twins 155
identity confusion 164–8, 185
ideology, assessment of 172, 173
Individual and Environment: Monozygotic Twins Reared Apart 40
inequality: and biological determinism 237; economic 236, 237
Inequality by Design 76
influence, mutual/MZT pairs 172–3
inheritance, genetic assumptions about 99
inherited: and heritability 78, 82; and heritable 78
injustice, and biological determinism 237
Institute for Behavioral Genetics, University of Colorado at Boulder 10
intelligence *see also* IQ: general intelligence (g) 52, 76, 89, 129, 131, 275; heredity for 29; and IQ 76; racial differences in 10
Intelligence Controversy, The 67
Intelligence, Heredity, and Environment 135
International Association of for the Advancement of Ethnology and Eugenics (IAAEE) 254
International Schizophrenia Consortium 231
intraclass correlation 276
Ioannidis, John 49, 200–1
IQ *see also* intelligence: decline of in population 121; genes for 3, 208, 220, 228, 233, 234; genetic heritability of 75; genetic influences on 54, 140; genetic theories of 64; and heredity 121; heritability estimates 232; heritability of 29, 51, 52–3, 63, 64, 68, 90, 121; and intelligence 76; molecular genetic research 232; psychometric approach to 76; racial differences in 10, 51, 53, 125; and social class 10, 51, 89, 121; and socioeconomic environments 99
IQ adoption studies, and selective placement 14
IQ Game, The 63, 76, 84
IQ QTL Project 223, 225
"IQs of Identical Twins Reared Apart" 52
IQ studies, MISTRA 86, 129–42, 146, 248
IQ tests 88–90; criticisms of 89–90; general intelligence (g) 129; Juel-Nielsen study 1965 41; MISTRA 129; as oppression against the poor 63; validity of 62–3, 70

Jackson, Don 63, 164
Jensen, Arthur 10, 16n.1, 51–3, 55, 66–7, 90, 114, 123
Jerry Levey and Mark Newman (Fireman Twins) 121–2
Jessie and Bess 18–19
Jim Twins 55–6, 59–60n.8, 103
Jinks, J. L. and Fulker, D. W. 84–5, 87, 114
John, Leslie 50
Johnson et al. 82, 138–9, 271
Johnson, Wendy 81, 86, 216
Jones, H. E. 156
Joseph, Jay 72–4
Journal of the American Academy of Child and Adolescent Psychiatry 198
Juel-Nielsen, Niels 40–8, 57, 62, 65–6, 68, 69, 74n.1, 86–7, 156, 268

Kaj and Robert 119
Kallmann, F. J. 267
Kamin, Leon: criticism of TRA studies 61–3, 69–70, 118; and Flint et al. 187; Kamin vs. Eysenck 67–8; and MISTRA data 136; and MISTRA researchers 124–5; *Science and Politics of I.Q., The* 48, 117
Kamin, L. J. and Goldberger, A. S. 71–2, 119, 134
Keller, Evelyn Fox 78
Kendler et al. 161, 162
Kendler, Kenneth 184–7, 252, 269

Kety et al. 14
kinship studies 64, 229, 276
Kirk et al. 190
Kirkpatrick et al. 208
Kline, Paul 93
Koch, Helen 165
Kringlen, E. 156, 165, 185, 270
Kühl, Stefan 254
Kupfer, David 181
Kupfer et al. 192

Langinvainio et al. 57–8
Latham, Jonathan 212, 214
Laughlin, Harry 253
Lerner, Richard 4, 251
Lewontin et al. 69–70, 76–7
Lewontin, Richard 69–70, 78, 85, 236
lies, of twins 71, 119 *see also* deceptions
literature, on IQ heritability 63
Loehlin, J. C. and Nichols, R. C. 268
Loehlin, John 85, 155, 268
Luxenburger, Hans 180
Lykken, David 53, 106, 112, 120–1, 148n.7, 256
Lynn, Richard 253, 257, 258
Lyons et al. 269
Lytton, Hugh 188

Maes et al. 270
"Mainstream Science on Intelligence" statement 53
manic-depressive disease 180 *see also* bipolar disorder
Manolio et al. 211, 212
Manolio, Teri 211
Martin et al. 158, 270
Martin, Nicholas 85
McClearn et al. 225
McClearn, Gerald 188–9
McCourt et al. 137
McCrea et al. 238
McCrea, Robert 238
McGue et al. 112, 134–5
McGue, M. and Bouchard, T. J. Jr. 113–14, 117, 131, 136, 216
McGue, Matt 53, 256
McGuffin et al. 226
McGuire, S. and Segal, N. L. 272
Mealey, Linda 125
Meany, Michael 85

medical disorders *see* psychiatric disorders
Medland, S. E. and Hatemi, P. K. 168, 271
Meehl, Paul 134
Mendelian inheritance 276
mental disorders: heredity of 237; as socially acquired maladjustments 196
Merikangas, K. R. and Risch, N. 223
Mill Hill Vocabulary Scale 29, 129
minimum contact 105
Minnesota Multiphasic Personality Inventory (MMPI) 93, 143
Minnesota Study of Twins Reared Apart (MISTRA) *see* MISTRA
Mirage of a Space Between Nature and Nurture, The 78
Mischel, Walter 91
Mismeasure of Man, The 188
missing GCTA heritability position 232
Missing Gene, The 212, 251
missing heritability explanation 210–16, 229, 230, 233, 250, 276
MISTRA 53–7; 16PF personality correlations 143, 146; age/sex confounds 117–18; assumptions 86, 107, 108, 113–15, 130, 142, 147; bias in 115–17, 126, 127; circular reasoning 113, 114, 160; and Colorado Adoption Project (CAP) 264; conclusions favoring genetics 109–13; confirmation bias 120–2; control group 107–9, 130, 131, 132, 139, 146; degree of separation of twins 70, 71–2; DZA IQ correlations/reporting of 134–41; evaluation of cognitive ability studies 141–2; evaluation of personality studies 145; failure to demonstrate genetic influences 147; failure to make data available 71, 122–6, 127, 132–3, 134, 141, 143, 146, 248–9; funding of 253–8; genetic interpretations/invalidity of 142; heritability estimates 110, 145; IQ studies 88, 129–42, 146, 147, 248; and the media 247; and missing heritability 214–16; model-fitting 83, 87, 107, 110, 111, 113, 115, 130, 131, 133, 144, 147;

peer-review 111; personality studies 93, 143–6, 147, 248; questionable basis of 126–7; Raven IQ correlations 138, 146; recruitment bias 70, 115–17, 126; researchers and Kamin 124–5; sample 104–7, 120, 138–9; special mental abilities 129–30, 133; as TRA study 64; use of findings by disreputable groups 125–6; work attitudes 94; work values study 148n.8

model-fitting: assumptions 138; biometrical 82–7; Colorado Adoption Project (CAP) 261; and heritability 262–3; MISTRA 83, 87, 107, 110, 111, 113, 115, 130, 131, 133, 144, 147; term 276

Models of Madness 190

molecular biology, and behavior 224

molecular genetic research: and behavioral genetics 15–16; failure of 3, 10, 207, 222, 223–34, 250; misleading claims of 200; of personality 210; schizophrenia 231; term 15, 277; and twin studies 220

monozygotic (MZ, identical) twins 277

Monozygotic Twins Brought up Apart and Brought up Together 118–19

Moore, David 77

morbidity risk 12

Morgeson et al. 91–2

Morris-Yates, A. 186

Muller, H. J. 18

Multidimensional Personality Questionnaire (MPQ) 143

multifactorial complex disorder 277

multiple measure approach 130

Munich School 11, 12, 29

Munsinger, Harry 14

MZA correlations: genetic factors 126, 133, 144; and heritability estimates 111–12, 126, 127n.1, 131, 139; and shared genes 129; v. DZA correlations 108–9, 110–11

MZA family environments, socioeconomic range of 97

MZA pairs: cohort effects 95–7, 103, 110; cultural influences 110; environmental influences of 96–8; extent of separation/different environments 94–9, 103, 109–10, 115, 118–19, 127

MZA study, Popenoe–Muller pair 18–19

MZ, identical twins 277

MZ pairs reared together *see* MZT

MZT–DZT pairs: attachment 164–8, 185; comparisons 154, 249; concordance rates/environmental factors 186; environments 155, 160, 164, 176, 186, 249; equal environment assumption (EEA) 154, 162, 175, 182–9, 249, 267–72

MZT–DZT twin method, genetic interpretations 177

MZT pairs, similar experiences/mutual influence 172–4

MZ twins reared apart *see* MZA

Names and Faces-Immediate tests 83

narrow heritability 77

National Human Genome Research Institute 211

Nature 211, 233

Nature, Nurture, and Psychology 134

nature–nurture debate 3–4, 54, 88, 247, 260

nature terms 4

Nazi era 8, 12, 201, 203n.7, 254

Nazi groups, use of MISTRA findings 125

Nazism: scientific supporters of 254; United Kingdom 255

Neel, J. V. and Schull, W. J. 156

newborn screening, genome sequencing 232

Newman et al. 43, 116, 117, 136, 155

Newman, Freeman, and Holzinger (1937), TRA study 20–8, 62, 65, 68, 74n.1, 95

Newman, Horatio 19, 116

non-genetic influences, behavioral characteristics 109, 177

Nordic supremacy 254

Northern League 255

Not in Their Genes 69

novelty seeking 226

nurture terms 4

oppression against the poor, IQ tests as 63
organizational psychologists 92
Origins of Human Potential, The 70
Osborn, Frederick 257

Palle and Peter 66
Parisi, Paolo 8, 16n.2, 270
Pearson, Roger 255
Pedersen et al. 83, 116
pedigree 277
peer-review, MISTRA 111
Penguin Dictionary of Psychology 87
personal distress, genetic explanations 197
personality: and culture 92–3; Five Factor theory of 238; genes for 3, 208–9, 226, 234; genetic factors 30, 41, 54, 55, 143–6, 265; heredity for 29, 145; lack of genetic influence 260–1, 265; and MISTRA study 93, 143–6, 147, 248; molecular genetic research of 210; twin studies 162
personality publications, MISTRA 144–6
personality testing, and social/political oppression 93
personality tests 20, 29, 41, 91–4, 277
personality traits 91, 92, 145–6, 226, 238
pharmaceutical industry, need for twin research 236, 252
phenotype 277
phenylketonuria (PKU) 79, 277
physical appearance, and political attitudes 174
pinkie finger curling, gene for 121–2
Pioneer Fund 102, 253–8
Plomin, DeFries, et al. 209, 231
Plomin et al. (1976) 268
Plomin et al. (1977) 263
Plomin et al. (1990) 83, 100n.3, 111, 263, 269
Plomin et al. (1994) 225
Plomin et al. (1997) 100n.3
Plomin et al. (1998) 143, 260, 262, 264, 265
Plomin et al. (2008) 228
Plomin et al. (2013) 158, 169, 222, 230, 272

Plomin, R. and Asbury, K. 228
Plomin, R. and Bergeman, C. S. 225
Plomin, R. and Crabbe, J. 226
Plomin, R. and Davis, O. S. P. 228
Plomin, R. and DeFries, J. C. 260, 263
Plomin, R. and McGuffin, P. 227
Plomin, R. and Rende, R. 224
Plomin, R. and Simpson, M. A. 231
Plomin, Robert 10, 11, 53, 76, 83, 149n.9, 213–14, 217, 223–34, 250
political attitudes, and physical appearance 174
political ideology, and genetic factors 171, 251
political interests, promoting genetic theories 236
political oppression, and personality testing 93
political science: and genetic research 157, 169, 171–6, 177; twin method (twins reared together) 177n.4; twin research in 168
political temperament, and environments 173
politics: of eugenics 203n.7; and genetic determinism 212
Politics of Schizophrenia, The 197
polygenic disorder 277
polymorphism 277
Popenoe–Muller pair, MZA study 18–19
Popenoe, P. and Johnson, R. 237
Popenoe, Paul 18
population, decline in IQ of 121
postnatal environmental influences, twin behavior 15
post-traumatic stress disorder (PTSD) 161, 163, 195
predisposition-stress (diathesis-stress) theory 180, 277
prenatal (intrauterine) environmental differences 174–5
Prescott et al. 270
Proctor, Robert 5
pseudoscience 277
psychiatric diagnoses: problems with 189–93; reliability/validity of 201
psychiatric disorders: and childhood adversities 199; and environmental factors 236, 250; and environments 235, 236; genes

for 3, 209, 234, 250; genetic factors 180, 181–2; and genetics 238, 252; and heritability 80–1; predisposition-stress (diathesis-stress) theory 180; rare variants underlying 210–11
psychiatric genetics: adoption studies 13–14; failure of 198–200, 220; family studies 11–12; family studies v. twin method 170; field 6, 180–1; molecular genetic research 15–16; as a null field? 200–1; and racial hygienists 201; reared-apart twin studies 15; term 277; twin method (twins reared together) 12–13; twin studies 179
psychiatric labels 191, 197
psychiatric molecular genetic research, failure of 223–34
psychiatric twin research: defenses of 187; equal environment assumption (EEA) in 182–9; and MZT–DZT comparisons 249
psychiatry: American 191; assumptions of genetic theories in 196–8; gene discovery claims in 182; need for twin research 252; term 277
psychiatry genetic research, reliability/validity of 189–91
psychiatry research, twin method 154
psychological functioning 196
psychological research, twin method 154
psychological traits, genetic factors 145
psychometric/behavioral genetic perspective 100
psychometrics 9, 76–7, 277
psychometric tests, measuring personality traits 145–6
psychometrists, defined 100n.1
psychopathology: behavioral genetic research 224, 227; developmental 199–200
psychopharmaceutical industry, need for twin research 236, 252
psychosis, and environmental factors 194–6
Purcell, Sean 83, 86

quantitative genetic research 10, 223
quantitative genetics 278
quantitative genetic theory 142
quantitative trait loci (QTLs) 223, 278

race, and genetics 125
Race, Evolution, and Behavior: A Life History Perspective 258
races, genetic superiority of 237
racial differences: genetic factors 125; in IQ 10, 51, 53, 125
racial discrimination, and twin studies 8, 16n.2
racial group differences 52, 53, 257
racial hygiene 8, 254
racial hygienists, and psychiatric genetics 201
racial research 256
racial superiority, white 255
racism, scientific 252, 254 *see also* black people; eugenics
racist arguments, and craniometry 89
random assignment 87–8
randomization, lack of/TRA studies 70
Rapaport's Word Association Test 41
rare variants 210–11
Raven IQ correlations, MISTRA 138, 146
Raven IQ test 129, 130, 140
Raven Progressive Matrices 41, 88, 130
Read, John 99, 190, 194, 195
reared-apart twins, degree of separation 24–8, 30–40, 44–8, 58, 62, 63–4, 65, 69–70
reared-apart twin studies 15
reared-together twins 153–4
rearing environments, assessment of 106
recruitment bias, MISTRA 70, 115–17, 126
reductionism 278
reliability: of psychiatric diagnoses 201; of psychiatric genetic research 189–91
reproduction, and eugenics 7
Research Agenda for DSM-V, A 191
research funding: genetic/biological research bias 238; of MISTRA 253–8
Richardson, Ken 70–1, 86, 89
Ridley, Matt 55
right-wing authoritarianism 137
Rorschach's Test 41

INDEX

Rose, Richard 68–9
Rose, Steven 69–70, 80, 197
Rossi, Michael 103, 120, 126
Rowe, D. C. 269
Rüdin, Ernst 11, 12, 180, 201, 203n.7
Rushton, J. Philippe 52, 257–8
Rutter et al. 269
Rutter, M. and Plomin, R. 226
Rutter, Michael 9, 85–6, 271

sample, MISTRA 104–7, 120, 138–9
sampling bias 21–4, 29, 62, 65, 66, 72, 104
Scarr, S. and Carter-Saltzman, L. 88, 155, 269
Scarr, Sandra 10, 55, 268
schizophrenia: adoption studies 14; classic diagnosis of 193–8; in contemporary psychiatry 250; and environmental factors 194–6; genes for 224, 227, 235n.2; as a genetic disorder 14; molecular genetic research 231; morbidity risk 12; pooled concordance rates 185; twin studies 161, 180
Science 104, 119, 124, 125, 131–2, 133, 139, 140, 143, 144, 145, 224, 225, 226, 248, 253, 256, 263
science: fraud in/misconduct 48–50, 59n.6; as interpretation of data 103; soft 103
Science and Politics of I.Q., The 48, 61, 63, 69, 117, 187
Sciences, The 135
Scientific American 234
Segal, Nancy: and bias in MISTRA 117, 127; and Colorado Adoption Project (CAP) 259; and difference between MZA/DZA pairs 111; and differences in MISTRA team 120–1; and DZA correlations 137–8; emotional closeness of MZT pairs 168; equal environment assumption (EEA) 270; and failure to make data available 124, 125, 127, 141, 143; and funding of MISTRA 253; genetic influences on traits 83, 142, 215; and gluten sensitivity 80–1; and IQ in MISTRA 129, 132, 137–8; MISTRA personality studies 114, 143; MISTRA's contribution to psychology 146; model-fitting 114; model-fitting analyses 86; molecular genetic advances 215; and MZA-DZA correlations 130; and MZA twins separated early 112; and MZT–DZT comparisons 154; and pinkie-curling styles 122–3; on Pioneer Fund 102–3, 256–7; and sample size 139–40; and twins making own environments 109
Segal, N. L. and Johnson, W. 139, 158, 271
selective breeding 7, 253
selective placement, adoption 13–14, 106, 277
Self-Rating Questionnaire (SRQ) 29
self-report personality tests 278
separated twin study *see* twins reared-apart (TRA) studies
Shields, James: 1954 MZT–DZT study 165, 267; 1962 TRA study 28–40, 57, 62, 65, 68, 74n.1, 85, 110, 116, 118–19, 161, 175
Siemens, Hermann 154
similar treatment, MZT pairs 173–4
single-nucleotide polymorphisms (SNPs) 210, 276, 278
16PF personality correlations, MISTRA 143, 146
Slater, Eliot 29
Slife, Brent 104
Smith et al. 157, 171, 272
social classes: and economic inequality 237; and IQ 10, 51, 89, 121
social conditions, and illness 236
social control, and psychiatric labels 197
social distress, genetic explanations 197
socially disapproved behavior 3, 12
social oppression, and personality testing 93
social order, and genetic determinism 212
social perspective, psychological functioning 196
social policies, limitations of psychology/biology 252
social science 6, 103–4, 157
socioeconomic environments, and IQ 99

socioeconomic range, of MZA family environments 97
soft science 103
special mental abilities 129–30, 133, 278
spectrum disorder diagnoses 14
Stapel, Diederik 49–50, 123
statistical modelling 85–6
status quo, maintaining 237–8
sterilization, compulsory 253
sterilization, eugenics 258
Sternberg, Robert 135
Stoolmiller, Mike 97
Sturgis et al. 159, 272
Suhay et al. 171
Swedish Adoption/Twin Study on Aging (SATSA) 57, 70, 71–2, 83, 87, 137, 260
Szasz, Thomas 194

Taylor, Howard 6, 58, 63–4, 75, 76, 84, 87, 90, 114
Tellegen, Auke 53, 120
Tellegen et al. 111, 144
Texas Adoption Project 255
thalidomide-related birth defects 175
Three laws of behavior genetics 11
"Three Laws of Behavior Genetics and What They Mean" 213
Tienari, P. 156, 157
"Toward Behavioral Genomics" 226–7
trait-relevant environmental factors 161–2
traits, heritability of 68
TRA research, cautions relating to 68–9
TRA researchers, use of 'apart' 103
TRA studies *see also* MISTRA: access to data 126; Arthur Jenson controversy 51–3; bias in 68, 116; criticisms of 61–74, 94; Cyril Burt Scandal 48–50; degree of MZA separation 118; and genetic theories of IQ 64; IQ correlations/cohort effects 117; Juel-Nielsen 1965 40–8; need for control groups 69, 72, 74; Newman, Freeman, and Holzinger, 1937 20–8; problem areas in 73; required features of 67; Shields, 1962 *see* Shields, James; validity of 154

Troublesome Inheritance, A 51
True et al. 163
Trzaskowski et al. 209, 218, 219, 232
Tucker, William 254, 257
Turkheimer, Eric 11, 81, 209, 210, 213, 217, 232
twin-based approach, and age/sex effects 117–18
twin behavior, postnatal environmental influences 15
twin data, genetic interpretations of 251
twin method (twins reared together) 12–13; assumptions 154; and Colorado Adoption Project (CAP) 263–4; equal environment assumption (EEA) 278; fallacy of 156–8; and family studies 168–9, 170; MZT–DZT comparisons 177; MZTs resemblance findings 176–7; political science 177n.4; psychiatric genetics 12–13; psychiatry research 154; psychological research 154; term 278; validity of 158–64, 168
twin research: environmental bias in 188; and eugenics 7, 252; evaluation of 251–2; extent of 5; historical background 7–9; in political science 168; problems with 247; psychiatry/pharmaceutical industry's need for 236, 252
twins: creating own environments 267–72; emotional closeness of 165, 168; exaggeration/deceptions of 22–3, 56–7, 118–19; and identity 155; lies of 71, 119
twin samples, volunteer 106
Twins: An Investigation into the Strange Coincidences in the Lives of Separated Twins 55–6
twin's answers, personality tests 93–4
Twins: A Study of Heredity and Environment 20
twin separation, contact time formula 104–5
twins reared-apart (TRA) studies 15, 147, 278
twin studies: and behavioral/psychiatric genetics 170; and molecular genetic research 220; personality 162; problems with

247; psychiatric genetics 179; and racial discrimination 8, 16n.2; schizophrenia 161, 180

unconscious experimenter bias 62
unconscious rater bias 104
uncorrelated environments 95
United Kingdom, Nazism 255
United States, eugenics 18, 254
University of California at Berkeley 51
University of Colorado at Boulder, Institute for Behavioral Genetics 10

validity: of heritability estimates 62–3, 68, 70; of IQ tests 62–3, 70; of psychiatric diagnoses 201; of psychiatric genetic research 189–91; of twin method 158–64, 168
Vandenberg, S. V. 268
variance 278
variants, genetic 210–11
variation, and cause 78–80
Vernon, Tony 256
Vinkhuyzen et al. 218
volunteers, use of/as risky 106
Wade, Nicholas 51
Wahlsten, Douglas 78, 252

Watson, James 238
Watson, Peter 55, 59–60n.8
Wechsler Adult Intelligence Scale (WAIS) 88, 129, 133, 138, 140
Wechsler-Bellevue Intelligence Scale 41
Wellcome Trust Centre for Human Genetics 187
Wetzel, Norbert 191
Weyher, Harry 257
White Power 255
white racial superiority 255
white supremacist, use of MISTRA findings 125
Wicherts, Jelte M. 50
Williams, Richard 104
Wilson, Allison 212, 214
Wilson-Patterson Index 172, 177n.6
Woodworth-Mathews test 21
Woodworth, R. S. 155, 156
work attitudes, MISTRA 94
work values study, MISTRA 148n.8
World War II, and twin studies 8
Wright, William 257

Yang et al. 216, 217

zygosity 15, 278